# COMPLETE
# TRIATHLON
# GUIDE

**USA TRIATHLON**

**COMPILED BY TRIATHLON'S NATIONAL GOVERNING BODY**

**HUMAN KINETICS**

D1473216

Library of Congress Cataloging-in-Publication Data

Complete triathlon guide / USA Triathlon.
    p. cm.
Includes bibliographical references.
ISBN 978-1-4504-1260-5 (soft cover) -- ISBN 1-4504-1260-2 (soft cover)
1. Triathlon--Training. I. USA Triathlon.
GV1060.73.C64 2012
796.42'57--dc23
                            2011052796

ISBN-10: 1-4504-1260-2 (print)
ISBN-13: 978-1-4504-1260-5 (print)

**Acquisitions Editor:** Tom Heine; **Developmental Editor:** Laura Floch; **Assistant Editor:** Elizabeth Evans; **Copyeditor:** Patricia L. MacDonald; **Permissions Manager:** Martha Gullo; **Graphic Designer:** Bob Reuther; **Graphic Artist:** Kim McFarland; **Photographer (cover):** Mario Cantu (left and right), David Sanders (middle); **Photographer (interior):** © Human Kinetics, unless otherwise noted, © Cynthia Hamilton, pp. 36-42 and © Vaughan Photography, pp. 51, 54-55; **Visual Production Assistant:** Joyce Brumfield; **Photo Production Manager:** Jason Allen; **Art Manager:** Kelly Hendren; **Associate Art Manager:** Alan L. Wilborn; **Illustrations:** © Human Kinetics; **Printer:** McNaughton & Gunn

Human Kinetics books are available at special discounts for bulk purchase. Special editions or book excerpts can also be created to specification. For details, contact the Special Sales Manager at Human Kinetics.

Printed in the United States of America          10   9   8   7   6   5   4   3   2   1

The paper in this book is certified under a sustainable forestry program.

**Human Kinetics**
Website: www.HumanKinetics.com

*United States:* Human Kinetics
P.O. Box 5076
Champaign, IL 61825-5076
800-747-4457
e-mail: humank@hkusa.com

*Canada:* Human Kinetics
475 Devonshire Road Unit 100
Windsor, ON N8Y 2L5
800-465-7301 (in Canada only)
e-mail: info@hkcanada.com

*Europe:* Human Kinetics
107 Bradford Road
Stanningley
Leeds LS28 6AT, United Kingdom
+44 (0) 113 255 5665
e-mail: hk@hkeurope.com

*Australia:* Human Kinetics
57A Price Avenue
Lower Mitcham, South Australia 5062
08 8372 0999
e-mail: info@hkaustralia.com

*New Zealand:* Human Kinetics
P.O. Box 80
Torrens Park, South Australia 5062
0800 222 062
e-mail: info@hknewzealand.com

E5492

# COMPLETE
# TRIATHLON
# GUIDE

# CONTENTS

# INTRODUCTION

Welcome to *Complete Triathlon Guide*. The sport of triathlon is growing at a tremendous rate as more and more people participate in triathlons to stay healthy, get fit, and have fun. Triathletes are highly motivated, and they want to learn everything they can about the sport to help themselves become better athletes. Training for triathlons is a challenge because of the unique balance needed in swimming, biking, and running in order to achieve success. This book provides athletes and coaches of all skill and experience levels the best training information and racing strategies available. It is an absolute must-have resource for coaches and athletes who are serious about taking performance to the next level or those wanting to learn more about the sport. *Complete Triathlon Guide* is filled with training tips and information from the best-known experts in the triathlon field.

When we started discussing the possibility of putting this book together, we were excited to have the leaders of triathlon coaching, training, and racing willing to write a chapter on a topic they are best known for. Each of these authors has enough knowledge and expertise to write their own books, and many have, so we are grateful to each of them for sharing a piece of their knowledge in this book.

Part I, Training, includes chapters 1 through 10. Chapter 1 focuses on developing your seasonal training plan and understanding periodization. Chapter 2 discusses how to customize training for special groups including beginners, youth, and masters and female athletes. Chapter 3 introduces you to yoga by talking about the benefits of yoga and types of classes while also providing several yoga poses that can be practiced at home. Chapter 4 helps you understand how to incorporate strength training for triathletes by covering resistance training concepts, organizing a strength training program for triathlon, and explaining specific strength training exercises that can improve a triathlete's fitness and performance.

As we move into chapter 5, we start getting into sport-specific training by covering swimming pool workouts for open water including the warm-up, technique work, main set, and cool-down. Chapter 6 discusses training for triathlon biking, while chapter 7 gets into the specifics of triathlon run training. Chapter 8 is dedicated to helping you understand overtraining and recovery, how to balance stress and recovery, and how to anticipate and prevent overtraining. Chapter 9 sets the foundation for the book as it discusses exercise physiology, covering the energy, muscular, and cardiorespiratory systems, and shows how manipulating the training loads affects physiological adaptations. Chapter 10 will teach you several key points about tapering including managing the training load during the taper, enhancing recovery during the taper, managing nutrition and hydration during the taper, and other details related to tapering.

Part II, Technique, includes chapters 11 through 15. Chapter 11 discusses bike fitting and mounting, essential skills for the road, and race-day skills. Chapter 12 covers how to set, improve, manage, maintain, and train your bike and run cadences. Chapter 13 goes over the key concepts of how to assess your running form including head, neck, and eye position; breathing; and head-to-toe body position. Chapter 14 explains the importance of setting up your transitions correctly, how to move from the swim to the bike and the bike to the run quickly, and how to have a great swim start. Chapter 15 focuses on how to reduce drag and create propulsion in the water by using body position and an efficient swim stroke.

Part III, Competitive Strategy, includes chapters 16 through 20. Chapter 16 covers everything you need to know about open-water training, tactical race aspects, rules, prerace warm-up, and specific swim tactics. Chapter 17 helps you understand the differences between cycling in a nondrafting race versus a drafting race as well as the skills used in each. Chapter 18 discusses how important it is to understand your limits when it comes to training and racing for triathlons as well as how to strengthen your weaknesses, increase your strengths, and individualize your training. Chapter 19 focuses on getting you mentally prepared for race day by evaluating your mental skills, describing mental skills strategies, and teaching you how to practice mental skills. Chapter 20 helps you prepare for traveling to a race by teaching you how to pack your bike and race gear, how to travel comfortably, and how to arrive at your destination relaxed and ready to race.

Part IV, The Triathlon Lifestyle, includes chapters 21 through 29. Chapter 21 provides you with strategies to help you fit training into your daily schedule while balancing your work and personal life by using time management skills and building a support network. Chapter 22 is a comprehensive discussion of the technological milestones that have been key to triathlon development and how to choose the best swim, bike, and run gear to match your skill level. Chapter 23 discusses what qualities you should look for in a coach, from education and background to philosophy and programs, as well as how a coach can help you with physical and mental skills, fitness assessments, and testing and time management.

Chapter 24 is dedicated to helping you promote an athletic childhood for the children in your life, how to get kids started in triathlon, and how to create champions of sport and life. Chapter 25 covers the most common injuries seen in triathletes, including specific swimming, cycling, and running injuries, and how to treat injuries and when to seek a medical professional's advice. Chapter 26 explains how to use the nutrition periodization concept and how to eat based on your physical activity and what phase of training you are in. Chapter 27 discusses the physiological role of water and hydration and the specific fluid needs for athletes before, during, and after training and competition. This chapter also covers the adverse health effects related to hydration. Chapter 28 covers other multisport activities beyond just triathlon including duathlon, off-road triathlon, winter triathlon, and adventure racing. Chapter 29 covers how to assess your athletic range and depth of fitness and how to be a lifelong triathlete through safe and effective training.

Much of a triathlete's swim training will take place in a pool. Internationally, both short-course and long-course pools are measured in meters, and pools in the United States are moving toward this standard. For this reason, meters is the unit of measure we have chosen for pool distances. However, we realize that some readers will be training in yard pools. In this case, readers can swim the same number of yards as meters stated.

This book is a basic guide and resource for the safe and effective development of a comprehensive triathlon training and racing program. It is an absolute must-have resource for coaches and athletes who are interested in their first triathlon or competing in their 50th triathlon. It is loaded with invaluable training information that experts in this book have spent years developing. The authors hope that athletes, coaches, and triathlon enthusiasts will gain an appreciation and a better understanding of what it takes to train for and compete in a triathlon. We hope you enjoy the book!

# PART I

# Training

# CHAPTER 1

# Developing Your Seasonal Training Plan

## Sharone Aharon

Just like any project we do in life, whether it's to plan a trip, build a tree house, or start a business, careful planning will be a critical step and most likely will make the difference between success and failure. Athletic performance, and in this case, triathlon training, is no different. Developing a training plan is a crucial step in maximizing performance for every athlete. Doing it well will help you identify clear goals, understand your current level of readiness, and establish an accurate training regimen. The annual plan should be your training road map. It should be the instrument that guides training and facilitates improvement in technical, physiological, and psychological abilities. Planning is by far the most important tool you have regardless of your level of knowledge and experience. The planning process requires you to take a realistic look at your current position on a frequent basis throughout the season. It requires you to acquire new information and then make decisions on how you are going to train.

The objective of every training program is to ensure peak performance on a specific date. This is a challenging task that is often hard to achieve. For example, insufficient rest in the training plan will most likely cause the athlete to reach peak performance before the desired race date. On the other hand, not enough training will most likely result in peak performance after the desired race date. Knowledge, a methodical approach, and experience are the key factors in building that plan. Poor planning will lead to an inaccurate peak performance and a decrease in motivation, and it can dramatically increase the chances for injury and overtraining.

Periodization is the gold standard of developing an annual training plan. Knowing your goals and understanding your current level of fitness make up the first step of a successful plan. Although the concept of periodization and the development of a yearly plan vary a bit from one sport to another and even between coaches within a sport, the basics are still the same. I will try to convey them to you in this chapter.

# Understanding Periodization

The term *periodization* comes from *period* and means dividing a certain amount of time, in this case the training year, into smaller, easier-to-manage phases. The periodization concept is not new and was used in many forms as far back as the ancient Olympic Games. Many coaches, in a variety of sports, use the periodization concept, although the names, number, and length of phases in the plans might be slightly different. The most common periodization refers to three segments of time that repeat themselves and differ by size: macrocycle, mesocycle, and microcycle.

## Macrocycle

The macrocycle is a long stretch of training that focuses on accomplishing a major and important overall goal or a race. For example, if the Chicago Triathlon is your most important race of the season, the time from the first day of training at the beginning of the season until that race will be what you consider your macrocycle. A macrocycle is then made up of a number of different small- and medium-size phases and covers a period of a few weeks to 11 months.

For most athletes, and especially beginners, a macrocycle covers the entire racing season, focusing on one big race for the year and the development of basic physical and technical skills. More advanced and elite athletes will have two or three macrocycles per racing season; elite athletes race multiple important races per season because they may need to accumulate points or qualify for the championship race. The number of macrocycles mostly depends on the number of times these athletes need to reach peak performance within a given racing season. Elite athletes preparing for Olympic competition often use macrocycles to represent a 4-year cycle, planning different or progressive goals for each of the 4 years.

## Mesocycle

The mesocycle can be a confusing concept, as its definition might be different from one coach to another. In general, the mesocycle is a shorter block of training within the macrocycle that focuses on achieving a particular goal. A mesocycle usually covers 3 to 16 weeks and will repeat a few times within a macrocycle, each time with a different training objective or goal. There are three mesocycles, or phases, that coaches often use within the annual training plan: preparatory, competitive, and transition. These phases can be (and most of the time are) divided into smaller, more specific subphases because of the different training objectives for each.

The preparatory phase is the period that establishes the physical, technical, and psychological base from which the next phase, the competitive phase, is developed. The preparatory phase is divided into general and specific preparation subphases. The general preparatory subphase focuses on developing high-level conditioning to tolerate the demands of both training and competition. The specific preparatory subphase also has the objective of elevating athletic working capacity specific to the demands of your race. Some coaches call these subphases "prep" and "build." The next phase, the competitive phase, is divided into precompetitive and competitive subphases. The objective of this phase is to perfect all training factors to ensure successful racing. The precompetitive subphase uses racing to test your ability. It's an objective feedback for your training and level of preparation. The competitive subphase is dedicated to maximizing your fitness for maximum performance. Finally, the third phase, called the transition phase, is the rest and rejuvenation phase in between training cycles or seasons.

The size of each mesocycle, or phase, is different and is mostly related to the training objective for that particular phase of training and its position within the race schedule. In the preparatory phase, the objective is to develop technique, endurance, and an overall conditioning foundation. These elements take a long time to develop, and therefore the preparatory phase will be the longest phase of your annual training plan. The competitive phase is shorter as the focus is on racing, which is very stressful, and therefore the amount of time you can be in that phase without detrimental effect on your body is limited. You will learn more about how to build the training phases in the section on dividing your season into training periods later in this chapter.

Keep in mind that the level of the athlete will also influence the length of each phase. For example, a beginner athlete most likely will have a very long preparatory phase, up to 22 weeks, if needed, to develop a strong foundation that will enable him to endure the load of progressive, more advanced training. On the other hand, an advanced athlete who has been training for a few years has already developed a strong foundation and may need only 12 to 16 weeks to get there, and therefore she can move to the competitive phase of training more quickly.

Table 1.1 provides general guidelines on how to divide the training season (macrocycle) into mesocycles and what the length, intensity, and volume of each phase would be. Table 1.2 provides general guidelines of what the focus of training in each mesocycle should be. Although the focus in each of these phases is mostly the same for every athlete, the length, intensity, and recovery time of each period will change based on the athlete's goals and athletic experience and the time the athlete needs to adapt to the training stress.

### TABLE 1.1

## Division of Annual Training Plan Into Phases and Training Cycles

| Phase | Subphase | Length in weeks* | Intensity | Training volume |
|---|---|---|---|---|
| *Preparatory* | *General preparation (prep and base)* | 12 to 20 | Very little | Low |
| | *Specific preparation (build)* | 4 to 12 | Moderate | Moderate to high |
| *Competitive* | *Precompetitive (peak or taper)* | 3 to 8 | Heavy | Moderate |
| | *Competitive (race)* | 1 to 3 | Very heavy | Low |
| *Transition* | | Few days to 6 weeks | Very little | Low |

*22-49 total weeks

TABLE 1.2

# General Training Focus Guidelines for Each Mesocycle

| Phase | Subphase | Training focus |
|---|---|---|
| *Preparatory* | *General preparation* | Focus is on developing a strong foundation: general aerobic endurance, muscular strength, and technique in all sports. The progression is mostly by increasing volume in aerobic intensity. This phase starts at the beginning of the annual training plan and lasts 12 to 20 weeks. In case of more than one competitive period, this phase may repeat itself after the first competition but in a shorter fashion to rebuild the fitness foundation. |
| | *Specific preparation* | Focus is on a continuation of the general preparation phase and the systems that are specifically needed for the targeted race: muscular endurance, anaerobic endurance, and power. This period lasts 4 to 12 weeks, and depending on the number of times the athlete needs to reach peak performance, this period may repeat itself later in the season. |
| *Competitive* | *Precompetitive* | Focus is on race-pace fitness, race strategy, race-specific skills, and the overall demand of the competitive period. Intensity, frequency, and training duration are manipulated to achieve the objectives of this phase. The common training methodology in this phase is to reduce frequency and duration of training while maintaining or even increasing training intensity, resulting in physiological and psychological recovery, allowing the achievement of a higher fitness level. This period may last 3 to 8 weeks and will repeat itself every time the athlete needs to reach peak performance. |
| | *Competitive* | Focus is to maintain race-pace fitness and promote complete physical and mental readiness. This period is determined by the schedule of main competition and lasts 1 to 3 weeks based on whether the athlete must peak for one race or several races over a few consecutive weeks. During this phase and before major competition, coaches and athletes should have two major focus points. The first point is unloading or taper, which is generally marked by lower volumes and intensities of training. This step allows the body to fully recover and promotes a supercompensation effect. The second focus point is on race special preparation, during which race-specific technical abilities are developed. |
| *Transition* | | Focus in this phase is rest and rejuvenation of physical and mental systems. This active recovery period is characterized by low workload and little to no organized training regimen. At the end of this period and at the start of a new training cycle, the athlete may return to the general or specific preparatory phase. This phase lasts a few days to 6 weeks depending on whether the phase is located in the middle of the season after a competition and before the next training cycle or at the end of the season. |

## *Microcycle*

A microcycle is the basic training phase that repeats itself within the annual plan. The microcycle is the smallest training period within the annual training plan, and it is structured according to the objectives, volume, and intensity of each mesocycle. The microcycle is probably the most important and functional unit of training, as its structure and content determine the quality of the training process. A microcycle can last for 3 to 10 days, but in most cases, it refers to the weekly training schedule. The progression of the microcycles within a mesocycle has to take into consideration the important balance between work and rest. Too much work without appropriate rest will lead to overtraining and injuries. On the other hand, too little work with too much rest will lead to underperformance. The common ratios of work to rest in a microcycle are 3:1 or 2:1; however, in some extreme cases of heavy-load weeks (the combined stress produced by volume and intensity on the body), a 1:1 work-to-rest ratio is used. Work-to-rest cycles are called training blocks.

You should first plan each microcycle, rather than plan individual workouts, and start by taking into consideration the physiological adaptation you are looking for during a particular training phase. For example, in the preparatory phase, your microcycles will be focused on developing endurance; therefore the key workouts of those weeks should be long and of endurance-promoting intensity. In the competitive phase, your objective is to develop speed; therefore your workouts will be shorter in nature and at a much higher intensity. Thus, make sure the order of the training sessions within the week promotes the desired training effect for the week and is relevant to the training objective. In the preparatory phase, you should plan short, high-intensity workouts before long, steady-state workouts, with a recovery day between these days. However, during the precompetitive phase, you may change the weekly schedule a bit; instead of having a recovery day between two hard days, plan the week with a high-intensity day followed by a long-endurance day, and then schedule a recovery day. Doing so increases the physiological and psychological stress on the body and develops a higher level of fitness that is appropriate for this period in the annual plan. You'll learn more about how to plan your weekly schedule later in this chapter.

The structure of the microcycle should also be based on training principles (i.e., developing general fitness before specific fitness; load progression that is specific to the level of the athlete; and a recovery period to reduce fatigue, energize the body, and provide time for fitness adaptation) while considering your ability, your past progress in training, and training and facility resources. Never develop more than three or four detailed microcycles at a time, as progression is not always as linear as you might predict. In addition, assess progress frequently, since progression and the training effect are highly individual and greatly differ from athlete to athlete.

Furthermore, training sessions scheduled within the microcycle should change from phase to phase based on the demand you want and to ensure progress. The physiological and psychological demands on the body should change every 4 to 6 weeks to ensure continued fitness development. This could be done simply by changing your weekly schedule around: Move the swim workouts one day forward and the run workouts one day back, switch your long bike workout day with your long run day, lift weights early in the day rather than late in the day, or just change the position of your rest day. These minor changes can have a great effect on the training stimulus. In addition, as we mentioned earlier, think of the delicate balance you need between the work done and the rest that is necessary to achieve these adaptations within a training week.

# Developing an Annual Training Plan

Now that you have a conceptual understanding of the building blocks of the annual training plan, you can start planning your racing season using periodization concepts and build your individual annual training plan. Applying periodization concepts to the process of building an annual training plan simply means developing a plan with training blocks where each block prepares the athlete for the next more advanced and more specific training period. Be patient, and be careful not to rush through the phases. Insufficient training in the preparation phase will result in the inability to maximize performance and will produce a higher risk of injury.

The best time to engage in building the yearly plan is a few weeks into the transition phase, just before the beginning of the new training season. It is essential to take a few weeks off after the last major competition to make sure you are mentally and emotionally recovered and can be objective in your planning process. Although it is tempting to find immediate solutions to last year's shortcomings, patience will produce a better plan.

There are two major steps in putting together the annual plan. The first step is to analyze past performance and set goals and training objectives for the forthcoming season. This is a very important part that can easily be overlooked. At the end of this step, you should have a clear understanding of your true strengths and weaknesses, be clear about your racing goals for the season, and finally, know what actions you need to take to achieve these goals.

After you do this, the second step is laying down your goals and objectives and defining your training blocks. At the end of this step you will have a clear picture of your race calendar, know what your training blocks are and how long they are, know when your benchmark tests are going to be (you'll learn more about these later in this chapter), and lastly, know the structure of your weekly training schedule.

## *Analyze Past Performance*

To properly and accurately plan for peak performance for the upcoming year, it is essential to look at and understand your performance from the previous year or two. Past performance analysis should include past races, benchmark tests, and how they relate to the training plan. What worked? What did not? How consistent were you with the plan, and what effect did the training phases have on your performance? Doing this step well will help you identify your triathlon strengths and weaknesses and then adjust your new training program accordingly. If, for example, your bike segment on race day is consistently slower than that of your competition, you may want to add some bike-specific training blocks in the preparatory phase of the upcoming season. However, if you dedicated a significant amount of time to bike-focused training last season and still did not progress very much, you may have to look into changing your workout protocols and progression or changing your bike position or even your bike.

Pay particular attention to last year's benchmark testing. Did you progress from test to test? Did the benchmark test consistently predict your race result or have no relevance to how well you did in your key races? If, for example, you were able to show progress from test to test but didn't improve your performance on race day, you may be using the wrong test or you might need to add race-specific workouts in order to convert your workout fitness to race fitness. In addition, you may find that you need to change your testing protocols altogether because they may not be relevant to the fitness you are building. This process is critical and will play a major factor in this season's training objectives.

## Set Goals and Training Objectives

Goals and training objectives are related but represent two different things. A goal is your destination (e.g., your key race, when you are going to do this race, and what the desired finish time or position in this race will be). Objectives are the milestones you need to reach in order to achieve your goal. Objectives are smaller goals that are derived from your major goal, and achieving them will increase your chances of achieving your major goal.

Setting goals can be tricky, and it should be done with proper balance between your emotions and reality. Your goal should be in line with your current athletic position and the time and resources you have for training on the one hand, but it has to stretch you on the other. A goal that is realistic but too easy to accomplish will not motivate you to go out and train. An unrealistic goal that is so far from your current athletic ability can be discouraging and can cause a great amount of stress. For the same reason, your goal should be believable. You need to know you can accomplish the goal in order to bring up the necessary energy to work toward it. If you can't make yourself believe in your goal, you will not make the effort to train for it. Setting bad goals can be the cause of anxiety and stress; setting good goals will provide you with a sense of satisfaction, confidence, and calm—great assets when you are about to engage in endurance training and especially demanding and time-consuming triathlon training. It takes a great amount of courage and inner control to pick the right goals. Here are two principles that can guide you toward setting good goals:

1. *Make your goal specific and measurable.* For example, your goal may be to finish the Chicago Triathlon with a time of 2:05:00 or better. This goal gives you all the details you need. You now know what you want to do and when.

2. *Make your goal stretchable and believable.* For example, a time of 2:05:00 for the Chicago Triathlon should be a finishing time that you have never achieved before. However, you know that if you work hard and improve certain factors in your readiness, you can achieve it.

Once you have set your goals, you then need to set up objectives for your training plan. As mentioned already, objectives are the milestones or smaller goals you need to hit in order to make your major goal possible. Using the Chicago Triathlon time of 2:05:00 as an example, these subgoals should be derived from analyzing your past performance and determining your needs based on your strengths and weaknesses. Finally, your objectives will guide the training you need in order to improve your weaknesses and build on your strengths. Just like goals, training objectives need to be specific, measurable, stretchable, and believable and should be written in the same manner. Figure 1.1 gives you an example of what your goals and objectives may look like.

**FIGURE 1.1**

**Sample training plan goals and objectives.**

| Goals | Objectives |
|---|---|
| Improve my 1,500 m swim time by 1:20 | • Take a swim technique course by April 30<br>• Complete three swim-focused training blocks by May 31 |
| Improve muscular endurance on the bike | • Increase my functional threshold power to 250 W by April 30<br>• Complete a 40K bike time trial under 1 hour by June 15 |
| Run 10K off the bike under 38:30 | • Run 8K or more at 30 min race-pace effort by May<br>• Run the Lincoln Park Zoo 10K in 35:50 or faster on June 26 |

Figure 1.2 is a blank template you can use to define your own goals and objectives. As you can see, you first write down your top three goals, and within each of these three goals, you list three related objectives to help you meet that overall goal.

**FIGURE 1.2**

**Goal and objective template.**

| Goals | | Objectives | |
|---|---|---|---|
| 1 | | A | |
| | | B | |
| | | C | |
| 2 | | A | |
| | | B | |
| | | C | |
| 3 | | A | |
| | | B | |
| | | C | |

From USAT, 2012, *Complete triathlon guide* (Champaign, IL: Human Kinetics).

## Develop Your Race Calendar

The race calendar is what drives the annual training plan. The races you select to do should first and foremost support your needs, level of development, conditioning, and psychological readiness. Before we begin, note that a blank training plan template has been included at the end of this chapter; see figure 1.3 on page 15).

Your key races (let's call these your A races) are the major factor and the most influential element in your periodization. Place your key races on the annual training plan template first. Your secondary and training races (let's call these your B and C races, respectively) will have lesser effect on your periodization, although they play an important role in your race preparation and fitness development for the upcoming key races. These races will be spread out mostly in the competitive phase at strategic times on the training plan template, including the end of a training block (three to eight microcycles) and 1 or 2 weeks before major competition.

Races should not be scheduled early in the preparation phase because the focus of training at this time is to develop basic fitness and skills. In addition, races impose extreme load on the body and may cause injuries if done too early in the preparatory phase. Secondary races should be scheduled in the annual plan to mirror the progression in training load toward the goal race. For example, if running is a major limitation and you want to use a half-marathon race as a B race, you should schedule the race far into the preparatory phase of the training plan, allowing sufficient time for proper training. The number of B and C races you schedule should be determined by your fitness level and your ability to recover and return to training after each race. Too many races on your schedule will interrupt your training and lead to premature peak performance. Too few races will lead to less-than-optimal performance at your major and most important race. In addition, proper taper and recovery must be built into the training plan, especially after B and C races that lead to your A race. More information about recovery is found in chapter 8, and tapering is covered in chapter 10. It is recommended that beginner and less experienced athletes reach peak performance once in their first and even second seasons and dedicate most of their training time to building basic endurance, strength, and skills. More advanced and experienced athletes may reach peak performance more often.

Once the race calendar is determined, try not to change it because the entire training plan is based on that schedule. In the event you need to change your race calendar, you may have to reset your training phases. If you are skipping or adding a B or C race, then a small adjustment in your plan may be sufficient. However, if it is an A race, you may have to reevaluate the entire plan, but stay true to your goals and training objectives.

## Divide Your Season Into Training Periods

Setting up your training period and the progression slope from period to period is the most important task in building your annual plan. Figure 1.3 on page 15 should help you set up your training phases and the number of weeks you should schedule for each phase. Training periods should be determined based on your race calendar and the number of times you want to reach peak performance in the upcoming season.

Again using figure 1.3, your annual training plan template, divide the season into phases by first making it useful for the current calendar year. In the date of the week column, place the date for each Monday for the entire year, starting with the first Monday of your training plan. Next, add the month's name in the month column to the left of the first Monday of that month. Now you are ready to use the template for the current year. Place your races on the calendar, with the option of using different colors to differentiate between the importance of each of the races (e.g., A, B, or C race). Moving back from your key race (or in the case of more than one peak performance, from your first peak performance), start filling in the weekly focus column. For the competitive phase, start by setting up 2 or 3 weeks for the race period, then 3 to 8 weeks for the precompetitive phase.

For the preparatory phase, I suggest starting at the beginning of the training season with 3 to 5 weeks of acclimation, building your load from your transition-phase fitness level. Next, start marking training blocks of 3- or 4-week cycles until you meet the precompetitive phase on your plan. Early in the season, you may be able to endure a 4-week training cycle because the load of each week is somewhat low. Later in the season, as the demand of each training week increases, you may have to use a 3-week training cycle. You may also need to adjust the number of weeks in the last training block because the weeks of the training year might not divide exactly into your cycles. Once you are finished planning toward your first A race, you should do the same from the second A race. Continue dividing the season all the way down to the level of the microcycle.

Your next step is to assess your starting abilities. This can be done by asking yourself three simple questions:

1. What is the distance I can currently swim?
2. How long can I comfortably bike in time?
3. How long can I comfortably run in time?

These starting abilities will give you an idea of the required length of each workout in the first few weeks. My suggestion is to start at a lower volume than you are currently capable of; the combined effect of having a new and complete training routine may make the load much higher, and therefore a stand-alone 60-minute run might feel much harder within a full training program.

Next you should set up your weekly schedule. Start by choosing your day off, and then schedule your swimming days, biking days, running days, and weightlifting days. In most cases you want a day of easy recovery between high-intensity days. However, as mentioned earlier, that might change as you progress into more advanced stages in the plan.

Last, mark your mesocycles to the left of the month column, based on descriptions you put in the weekly cycle for each week and training block. As you can see, the planning of your season and the focus of each training block start from the end and go backward and are determined by the A race, your training objectives, and your level of fitness and experience.

As mentioned earlier, the progression slope normally includes 3- or 4-week cycles, but depending on the training phase, a 2-week cycle is used as well. Starting at the beginning of the preparatory phase, the first week in a 3-week cycle will have a training volume of about 30 to 40 percent of your maximum load. In the second week, the training volume will increase by 10 to 20 percent, and in the third week, the volume will drop by about 6 to 7 percent. Continue to progressively increase the training this way through the preparatory phase, maximizing your training volume toward the end of the general preparatory phase and the beginning of the specific preparatory phase, and stay that way for a period of one to three cycles. At that point, volume will start to decrease by about 5 to 10 percent per cycle and will stay at about 75 to 80 percent throughout the competitive phase. During taper, volume will decrease to about 50 percent of the maximum load.

On the other hand, intensity trails volume throughout the annual plan, starting at about 25 percent of maximum load, and stays around that level for 3 or 4 weeks. After that, intensity increases by about 15 percent every two or three training cycles, in the same way training volume increases and reaches its highest levels at the end of the specific preparatory phase. At that point, intensity levels will be just under volume levels and in some cases may match volume levels. During the precompetitive and competitive phases, intensity will stay around the same level, with slight variation to allow recovery and high-intensity race-simulation cycles. Toward the end of the competitive phase, training intensity should drop down to around 60 percent.

The ultimate goal of every athlete is to reach peak performance in key races throughout the season. You will achieve this goal through careful planning and proper progression of the training cycles in your annual plan. In the early part of the season, during the preparatory and competitive phase, you build your technical, physiological, and mental foundation. The last part of the competitive phase is where you start the process of peaking. Peaking, or taper, is achieved by manipulating volume, frequency, and intensity during the last one to four microcycles to reduce overall training load and maximize adaptation. Proper taper can be achieved by systematically reducing physiological and psychological fatigue while maintaining a high level of sport-specific fitness. Taper should last 1 to 4 weeks depending on the athlete, the pretaper load, and the race distance. In most cases an Ironman taper will last 3 or 4 weeks, and taper for an Olympic-distance triathlon leading to major competition will last 1 or 2 weeks. During taper you should maintain training intensity to prevent detraining, decrease training volume by 40 to 60 percent of the pretaper volumes, and keep the frequency of your training sessions at around 80 percent of pretaper frequency. Proper taper should lead to about a 3 percent improvement in performance.

## Set Up Benchmark Testing

Testing is a critical and integral part of the annual plan and should be performed throughout the season systematically and consistently. The main objectives of the tests are to determine your strengths and weaknesses; monitor your progress; and produce data that will allow you to calculate training zones, pace, and load. Test results should steer the training program and keep you on course toward reaching your goals. Baseline testing should be performed in each sport 3 to 5 weeks from the beginning of the program. Follow-up testing should be scheduled every 3 to 10 weeks after that.

For testing to produce meaningful results, make sure you test what you train or for data you may need for future training to calculate heart rate training zone or pace and power zones. Don't train aerobically and look for progress at anaerobic endurance levels. In addition, make sure your training objectives are lined up with your goal. There are many lab and field tests that let you compare your performance against standards to see where you stand. However, don't hesitate to use one of your favorite workouts as your test; a certain bike loop or a swim workout that always feels good can be a great measure of progress.

The timing of the tests is critical for producing accurate results. Most of your testing should be done in the preparatory phase to make sure your training produces the adaptation you are looking for. During the competitive phase, it is much harder to find the time for testing and to produce accurate results. The best time to test is at the end of or right after the recovery week of a certain training block.

### Build Your Weekly Training Schedule

As you learned earlier, the microcycle, or in other words, the weekly training schedule, is by far the most important period of the training program. Its design and content are the cornerstone of the annual training plan. You should consider the weekly schedule as a 7-day training program (could be as little as 3 and up to 10, but 7 days is most common) for achieving a predecided training adaptation. Based on the goals and objectives you set for the season, your weekly schedule should change from one training phase to another in order to promote different training loads. Another important factor in scheduling your workouts is the balance between work and rate of recovery. Too much load with too little rest will lead to injury and overtraining. On the other hand, too little load and too much rest will slow your progress dramatically and will prevent you from reaching peak performance.

There are many approaches to developing an annual training plan. Find or build the one that works best for you. Not having an annual training plan would be like walking in the dark and not understanding why you can't see anything. Without a training plan, you will have no direction and will produce poor, or at best unpredictable, results. You should take the time at the beginning of the year to gather the proper information, establish goals, set objectives, and build a detailed annual training plan.

# Annual Training Plan Template

An annual training plan template will help you record and organize the information you gathered as well as plan the training phases down to the level of the training session. Figure 1.3 shows the template I have developed that works best for my needs. The template contains the yearly calendar by weeks and allows you to plan the year down to your weekly schedule and your individual workouts. It also allows you to change the plan from phase to phase and add any necessary information you might need in order to build a complete yearly plan.

FIGURE 1.3

# Annual training plan template.

Name: _____ Year: _____

### Weekly schedule

| | M | T | W | Th | F | Sa | Su |
|---|---|---|---|---|---|---|---|
| Swim | | | | | | | |
| Bike | | | | | | | |
| Run | | | | | | | |
| Strength training | | | | | | | |

| | Start of season training ability (beginner, intermediate, advanced) | Strength level (excellent, good, fair, poor) |
|---|---|---|
| Swim | | |
| Bike | | |
| Run | | |

| Phase | Month | Date of the week | Swim sessions | Bike sessions | Run sessions | Strength training | Weekly Focus | Race name and date |
|---|---|---|---|---|---|---|---|---|
| | | | | | | | | |

**Workout Codes**

| | | | | | |
|---|---|---|---|---|---|
| A | Aerobic | TC | Technique session | — | _____ |
| T | Tempo | T1 | Swim/bike session | — | _____ |
| TH | Threshold | T2 | Bike/run session | — | _____ |
| VO | $\dot{V}O_2$max effort | TR | Transition run | — | _____ |
| MX | Max effort | OP | Open-water swim | — | _____ |
| F | Fartlek | | | | |
| R | Recovery | | | | |

From USAT, 2012, *Complete triathlon guide* (Champaign, IL: Human Kinetics).

# CHAPTER 2

# Customizing Training for Specific Groups

## Christine Palmquist

As a good coach tackles the challenge of solving each athlete's training puzzle, he soon learns that every athlete is unique and requires a training program specific to that athlete's strengths and limitations. Excellent coaches prescribe specific training to fit each athlete. Beyond the individual differences seen between every triathlete, however, good coaches also need to account for the special characteristics found within some triathlete populations—such as beginners, youth, and female or masters athletes. A strong knowledge of how these special athletes may differ from the typical adult male athlete can help a coach avoid potential problems.

Although triathletes from all populations share far more similarities than differences, the coach must still consider each athlete as an individual. This chapter addresses potential differences and similarities between athlete groups and gives training examples of how to help all athletes succeed at their goals.

## Coaching Beginner Athletes

For a coach, there is nothing quite like guiding a beginner to her first triathlon finish line. A coach of beginners has the privilege to be partner and witness to a truly life-changing event in that new triathlete's life. It can be every bit as rewarding as the opportunity to coach an elite athlete to a podium finish. It can also be just as challenging.

### Focus for Beginners

Triathlon is a thriving, growing sport. In the first nine months of 2011, USAT licensed 57,555 new members and sanctioned 641 new races (out of 2,353) in 2011. A beginner's training should focus first on development of the skills and endurance necessary to complete the goal event safely and enjoyably. The beginner athlete's training and racing journey should help him develop a love for the sport and the desire to continue with future competitions.

In short, the keys to success for beginners are as follows:

- Allow them to give input on training scheduling.
- Give them training sessions that are short and easy enough to ensure completion.
- Early weeks are mostly about learning how to train, not about building fitness, so be patient.
- Avoid pace- or time-based goals.
- Focus on teaching skills and building the fitness required to safely complete the race.

## Allow Input on Training Schedules

Beginners may have never before experienced structured training. Remember, these are independent adults, accustomed to programming their own schedules. They may initially feel uncomfortable at the loss of this control. It is important to communicate often with them about how the training is fitting into their lives. Get their input, and give them back a little control over how the training days and weeks look. Allow your beginning athletes to tell you which times are best for training each day of the week, and give them a chance to update this as often as needed. As a result, you will prescribe training that will fit into their schedules. This will make it more likely that they will complete most of their training and feel confident and positive about it. Realize they will change their minds often as they find out more about how pools, bikes, and running shoes fit into their work and family lives. Take it one week at a time during the early weeks, and remain extremely flexible.

## Keep Training Sessions Manageable

Any coach who has spent recent seasons with veteran triathletes will tend to overestimate how much of a training load to give a beginner. Although an easy training session for a seasoned triathlete might mean an hour swim, bike, or run, a beginner might need to start with extremely short sessions that hardly warrant a shower. For example, a beginner runner might complete only 10 minutes of running in an early-season training session, or a swim for a beginner might mean a lesson with technique focus and only 200 to 300 meters of swimming. Although your beginners may express the enthusiasm to go farther in these initial sessions, make sure to design training sessions they can complete successfully, with the desire to do more on the next day. Start transitioning them into the routine of a triathlete one tiny step at a time. Allow them to spend part of their early training time investigating the pool, learning how to hook a bike up to the trainer, getting a proper bike fit and a comfortable saddle, and acquiring proper clothing and footwear for every session. Err on the side of too little training rather than defeating them right away. Ensure they feel early success as they begin their journey to that first race.

## Teach How to Train

Beginners approach their first triathlon with an overwhelming mixture of emotions. There is a mountain of equipment to acquire and learn how to use. The coach may need to teach swim technique and help the athletes overcome very real swimming fears. The majority of beginner triathletes are tentative or new cyclists, requiring thorough guidance on where and how to ride their (often new) bikes. Coaching these athletes through the run segment means teaching them proper nutrition, hydration, and pacing strategies to maintain their strength through to the finish line. The most important strategy for coaching beginners is to assume they have absolutely no knowledge or experience with any triathlon discipline. Start from zero and provide clear, detailed instructions, and anticipate misunderstandings. This is a time when the two-way communication of a personal coaching session or phone call may address all an athlete's questions better than an e-mail.

## Avoid Pace Goals

Race results and pace- or time-based goals should be pushed aside because the ultimate goal for beginner athletes is to gain the skills and strength to safely finish the race. A beginner should be focused on crossing the finish line feeling strong rather than on holding a certain speed on the bike or during the run. Examples of good first-race goals include the following: Stay calm during the swim; drink a bottle of water during the bike; hold back to an easy jog for the first mile of the run. The beginner athlete has control over achieving goals such as these and by doing so will have a better race overall.

## Teach Skills

Beginner triathletes will have successful first races if they have the skills to race safely and the endurance to make it to the finish line. Speed is not nearly as important at the beginner stage of development. Instead, have athletes spend training time practicing how to set up a transition area. They should practice efficient transitions frequently in the weeks leading up to their race. They should learn how to change a flat tire and have basic knowledge to maintain their bikes. Beginners need open-water experience under supervised and safe conditions. You will have to teach them about triathlon-specific clothing and equipment and how to use them. Coaches must help new athletes learn how to drink and fuel before, during, and after training and racing situations. Training sessions should address mental skills, pacing strategies, and the basics of training language and training zones. Coaching a beginner is a wonderful challenge. It is very gratifying for both coach and athlete to cross that first finish line.

## *Training Considerations for Beginners*

Prescribing training for beginners means designing short workouts at an easy intensity to introduce the new athletes to each mode of training. The first swim workouts should be swim lessons. The first bike workouts should be bike fits and equipment checks. The first run workouts for beginner runners should be run–walk patterns based on their experience and fitness. Total training time for the first several weeks might be six to nine training sessions, each lasting about 30 to 60 minutes, for a total of 3 to 7 hours. A beginner's first week might be as simple as the weekly plan shown in figure 2.1.

If your beginner athlete gets through these first several weeks, he will have the confidence and excitement to continue and to build from here toward the race distances. After a few weeks, the athlete will be ready to progress to workouts that begin to resemble the race he is training for. These workouts will continue to hone the athlete's triathlon skills as well as build his ability to endure longer swims, bikes, and runs. In the water, the athlete should work toward the ability to swim the race distance nonstop in the pool and in the open water. If swimming is a weakness for the athlete, the coach should include more frequent swims—maybe four or five swims a week to advance the athlete's swimming endurance more rapidly. Training should progressively work the athlete up to race distance on the bike. And in run training sessions, the athlete should lengthen his continuous runs as well as practice the run–walk pattern (if necessary) he will use to complete the race distance.

**FIGURE 2.1**

## Sample beginner training plan for weeks 1-3.

|  | Monday | Tuesday | Wednesday | Thursday | Friday | Saturday | Sunday |
|---|---|---|---|---|---|---|---|
| *Swim* | Swim lesson (30 min) | | | Swim lesson (30 min) | | | Day off |
| *Bike* | | Easy ride; bike check (30 min) | | | Easy ride; handling skills (30 min) | | |
| *Run* | | | Alternating run–walk (30 min) | | | Alternating run–walk (30 min) | |

The number of training sessions per week will remain about the same as in the early weeks (six to nine sessions per week). However, the length of many sessions may increase slightly, with most workout sessions being 30 to 90 minutes. Total training time for a typical week will be in the 5- to 10-hour range for most beginners. A beginner's training plan for these weeks may look like the plan in figure 2.2.

**FIGURE 2.2**

## Sample beginner training plan for weeks 4-12.

|  | Monday | Tuesday | Wednesday | Thursday | Friday | Saturday | Sunday |
|---|---|---|---|---|---|---|---|
| *Swim* | 3 × 400 at moderate effort; practice sighting once per length (45 min) | | 20 min continuous swim; practice sighting once per length (45 min) | | Open-water practice swim with a buddy; practice sighting (30 min) | | Day off |
| *Bike* | | Bike in rolling hills; bike the uphills strongly (45 min) | | Easy ride, quick cadence; aim for 90 rpm cadence for most of this ride (45 min) | | Long ride for 75-90 min at a steady pace; practice drinking while riding (90 min) | |
| *Run* | Easy run–walk (intervals of run 4.5 min and walk 30 sec); practice drinking during walk breaks (45 min) | | 4 × 60 sec uphill repeats at a strong pace; walk down the hill after each for recovery (45 min) | | Easy and continuous run with 30 sec walk breaks (up to 4) when needed (45 min) | Easy transition run immediately after bike ride; get used to making the transition (10 min) | |

As you move within 3 or 4 weeks of race day (late in the competitive phase of training), the athlete should be able to complete stand-alone swims, bikes, and runs that equal the race distance. The athlete also needs to complete some swim–bike and bike–run "bricks" that come close to race distance. The triathlon term *brick* means to complete two or more triathlon disciplines within a training session. The athlete might do a race-paced swim followed by a bike training session, with a very short transition in between the two workouts. Bike–run bricks are very important to teach the new athlete what it feels like to run on legs already fatigued from biking. The coach should teach proper race-day nutrition and race pacing and have the athlete practice these during race-simulation bricks. Three weeks before the race, your beginner's training might look like the weekly plan in figure 2.3.

**FIGURE 2.3**

### Sample beginner training plan 3 weeks before race.

| | Monday | Tuesday | Wednesday | Thursday | Friday | Saturday (race-specific brick) | Sunday |
|---|---|---|---|---|---|---|---|
| **Swim** | 4 × 200 m, steady effort (45 min) | | | 3 × 500 m, steady effort (60 min) | Day off | Race-distance continuous swim (30 min) | |
| **Bike** | | Easy ride (30 min) | | | | Moderate ride (30 min) | Steady ride (60 min) |
| **Run** | Alternating run–walk (30 min) | | Alternating run–walk (30 min) | | | Alternating run–walk (30 min) | |

The last two taper weeks will be for the athlete to rest, practice transitions, gather and tune up equipment, and finish discussions about nutrition and pacing. The coach should plan to spend some extra time on the phone or in person during race week to talk through every step. It is important to help the athlete visualize the good and bad moments of a typical race and how to react appropriately. Finally, be sure she knows you are rooting for her and are proud of her efforts. Then step back and watch the joy on her face when she finishes.

# Coaching Youth Athletes

Youth triathlon is a rapidly expanding sport. There were 42,626 youth USAT members in 2011; approximately 29.07 percent of all USAT members are aged 7 to 19. Race directors are providing more kid triathlons, with safe courses and age-appropriate distances for kids as young as early elementary school. Youth triathlon teams are developing across the country, providing opportunities for these young athletes to train together and be part of a coached team. But, remember, young athletes are not simply small-sized adults. There are many differences to consider when creating training sessions for these special triathletes. Note that chapter 24 covers coaching youth athletes in more detail.

## Focus for Youth

Some of the unique considerations when coaching young athletes include, but are not limited to, safety, fear, motor coordination, maturity, attention span, physical reactions to weather conditions, parental fears, growth issues, nutrition, competition with other sports, group dynamics, team building, confidence building, developmental readiness, and basic skills for all three sports plus transitions. A youth coach should not be a beginner coach. This group warrants an experienced coach, knowledgeable in how to properly coach young athletes, who will be present at all training sessions. Any coach willing to take on these youngest, most special triathletes will realize quickly that this group can be the most challenging and most rewarding group of all to guide. After all these considerations, however, the highest priority for coaching young athletes is to nourish a new love for the sport. If a young triathlete loves triathlon, then he will love the practice and learning involved in training. In short, the keys to success for youth are as follows:

■ Develop skills and speed.

■ Ensure safety.

■ Keep training fun.

■ Maintain open communication.

■ Educate on proper nutrition.

### Develop Skills and Speed

A coach's first priority with young athletes is to help them develop skills. Practice sessions with elementary and middle school youth should involve skill drills at every session. Running drills to develop proper form, cycling drills to improve bike handling, and swimming drills to develop proper stroke technique should provide the foundation for each practice. Young athletes are physiologically primed to learn skills more rapidly during these years.

Coaches must realize that motor patterns are most easily learned at a young age. Once learned, these motor patterns are stored in the central nervous system. A young athlete who practices and learns speed will develop into a faster older athlete. In addition, youth is the prime time to develop certain types of muscle fibers, especially fast-twitch fibers, and the neuromuscular patterns required to be fast. Therefore, young athletes should spend much of their practice time doing short sprints to develop speed and economy of movement.

Remember, too, that as young athletes grow, their bones grow first, followed eventually by the surrounding soft tissue (muscles and ligaments), which can be weakened and stressed as a result. Coaches should be aware of their athletes' growth spurts and reduce training stress during those periods. And during growth spurts, the kids, parents, and coaches should expect to see the athletes take a step backward in terms of training and speed. A coach should also recognize and respect that there are early developers and late developers. The coach must take care to not give early developers more attention and recognition. Late developers can often become the most talented athletes with a patient and motivating coach.

Young athletes have a much more difficult time sustaining a strong effort for several minutes than adults because of their low economy of motion, inability to release body heat, and low ability to store and use muscular glycogen. Youth athletes have a lower cardiac output and a lower $\dot{V}O_2$max than adult athletes. Their heart rates are much higher during rest and during activity. All these things begin to improve as the young athletes reach and surpass puberty, but for preadolescent athletes, adultlike endurance training and adult endurance races are not appropriate. It is important to find age-appropriate race distances and to focus more on fun and short speed than to assign grueling intervals during triathlon practices.

## Ensure Safety

When training young athletes, the coach must consider every potential safety hazard. Young triathletes should pass a swim screening and swim regularly. Membership in a youth swim team is a great start for the youngest triathletes because it gives kids good instruction in technique, practice at swimming in a racing situation, practice at swimming in a crowded lane, and plenty of training. Even with a swim team background, any swimmer can panic at her first open-water swim. Therefore, open-water swim practices are crucial, and a coach should conduct them regularly in a safety-conscious environment, with lifeguard supervision and enough adults to thoroughly watch and assist each swimmer.

Cycling is the other potentially dangerous sport. Most youth triathletes will eventually crash. Therefore, have a good first aid kit and an emergency plan. Youth must cycle in an area that is completely safe from traffic and free of hilly terrain that is beyond their bike-handling capabilities. If the riders are on a bike trail, the coach will need to teach them how to pass pedestrians politely and safely. When riding in groups, the coach will have to combine riders of similar abilities and consider who may need to ride alone or with more space around them to be safe. Adult riders should ride with each small group of kids. When coaching youth riders, a coach will need to teach each athlete how to brake safely, when and how to shift gears, how to turn corners and make cone turns, how to draft, how to speak to other riders regarding stopping or slowing, and how to properly wear a helmet.

Safe running training for kids just requires a safe course. Make sure the footing is good, and look for a training venue that offers a variety of running surfaces (trails, grass, asphalt, hills). The course should be safe from traffic and easily monitored by the coach. Runners should each pair with one or more buddies for their runs.

A good youth coach will also be ready to modify training for all sorts of weather situations. The coach should have a bad weather plan and be ready to use it at the first sign of lightning. Young athletes do not sweat as efficiently as adults do and are more susceptible to heat-related illness. Conversely, young athletes are also more susceptible to hypothermia. The coach needs to teach athletes how to adjust to weather conditions with proper hydration and clothing choices.

## Keep Training Fun

A good youth coach will incorporate games and fun challenges in every practice session. Games are the best way to increase the amount of high-quality running in a practice. Games strengthen teams, help with short attention spans, develop speed and agility skills, and help nurture that love for triathlon that is so important for the development of a great young triathlete.

Contests and practice races are good ways to motivate young triathletes. For example, put up a map of the United States, and tally team weekly running miles to "cross the country"; have a weekly race or time trial, with a frozen fruit bar for all finishers; pick an athlete of the week, and reward him with a small prize; or give each kid a nickname that matches her personality and conveys strength, skill, or speed. And above all, a good coach will hammer the theme of *team*. Team games, team colors, team songs, and team cheers all remind these athletes they are training and racing for their team as well as for themselves.

## Maintain Open Communication

Communication is critical for a good working relationship between coach, athlete, and parents. The coach should communicate to athletes and their parents by phone or by e-mail at least weekly about upcoming training sessions, racing schedules, and any other group concerns. The coach who sends personalized e-mails to each athlete regarding individual goals and accomplishments will make all the athletes feel special and involved in their growth as triathletes.

## Educate on Proper Nutrition

Coaches should educate youth on how to properly fuel their training and racing. Without good nutrition, all the training will go to waste, and the youth athletes can suffer health problems. A good coach will teach kids the information they need in order to choose energy-packed, healthful foods that will give them strength and health. The youngest competitors and their parents may not understand the importance of hydration and food before, during, and after workouts. Kids tend to choose foods based on taste, appearance, and availability, so teaching them to plan their breakfasts and pack healthy snacks is important. Kids do not have a sensitive thirst signal to tell them to drink. Hydration education is crucial. The coach can hand out clear water bottles marked in two-ounce (60 ml) increments to help kids learn the concept of hydration volume and practice drinking regularly.

Nutrition coaching becomes even more complex when athletes begin to go through adolescence. Female athletes will naturally grow and gain body fat during adolescence, and each girl may become very conscious of her new curves and the loss of running speed due to weight gain. The coach needs to emphasize that this is normal and help guide the athletes through this period with a base of how to properly stay fueled. Boys may go through a similar stage where they gain weight before they grow taller. One insensitive comment by the coach about "getting big" or "needing to lose weight" can send a kid spiraling toward a long-term eating disorder. The coach, as a respected authority figure, can make a positive difference during this awkward time with good information and advice.

## *Training Considerations for Youth*

Early-season workouts (preparatory phase) should introduce a training routine that will remain consistent throughout the season. Training sessions should start on time but with a "sponge" activity that allows latecomers (usually not the young athletes' fault) to join practice without disruption. Functional dynamic warm-up and stretching routines are good for the first 10 to 15 minutes of practice. After the team learns the routine, the older athletes can take turns leading the warm-up while the coach says hello to each athlete and explains the workout for the day.

Early in the season, training should be preparatory by starting easy and progressing according to the child's abilities and skills. It is better to be too conservative with training than to risk burnout or injury with these new athletes. Coaches should make sure their young athletes are recovering well and remaining positive about going to practice. If not, these are sure signs that training should be reduced for more rest.

A youth coach must remember that kids can build fitness very quickly. The coach can save the toughest workouts for the competitive season and spend the early, precompetitive months building skills, safe habits, speed, strength, and confidence in the athletes. Appropriate weekly training hours range from 4 to 8.5 hours of training for athletes 12 and under, and up to 16 hours for athletes older than 12. Young athletes should spend about half of their training time swimming, as swimming skills require much practice, and the nonimpact nature of swimming is the best place to build endurance. Typical swim team workouts are usually age appropriate and excellent for young triathletes.

Young triathletes should frequently practice bricks that come close to their race distance, allowing them to complete two or more triathlon disciplines within a training session. This gives them a chance to practice the skill of transitioning from swim to bike and then from bike to run. In addition, skills such as getting shoes and helmets on and mounting and dismounting a bike can be difficult for young athletes, so transition practice helps them gain valuable experience. And finally, even the youngest triathletes need some strength training. However, it should come in the form of exercises that help the young athletes move their own body weight with good strength and balance. Dynamic warm-up running exercises, jump rope, simple plyometrics such as hopping and skipping, and hill repeats are all good strength-building practices.

An early-season training week for youth age 12 and under gives them an opportunity to swim, bike, run, practice transitions, and build strength three times each per week. The week may look like the plan in figure 2.4, whereas an early-season training week

**FIGURE 2.4**

## Sample 12-and-under youth training plan for an early-season week.

|  | Monday | Tuesday | Wednesday | Thursday | Friday | Saturday | Sunday |
|---|---|---|---|---|---|---|---|
| *Swim* | Typical swim team practice working on stroke, drills, speed, and endurance (60-90 min) |  | Typical swim team practice working on stroke, drills, speed, and endurance (60-90 min) |  | Typical swim team practice working on stroke, drills, speed, and endurance (60-90 min) |  | Day off |
| *Bike* |  | Skills and speed (35 min) |  | Skills and endurance (35 min) |  | Bike–run bricks (30 min) |  |
| *Run* |  | Skills and endurance (30 min) |  | Skills and speed (30 min) |  | Bike–run bricks and skills (30 min) |  |
| *Transitions* |  | 10 min |  | 10 min |  | 15 min |  |
| *Strength* |  | 15 min |  | 15 min |  | 10 min |  |

for athletes over 12 may look more like the plan in figure 2.5. As young triathletes transition into over-12 training, be patient because some of the younger members of this age group may still do better with the lighter 12-and-under schedule. The triathletes who are ready can handle four sessions of swim, bike, and run each week, with three functional strength sessions per week and short transition practices as needed.

## FIGURE 2.5

### Sample over-12 youth training plan for an early-season week.

| | Monday | Tuesday | Wednesday | Thursday | Friday | Saturday | Sunday |
|---|---|---|---|---|---|---|---|
| *Swim* | Endurance (60 min) | Speed (60 min) | | Force (60 min) | Speed (60 min) | | Day off |
| *Bike* | | Skills (60 min) | Speed (45 min) | Strength (60 min) | | Speed (60 min) | |
| *Run* | Tempo (45 min) | | Tempo (50 min) | | Easy (45 min) | Speed (45 min) | |
| *Transitions* | | | 10 min | | | 15 min | |
| *Strength* | 15 min | | 15 min | | 15 min | | |

During the competitive phase, the athletes should perform two or three race-specific workouts per week. Race-specific workouts give the athletes a chance to practice race pace and race distances in practice. In these workouts, the coach should frequently pace the athletes at race-goal pace. Races may be substituted occasionally for such workouts, but be careful not to race too often (racing is mentally and physically draining). Overall training volume should decrease during the competitive season to allow extra rest and recovery from these important workouts.

A competitive-phase training week for youth 12 and under will have easier midweek practices to allow recovery for the weekend races or race-simulation practices, as shown in figure 2.6. A competitive training week for triathletes older than 12 is built on the same philosophy of harder races or race simulations followed by easier practices and opportunities for recovery, as shown in figure 2.7.

For the purposes of this book, these training week examples are very general. In reality, the coach will need to adapt training to each athlete's skills and weaknesses and carefully monitor the energy level of each athlete. The coach should promote balance between school, family, fun, and training. A happy athlete is a strong athlete.

FIGURE 2.6

## Sample 12-and-under youth training plan for a competitive-season week.

|  | Monday | Tuesday | Wednesday | Thursday | Friday | Saturday* | Sunday |
|---|---|---|---|---|---|---|---|
| *Swim* | Speed and skills (60 min) |  | Endurance and skills (60 min) |  | Strength and skills (60 min) | Race or race-simulation workout (30-60 min) | Day off |
| *Bike* |  | Bricks and skills (35 min) |  | Endurance and speed (35 min) |  | Race or race-simulation work-out (30-60 min) |  |
| *Run* |  | Bricks and skills (30 min) |  | Speed and skills (30 min) |  | Race or race-simulation work-out (30-60 min) |  |
| *Transitions* |  | 15 min |  | 15 min |  | 15 min |  |
| *Strength* |  | 5 min |  | 5 min |  | 5 min |  |

*The training scheduled for this day may be replaced by a formal race.

FIGURE 2.7

## Sample over-12 youth training plan for a competitive-season week.

|  | Monday | Tuesday | Wednesday | Thursday | Friday | Saturday* | Sunday |
|---|---|---|---|---|---|---|---|
| *Swim* | Speed (60 min) | Endurance and skills (60 min) |  | Force and skills (60 min) |  | Race or race-simulation workout (30-60 min) | Day off |
| *Bike* |  | Strong group ride with sprints and race-pace efforts (60 min) | Easy ride; skills (45 min) | Endurance and skills (60 min) |  | Race or race-simulation workout (30-60 min) |  |
| *Run* | Speed and skills (45 min) |  | Race-pace run; skills (50 min) |  | Easy run (45 min) | Race or race-simulation workout (30-60 min) |  |
| *Transitions* |  |  | 10 min |  |  | 15 min |  |
| *Strength* | 5 min |  | 5 min |  | 5 min |  |  |

*The training scheduled for this day may be replaced by a formal race.

# Coaching Masters Athletes

In triathlon, a masters athlete is one who is aged 40 or older. As of the end of 2011, 39 percent of USAT annual members met this criterion. In fact, the largest single age group for both female and male USAT annual members is the 40 to 44 age group. Masters athletes may have more time and disposable income for racing than their younger counterparts. However, it doesn't matter how hard we try to stay young, as we grow older there are certain undeniable physiological changes in our bodies. The good news is that proper training can delay or diminish these changes.

## *Focus for Masters*

A masters athlete's training focus should be on the quality of each training session combined with the opportunity to recover and rest adequately before the next session. Masters athletes should spend less time doing long, slow endurance workouts and more time preserving their speed with harder training and racing efforts. Triathletes 40 and older often have extensive racing and training experience, and they can use this knowledge to race and train more successfully.

Coaches can ask masters to talk through past races to find out what went well and to learn from mistakes. Masters athletes may also have the maturity to approach training and racing in the most healthy and balanced manner, and they may have more time and money to devote to their racing passions. These advantages mean that some endurance masters athletes can still set new personal bests well into their 50s. In short, the keys to success for masters are as follows:

- Strength train regularly.
- Plan adequate recovery.
- Be aware of the injury potential.

### Strength Train Regularly

Sometime in our late 20s, all adults begin to lose muscle. This yearly degenerative loss of .5 to 1 percent of skeletal muscle is called sarcopenia. Fortunately, exercise and strength training have been shown to slow the rate of degeneration (Taaffe 2006). This is crucial information for designing proper training for this special group of athletes. Masters athletes should regularly incorporate strength training into their training programs. Two or three strength sessions per week will help a masters athlete maintain strength, balance, and speed.

### Plan Adequate Recovery

Masters athletes require more recovery time from training sessions. Athletes 40 and older need more rest days and rest weeks built into their training plans. Where 30-year-old athletes might be able to build their training for 3 weeks in a row before needing a rest week, masters athletes might need a rest week as early as after 1 week of training. Because of this increased need for recovery, masters athletes should cut running days (because of their high impact) down to a minimum—often to just 3 days a week to allow for the balance of adaptation and recovery.

## Be Aware of the Injury Potential

By the time an athlete has reached her 40s, she has probably experienced a wide range of injuries from training and racing. Some of these injuries may become chronic as the athlete ages through degeneration or long-term weakness. The coach needs to prescribe weekly strength and stretching training sessions derived from rehabilitation experts to address muscular imbalances and tightness. The coach must also optimize training volume to allow the masters athlete enough rest for adequate recovery between hard training sessions. Masters athletes generally do best on a lower training volume, with a higher percentage of time spent doing high-intensity or force and strength work.

There is also good news about masters and injury potential. Masters athletes are more likely to be wise about injuries. They have experienced enough of them to know when to stop a training session, take a rest day, or slow down the pace of a workout to avoid injury. If they become injured, they are more likely to know how to heal and have a pool of trusted resources to consult. Many masters remain more injury free in their older years than when younger.

## *Training Considerations for Masters*

Masters often have a large base of cumulative years of endurance training. They have adapted physiologically from all the years of steady biking, swimming, and running and have built their base. Therefore, they may need less base-building time than younger or less experienced athletes.

If an athlete wants to keep his ability to race strongly at shorter distances, he must continue to do high-intensity workouts and races. The biggest contributor to age-related loss of performance may be loss of aerobic capacity ($\dot{V}O_2$max) along with loss of speed and power at lactate threshold. Although there is not much available research on the topic, it appears that masters athletes can maintain their aerobic capacity, lactate threshold capacity, and economy until sometime in their 50s *if* they continue with focused training and racing at a high level (Trappe et al. 1996).

One study that followed 27 elite endurance athletes over 15 years found that the most active athletes (those who raced shorter races regularly) managed to maintain or even improve their aerobic capacities over the 15 years (Marti and Howald 1990). Conversely, recreational athletes tended to lose aerobic capacity at an average rate of 1 percent per year. Those that became sedentary lost 1.6 percent of their aerobic capacity per year. It appears that frequent race-paced efforts (anaerobic threshold) in training and races help sustain aerobic capacity as we age. Another study tracked the decreasing performance of top triathletes in older age groups at the Triathlon World Championships in 2006 and 2007 (Lepers et al. 2010). Of the three sports, cycling showed the least amount of decline as the age groups became older. Swimming was next, and running showed the greatest performance decline. But the most interesting finding was that the short-course athletes showed the least decline in aerobic capacity, or $\dot{V}O_2$max. Ironman-distance athletes showed the greatest declines. This finding seems to indicate that masters athletes must include high-intensity training and short-course racing in their regimes to fight off the natural decrease in aerobic capacity that comes with age.

An example of masters-specific high-intensity training is starting with a 1- to 3-month series of intervals done at lactate threshold or just below, building the total interval time per workout up to 20 to 40 minutes. For example, an early interval session might be 3 × 3:00 at 1-hour race pace. Each week the intervals would increase in volume. An example of a late interval session would be 4 × 10:00 at 1-hour race pace. These intervals could be translated to swim, bike, or run workouts—one for each discipline each week. If the masters athlete completes these with no trouble, she is ready for a series of aerobic-capacity intervals ($\dot{V}O_2$max). Figure 2.8 shows a sample week of aerobic-capacity training for the late competitive phase of training, along with strength training workouts. After this aerobic capacity and strength phase, the athlete should do more and more race-simulation workouts, building toward race distances. For example, the masters athlete might do a 1-hour bike ride with intervals done at goal pace followed by a quick transition to a run done at goal pace.

Athletes are capable of achieving their best race performances after the age of 40. Training needs to address the maintenance of strength and speed rather than involve nothing but easy endurance efforts. Masters athletes can use their experience to make the most of their training journey. A successful training plan will result in healthy, strong athletes who maintain performance or lessen declines well into their 50s.

**FIGURE 2.8**

### Sample aerobic-capacity training plan for a masters athlete.

|          | Monday | Tuesday | Wednesday | Thursday | Friday | Saturday | Sunday |
|----------|--------|---------|-----------|----------|--------|----------|--------|
| *Swim* | Endurance (60 min) | | | 6 × 300 fast with 100 m easy swim after each for recovery (60 min) | | Force and endurance (60 min) | Day off |
| *Bike* | | 5 × 5:00 at $\dot{V}O_2$max with 5:00 easy spin after each for recovery (90 min) | | Hills (60 min) | | Endurance (120 min) | |
| *Run* | | Easy transition run immediately after completing bike ride (15 min) | Endurance (75 min) | | 3 × 3:00 at $\dot{V}O_2$max with 3:00 easy jog after each for recovery) (45 min) | | |
| *Strength* | Muscular imbalances (30 min) | | Power, low reps (30 min) | | Core (20 min) | | |

# Coaching Female Athletes

As of 2011, 38.46 percent of all USAT annual members were female (56,404 women). Talk to most experienced coaches and they will tell you there are few characteristics associated uniquely with one gender or the other (aside from pregnancy and associated issues), so there really isn't such a thing as a "female athlete" training plan. Rather, coaches should look at athletes individually, considering their strengths, weaknesses, and goals—not gender—when guiding them. However, there are some basic physiological, nutrition, and medical gender differences that coaches must consider when training females. Female athletes approach training and racing with different mental skills as well.

## *Female Physiological Concerns*

Women have less muscle mass than most men. Female athletes must perform regular strength training to help slow the loss of muscle mass as they age to preserve that smaller initial amount of muscle. Exercises that stabilize the pelvis, shoulders, knees, and core are very important for women because they address the effects of the wider hips and larger hip–knee angles of the average woman's body. Women who have the strength to keep their joints stable during running are much less susceptible to injury. Stable joints also lead to more efficient running, cycling, and swimming.

In addition, female athletes need access to a qualified bike-fit specialist. Women sometimes do not fit well on bikes designed with the male torso and leg lengths in mind. Bike manufacturers are beginning to realize this and offer bikes designed for women; a good bike fit is the most important component of optimizing rider performance.

## *Female Nutrition Concerns*

All endurance athletes are susceptible to running a calorie deficit during high-volume or high-intensity training blocks. All athletes may be susceptible to disordered eating, although it is arguably far more prevalent in the female athlete. Both disordered eating and accidentally inadequate nutrition in women can lead to the female athlete triad, a gender-unique medical issue that can have serious health implications. The triad begins with inadequate nutrition, disordered eating, or both and progresses to amenorrhea (the absence of menstruation) and then osteoporosis. These are difficult issues to address as a coach. Female athletes may not be honest about these highly personal topics with a coach. When they are, most coaches are not qualified to fully address them. This is an appropriate time to refer these athletes to an expert you trust, then work as a team with that expert to coordinate training with nutrition goals. Of course, coaches should never promote thinness as a training objective. Instead, coaches should give athletes solid, general, proven advice on how to fuel their training and racing.

## *Female Medical Concerns*

Female runners tend to be more susceptible to training injuries. Commonly documented reasons for this include the structure of a woman's body, with its wider pelvis and therefore greater angle from the knee up to the pelvis area. This can lead to increased patellofemoral injuries and iliotibial band syndrome. Females also tend to have loose ligaments—possibly due to the impact of estrogen. Loose ligaments mean hypermobile joints that are not as well supported by soft tissue connections. This can also result in a higher chance of injuries. Most of these injuries can be resolved and prevented with specific strength training targeted at strengthening the weaker muscles that stabilize the hip and the knee.

Women are more susceptible to stress fractures and anemia than are men. Remind all athletes to consume a diet rich in calcium, iron, and vitamin D, and urge female athletes to be checked for signs of anemia with annual blood tests. Supplement with iron *only* when under medical supervision, as it can be harmful in excess. Stress fractures are often a result of inadequate nutrition or the female athlete triad.

If a female athlete becomes pregnant, she should defer to her doctor for guidance on how it will affect her activity. Pregnancy affects every athlete differently. Some women are able to run, bike, and swim until near the end of their pregnancies with a physician's guidance. Others find they really need to back off from training for much of their pregnancies. Every woman should consider the safety of each activity done while pregnant as well as how the activity contributes to her and her baby's health and well-being.

## Female Mental Concerns

"I've found that women are much better at following the race plan—sometimes too good. Even if they have what it takes to go faster on race day, they will often hold back and follow their plan," says Joe Friel, coach and author of many books on endurance training. "Men, on the other hand, start with the notion they are going to 'beat' the plan." So, good coaching may mean convincing female athletes to take justified risks when warranted. Assign them to take a specific risk in a C or a B race. (For example, have them push harder than normal for the bike segment to see how it affects the run. Convince them that *learning* is the goal for this race, not overall time. Give them permission to fail when taking a calculated risk.)

When coaching a woman, also consider her background and experiences as a female athlete. Has she had opportunities as an athlete, or were there times when she was not supported in her sporting endeavors? Many women were never brought up to think of themselves as athletes. Sometimes, a coach's main objective with these women is to get them to that point—to where they dare to describe themselves as "an athlete." Once there, the possibilities are endless. But until then, how can a woman race to her potential if she does not yet have that fundamental belief that she belongs in the race?

In addition, female athletes frequently struggle to balance work, family, and training—as do male athletes. Without balance, a female athlete will never reach her potential. Coaches should plan rest days, vacations, big work weeks, and time for children and spouses into all athletes' days, weeks, seasons, and annual training plans. An athlete's career should revolve around having no regrets. When she is retired from racing and is reminiscing about this part of her life, what will seem important after all those years? Time with loved ones; full involvement with her children; energy spent on other activities that provide emotional, spiritual, and social balance in her life—these should all be good memories along with the memories of training and racing well.

Every triathlete is a unique person with unique skills, weaknesses, schedules, energy levels, goals, and life circumstances. A good coach will understand each athlete and prescribe the training that will help him reach his potential.

# CHAPTER 3

# Yoga and Flexibility for Triathletes

## Sage Rountree

As yoga grows more and more accessible to Western athletes, more and more people are using it as an important part of training. Yoga's benefits include increased strength, flexibility, and focus, on both physical and mental levels. Although the physical practice of yoga is the entry point for most practitioners, the system of yoga includes other practices, such as meditation and breath exercises, that directly benefit athletes. For a primer on yoga philosophy as it applies to endurance sports training and racing, please see my book *The Athlete's Guide to Yoga: An Integrated Approach to Strength, Flexibility, and Focus* (2008).

## Benefits of Yoga

Yoga works to bring your system into balance, and this balance plays out along many lines. On the physical level, yoga can hone your sense of balance, keeping you upright if your bike wavers or you misstep while running. It can also keep balance between opposing muscle groups, by working to strengthen the weaker muscles and to stretch the tighter ones. This muscular balance is critical for the prevention of overuse injuries, which occur when the system is out of balance, either because the physical demands placed on the system were too strong to be balanced with the recovery allotted, or because one group of muscles was stronger or tighter than another.

Yoga also confers a sense of balance between the body and mind, as a yoga practice gives athletes the space to see how their bodies and minds relate, specifically how they interact with the breath. As both an involuntary and a voluntary process, the breath powerfully connects the needs of the physical body (oxygen in, carbon dioxide out) and the abilities of the mind (deep breathing is relaxing; we can control the breath to accommodate various paces in the swim, bike, and run). When we tune in to the breath, we can see what the state of the body is and begin to learn what we need. Sometimes, that answer is more work; often, that answer is more rest. This self-awareness is an important part of training. Athletes often cleave to a set training plan even when it is not working for them, to the detriment of their recovery and therefore to their performance in workouts and races.

# Types of Yoga

Whether you are practicing yoga in a class setting or on your own at home, you'll need to be sure your practice is complementing your training rather than simply acting as an extension of it. You're probably putting a lot of care into the work you do swimming, cycling, and running. Be careful that your yoga practice doesn't sabotage your training but instead supports it. That means choosing classes wisely and modifying where necessary. Although the general fitness-minded yoga student might come to class for a workout, the athlete in training has different needs: a chance to relax and recover from the work of training, and to shore up weak areas in the body that have not been addressed in the weight room or in physical therapy. Sweating and pushing the limits may not serve the season's or week's goals, so be careful not to be swept into a more-is-more mentality.

When choosing a class or a sequence for home practice, check that your yoga is periodized in inverse proportion to the intensity of your training. That is, when your training is less intense and easier, during the transition and preparatory phases, you can include a more vigorous, strength-building practice. In fact, at this time of the year, yoga might be a direct complement to or even a replacement for a strength workout. As you begin to build toward your key races, though, the intensity of the practice should lighten. During this time, you'll focus on maintaining flexibility and recovering between your key workouts. And as you reach your physical peak in the competition phase, the intensity of your yoga practice must be lighter still. This is a good time to take restorative yoga classes or to focus on focus itself by practicing breath exercises and meditation. These will bolster the work of mental training in preparation for your race.

Here is some advice on ways to choose the classes and home practice that will best support your triathlon and life goals. Remember that yoga is not a competitive sport; use it as time to balance the work of doing and to rest in simply being.

## Yoga Classes

Classes are the best place to learn yoga, as you will have a teacher's feedback about your alignment and you'll be far from the distractions of home. Even small towns these days have yoga studios, and there is good yoga to be found at gyms, too. There is no universal system for labeling and describing classes, so you'll need to keep room for trial and error as you find the right class for you. As an athlete, you are looking for a class that complements your training. This means that although you might enjoy a warm, vigorous, flowing class during your off-season, you'll need to dial back this practice as you get closer to your peak races. For competitive athletes, it can be tough to control the intensity and hold back in class, even when it's the best idea. A competitive athlete often believes any options offered to increase the work or stretch in a pose must be tried, but this is not the best approach, as it can lead to overstretching or interfere with recovery.

Following is a list of terms you'll see on a typical studio schedule:

- *anusara*—An alignment-oriented approach developed by American John Friend, anusara focuses on "heart openers," specifically back bends, which in their more gentle forms are of good use to athletes, especially triathletes who spend hours each week riding in aerobars or sitting at desks.

- *ashtanga*—Usually taught in primary-series or mysore (uncued) classes, this rigorous approach takes athletes through a set sequence of poses linked by vinyasa, or flowing movements. Because it is a power-based practice, ashtanga is best kept for the off-season or for the seasoned yogi.
- *bikram*—A franchised style of hot yoga, this style includes 26 specific poses in a room heated to more than 100 degrees Fahrenheit (38 degrees Celsius).
- *hatha*—Although this term once meant any physical practice of yoga asana, or poses, it now connotes a slower-paced class with poses held static.
- *Iyengar*—Classes emphasize precise alignment, using props to accommodate each practitioner. Certified Iyengar teachers have detailed knowledge of anatomy and can be an important resource for athletes.
- *restorative*—A gentle, prop-supported practice concerned less with stretching than with helping the nervous system relax. This is a great choice for a rest day or for the competitive period of training.
- *vinyasa*—Often associated with flow and power, vinyasa involves moving dynamically through a sequence of poses, often in conjunction with the breath. Depending on the teacher and the level, this will be a faster-paced class and is often best kept for the transition and preparatory periods or for those with more experience mixing yoga and training.

---

### ▶ Hot Yoga

Depending on your geographic region, you might find that some or virtually all of the yoga available to you is "hot yoga," practiced in a heated room. Fans of hot yoga love the intensity of the heat and its challenge, and they argue that the heat cultivates flexibility. For an athlete in serious training, hot yoga creates some concerns, and it should be approached with caution.

If you choose to practice hot yoga, pay special attention to your hydration before, during, and after class. Many athletes exist in a dehydrated state to begin with; adding heat can only exacerbate this condition. Beware also of a false sense of suppleness. In the heat, you may find yourself pushing into stretches that are actually too far past your natural range of motion. Take care, lest you injure yourself.

Finally—and this is good advice for any class—trust your own body. The language of some hot yoga classes is extreme, exhorting you to push, to do more, to go beyond your flexibility. Don't. Set your intention to practice safely, to leave out things that seem inappropriate for your body and your stage in the training cycle. Then stay aligned with that intention.

---

## Home Practice

Your home practice is an integral part of your training, and being regular in your home practice will have a direct positive effect on your performance in triathlon, just as being regular with other elements of your training does. Home practice gives you the time to personalize your practice, shore up your weaknesses, and get to know your body. Consistency is key to seeing benefits. Your home practice can consist of a

5-minute routine or a 50-minute routine. Over time, you'll see what works for you and what addresses your needs. Be sure you try poses, meditations, and breath exercises that are difficult for you instead of playing only to your strengths. By addressing your weaknesses in home practice, you'll become a more well-rounded athlete and person.

If you feel adrift when you begin a home practice, there are many resources available. The poses described in this chapter can be a starting point, as can DVDs and online classes. (My weekly yoga for athletes class is available to stream online at YogaVibes.com, for example.) Books can help, too; my book *The Athlete's Pocket Guide to Yoga* (2009) is spiral-bound to lie flat and contains 50 routines of specific use to endurance athletes.

Just as you need to take care in class, you should be aware of your appropriate edge during home practice, too. Pay attention to your breath, and let it be your guide. A choppy breath or an impulse to hold your breath is a sign of pushing too far.

# Yoga Poses

This section includes some poses you'll see in class and can use in your home practice, with brief explanations of why and how to practice them. These poses can be practiced on their own or combined to create a full-body routine appropriate for practice after a training session in the base and build periods (and, in lighter expression, during the peak). For specific sequence ideas, please see my book *The Athlete's Pocket Guide to Yoga* or my online classes at YogaVibes.com.

## Mountain

The base of all other yoga poses, mountain also promotes ideal alignment for balance in the water and on the road. Learn the pose well, and check your form in the mirror and by asking your teacher for feedback. During your practice and during your training, periodically come back to your best mountain-pose alignment, and you'll find ways to get more efficient and economical in your energy use, thus increasing your endurance.

To take mountain pose (see figure 3.1), stand tall with your feet under your hips. This will probably place your feet about a fist's width apart, where they would land relative to your hips if you were running. Your hip points, knees, and feet should line up perpendicular to the ground. Balance your pelvis in a neutral position, eliminating any tilt forward or backward. Let your spine grow long, relax your shoulders, and drop your chin slightly. You should feel steady and strong.

**FIGURE 3.1**    **Mountain pose.**

# Back Bends

Back bends open the front of the body, which grows tight as we sit in car seats, at desks, and on our bikes, and at the same time they strengthen the back muscles that are overstretched as we hunch forward. Back bends done from a prone position (on the belly) emphasize the strengthening element of the motion and are a necessary precursor to other, deeper back bends.

For locust pose (see figure 3.2), rest on your belly and take mountain-pose alignment, holding your pelvis in a neutral position to protect the lower back. On an inhalation, lift your legs straight back behind you, and use your back muscles to pull your upper body off the ground. Hands can be alongside your hips, hover under your shoulders, or reach out along the floor overhead. Hold your shoulder blades down low on your back as you breathe. For bow pose (see figure 3.3), rest on your belly and reach your hands for your feet or ankles. On an inhalation, kick your feet into your hands, and lift up into a back bend. Your pelvis stays down and neutrally aligned; your chest lifts off the floor. Hold your neck relaxed as you breathe here.

FIGURE 3.2    **Locust.**

FIGURE 3.3    **Bow.**

## Planks

The plank position cultivates core strength by challenging the body to maintain mountain-pose alignment in a different relationship to gravity. Planks can be done on the hands or the forearms, in downward-facing, side-facing, and even upward-facing positions.

For the downward-facing plank (see figure 3.4), position your hands or your elbows under your shoulders, the balls of the feet on the floor, and assume mountain-pose alignment all along the body. Don't let your hips sag, and don't lift your shoulders too high.

For side plank (see figure 3.5), rotate to one side, flexing your feet. You can have the foot of the top leg in front of the bottom leg, stacked on top of it, or placed on the ground in front of or behind the bottom leg's knee. This can be done on the palm or, for greater shoulder stabilization, on the elbow and forearm.

FIGURE 3.4　　**Downward-facing plank.**

FIGURE 3.5　　**Side plank.**

For upward-facing plank (see figure 3.6), position the hands under the shoulders, fingertips facing forward and belly up, and lift the hips off the ground. For less intensity, keep your knees bent; for more, work to straighten the legs and reach your toes to the floor.

FIGURE 3.6    **Upward-facing plank.**

## Lunges

The lunge balances the musculature of the hips. Longer holds increase flexibility in the hip flexors and hamstrings, while moving into and out of a lunge strengthens the glutes and hip stabilizers while increasing balance.

Do a split-stance lunge with your legs. Check that the knee of the front leg is directly over the foot so that the shin is perpendicular to the ground. You can be on the ball of the back-leg foot (see figure 3.7), or you can lower that back knee to the ground. Hands can be on the floor, on the knee, or overhead. Hips and shoulders are squared forward.

FIGURE 3.7    **Lunge.**

## Forward Folds

Forward folds stretch the back of the body, from the calves and hamstrings to the muscles of the back and neck. They make a nice complement and counterpose to back bends.

In all forward folds, the action should begin from the pelvis, which must tilt forward so that the fold isn't taken too deeply into the lumbar spine of the lower back. Whether you are in a standing forward fold (see figure 3.8) or a seated forward fold (see figure 3.9), you should feel your hip points moving forward into the pose instead of simply bending forward from the waistline. If forward folds feel intense, bend your knees to protect your hamstrings.

FIGURE 3.8　　**Standing forward fold.**

FIGURE 3.9　　**Seated forward fold.**

## Twists

Twists wring out the spine, maintaining rotational range of motion and stretching the chest and hips, which frame the top and bottom of the spinal column. When practiced until they feel even, twists bring balance to bodies that are more comfortable rotating in one direction than the other, which makes triathlon-specific actions such as bilateral breathing in swimming more easy.

A reclining twist (see figure 3.10) is a gentle, pleasant way to stretch the hips, spine, and chest. Lying on your back, bend your knees and drop them to one side. For more intensity, keep the legs stacked and active as you hold your shoulders level against the ground. For less, let your legs relax. You can slide them away from your shoulders. Variations include straightening the bottom leg and keeping only the top leg bent at the knee, or wrapping the top-leg knee around the bottom-leg knee.

FIGURE 3.10　　**Reclining twist.**

## Inversions

Inversions change the body's relationship with gravity, inviting a new perspective and helping calm the nervous system. Additionally, they help drain excess fluids from the legs, useful for recovery.

Inversions such as headstand and shoulder stand are best learned under the supervision of an experienced teacher, as they can put undue stress on the neck if practiced incorrectly. A safe alternative is happy baby pose (see figure 3.11), an upside-down squat. Resting on your back, take your knees wide and lower them toward your armpits as you hold your hamstrings, calves, ankles, or feet with your hands. Your tailbone and head should both stay down on the ground. A deeper but also safe inversion is taking a position with your legs up the wall (see figure 3.12) or your calves resting on a chair, seat cushion, or coffee table (see figure 3.13). In either, move toward the prop until your knees are over your hips, and take a comfortable arm position to encourage a gentle release across the chest.

FIGURE 3.11    **Happy baby.**

FIGURE 3.12    **Legs up the wall.**

FIGURE 3.13    **Legs to a chair.**

## Resting

Rest is where the gains of exercise occur, as the body repairs itself and supercompensates, growing back stronger in anticipation of an increased workload. Without rest, you will not thrive as an athlete. Resting at the end of a yoga routine or as a stand-alone practice will help you recover faster and more completely, bringing balance into your nervous system and your life.

For corpse pose (see figure 3.14), rest on your back, with your spine neutral and your arms and legs spread. Relax everywhere as you rest and breathe. As you notice tension or thoughts intruding, release and let go.

FIGURE 3.14    **Corpse.**

Beyond the physical benefits of the practice, yoga can teach you equanimity, maintaining a sense of balance even in the face of changing circumstance. This comes in extremely handy both in triathlon and in life. Some of this benefit comes organically through the physical practice; some comes through studying breath exercises and meditation. Seek out local resources by talking to the owners of your local yoga studios. A regular yoga practice will bring longevity, appreciation, and balance to your training and improve the quality of your life.

# CHAPTER 4

# Strength Training for Triathletes

### George M. Dallam, PhD

There is a long, ongoing debate among sport scientists, coaches, and athletes concerning the value of strength training for endurance athletics. The early science attempting to examine this issue did little to resolve the debate, as studies found both potential benefit and negligible value. However, more recent and effective research examining this question supports strength training as a critical component of an overall training program for endurance sports, particularly when performed using the right kinds of exercises, using adequate resistance, and in conjunction with more typical triathlon training. The improvement for a triathlete who becomes stronger in swimming, cycling, and running comes through better movement economy—which basically means you can move more easily using less energy once you are stronger in a movement pattern.

However, to efficiently improve strength and movement economy, well-trained adults are most likely to have success with training exercises involving high resistances and high power outputs. Studies of strength training in conjunction with endurance running show that improved strength offers a significant avenue for running improvement when compared with training programs using running alone. The exercises used most commonly in these studies involve variations of the basic squat, the Olympic lifts, and various jumping and plyometric movements, all of which train you to move in patterns similar to running itself, a concept sport scientists refer to as movement specificity. Applying resistance to these kinds of movements increases both strength and functionality in comparison to traditional machine-based movements. Improved functionality offsets the natural losses in movement capability that often occur when doing repetitive triathlon training alone. Of course these mobility losses are made even worse if you sit for extended periods every day.

A few recent cycling studies using similar exercises illustrate the potential benefit of heavy resistance training for this sport as well. A small number of studies have also shown a positive relationship between swimming-specific strength exercises and swimming performance, although numerous studies using more conventional strength training exercises show little or no effect on swimming performances. The successful studies tended to use movement patterns similar to those created by swim benches such as the Vasa Trainer, which emphasize the high-elbow "catch" position so critical for effective swimming, as well as a variety of functional movements that target core and upper body mobility generally. Some studies have also applied in-water resistance devices directly to swimming. Two key elements of the studies showing a successful transfer of improved strength to improved endurance performance seem to be (1) the specificity of the movements used for training and (2) the examination of actual endurance performance as an outcome instead of more typically analyzed physiological outcomes, such as improved $\dot{V}O_2$max and lactate threshold. A reasonable conclusion for the competitive triathlete is that resistance training using the most appropriate movement-specific and functional exercises with adequate loading can benefit performance in swimming, cycling, and running beyond that obtainable using conventional endurance training methods alone.

This chapter attempts to highlight the key training methodologies and specific exercises most useful for achieving the twin outcomes of improved performance and reduced injury in training triathletes.

# Strength Training Components

Triathletes and coaches seek first and foremost to use a training process as a means of performance improvement. To effectively apply resistance training for this purpose, athletes and coaches must consider the following components when designing a strength training program.

## *Specificity*

For improvements in strength and power to have maximum transfer to the ability to swim, cycle, and run at greater speeds over racing distances, it is necessary to train the movement itself rather than simply the muscles involved. This concept is referred to as training specificity. To ensure training specificity in a chosen resistance training movement, you should consider the following factors: the pattern of total-body movement; the range of motion used during force application and recovery; the speed at which the movement pattern occurs in performance; the nature of the muscle contractions involved; the nature of the movement pattern (i.e., simultaneous versus sequential); the relationship of the movement pattern to gravity and the ground, water, or bicycle; and finally the nature of the force impulse generated with each repetition of the movement pattern resulting in forward motion.

In running, for example, the movement pattern requires the body to fall forward, with each step efficiently absorbing the force of gravity at foot strike through a total-body posture and then returning the absorbed force through elastic recoil as the foot is lifted from the ground and the center of mass is shifted to the opposite side of the body. The force-application impulse occurs in microseconds over a very limited range of motion yet involves the entire body musculature, much of which is contracting either eccentrically to absorb force or isometrically for stabilization. At the point of force application (foot strike), the movement is entirely simultaneous in nature, meaning all joints move together at one time. The majority of these factors are present when you perform a squat, particularly when doing so with one leg. This movement pattern simulates the body position during the support phase of running, in which eccentric (lengthening) muscle contractions occur to support the body and simultaneous muscle activations are required because of the addition of significant resistance. The factors may be even more specifically present when you perform a box jump. A box jump requires a relatively high movement speed similar to that which occurs during support in running, hence the high degree of positive effect on running performance when these exercises are used for strength training.

However, you should also consider the following Latin proverb when employing movement specificity to highly repetitive movement patterns having a limited range of motion, such as swimming, cycling, and running: "What nourishes me also destroys me." This could be interpreted as meaning that too much specificity of movement in resistance training, while improving speed initially, may also create conditions that eventually alter movement patterns and create injury.

## Muscle Balance

When the human body functions optimally, each joint is controlled by an appropriate force-couple relationship between the opposing muscle groups that move and stabilize the joint. Unfortunately, highly repetitive movements favor the development of one side of the force couple (the one that propels us forward) over the other (the one that returns each joint to its original position). The result is a change in the basic postural position of the joint over time and ultimately a loss in its movement capability. This phenomenon also occurs when you sustain unusual body postures during both your athletic performance (think of your aerobar shoulder position) and your daily activities (think of your sitting position at a computer). Consequently, when identifying resistance training movements for triathlon, you should also consider the recovery aspect of each motion as well as the repetitive body postures employed. Of course the effect of repetitive movement patterns and body postures can also be seen by examining resting body posture while sitting or standing.

Continuing with the running example in the previous section, although a squat is very specific to the force-producing aspect of running, it is very nonspecific to the recovery motion because the leg is not lifted from the ground. In running, you apply gravity as a driving force in the next support-leg position by shifting your center of mass and body weight off the previous support leg as you remove that foot from the ground. This weight shift and foot lift combination should therefore become its own specific exercise in a movement-specific strength training program for running. Consequently, hopping exercises and ankle-pulling exercises are very specific for this aspect of the movement and should be paired with the force-producing exercises. As a result, an effective strength training program includes some form of squatting and depth jumps as well as some form of hopping and leg pulls in order to develop or maintain balanced strength of both the support and recovery aspects of running technique. The importance of balanced strength development is further described in the next section.

## Functionality

When you move in swimming, cycling, and running, you regulate and integrate the entire body musculature in ways that require an intricate sequencing, timing, and firing of muscle groups, which results in optimal function of all of your joints. When one or more joints and associated muscle force-couples fail to perform correctly, other muscles and joints have to carry a greater role. This is referred to as a compensatory movement. When forced into using compensatory movement patterns, you fail to achieve the degree of control, range of motion, and optimal force application necessary to produce elegant and effective swimming, cycling, and running movements, and so your performance suffers. Even worse, altered movement patterns often overload the compensating joints and muscles and produce the kinds of chronic injuries that end triathlon careers or result in surgical interventions. A classic example is the loss of stabilization force necessary to hold the pelvis laterally in an upright position as the athlete absorbs force while landing on each foot in running. The result is a falling and twisting pelvis during the ground support period, which both dissipates force that could be absorbed as well as forces the hip, knee, and ankle joints into further compensatory movements to propel the body forward. The athlete often loses needed muscle activity, in this example in the medial gluteus, by sitting so much of the time that the muscle becomes inactive.

However, once the most typical compensatory movement patterns that develop with repetitive swimming, cycling, and running are identified, correcting them by applying appropriate functional training exercises—the basis of modern concepts in physical therapy—is relatively effective. Further, it is certainly logical, although as yet unproven scientifically, that the proactive use of such exercises might not only prevent the development of injuries in the first place but also improve performance and technique in the uninjured as well.

## Strength and Power

A person's strength in a movement pattern is defined by the ability to produce a force against a resistance to cause movement, regardless of the time involved. This concept defines the capacity to do work using the following equation:

Work = force × distance

However, each force application in efficient swimming, cycling, and running must occur very rapidly over a brief period of time, and so the rate at which force is applied is also critical. This is known as power (the rate of work) and is defined by the following equation:

Power = force × distance/time

As a result, both the ability to apply force and the rate at which force can be applied are important for generating greater speed in swimming, cycling, and running. However, the optimal training conditions for strength and power development vary somewhat. Strength is trained optimally using very heavy resistance, which necessitates slower movement. Rapid force application, or power, is trained best using lesser resistances that can be moved at speeds comparable to those in the movement itself. Both facets of the process—force and movement speed—can be trained independently, however, and so both approaches can and should be used in a training program. You might think about the overall process as follows: You first seek to increase strength by adding resistance to your movements, but you sacrifice movement speed in the process. However, as you build greater strength, you reestablish speed to heighten power output.

This concept can be applied to a single training exercise, such as the squat, by manipulating the resistance used and the intent of the exercise. Training sessions for the squat can be varied by using both heavier weights to develop strength and relatively lighter weights to develop power (by performing the squats explosively). This process can be further augmented by jumping movements similar to squats in order to work at movement speeds equivalent to those used when running or cycling.

## Stabilization

At the moment of force application in running, cycling, and swimming, a large number of muscles in the body contract against one another to simply hold portions of the skeletal system in place so that other portions of the body can push against them. This is the basic concept of stabilization in a lever system. When one lever in a system is held in place, the lever working against it can work with greater efficiency. It is commonly thought that most of our important stabilization in locomotion occurs in the torso, which is sometimes referred to as the core muscle set; however, stabilization in swimming, cycling, and running is more often a total-body function. This component is trained effectively using functional movements that require dynamic stabilization, such as alternate lunges with the upper body held upright.

# Organizing a Strength Training Program for Triathlon

Use the following three steps to design a resistance training program that improves performance and prevents injury: (1) Select a group of exercises that create greater strength, peak power, and functionality in swimming, cycling, and running, with minimum training time and maximum efficiency; (2) develop a cyclic training plan that will create sustained improvements in strength and power while maintaining or promoting greater functionality over time, scheduling the training to augment your basic swim, cycle, and run training; and (3) determine a specific plan for guiding the intensity and volume of training to maximize the adaptive response.

## Select Strength Training Exercises

When organizing a strength training program, you should select a force-application and related recovery exercise each for swimming, cycling, and running along with three basic functional movement exercises (strength training exercises are described beginning on page 51). Force-application exercises simulate the movement to propel the body forward. In running, this happens during the support phase as your falling body weight is absorbed; in cycling, it happens as the pedal is projected downward in the pedaling "circle" by your shifting body weight; and in crawl-stroke swimming, it happens as the body weight is placed on the "catch," or support, of the leading arm.

Recovery refers to the phase in which you resume the body posture used for force production on the opposite side of your body so you can perform the movement again. In running, this occurs as you lift your support foot and shift body weight onto the opposite and descending leg; in cycling, this occurs as you unweight, or "get out of the way of," the ascending pedal, allowing your body weight to shift onto the opposite descending pedal; and in crawl-stroke swimming, recovery occurs as you lift the trailing arm and position it to drop into the water forward of your head, thereby initiating the next successive body roll.

Unfortunately, complex locomotion patterns, particularly swimming, can never be completely duplicated using only a few exercises. Further, the potential list of functional movement patterns that may be beneficial for a given individual triathlete is continually expanding. Given greater time and commitment, the next step is to add additional movement-specific paired exercises (force and recovery) for each discipline along with additional functional exercises to address specific aspects of body mobility that may become compromised through the normal triathlon training process. As you develop improved functionality and increased strength, the addition of plyometric exercises (e.g., box jumps, long jumps) will further augment improvements in your running, particularly because of the inherently different way in which force is applied in this movement pattern.

## Incorporate Strength Training Into the Overall Training Plan

A common mistake is to do strength training only in the off-season. The fallacy of this approach is that while strength and power may improve during this relatively short period of time, the loss in strength that occurs through the considerably longer in-season period, if no significant stimulus for strength is included, results in a net no change or loss in strength year to year. This happens because detraining occurs at a faster rate than the adaptive process associated with training. If you accept the now well-established science that movement-specific strength is a vital component of overall endurance performance, it only makes sense to utilize a year-round training process that allows improvements in strength from year to year.

The published scientific literature examining how weight training should best be organized in an overall periodization approach to training is sparse; however, it does suggest that an undulating approach may be superior to a linear one. In an undulating approach, various intensities of training are regularly alternated in shorter training cycles, much in the way that successful endurance athletes alternate endurance sport training sessions focused on endurance, race pace, and speed on a regular cyclic basis. In a linear approach, each area of emphasis is trained in isolation over extended blocks of time.

You can also create a longer-term cyclic periodization plan or macrocycle in an undulating approach by varying the exercises employed in the phases, typically moving from more general exercises, such as the half squat, to more movement-specific exercises, such as the single-leg quarter squat. Finally, the training plan, when carried out throughout a full training year, will by necessity have to include periods of strength and power maintenance versus progression so that more specific swim, cycle, and run training progressions can be adapted to more successfully. This is accomplished by simply maintaining the current stimulus level (the weight and sets you are currently adapted to completing without undue fatigue) and by reducing the frequency of sessions if necessary.

The most emphasized areas in endurance sport resistance training are peak strength, peak power, and anaerobic endurance. To these one might add the emerging concept of functionality, although that might just as easily be more directly integrated into the other areas of emphasis, depending on one's time and equipment limitations.

An example of a resistance training microcycle carried out over 7 days might look like this:

- ▪ *Day 1*: Strength emphasis and functional training
- ▪ *Day 2*: Power emphasis and functional training
- ▪ *Day 3*: Anaerobic endurance emphasis and functional training
- ▪ *Day 4*: Day off
- ▪ *Day 5*: Strength emphasis and functional training
- ▪ *Day 6*: Power emphasis and functional training
- ▪ *Day 7*: Anaerobic endurance emphasis and functional training

As you can see, these sessions are separated by a minimum of a full day for recovery, but they can still be effective even when performed 2 or 3 days apart once an athlete adapts to relatively high resistance levels. Unfortunately, the best placement of resistance training sessions relative to endurance training sessions on the same day has not been established. In my experience, resistance training performance is influenced less by fatigue created by prior endurance training sessions than vice versa, and so resistance training should be carried out last in a day whenever possible. In addition, the lower sustained metabolic intensity of resistance training allows for a gradual cool-down when such sessions directly follow endurance training, and no warm-up is required for the resistance training session. Finally, by placing the functional training movements last, an athlete leaves the training process having regained mobility rather than the opposite.

The higher intensity of resistance training can also be used before endurance training to augment performance. This works best when an athlete is highly adapted to the resistance training and uses reduced training volumes to prevent significant fatigue. The high-level neuromuscular stimulus before endurance training seemingly results in an acute stimulating effect, improving the capacity to swim, cycle, or run afterward.

## Determine Intensity of the Training Sessions

Typically, strength training intensity is based on percentages of your one-repetition maximum (1RM), meaning the weight you can successfully move in a given exercise only one time. Typically, strength is developed using weights in excess of 85 percent of 1RM, with repetitions of 6 or fewer. Peak short-term power is developed using lighter weight in the range of 30 to 70 percent of 1RM, with repetitions of 4 to 6 done as explosively as possible. Short anaerobic endurance can be developed using weights in the range of 40 to 60 percent of 1RM, completing repetitions over 30 to 60 seconds, or typically between 10 and 20 repetitions. Finally, functional exercises are completed using very minimal resistance (often initially only body weight or light poles for overhead extension), with an emphasis placed almost entirely on balance and technique. Of course over time significant resistance can be used in these exercises as well. Following are examples of squat training sessions focused on strength, power, anaerobic endurance, and functionality, respectively.

The nomenclature used next, such as 1 × 10 reps at 80 percent of 1RM, refers to the number of sets (i.e., 1) and the repetitions of each set (i.e., 10) at the target intensity based on an athlete's known or estimated 1RM value in that exercise. As an example of the intensity, an athlete who can lift 200 pounds (91 kg) once in the given exercise would then use 80 percent of 200 pounds (160 pounds, or 73 kg) in each set.

### Strength Session

Using a half squat or a single-leg quarter squat, perform the following:

- 1 × 10 reps at 70 percent of 1RM
- 1 × 10 reps at 80 percent of 1RM
- 3 × 5 reps at 85 percent of 1RM

### Power Session

Using a half squat or a single-leg quarter squat, perform the following:

- 1 × 10 reps at 70 percent of 1RM
- 1 × 10 reps at 80 percent of 1RM
- 3 × 6 reps at 50 percent of 1RM (at maximum speed using timed sets)

### Anaerobic Endurance Session

Using a half squat or a single-leg quarter squat, perform the following:

- 1 × 10 reps at 70 percent of 1RM
- 1 × 10 reps at 80 percent of 1RM
- 1 × 20 reps at 50 percent of 1RM

### Functional Training Session

Using an extended-arm full squat, perform the following:

- 3 × 10 reps, with pole maintained overhead and body kept in appropriate alignment

The approach to creating training targets used in the previous examples presumes you will complete only the targeted number of repetitions at the target weight and then make increases in the target weight as the 1RM increases over time. Of course another traditional approach to training is to use failure sets, whereby you lift a given weight until the last repetition cannot be completed successfully. However, limited research suggests that the adaptive response to more controlled training (using fewer reps at a weight level less than that necessary to produce failure) is superior, meaning that trainees experience greater improvements over time. From a practical perspective this is very likely the result of reduced exertional pain, less posttraining fatigue, and a greater amount of the specific neuromuscular stimulus desired. The last comment may seem contradictory; however, shorter training sets at a given weight allow the completion of a greater total number of sets and repetitions of the movement with less fatigue. Even though many associate the pain of failure sets with improvement, the actual stimulus for neuromuscular adaptation lies primarily in the total work completed and the forces used to accomplish the work rather than in the pain and acidity experienced with each set.

# Strength Training Exercises

Following are training exercises for each discipline, classified by movement specificity versus functionality. The intent is to provide an accessible group of exercises that can be used in conjunction with one another to achieve improved triathlon performance in a time-efficient manner.

In general, the following two principles should be put into practice when performing any of these exercises. First, you should always maintain optimal body posture during the exercise. Important points involve drawing the pelvis (or belly button) in by activating the gluteal muscles and flattening the abdominal muscles so you have a normal curve in your low back; pulling the shoulders back and together to hold the thoracic vertebrae in a normal curve by activating the midback muscles; and elevating and aligning the head to hold the cervical vertebrae in a normal curve. In this way, each exercise also helps develop optimal posture rather than further degrade it. Second, you should always attempt to align joints with the intended direction of force in each exercise. A critical example is the alignment of the hip so that the knee tracks correctly over each foot while weight bearing during exercises such as squats, lunges, and jumps.

## *Swimming-Specific Strength Training Exercises*

These basic exercises develop both the force-producing and recovery aspects of the crawl stroke in swimming, the most commonly used stroke during the swim leg of triathlons.

### Two-Arm High-Elbow Cable Pull

This exercise develops the catch and pull in crawl-stroke swimming. It is best done on a sliding bench as pictured; however, it can also be done using a cable machine. To perform this exercise, lie facedown on the sliding bench, with the hands held in flexed position as when swimming and the elbows raised above the hands, keeping the elbows high, or forward (see figure 4.1a). Then, attempt to push the hands down, keeping the elbows up (see figure 4.1b).

**FIGURE 4.1**
**Two-arm high-elbow cable pull.**

## Two-Arm Lateral Raise and Extension

This exercise develops the recovery movement pattern in crawl-stroke swimming that pulls the hands from the hips to the extension position in the water. To perform this exercise, stand with feet shoulder-width apart and knees slightly bent. Hold the arms at the waist with elbows flexed, a dumbbell in each hand (see figure 4.2a). Lift the arms simultaneously to a position at shoulder level (see figure 4.2b) and then to full extension overhead (see figure 4.2c). The elbows are flexed from the beginning of the lift until the transition to full extension overhead, as during the high-elbow recovery in swimming.

**FIGURE 4.2** **Two-arm lateral raise and extension.**

## *Cycling-Specific Strength Training Exercises*

These basic exercises develop both the force-producing and recovery aspects of the pedal stroke in seated cycling.

## Parallel Squat

This exercise trains the cycling force-producing movements effectively. This movement uses a range of motion in the hip and knee specific to cycling as well as provides a greater general mobility stimulus and total-body muscle activation. To perform this exercise, stand with feet shoulder-width apart, with feet pointing forward and a barbell supported across your shoulders (see figure 4.3a). Lower the hips until the thighs reach a parallel, or close to parallel, alignment with the ground while maintaining the normal curvature of the lower spine, an upright head position, and your weight balanced evenly across your feet (see figure 4.3b). It is important to keep the center of the ankles, hips, shoulders, and head in alignment. Once this alignment changes in the movement, you are beginning to compensate for limitations in either strength or range of motion in one or more joints.

**FIGURE 4.3** **Parallel squat.**

## Seated Leg Curl

This relatively simple exercise trains the cycling recovery movement effectively. To maintain muscle balance, the movement employs the paired muscle groups used in conjunction with the parallel squat exercise just described. To perform the exercise, assume an upright seated position at a leg-curl machine (see figure 4.4a), and simply pull the heels toward the buttocks (see figure 4.4b). Special care should be taken to maintain neutral alignment of the kneecap with the feet during the movement. When appropriate equipment is available, it is possible to use a contralateral, or alternating-sides, approach for greater movement specificity.

FIGURE 4.4
**Seated leg curl.**

# Running-Specific Strength Training Exercises

The basic strength training exercises described first develop both the force-producing and recovery aspects of running technique. The plyometric and jumping exercises further develop both the ability to apply forces very rapidly and the dynamic balance so vital for efficient running.

## Single-Leg Quarter Squat

This version of the squat is very specific to the force-application absorption phase of running during ground support. The exercise can be done with light or no weight to stimulate improved pelvic control as well as with heavy weight to stimulate strength, once pelvic control is established. For the weighted version, use a Smith machine or similar support rack for squatting and a board or box to stand on (the board creates an elevated position for standing on the ball of the foot). To perform the weighted version of this exercise, stand on one leg (as in running during support) with a level pelvis (see figure 4.5a). Lower the hips, just as in two-leg squats, keeping the pelvis level (see figure 4.5b), then push up to the start position. The support-leg knee should track directly over the support foot, with the body weight placed on the ball of the foot as in running support. The nonsupport leg should be held in a flexed position as in recovery during running. Lower approximately half the distance of a more typical parallel squat in a way that simulates the movements that occur as you land on the ground with each foot during running. Change legs and repeat.

**FIGURE 4.5**　　**Single-leg quarter squat.**

## Vertical Ankle Pulls With Resistance

This exercise trains the recovery pattern of the leg during effective running technique. To perform this exercise correctly, use either ankle weights or a plyometric box and cable, with adequate movement range from a point near the ground so the ankle movement can be as near to vertical as possible. To perform this exercise, stand on one leg (as in running during support) with the knee of the support leg bent, the pelvis neutral, and the head and upper torso upright. Pull the nonsupport ankle vertically from the ground to the bottom of the pelvis, the knee and hip flexing simultaneously (see figure 4.6), and then allow the ankle to fall to the ground again, initiating the next repetition as quickly as possible as the foot touches the floor. The ankle should travel in a nearly vertical line with each repetition. Try to cover a full range of motion, with the ankle tucked under the buttocks at the top of the movement as seen in the leg actions of runners moving at peak velocity. Repeat the exercise using the opposite leg.

**FIGURE 4.6**    **Vertical ankle pulls with resistance.**

# Double- and Single-Leg Box Jumps

Plyometric depth jumps simulate the total-body actions taken as the body falls to the ground with each running step and the feet rapidly move into recovery. These exercises augment our ability to apply very high forces very rapidly by prestretching the propulsive muscles during the landing. This activates the stretch reflex, which increases the responding muscle contraction forces as you leave the ground, assuming you do so rapidly.

To perform this exercise, stand on an elevated box in a running-specific support position on both legs (see figure 4.7*a* for an example of this position for the double-leg jump), simply drop to the ground (see figure 4.7*b* for an example of this position for the double-leg jump), and then lift the legs and ankles as quickly as possible at contact to return to the box. Land in a "soft" position, with knees bent, pelvis neutral, and head and upper torso upright. The key element of an effective depth jump is removing the feet from the floor as quickly as possible instead of landing, pausing, and then jumping. As you develop greater coordination in the exercise, loading can be increased by adding resistance (a weight vest is best), by increasing jump height, or doing both. The exercise can also be performed on a single leg once adequate strength and balance are developed, making it even more running specific.

FIGURE 4.7     **Double-leg depth box plyometric jumps.**

## Double- and Single-Leg Long Jumps

Repetitive long jumps develop total-body coordination, which creates greater transfer to the steps taken in running. A plyometric effect is also achieved when the jumps are done in rapid succession. Successive jumps also require a more vertical body action, which simulates running mechanics. To perform this exercise, begin standing in a running-specific support position. Initiate the jump sequence by allowing the body to begin falling forward, simultaneously crouching slightly (see figure 4.8*a* for an example of this position for a double-leg jump), and then lifting the feet from the ground vertically as in depth jumps (see figure 4.8*b* for an example of this position for a double-leg jump). Land softly on the balls of the feet on each successive jump, initiating the next jump in turn by rapidly lifting the ankles.

The emphasis should be on rapid vertical foot removal with each successive contact, as in depth jumps, as well as balance versus maximum distance on each jump. You will have to work harder than during depth jumps to keep the body upright with each jump by activating your core muscles more forcefully. The exercise can also be performed on a single leg once adequate strength and balance are developed, making it even more running specific.

**FIGURE 4.8** **Double-leg long jumps.**

## *Functional Strength Training Exercises*

These basic exercises develop general mobility, balance, and strength in movement patterns that are often impaired by extensive swimming, cycling, and running training.

# Extended-Arm Full Squat

This squat variation is the king of all general functional training movements. It serves as both an assessment technique to identify existing compensatory movement patterns and as a training exercise to correct deficiencies. To perform this exercise successfully, you must have virtually all sagittal plane (forward–backward) joint actions in working order. Most experienced triathletes will initially be deficient in the hip, ankle, and shoulder extension mobility necessary to successfully complete the movement. That said, the ability to squat fully to the ground without difficulty is a basic evolutionary skill most of us are likely capable of performing but have lost thanks to the modern world of chairs. Once this movement capability is regained, running, cycling, and swimming performance and injury resistance are often greatly improved.

This exercise is commonly used by physical therapists, coaches, and trainers to test total-body functionality, and it should be used by triathletes in this manner as well. As joint movement limitations and the resulting compensatory movements are identified, they can be addressed using a combination of stretching, muscle strengthening, and dynamic warm-up techniques to mobilize the joints functioning suboptimally. When the full squatting movement can be successfully completed, it can be used by itself to maintain normal joint function and to gradually improve strength and body control.

To perform this exercise, stand in the normal beginning position for a squat, with arms overhead, holding a lightweight pole (see figure 4.9a). Grasp the pole just outside of shoulder width or at a width where a 90-degree angle is created when you let the pole touch the top of your head. Keeping the arms over and behind your head, lower your hips just as in conventional squats, going as deeply as possible (see figure 4.9b), and then push up to the original starting position.

**FIGURE 4.9**    **Extended-arm full squat.**

## Extended-Arm Forward, Lateral, and Back Lunges

This general functional movement series for the entire body develops full hip mobility as well as upper body stabilization and balance. To perform this exercise, stand in the normal beginning position for a squat, with arms overhead, holding a lightweight pole, as shown in the previous exercise. Begin by stepping forward with a single leg into the lunge position (the knee of the rear leg nearly touching the ground in the process), keeping the upper body upright, with arms extended (see figure 4.10a), and then push back up to the start position. Attempt to step on a line near the center of the body, being sure to track the knee directly over the extended foot. Repeat the movement with the opposite leg. Next step laterally, flexing the extended knee and keeping the pelvis neutral (see figure 4.10b), and then push back to the start position. Repeat the movement with the opposite leg. Finally step backward, flexing the forward leg now (see figure 4.10c), and then push back up to the start position. Repeat with the opposite leg for one full repetition of the series. These movements can be increased in difficulty and the total-body coordination required by adding a shoulder press to each step as well as by adding torso rotations to the front and back lunges.

**FIGURE 4.10**   Extended-arm (*a*) forward, (*b*) lateral, and (*c*) back lunge.

Although it is certainly true that beginning triathletes will see their greatest improvement in the sport simply by adapting to increased amounts of swimming, cycling, and running, the ability to increase movement-specific strength and injury resistance eventually paves the way to performance improvements and continued participation in the triathlon. The intelligent and consistent application of a resistance training program using movement-specific exercises in combination with injury-preventing functional training exercises can take triathletes to the next level of performance as well as ensure their ability to compete successfully for decades to come.

# CHAPTER 5

# Training for Triathlon Swimming

## Steve Tarpinian

Although the swim portion of the triathlon is in open water (with the exception of pool triathlons), pool swimming is an essential ingredient for preparing for open-water swimming because technique is best refined in a pool, where the conditions will not distract an athlete's focus. Also, no matter how well you measure the distance in open water, it is never exact, and for that reason speed and efficiency are best quantified in a pool. Interval work is an essential part of swim training, and the pool is best for accurate high-quality interval training. And last, for the large majority of athletes, open-water swimming is not an available option for consistent training because of geography.

## Key Elements of a Pool Workout

All training in the pool should include the following components to maximize its effectiveness:

- Warm-up
- Technique work
- Main set
- Cool-down

### Warm-Up

One purpose of the warm-up for swim training is to get the athletes acclimated to the water temperature. For this reason, the colder a pool is, the longer you will need to warm up. The other reasons for the warm-up are the same as for other sports—to increase heart rate, increase blood flow to the muscles, and prepare mentally for the training session. Typically, 5 to 15 minutes is sufficient and can be accomplished by all freestyle or a combination of freestyle and off strokes (see What Are Off Strokes? for more information). In general, you will focus on your technique in the next part of the workout; however, the warm-up is still a good time to work on breathing smoothly and easily and to become as relaxed as possible for the upcoming technique work.

▶ **Pool Safety Reminders**

When swimming or training in a pool, some basic safety precautions should always be taken. Following are a few key reminders:

■ *Diving*. Most pools allow diving only in the deep end and when supervised, so when in doubt enter feetfirst.

■ *Using lane lines and flags*. Most pools have warning flags 5 meters from the wall to let you know you are approaching the wall. In addition, pool lane-line colors switch from alternating colors to a solid color at this same point so you can see to your side and do not need to turn to look for the wall. If your pool has these, you can roll over on your front at that point and swim in to the wall. If there are no such indicators at your pool, find a way to ensure you do not hit your head.

■ *Sharing lanes*. It is customary to share lanes when doing laps in a pool. Usually when only two swimmers are in a lane, they will split the lane (each swimmer stays on her respective side). When there are more than two swimmers, circle swimming is the method to use. Swimmers always stay on the right-hand side of the lane so that at each wall, the swimmer moves over to swim on the opposite side as on the previous length. This works particularly well when the swimmers are similar in speed. If the swimmers' speeds vary, then the faster swimmers will need to pass the slower ones, and this can be done in either of two ways. First, a faster swimmer can tap the feet of the swimmer he wants to pass, and that swimmer can let him pass at the wall; second, the faster swimmer can swim in the middle of the lane to go around the slower swimmer. The latter method should be done carefully. If another swimmer is doing the same thing coming the other way, a painful head-to-head meeting can occur. Always be careful when passing other swimmers in the pool.

## Technique Work

Technique work is the part of swim training where an athlete focuses on any improvements or refinements to her swimming technique. There is more technique involved in swimming than in biking or running. Ultimately a swimmer's performance is limited by her technique, not by her training. In addition, water has a much higher drag coefficient (as opposed to air during running and biking), so small changes in body position and angles can have big effects on performance. As a swimmer advances, some technique training can be done at a faster pace, allowing for physiological adaptations as well as technical benefits. For these reasons, do your best to not skip drills; if you have to skip any part of the workout, go without a main set.

This chapter describes drills that address the most common areas to improve and master for efficient freestyle (chapter 15 focuses on troubleshooting your freestyle). Remember these are general drills and can be substituted with a set created specifically for a particular swimmer if that swimmer has the opportunity to work with a coach who can properly design one. Also, although many different pieces of equipment are available to assist with swim training, very few are as essential as a swimsuit, swim cap (if hair is long), and swim goggles. Other than these obvious essentials, there is only one additional item a swimmer should have in his swim bag, and that is short-blade fins.

---

### ▶ What Are Off Strokes?

All swimming styles other than front crawl (freestyle) are collectively called the off strokes. These include backstroke, breaststroke, and butterfly. Other than to impress your friends, it is not necessary to master the butterfly stroke—the most strenuous of the four swim styles—in order to be a good triathlon swimmer. However, being able to proficiently swim backstroke and breaststroke can sometimes come in handy for navigation purposes when swimming in open water. Backstroke can be helpful when the sun is in your eyes and you need to see where you are coming from to get a better idea of where to go. Backstroke can also be used to adjust swim goggles or take a short break from timing breathing, which for many beginners is the biggest challenge of freestyle. Breaststroke can be used when the water is wavy and you need to lift your head higher to be able to see over the waves. In addition, breaststroke is the least strenuous of the four strokes so it allows an easier intensity for tired swimmers.

---

These types of fins are very helpful for technique work in order to perform the drills properly. They provide a little bit of extra propulsion, which helps you maintain a good body position during drills. In addition, the fins make you more aware of your feet and legs, helping keep them in the slipstream of your body so you don't kick too big or too wide. The fist drill (page 67) is the only drill where you should not use fins, and the reason is that you want to struggle a little to force yourself to pull with your forearms so you learn to bend the elbow early.

Also note there are many other tools that can be used in swimming, and some are helpful when used properly, but some can lead to injury. An example is paddles designed to add resistance to the underwater pull, thereby making the swimmer stronger. If the swimmer's technique is poor (e.g., arm crossing over the middle of the body, which is fairly common), this added resistance can very easily create a shoulder injury. A safer way to develop more power in the pull and also work on technique is to do sport-specific dryland training with resistance cords.

Following are 11 freestyle drills every swimmer should know and do regularly. The first 5 focus on body position and rotation in order to improve the streamlined position. You will notice they are mostly kicking drills, with little to no use of the arms. This is because you need to learn how to use your kick and core to rotate. This is not about kicking hard, but efficiently and in the correct fashion. The last 6 drills focus on the arm cycle (often referred to as the pull or stroke). They will directly increase your propulsion. There is a definite reason for the order—each drill builds on the one before, so it is best to perform them in the suggested order.

You should strive to complete 10 sets of 50 meters for each of these drills (excluding the vertical kicking drill, which is done stationary for 1 minute) to create a comprehensive overall technique-work segment in the pool. Precision is paramount. Rest for 10 to 20 seconds between each 50 meters so you can not only recover physically but also remind yourself to visualize before actually pushing off the wall; mental focus while doing these drills is crucial. The key to success during drills is to do them properly so the desired effect is achieved. Often athletes do drills and make the same technique mistakes as they make in their swimming and therefore see no improvement.

## Vertical Kicking Drill

The purpose of this drill is to make the kick efficient and improve long-axis rotation. From a vertical position with your arms at your sides, use a flutter kick to keep your head above the water. This is the part of the drill where you work on your kick. You can even look down at your legs and make sure you are not bending the knees too much or bending forward at the waist. Utilize the upper muscles of the leg, and make small fast movements. At first this may be hard to do for even 30 seconds, but try to work your way up to 1 minute.

Once this is comfortably achieved, you can start to work on your long-axis rotation. From the same vertical kicking position, rotate 90 degrees every 3 to 5 seconds to work on rotating from kick and core. Rotate the entire body as a unit from the kick and hips, 90 degrees to the right and then back to center, then 90 degrees to the left and back to center again. Repeat this for another minute, and focus on starting the rotation from the kick and hips, not the upper body.

## Corkscrew Drill

This drill helps you find a balanced and comfortable body position and improves your long-axis rotation. This is the same drill as vertical kicking, only you move into the horizontal plane as you progress toward swimming. Keep your hands at your sides, and again focus on turning the body from your kick and hips; do not lead with the head and shoulders. For this drill, rotate your body 180 degrees so you are either on your belly or your back. Keep your head back and hips up to have an aligned body position when on your back. You should be looking either at the ceiling (when on your back) or at the bottom of the pool (when on your belly). Be sure to take your time, and breathe out when your head is facing down; when your head is facing up, try to relax and breathe normally. You can stay on your back or belly as long as you like until you feel ready to rotate properly. Remember to be careful when reaching the end of the pool.

## Kick on Side Drill

This is a great drill for working on body position. This side position is one of the most streamlined forms a human can take in the water. The objective here is to get comfortable with the head lying on the shoulder and having one goggle in and one out of the water. This is the ideal position for your head when you breathe.

To do this drill, lie on your side, with your bottom arm stretched out and your ear pressing onto the shoulder. This arm should be just under the surface of the water, with the hand parallel to the bottom of the pool. The top arm should be on your side. Do a flutter kick, and strive to maintain one goggle in and one goggle out of the water. The natural tendency is to start lifting the head to get the mouth out of the water to breathe. This actually makes you sink and work harder. If breathing while keeping a good head position is difficult, simply roll your head and look up to allow your mouth and nose to clear the water and enable you to breathe.

## Kick on Side Drill With One Stroke

This drill works the body position and also the rotation. You are again progressing toward swimming whole or regular freestyle. In this drill, you perform the kick on side drill, as just described, but every 5 seconds or so, you make a recovery with the trailing arm and pull with the leading arm as you rotate over to the other side. The focus needs to be on making a smooth rotation and keeping the body in alignment. The best way to do that is to start the recovery first and stay on your side until your hand passes your face, then start to bend the elbow of the leading arm; as the recovering arm enters the water, pull with the other arm and roll over to the other side. Keep your neck in alignment with your spine (do not lift the head) as though the long axis is coming out of the top of your head. Repeat over to the other side. Take your time; at first you may do only one rotation per length.

## Kick on Side Drill With Three Strokes

This drill also works the body position and rotation in another step toward full freestyle swimming. This drill is the same as the previous one-stroke kick on side drill, but this time three strokes are used to rotate from one side to the other. Really focus on an integrated rotation in each stroke, driving it with your kick and hips, not the head and shoulders.

## Catch-Up Drill

This drill is great for working on exchanging one arm for the other in front of the head, ensuring there is always an arm in front of the head to glide out on. This makes the body longer, and in general, a longer body moves faster. Think of the long hull design of speedboats. In addition, the hands meeting in front of the head is a great reminder to pull and rotate. If you breathe on both sides, this drill can balance out your rotation. You continue to glide out on the arm in front as you recover with the other arm. When both arms are fully extended in front of your head, you then pull with the opposing arm. When first doing this drill, it is helpful to keep both arms in front of your head and kick awhile before switching arms. This gives you time to visualize a good pull with early elbow bending and good rotation during the power phase. As with all drills, take your time. The slower and more accurately you do these drills, the more you will retain when you swim fast.

## Fist Drill

This drill will specifically help you develop the early elbow bend at the beginning of your stroke. Many swimmers get little to no benefit from this drill because they lack the knowledge of how to perform it correctly. It must be done slowly and with very conscious thought about feeling pressure on your forearm as you begin your pull. This feedback shows you are indeed bending the elbow early enough to feel pressure on your forearm as you pull against the water. What this drill does is take the hand out of the pull. In a sense this forces you to bend the elbow to try to "catch" some water. If you rush the strokes, you will simply make the same errors you make in your regular swimming. Never do an entire length with fists. The dynamic feeling of opening the hands and feeling the added power from the higher elbow is the positive feedback that makes the change carry over to your regular stroke. Since you actually need to struggle through the water a bit to feel this pressure on the forearm, it is best to do this drill without fins, as mentioned previously.

## Sculling Drill

This is another drill for working on the beginning of your pull. Sculling is defined as moving a limb from side to side to create lift. It is the motion one uses for treading water. This subtle skill can be helpful in getting that elusive "feel" for the water swimmers talk about. The goal is to get a feeling of pressure on your arm from the fingertips to your elbow. To do this, push off and bend both arms at the elbows, and rotate your shoulders medially so your fingertips face the bottom of the pool. Then as though your forearm and hand form a paddle, hinge at the elbow and weave your hand and forearm in and out repeatedly for 3 to 5 seconds. Then swim normally and take a few breaths; when ready, repeat. While sculling, be sure to keep your neck neutral, and hence breathe only when you are taking the regular strokes between sculling.

## Single-Arm Drill

The purpose of this drill is to make the swimmer focus on only one arm at a time. To perform this drill, use only your right arm to swim one length and your left to swim the next. This drill is also used to work all five phases of the freestyle stroke (see Five Phases of the Freestyle Stroke for more information). It can be tricky because many swimmers try to work on all five phases at once, where nothing is really worked on specifically, and a swimmer can end up making the same mistakes in the drill as in his regular swimming. However, if you focus on only one aspect or phase for an entire two-length sequence (one arm in one direction and the other coming back) the results are amazing. When in doubt as to which phase to focus on, the early elbow bend at the beginning of the pull is your best choice because problems in this phase are very common, and every swimmer can benefit from improving it. If you have had your swimming analyzed on video and you can see in your mind's eye other flaws to correct, such as a poor entry or recovery, then do another two-length sequence focusing on just that phase.

## Catch-Up Drill With Thumb Scrape

This drill will ensure that you finish each stroke. Before you push off, extend your arm down your leg, and scrape your thumb on your thigh. At the finish of each pull, scrape your thigh

---

### ▶ Five Phases of the Freestyle Stroke

The freestyle stroke has five phases. Let's examine these a little more closely:

1. *Entry and extension.* In this phase, the hand enters the water and extends forward just under the surface, like putting on a long glove that is lying just under the surface of the water, parallel to the surface.

2. *Elbow bend or catch.* After the arm is fully extended, the next phase involves internally rotating the shoulder and bending the elbow. This prepares the forearm to be used as a paddle to apply force backward and propel you forward.

3. *Pull.* This is where the force is applied to the water, and the body then moves past the arm. It can also be termed the power phase since it is where the majority of the forward power and propulsion come from in swimming.

4. *Round-off and release.* When the pull is finished and the triceps have been used to extend the arm along the side of the body, it is time to externally rotate the shoulder, which releases the shoulder joint and allows the arm to move freely to the next phase.

5. *Recovery.* After the shoulder is released, the arm can then return back over the water to start the cycle again by going into the entry and extension phase.

in that same area. This is also the perfect drill to work on the release of the shoulder at the end of your stroke since with the touch you are sensitized to that part of the stroke.

## Catch-Up Drill With Fingertip Drag

This twist on the catch-up drill focuses on the recovery and entry of your stroke. For this drill, lie on your side and slowly drag your fingertips through the water's surface as you recover. Ideally, you should see the palm of your hand as it passes about 8 to 12 inches (20 to 30 cm) from the side of your head. Your fingertips stay in the water from the release phase of the stroke until the hand enters the water. After entry, the arm extends in front of the shoulder to full extension and meets the other outstretched arm.

---

### ▶ Min/Max Sets

Min/max sets are used to test an athlete's improvement in technique and efficiency. It is recommended to use min/max 50s once a month to play with your stroke efficiency. This is simply a set of 50s where you count your strokes and time yourself. Add the time and stroke count. That total now becomes your gauge of efficiency. Lower it. Create a PR (personal record), and play with speed and stroke length to see how low you can get that total of time and strokes. For example, let's say you swim a 50 meter in 40 seconds and take 45 strokes; the total is 85. On the next 50 you swim faster and go a 35 seconds, and it takes 48 strokes; the total is 83. Keep doing 50s, changing speeds and stroke rate to find the most efficient. As you improve your stroke, your PR on this will decrease. Have fun with it.

I recommend a set of 6 × 50 meters min/max at least once per month. Just counting strokes can be misleading since you can get a very low stroke count by overgliding and delaying strokes. What happens is you will become a slow swimmer who takes fewer strokes.

There are probably areas of your swimming that are inefficient or maybe even missing. A video analysis can usually show you what areas of your technique need more attention. If you have a straight arm pull, then an extra round of single-arm and fist drills will help. Most swimmers make a few very common errors. Seeing any of these in your video analysis allows you to focus on these areas, either through specific drills or a combination of drills that allow you to make changes. A follow-up video analysis and new PRs in the min/max drill are helpful to gauge your success and assure you that your technique training is working. Ideally, above- and below-water video footage is the best to see all aspects of a swimmer's technique; however, much can be garnered from the surface as long as there is a side view that allows a coach to see how your arm is pulling under the water.

---

## *Main Set*

The main set for a pool workout is what you may consider the actual "workout," and most often, it is created for a specific training purpose. It's termed *main set* because swim training is accomplished almost exclusively using interval training. Interval training in swimming is when a set distance is performed a number of times on a specific interval time. For example, if we use *R* for the number of times the distance is completed, *D* for the distance of each swim, and *T* for the interval time, then an interval set can be expressed as R × D on T. Using this formula, 10 × 100 on 2:00 means that every 2 minutes the athlete pushes off the wall and swims 100 (yards or meters depending on the pool), and this is done 10 times. If the athlete completes each swim in 1:42, she would then have 18 seconds' rest before starting the next one. Some coaches may use interval training in warm-ups, whereas almost all use them for technique work.

In the main set, intensity is the focal point rather than technique, so in many ways the workout is built around the main set, and interval training becomes the backbone of all swim training programs to help keep athletes aware of their pace and keep track of distance covered. Although the combinations of interval distance, number of repeats, and interval time are infinite, in general the following are the three types of main sets found in the weekly training plan of a good program:

- Short intervals including 25s, 50s, and 100s for building speed
- Medium intervals of 100, 200, 300, and 400 meters to build speed and endurance
- Long intervals of 500 meters or more to build endurance or a straight swim so the swimmer experiences race distances (in this case, the main set is technically not a set but rather a long swim done once)

Essentially, this means that if the overall focus of the workout is to build speed, then the main set should be intervals of a short distance so a high rate of speed can be maintained. If the overall focus of the workout is to build endurance, then a set of longer intervals with a relatively short rest period would fit the bill.

In some situations, such as for beginning swimmers or when the main goal is large gains in a swimmer's technique, in at least one session per week the main set should consist of technique drills in place of the various intervals (short, medium, long) listed previously. This could be a repeat of the drills performed in the technique-work portion of the workout, just one or two drills focusing on one particular aspect of technique to improve on, or different drills or a subset of drills that focus on one aspect of a swimmer's stroke. For example, let's say a particular swimmer needs to improve his underwater pull, especially the catch. To do this, the main set could consist of 20 × 50s as follows: 5 fist drills, 5 sculling drills, 5 single-arm drills, and 5 catch-up drills. Remember, simply doing the drills is not enough—doing them correctly is key. If a coach is not available, perhaps have a lifeguard or friend record you so you can assess whether you are performing the technique correctly.

## *Cool-Down*

The cool-down is the time to reduce heart rate slowly and return to easy breathing and good technique. The cool-down can also be a good time to practice strokes other than freestyle by adding several 50s of the breaststroke and backstroke. This not only helps your body cool down but also engages other muscles, relieving those used during your workout. Adding a drill or two to the cool-down helps finish each swim training session with optimal technique. Be careful not to skip this important part of the workout because it contributes to the success of your next workout. Successful training is done one step at a time, and every workout should prepare you for the next.

# Practicing Open-Water Techniques in the Pool

For swimmers who have little or no open-water swimming experience, drills in the pool to practice the techniques needed in open water can make the first few open-water swims much safer and more effective. In place of traditional main sets, at short, medium, and long intervals, the following can be used when the focus is to help a swimmer prepare for the open water.

These suggestions usually require a special arrangement with your pool's management and coaching or lifeguard staff since they involve utilizing more than one lane.

## *Sighting*

A key skill for a swimmer in open water is navigation, and to navigate well, a swimmer needs to sight often. You may think you swim straight in a pool, but you are unconsciously and continually correcting your course, by following the line on the bottom of the pool and seeing or hitting the lane lines. In open water, you do not have these helpful lines, lanes, and visibility; and what's more, you need to deal with currents from wind or tides, which can move you a little or a lot. To sight in open water, it is advised that you switch to the breaststroke or tread water while you assess where you are heading, and adjust as needed. Although this gets the job done, it will slow you down, and in a crowded swim, other swimmers may run into you. Because of these two drawbacks, you do not want to look too often, meaning you may swim off course for longer. The longer you swim off course, the farther the distance you swim, which of course is not ideal (more details about sighting can be found in chapter 16). Following are a few activities you can do to practice sighting in a pool:

- Perform 10 × 25s while incorporating sighting into your stroke. Sighting can be done by swimming a few strokes, looking up at a buoy or other object while still moving forward using a shorter freestyle stroke or the breaststroke with your head above water. You will want to sight in open water every third or fourth stroke. Be patient since it usually takes several sessions to get the hang of it. Beginners should hold off on this technique until they can easily swim a 500 straight. If a swimmer is struggling with breathing, then this drill will simply increase anxiety.

- Integrate sighting into efficient freestyle. As you might guess, this is the best method and of course the most difficult to master. Having said that, with a little practice at the pool you will get pretty good at it. The key is to lift your head only enough to have your eyes above the water (not high enough to breathe). Then as your arm comes past your head on the recovery, you drop your head and roll to the side to breathe as you would if you were not sighting. This way you do not compromise your body position by lifting your head all the way out of the water, yet you still get a view. Since this technique does not slow you down, you can view every two strokes; even if you do not see what you need to every single time, with this kind of frequency you can swim very straight.

- To practice sighting and passing (or being passed), you can do snake swims. The purpose of this exercise is to have a large group do a long continuous swim together and get practice sighting and passing (or being passed by) other swimmers. This requires utilizing multiple lanes and generally works best when the entire pool can be used. The swimmers line up from the fastest to the slowest and start about 5 to 10 seconds apart. The swimmers go down one side of the lane, come back in the other, and then push off into the adjacent lane and repeat, hence "snaking" their way through the pool. If you have a six-lane 25-meter pool, then each sequence through the pool is 300 meters. You can have a swim of 30 minutes, with the goal of getting in as many laps as possible. After finishing a 300-meter sequence, each swimmer gets out and walks back to the other side of the pool to do another 300-meter sequence.

## Drafting

Drafting is best practiced first in a pool and is actually part of any masters program by necessity of having multiple swimmers in a lane. The key to drafting is to swim as close to the swimmer in front of you as possible without hitting her feet with your hands. To accomplish this, you may have to alter your stroke and enter wider or slow down to maintain the correct position. Drafting works best when the swimmer in front is about 10 percent faster than you. Much faster and you will be going anaerobic to keep up; if she is the same speed or slower, you won't swim as fast as you are capable of. The concept is very similar to drafting in cycling. In cycling the energy savings can be 10 to 30 percent; in swimming it is more like 5 to 15 percent, which is still very significant.

Although drafting can be a great bonus, spending lots of energy trying to get behind the right person is foolhardy. The best approach is to swim your own race, and if you happen to notice a swimmer swimming about the same speed or maybe slightly faster or more aggressively, then you can slide behind that person and draft for a while. Always check two things: that he is swimming straight and that you are not working too hard or too easy to stay in that position. Swimming with several people in a lane at a group workout is the best way to practice drafting.

## Starts

Although deep-water and chest-deep starts can be practiced solo in a lane, it is even more effective if you take out a lane line or a few lane lines and get a group of six or more swimmers all treading water in close proximity before someone yells "go" or blows a whistle. The swimmers all race to the other end of the pool. This exercise requires a deep end. A chest-deep start can also be practiced from the shallow end of the pool. These drills give the swimmers the opportunity to practice starting while treading water and also with a group so they get used to the conditions of such starts, such as churning arms.

## Buoy Turns

Take out some lane lines, and put a buoy (this can be a lifeguard buoy attached to a line and a weight) about 5 meters from the wall. The swimmers (preferably a group of six or more) start at the other side of the pool and swim to and around the buoy and back. If it is possible to take out some lane lines and have a group of swimmers together, then practicing starts and buoy turns can be done as intervals. This is a fun workout that is ideal as a lead-in to open-water swimming both for beginners and advanced athletes. One of the main differences in the stroke technique of open-water swimmers in crowded races or rough conditions is that the recovery portion of the arm cycle needs to be higher and wider to help the swimmers clear waves and to keep them from getting hit by other swimmers' arms. These open-water techniques practiced in the pool help swimmers see the value of working on this type of "defensive" swimming.

# Swim Training Strategies

An important distinction between swimming and the other two sports in triathlon is that, in general, training intensity and frequency can be much higher for swimming than for the other sports since the water is very supportive to the body, and the risk of going too hard (intensity) or too often (frequency) is not an issue. This is advantageous because swimming frequently can help a swimmer learn new neuromuscular patterns. In addition, since gauging intensity is not as critical as in biking and running, pace and the swimmer's perceived effort can be relied on to define intensity, and the swimmer doesn't need to worry about monitoring physical aspects such as heart rate, which is difficult to determine in real time while swimming.

When designing a swim program for triathlon training, the phases of the season need to be taken into account before defining intensity and frequency. It would take an entire book to cover all the variables for the various phases of the season. In general, the earlier in the season, the easier the effort and the less rest an athlete should have in order to focus on building endurance. As competition approaches, the effort and rest time should increase to improve speed and pace.

Here is how a set of 10 × 100s would change in intensity and frequency for the six phases of the season just listed:

- *Prep phase*—The interval time would allow for a short rest, and the intensity would be defined as relatively easy. The set would be done once a week.

- *Base phase*—The set would be similar to the prep phase; however, the goal would be to do it more than once per week and perhaps even add volume (e.g., 12 × 100s).

- *Build phase*—The set would be done a few times per week with more volume. (e.g., 15 × 100s)

- *Peak/taper*—The set would be adjusted to a lower number of intervals, such as 1, 3, or 5 × 100s at a high intensity, for a long interval, and with lots of recovery.

- *Race phase*—The set would be done once per week, with the intensity and rest increased.

- *Off-season*—The off-season set can go in many directions depending on the goals of the athlete (e.g., it can morph into a technique set; it can be used to work on off strokes; it can ease back to the sets done in the prep-phase set to maintain a level of fitness). Also note that swimming is one of the best off-season activities because this is a great time to work on technique, the properties of the water are very restorative for muscles that have been overloaded from many miles of running and biking, and the risk of overuse injuries in swimming (other than shoulder tendinitis, perhaps, if stroke mechanics are off) is not an issue, so the more swimming the better!

In addition, test sets are helpful to keep athletes on track and to act as benchmarks for technique, speed, and endurance to ensure the desired training effects are taking place. An example of a good test set is 10 × 100s at a threshold pace (very intense) on an interval allowing for 10 to 15 seconds of rest in between. This is a good indicator of fitness because as an athlete gets in shape, she can go a faster average pace or decrease the interval time. If no improvement is indicated, this can tell you that training needs to be adjusted; it can also indicate the athlete is sick or overtrained or she has reached a plateau and needs to be patient. This is part of the art of coaching and sport—being able to distinguish what test sets and race results actually indicate and then adjust the training appropriately.

Other good test sets are time trials of key distances: 100, 200, 500, 1,000, 1,500, 2,000, and 3,000. PRs of these distances should be logged for any serious swimmer to chart his progress. These times (especially the longer ones, 1,500 to 3,000) can be used as a threshold pace to determine targets on interval sets. As an example, if an athlete goes 45 minutes for a 3,000-meter time trial, that would be a pace of 1:30 per 100. This would lead to the ability to prescribe a set of 10 × 100s on 1:45 for this athlete, with the goal of swimming each repeat in 1:30 or better, allowing for 15 seconds' or more rest for each one. This pace can then be used as a target for shorter intervals. As the time-trial pace increases, so does the workout pace.

This chapter covers the importance of a well-designed swim training plan for the pool, not only for getting swimmers ready for their first time in open water but also for showing seasoned veterans how essential it is to work on continual improvement in the swim discipline. The controlled environment of the pool is ideal for doing technique and open-water preparation drills in addition to correctly quantifying distances and times for training purposes. Eleven of the most popular and effective drills are explained so they can be implemented in the four-part workout template suggested. Some main sets are reviewed to assist the reader in creating effective main sets for different times of the season for swimmers of different levels. The reader should now be able to create an effective swim workout for any level of swimmer to prepare for participating in a triathlon.

One final caveat: No matter how well a swimmer does in the pool or how much open-water simulation she experiences, she should still do several practices in the open water in preparation for an event, especially for any first-timer, so the first time she swims in open water is not at an event.

# CHAPTER 6

# Training for Triathlon Biking

## Joe Friel

Many experienced triathletes believe that the key to a fast triathlon is bike fitness. They contend that being highly fit for the bike portion of the race allows them to hold back slightly, still go fast, and then start the run with relatively fresh legs. Those athletes who are less cycling fit may also finish the bike leg with a fast time, but they will experience greater fatigue during the run since they rode at a higher percentage of their fitness capacity.

To develop such excellent bike fitness, triathletes typically do about half of their training on the bike, and their longest workouts are also on the bike. The bottom line is that to race fast you must first become fast on the bike. How you can do that is the purpose of this chapter.

## Bike Training Components

Three workout components of training are critical for all triathletes' fitness and performance regardless of their levels of expertise: duration, frequency, and intensity.

### Duration

The duration of your bike training sessions, or how long your workouts are, depends on several things, the most basic of which is the distance of your goal race, meaning the longer the race, the longer the workout. Also, the time of the season determines how long your workouts need to be, which you learned about in chapter 1. Generally speaking, though, fast or high-intensity workouts are shorter than slow, low-intensity rides. But if forced to put a number on it, your longest ride, regardless of the race you are training for, should be at least 90 minutes. Half- and full-Ironman triathletes typically do rides that are two to four times that long. One such long ride each week is generally adequate for most triathletes given everything else they must fit into a training week along with work or school, family, and other commitments.

## Frequency

Novice triathletes typically ride two or three times a week. Experienced intermediate athletes usually ride three or four times a week. Advanced and competitive triathletes are on their bikes four to six times a week. For optimal bike fitness, you should ride at least three times a week. However, four rides in a week will produce even greater fitness even if the weekly volume remains unchanged. Interestingly, research tells us that beyond four workouts a week, there is a decreasing return on the investment of your time. In other words, your fitness will likely improve if you ride five or six times a week instead of four, but the rate of improvement is not nearly as great as the change from three to four. Competitive triathletes, however, are generally seeking every bit of fitness possible, so even though the return is small at five or more, they see the gain as fitness they otherwise would not have. Of course, there are limits to how often you train on the bike because of lifestyle conflicts and your capacity for training. If you have a very busy life or if you are easily fatigued, then you simply can't train as much.

## Intensity

For the novice triathlete, the key to improvement is duration—how long the workouts are. Unfortunately, many experienced athletes never give up that notion and continue to believe their improvement is tied more to how many miles or hours they do than anything else. Research tells us that as you gain experience and become more advanced, the key to performance is the intensity of your workouts. In other words, doing lots of slow miles will get you in pretty good shape when you first start training for triathlon, but to approach your potential as an experienced triathlete, the key is intensity.

This doesn't mean all your workouts on the bike should be done as hard and as fast as you can possibly go. That's counterproductive. *Intensity* as used here is related strictly to the demands of the event for which you are training. High intensity for a sprint-distance race is nothing like that for an Ironman triathlon. The advanced athlete should gradually do more on-bike training at or slightly above the intensity planned for the race. In other words, training intensity should gradually become more race-like as the season progresses.

In the preparatory phase, training is not race-like. A short-course triathlete will do a lot of bike training at an intensity well below race intensity at this time. A long-course triathlete may also do workouts that are unlike the planned intensity of the race. This could be fast intervals in the late preparatory phase. That's unlike the expected race intensity in a long-course event. But in the last 12 weeks before the goal race, the intensity of bike workouts for both short- and long-course triathletes will become more like that planned for the race. This means that the short-course athlete's workouts would become faster relative to the late base period, while the long-course triathlete would do more longer workouts at a moderate pace. Realize, however, that as you get closer to race day, only one or two bike workouts each week will be done at a race-like intensity, whereas the others will be for recovery and maintenance (this is discussed in more detail later in this chapter).

Speed, or pace, is a good measure of intensity for running, but it doesn't work on the bike, where wind, even a slight wind, plays a major role in how fast you go. Ride into a breeze and although you are working hard, your speed is low. On the other hand, get a bit of a tailwind and speed is quite fast while your effort may be very low. Better measures of biking intensity are rating of perceived exertion (RPE), heart rate, and power.

RPE is probably the easiest to use and understand. It is certainly the cheapest. Just subjectively rate how hard you are working while riding using a 1-to-10 scale, with 1 being very, very easy and 10 being very, very hard (see figure 9.2 on page 119 for the RPE scale). With a few weeks of experience you can get pretty good at this. The downside is you don't know if fitness is improving if RPE is all you have.

Heart rate–based training is very common in running and works just as well on the bike. All you need to do is establish zones based on functional threshold heart rate (FTHR). To find your FTHR, warm up and then ride for 30 minutes as hard as you can—just as if it were a race. Your average heart rate for the last 20 minutes of the 30 minutes is a fairly good predictor of your FTHR. All you need to do now is a bit of math using table 6.1 and you have your bike heart rate zones. Take the FTHR that you just found and multiply it by the percentage shown in the table (e.g., for zone 2, you'd multiply your FTHR by .81 to determine your heart rate for the low end of the zone and by .89 for the high end). You can continue this for the entire table to determine all six heart rate zones.

The downside of heart rate training is that if you don't compare your heart rate to something, you still don't know if fitness is improving. Heart rate by itself tells you nothing about fitness—or how fast you can go in a race. It tells you only how hard you are working. Even people who are very unfit have high heart rates when riding a bike. But they aren't fast. So with what can you compare heart rate to know if you are making progress? The answer is power.

Although power meters are expensive, at least when compared with heart rate monitors, they provide you with what's missing from both RPE and heart rate. Those measures of intensity tell you what your "input" is during a bike ride. A power meter tells you about "output"—what you are accomplishing given a certain RPE or heart rate. If you know input and output, you have all the information necessary to gauge changes in fitness.

**TABLE 6.1**

## FTHR Percentages and Heart Rate Zones for Bike Training

| % of FTHR | Heart rate zone |
|-----------|-----------------|
| <81% | Zone 1 |
| 81-89% | Zone 2 |
| 90-93% | Zone 3 |
| 94-102% | Zone 4 |
| 103-106% | Zone 5 |
| >106% | Zone 6 |

Power meters are no more complex or mysterious than heart rate monitors. To use a power meter, you set up zones similar to what you did for heart rate, only now you use functional threshold power (FTP). Similar to heart rate, FTP is the highest average power you can sustain during a 30-minute, all-out test on your bike. Just ride as hard and fast as you can for 30 minutes, and look to see what your average power was for the entire time when done. Using a scale similar to heart rate, you can set up your power zones using Dr. Andrew Coggan's system. You can take the FTHR you just determined and use that number to calculate your power zones using the percentages listed in table 6.2. For example, to calculate your power zone 1, multiply your FTHR by .55. Power zone 1 is anything below this number. To calculate your power zone 2, multiply your FTHR by .55 for the low end and .74 for the high end of the zone. You can continue this for all the zones listed in the table. The section on bike workouts later in this chapter describes the details of using these zones to gauge your workout intensity.

**TABLE 6.2**

## FTP Percentages and Power Zones for Bike Training

| % of FTP | Power zone |
|----------|------------|
| <55% | Zone 1 |
| 55-74% | Zone 2 |
| 75-89% | Zone 3 |
| 90-104% | Zone 4 |
| 105-120% | Zone 5 |
| >120% | Zone 6 |

Adapted, by permission, from H. Allen and A. Coggan, 2010, *Training and racing with a power meter,* 2nd ed. (Boulder, CO: VeloPress), 48.

## *Volume*

When workout duration and workout frequency are combined, the result is something called *volume*. This is how many hours, miles, or kilometers you do in a given period of time, such as a week.

So, what should your bike volume be when preparing for a race? If you do too much it means risking overtraining. Too little and you will not reach peak fitness. Getting bike volume just right is the goal, and there are a couple of guidelines you can follow.

The first has already been mentioned: About half of your total training time each week should be dedicated to the bike. That may vary quite a bit, however. In the early preparatory phase, you may ride less in order to devote more time to your swimming and running, especially if one of these is a limiter for you. And in the winter when early preparatory-phase training is common, the days are short and the weather can be challenging for riding a bike. At this time of year, saddle time may be far less than half your volume. On the other hand, in the summer you may do more than half your training on the bike.

Bike volume is also related to the event for which you are training. On average, across the season, minimum weekly bike training times range from about 3 to 5 hours depending on the race distance. Sprint- and Olympic-distance triathletes will typically train a minimum of 3 hours, with long-course triathletes doing a minimum of 5 hours in a week. Maximum bike volume is even more variable, typically ranging from 6 to 15 hours weekly. For the experienced triathlete, the key to success isn't so much how many hours are spent on the bike, but rather what is done with the bike time. In other words, intensity is the real determiner of success if you've been in the sport for some time.

## Specificity

Throughout the season, as your training progresses from the preparatory to the competitive phases, your bike training follows the specificity principle, meaning the duration and intensity of rides should become more like what you expect to do in the race. For the novice triathlete, the greater issue is duration. For the experienced triathlete, it's intensity.

Training for a sprint triathlon is nothing at all like training for a long-course race. Being fit and ready for one distance doesn't mean you are equally prepared for the other. The shorter the race distance, the higher your training intensity must be; the longer the race, the lower the intensity but the longer the bike workouts. Although long-course triathletes may ride long and steady at a variety of intensities in the preparatory phase, from very low to very high, in the competitive phase these long, steady rides are done at race intensity or slightly above. Such sessions may even involve intervals (e.g., three to six 20-minute intervals at or slightly greater than race intensity, with 5-minute recoveries). After a preparatory phase in which they developed aerobic fitness primarily with long rides, experienced sprint- and Olympic-distance triathletes typically do one bike interval workout each week in the preparatory phase. These intervals are done at or slightly greater than goal-race intensity. An example is three to five work intervals at race intensity for 6 minutes each, with 90-second, easy-spin recovery intervals. Again, the underlying idea of training is that your bike workouts should become increasingly like what you intend to do in the race as you get closer to race day.

## Recovery

Of course, it's also possible to train too much on the bike. Doing too much means you'll frequently experience excessive fatigue, and training quality will suffer. The idea is to increasingly train harder, which is called overreaching, while avoiding overtraining. Overtraining is overreaching taken to the extreme. The difference between overreaching and overtraining is moderation in training and adequate, well-timed rest. Let's take a look at how you can do that.

Training on the bike, just as in the other two disciplines, is made up of both hard workouts (high intensity, long duration, or both) and easy workouts (low intensity, short duration, or both). Most advanced triathletes include 3 to 6 workouts in a week in each of the three sports. Since they are typically doing in the neighborhood of 9 to 18 total workouts in a week, it's obvious that most must be easy. Of course, novice and intermediate triathletes do fewer workouts but also with a mix of hard and easy sessions.

So why do easy workouts? Why not just take the day off? Actually, that's probably the best option for newbies, but experienced triathletes seem to recover faster when doing light exercise. An easy ride or swim is a great way to get the blood flowing to remove the waste products of a previous workout. Running is not typically used to speed up recovery, however, since it is a bit stressful for the legs. An easy spin on the bike is also a good way to further ingrain pedaling skills, which enhances biking economy. As an athlete becomes more economical, fitness and race speed improve just as they would if aerobic capacity ($\dot{V}O_2$max) increased.

When the training load (volume or intensity) is high, fatigue accumulates. If you don't frequently shed that fatigue, your workout quality will decline, and you may eventually become overtrained. To prevent this, it's a good idea to periodically take several consecutive days of recovery. Older triathletes and those new to the sport generally should recover for a few days after about 2 weeks of hard training. Younger and experienced athletes can delay recovery until after 3 weeks of hard training. But if in doubt as to whether you need to recover more or less frequently, opt for resting every 3rd week.

Such a recovery period is 3 to 5 days long depending on how much fatigue has built up. During the recovery period, the workouts are short and of low intensity, primarily in zone 1. At the end of this break from hard training, you should feel rejuvenated and eager to train hard again. Use that sensation as a guide when deciding how long to make the recovery break.

# Bike Training Workouts

Once you understand the general philosophy of training with regard to duration, frequency, intensity, volume, specificity, and recovery, as described previously, the next step is what to do when it's time to go for a ride—the workouts.

When deciding how to work out each day, it helps to have a way of classifying the training sessions according to training purpose. For cycling, I am listing five types of triathlon-specific workouts based on the physical ability you want to improve: aerobic endurance, muscular force, speed skills, muscular endurance, and anaerobic endurance. See table 6.3 for a summary of these five workouts and what each requires (how the workouts can be organized into a training week is described in greater detail in a later section about the periods of the season).

**TABLE 6.3**

## Triathlon-Specific Bike Workouts and Requirements

| Type of bike workout | Workout requirements |
|---|---|
| Aerobic endurance (AE) | 1-4 hr steady at RPE 4 or at HR or power zone 2 |
| Muscular force (MF) | Weights, force reps, hilly rides |
| Speed skills (SS) | Drills: One-leg pedaling, spin-ups, shoe-top pedaling, relaxed high-cadence pedaling |
| Muscular endurance (ME) | 2 × 20 min in zone 3 with 5-min recoveries, 3-5 × 6 min in zone 4 with 90-sec recoveries, 20 min in zone 4 |
| Anaerobic endurance (AnE) | 5 × 3 min in zone 5 with 3-min recoveries (power meter preferred) |

## Aerobic Endurance Workout

The purpose of the aerobic endurance (AE) workout is to build a sound cardiorespiratory system by improving the function of your heart, lungs, blood, and blood vessels. This is the single most important type of workout for the triathlete since triathlons of all distances are relatively long-duration events demanding excellent aerobic endurance. If you don't have a sound platform of AE, none of the other abilities will do you any good. AE is the most basic and important workout for triathletes, from novices to elites.

An AE workout is done by riding for a long duration at a moderate intensity. How long the duration is depends on the event for which you are training. A triathlete training for a long-course race will do much longer workouts than someone training for a sprint-distance triathlon. Moderate intensity means zone 2 heart rate or power, or an RPE of about 4. So essentially all you do in an AE session is ride steadily for a long time. It's the simplest of all the bike workouts, yet it is the most critical for triathlon success.

AE workouts are the primary focus of the preparatory phase. You should do many of these sessions during this time. In the competitive phase, after AE has been thoroughly developed, these workouts take on a secondary importance as you maintain the ability with less frequent AE workouts. This allows you time to work on the more advanced race-specific abilities—muscular endurance and anaerobic endurance.

## Muscular Force Workout

Muscular force is the ability to overcome resistance. When riding a bike you typically face two types of resistance—wind resistance and gravity. Wind resistance has to do with aerodynamic drag. No matter how aerodynamic your position on the bike, drag will always be the most significant obstacle of going fast when the course is flat. Gravity replaces drag as the primary obstacle when going up a hill. The purpose of a muscular force (MF) workout is to develop an optimally strong muscular system so you can overcome these twin obstacles.

If your muscles aren't sufficiently strong, you will never be able to truly ride fast in a race. It's muscles that push the pedals down. Of course, it's also possible to be too strong. You don't need the muscles of a bodybuilder or powerlifter. Such a body is too big and would be a great disadvantage on a hilly course. As a triathlete, you need muscles that are strong but not bulky.

There are two general ways to develop muscular force. One is by lifting weights in a gym to build the primary movers on the bike. This primarily involves doing hip, knee, and ankle extension exercises such as squats, leg presses, step-ups, deadlifts, and lunges. The other way to develop muscular force is by doing on-bike force workouts. Very short intervals done in a big gear at a very high effort with long recoveries will do this. These are called "force reps": three sets of $3 \times 12$ pedal strokes at max effort done in a high gear with 3 minutes between reps and 5 to 10 minutes between sets. To do this, warm up first, and then shift into a high gear (such as $53 \times 14$); coast to a near stop, stay seated, and then drive the pedals down 12 times at maximal effort. Your heart rate monitor is no use for this workout. But a power meter is perfect for measuring what your power output (and therefore force) is. If you don't have a power meter, go by RPE 10 on each repetition. Pedal easily to recover for about 3 minutes after each repetition within a set. Between sets, recover with easy pedaling for at least 5 minutes and as much as 10. After a few such sessions, you will notice you are becoming measurably stronger on the bike.

There is one caveat: This is a high-reward workout, which also makes it high risk. Whenever a workout has a big payoff of significantly improved fitness, there is a risk of being injured. The most likely injury will be to the knees. To reduce the chance of succumbing to a season-ending injury, be conservative with force reps. Do this workout only once each week in the preparatory phase. The first time you do it, start with only one set of three reps. Make the effort on the first two reps RPE 6 and 8 as you test your knees and learn how to do the workout. Make only the third one a max effort with an RPE of 10. Assuming the first such session went well and there was no tenderness in your knees either during or after the workout, the next time you do force reps, do one set with all three reps at RPE 10. The following weeks you can add additional reps and sets as long as there have been no problems. Also, if you have a tendency toward knee injury, you are advised not to do force reps. In this case, however, you may be able to ride hilly courses, doing the climbs at a somewhat higher-than-normal intensity in order to overload your bike muscles.

As with AE, MF workouts are a primary focus of the preparatory phase, with one such bike-specific workout weekly (strength training in the gym is typically done twice weekly in the preparatory phase). In the competitive phase, MF is maintained by doing these workouts less frequently. Base-ability maintenance is discussed later in this chapter.

## Speed Skills Workout

There are many skills to develop in becoming a better cyclist, and this is the intention of a speed skills (SS) workout. Skills include those for climbing and descending hills and cornering. The most critical skill, however, for your success as a triathlete is pedaling.

Pedaling a bike seems like a no-brainer. After all, your shoes are clipped into pedals, and the pedals are attached to rigid crank arms that are fixed to the bottom bracket of the bike. The feet and legs have no choice but to make round circles. But some riders pedal more smoothly than others, wasting less energy. They are often referred to as "spinners." Those who are less efficient are often called "mashers." The difference between them is that spinners apply some degree of productive force (or at least no negative force) to the pedals throughout the entire circle; mashers just push down on the pedals and otherwise let their feet rest on the pedals throughout the remainder of the stroke. This requires the leg that is on the downstroke to lift the weight of the other, resting leg. Mashing is very inefficient, wasting a great deal of energy that could otherwise be used to produce effective power.

The key to becoming a spinner is learning to unweight the pedal throughout the recovery phase of the pedal stroke, from about the 6 o'clock position to 12 o'clock, and to apply a slight amount of tension to the chain at the top and bottom ranges. You can learn to do both of these with drills in the preparatory phase as you are developing fitness. SS drills may be done at any time and as a portion of any workout, such as a warm-up. They are an important part of training in the base period for triathletes of all abilities. Here are a few pedaling drills that are effective for many triathletes.

## Isolated-Leg Training Drill

This is the quintessential pedaling drill, the one you should do a lot in the early weeks of the preparatory phase. It's best done on an indoor trainer. Unclip one foot and rest it on a chair next to the bike so you pedal with only one leg. With the bike in a low (easy) gear, turn the crank at a comfortable cadence. The first thing you'll notice is that getting through the top of the stroke, the 12-o'clock position, is difficult. Focus on smoothing this top transition. At first you may last only a few seconds before the hip flexors fatigue. When that happens, switch to the other leg. When this leg fatigues, clip both feet in and pedal for a few minutes, applying what you have learned in the single-leg pedaling. Repeat the drill several times throughout the remainder of the workout.

## Top-Only Drill

This is a foot-focused drill. Pedal the bike by keeping the top of your foot in constant and firm contact with the inside, top of the shoe. Try not to push down on the pedal at all. The actual pedaling is done just with the upstroke. Don't apply excessive upward force. Make the pedaling movement gentle and smooth. Do this several times throughout the session for a few minutes at a time.

## Spin-Up Drill

During a ride, shift to a low (easy) gear, and gradually increase your cadence until it is so fast that you begin to bounce on the saddle. Then return to a normal cadence. It should take 30 seconds or so for each spin-up. The bouncing is because you have reached and gone slightly beyond your optimal high cadence. You bounce because your foot is still pushing down at the bottom of the stroke (6 o'clock position). And since the crank arm can't get any longer, as you push down your butt comes off the saddle. This drill is best done with a cadence meter on your pedal so you know what your top-end cadence is. The goal is to raise your highest, optimal cadence by learning to transition smoothly at the bottom of the stroke. Repeat this frequently throughout the workout.

## *Muscular Endurance Workout*

For the experienced triathlete, regardless of race distance, muscular endurance (ME) is the training ability that determines high performance. ME workouts closely simulate the demands of a triathlon, involving either relatively long intervals with short recoveries or long, steady-state efforts. The intensity is lactate (anaerobic) threshold or slightly below. This is heart rate or power zones 3 and 4 or RPE 6 to 8. Examples of such workouts follow:

- 2 to 6 × 20 minutes at zone 3 with 5-minute recoveries
- 3 to 5 × 6 minutes at zone 4 with 90-second recoveries
- 40 minutes steady in zone 3
- 20 minutes steady in zone 4

Zone 3 ME intervals are common in the early preparatory phase for all race distances. In the competitive phase, zone 3 intervals and steady-state rides are a standard workout for long-course triathletes. ME intervals and steady states in zone 4 are best done in the last part of the preparatory phase and continue into the competitive phase for sprint- and Olympic-distance racers. One of these bike workouts done weekly for several weeks will boost muscular endurance and prepare you for race intensity.

### Anaerobic Endurance Workout

An anaerobic endurance (AnE) workout is the most challenging type of workout and is intended only for the experienced triathlete. Although the potential reward is high when doing AnE workouts, the risk is also great. AnE workouts boost aerobic capacity ($\dot{V}O_2$max), raise the lactate (anaerobic) threshold, and improve pedaling economy. This is a standard workout for a high-performance triathlete in the build period. It should be done only once a week during this training period. Six to eight of these sessions done over 8 to 10 weeks have the potential to lift performance remarkably. The possible downside is injury, illness, mental burnout, and overtraining. You must be cautious with AnE intervals.

The AnE workout is simple: 5 × 3 minutes at zone 5 with 3-minute recoveries. Be sure to warm up well before starting this session by gradually raising your intensity to zone 3 and including a few brief and powerful accelerations. AnE intervals may be done on flat terrain or on a hill. They also work well on an indoor trainer, which eliminates such dangerous conditions as traffic, stoplights, potholes, and dogs. The AnE work intervals must be done in zone 5 to bring the desired results. A power meter or even a subjective rating of RPE is preferable to a heart rate monitor for this session. These intervals are so brief that heart rate will still be rising at the end of each interval and is unlikely to achieve zone 5. This generally causes athletes to go much too hard in the first part of the interval in an attempt to force the heart rate to rise faster. That, of course, makes the workout too hard, increases the risk of breaking down in some way, and prolongs recovery.

# Bike Training Strategies

Most triathletes train using a system called periodization, as you learned in chapter 1, where the season is divided into phases, or blocks of weeks, where each has a specific training purpose. These phases are often referred to as macrocycles, mesocycles, and microcycles. The macrocycle is the overall segment of training that is done toward one specific goal. Mesocycles break down the overall macrocycle into smaller blocks of time, typically the preparatory phase (which has two subphases, general preparation and specific preparation), the competitive phase (which has two subphases, precompetitive and competitive), and the transition phase, where an athlete rests and recovers between training cycles.

The purpose of periodization is to achieve high fitness and peak form for your most important races. The underlying theme of this method of training is that the workouts become increasingly similar to the A race you are training for the closer you get to the race. So in the preparatory phase, you may be doing workouts that are unlike the race. This could be riding long distances at a moderate effort and speed, doing drills to improve your pedaling skills, or even lifting weights. Typically, these things aren't done in a triathlon. In the competitive phase, the workouts take on a duration and intensity that are increasingly similar to the race. In the precompetitive period, you taper the volume of your training while doing mini-race simulations. And as the name implies, the competitive period is the last few days leading up to and including your race. Table 6.4 summarizes these periods, shows how long each period typically lasts, and lists the abilities to be trained in each period.

The following sections describe the details of the bike workouts for each period of the season and other pertinent activities of each period.

**TABLE 6.4**

## Bike Training Phases and Focus

| Training phase (mesocycle) | | Length (weeks) | Bike abilities to train or purpose of training |
|---|---|---|---|
| *Preparatory* | General preparation (prep and base) | 12 to 20 | Speed skills, aerobic endurance, muscular force, muscular endurance |
| | Specific preparation (build) | 4 to 12 | Muscular endurance, anaerobic endurance (maintain AE, MF, SS) |
| *Competitive* | Precompetitive (peak or taper) | 3 to 8 | Muscular endurance, anaerobic endurance |
| | Competitive (race) | 1 to 3 | Recovery, maintain ME and AnE |
| *Transition (off-season)* | | A few days to 6 weeks | Rejuvenation |

## *Bike Training in the Prep Phase*

The purpose of the prep phase is to prepare both physically and mentally for the base period and the return to serious training. You should have just wrapped up your previous season's transition period with approximately a 1- to 6-week break from serious training. During this break, you probably stayed fairly active, but the emphasis was on recovery to allow niggling injuries to heal while you recharged your batteries. It was more "play" than "training." Now in the prep phase, it's time to start back into training.

For the bike, three types of workouts will be done in the prep phase. In the order of importance they are speed skills, aerobic endurance, and muscular force (each is described previously in the section on bike training workouts). Figure 6.1 shows what a typical training week for bike workouts in the preparatory phase may look like.

**FIGURE 6.1**

### Sample prep-phase training week for the bike.

| Day | Bike workout focus |
| --- | --- |
| Day 1 | Day off bike or recovery ride or muscular force |
| Day 2 | Speed skills |
| Day 3 | Day off bike or recovery ride |
| Day 4 | Day off bike or muscular force |
| Day 5 | Day off bike or recovery ride |
| Day 6 | Day off bike or recovery ride |
| Day 7 | Aerobic endurance |

## Bike Training in the Base Period

Training for the bike in the winter north of about 40 degrees latitude is quite challenging because of inclement weather and short days. Cross-country skiing, snowshoeing, and other common winter sports are a great alternative in prep and the early weeks of the base period, but the closer you get to the race, the more like the race the workouts must become. Skiing and other winter sports are not the same as riding a bike. If you can't get on the road by the late base period, then the only alternative is an indoor trainer. It's simply a necessity.

In the base phase, the focus of the bike workouts is endurance, force, and speed skills. It is crucial to develop endurance and force during this phase because you will be using this fitness base to start the more challenging workouts of the build phase. Figure 6.2 shows what a typical training week for bike workouts in the base period may look like.

**FIGURE 6.2**

### Sample base-period training week for the bike.

| Day | Bike workout focus |
| --- | --- |
| Day 1 | Day off bike or recovery ride or muscular force |
| Day 2 | Speed skills and muscular endurance |
| Day 3 | Day off bike or recovery ride |
| Day 4 | Muscular force |
| Day 5 | Day off bike or recovery ride |
| Day 6 | Day off bike or recovery ride |
| Day 7 | Aerobic endurance (long duration) |

## Bike Training in the Build Period

This is when training must become narrowly focused on race performance. To make your workouts increasingly like what's expected of you in the race, the focus of training should be on muscular endurance and, perhaps, anaerobic endurance if you are racing short course. To make these workouts race-like, do them at or slightly above goal-race intensity. It's also a good idea to include some bike–run combination workouts (bricks) in the build period.

In the build period, you will also need to maintain aerobic endurance, muscular force, and speed skills. To maintain high levels of these abilities, all you need to do is include them occasionally in your training. To maintain AE, do one long ride each week. Early in the ride, do some ME training, and then finish with a long, steady zone 2 effort. MF can be maintained with high-intensity training, especially on hills. You may also want to sustain MF by doing strength maintenance work in the gym. To maintain SS, include pedaling drills in warm-ups and cool-downs. Figure 6.3 shows what a typical training week for bike workouts in the build period may look like.

**FIGURE 6.3**

### Sample build-period training week for the bike.

| Day | Bike workout focus |
|---|---|
| Day 1 | Day off bike or recovery ride or muscular force |
| Day 2 | Muscular endurance (maintain speed skills) |
| Day 3 | Day off bike or recovery ride |
| Day 4 | Anaerobic endurance (optional) or recovery ride or day off bike |
| Day 5 | Day off bike or recovery ride |
| Day 6 | Day off bike or recovery ride |
| Day 7 | Muscular endurance and aerobic endurance (long duration + short run) |

## Bike Training in the Peak Period

By the peak period, you are down to just 2 or 3 weeks until your race. This is sometimes called the taper period. Although that is descriptive of what happens to the duration and volume of your training, it leaves out the other critical element—intensity. Research has shown repeatedly that the keys to a successful peak period are increasing the amount of rest you get while doing just a few workouts that simulate the intensity of key portions of your targeted race. This latter could be race-like repeats on a hill that is similar to the one in your race. Or it could be long, flat sections where you expect a strong headwind and so must be very aerodynamic. Do these simulations two or three times each week in the peak period. The days between them are strictly for rest and recovery. Figure 6.4 shows what a typical training week for bike workouts in the peak period may look like.

FIGURE 6.4

### Sample peak-period training week for the bike.

| Day | Bike workout focus |
|-----|--------------------|
| Day 1 | Day off bike or recovery ride |
| Day 2 | Race simulation (brick: race-like bike portion) |
| Day 3 | Recovery ride |
| Day 4 | Recovery ride |
| Day 5 | Race simulation (brick: race-like bike portion) |
| Day 6 | Recovery ride or day off bike |
| Day 7 | Race simulation (brick: race-like bike portion) |

## Bike Training in the Race Period

The week of the race is a time to emphasize rest even more than in the peak period. Keep all workouts short, becoming shorter as the week progresses. On the bike, do three to five 90-second to 3-minute intervals at race intensity, with recoveries that are twice as long, two or three times this week. Figure 6.5 shows what a typical training week for bike workouts in the race period may look like.

FIGURE 6.5

### Sample race-period training week for the bike.

| Day | Bike workout focus |
|-----|--------------------|
| Day 1 | Day off bike or recovery ride |
| Day 2 | Muscular endurance (short) |
| Day 3 | Recovery ride |
| Day 4 | Anaerobic endurance (optional) or muscular endurance (short) |
| Day 5 | Day off bike or recovery ride (short) |
| Day 6 | Speed skills (very short) |
| Day 7 | Race |

Measuring progress toward your race goals can be done in many different ways. One of the simplest is to compare times, heart rates, or power for standard rides you do. You can also do field tests that simulate the expected intensity of your race. For example, a 30-minute time trial on a standard course done every 4 to 6 weeks will help gauge performance changes (and confirm your threshold heart rate and power). Perhaps the most precise way of gauging progress is to do a $\dot{V}O_2$max test every few weeks.

As mentioned at the start of this chapter, many consider the bike as the key to a fast triathlon. Good equipment and excellent bike fitness are necessary for a successful event. The more bike-fit and bike-ready you are, the more you can hold back on the bike, still produce a fast split, and leave enough in the tank to have a fast run. Also important is a long-term plan so your bike workouts become increasingly like your goal race as you proceed through the season.

# CHAPTER 7

# Training for Triathlon Running

## Sergio Borges

Running in triathlon is completely different from pure road racing. In triathlon, since swimming and cycling come before the run, athletes have a limited range of motion in their legs caused by tight and overused muscles (e.g., hip flexors, hamstrings, quads). This limited range of motion will prevent athletes from bringing their legs as high during the recovery phase and from bringing their knees as high during the propulsion phase. Therefore, the stride length gets shorter, and the athletes run slower. In addition, the aerobic system is taxed from the swim and bike, also increasing fatigue. This chapter explains how to train for triathlon running, helping you be more effective and race faster while minimizing injuries.

## Run Training Components

It's important to understand the components of training when designing your training plan for triathlon running. If you're looking to improve your run, each of the following components needs to be part of your training, but they are forgotten by many athletes—especially the first two—because most just want to put on their shoes and head out the door.

### Sport-Specific Motor Patterns

Motor patterns are neural networks that endogenously (i.e., without rhythmic sensory or central input) produce rhythmic patterned outputs or "neural circuits" that generate periodic motor commands for rhythmic movements such as locomotion. In simpler terms, they are particular sequences of muscle movements directed to accomplishing an external purpose. A great way to improve your motor patterns in running is through repetition. By repeating certain training sets over a number of weeks, you learn to do the following.

### Improve Motor Skills

Via specific training sessions using a flat treadmill (0 percent incline helps you move forward more easily), you can work on increasing stride rate, thereby reducing the time spent on the ground and causing less eccentric load on your quads. You'll "program your body" to perform the way you want.

### Train Concentration Skills

Repeating the same workout with the same effort and duration allows you to shift emphasis from aerobic levels of effort to form. Repetition training encourages you to develop greater levels of focus and concentration that will help you in racing and increase the effectiveness of your workouts.

### Develop Intuition

Over time, athletes who train with repetitions develop a keen ability to feel how they are doing on any given day, through factors such as muscle soreness, fatigue, energy levels, and motivation.

### Anticipate Training

Repetition provides a predictable and structured routine that you can adhere to without compromising sound training principles, while making more efficient use of your time. This is especially true for age-group, or amateur, triathletes.

### Track Performance

With repetitions, you don't need to undergo physiological testing or test yourself over race distances in training—instead, your training ensures that you can track your improvements in each sport every week.

### Gauge Fatigue

The interactive process means you learn quickly how to determine whether on one of "those" days you are truly tired and need rest or are merely "off."

### Build Consistency

Repetition training also helps you accurately interpret your body's signals over time and to better apply these to maintain training consistency.

## Stride Rate

Efficiency in triathlon running comes from the ability to run fast on fatigued and tight legs. To be able to do this, you must develop a naturally high leg turnover (about 94 to 96 steps per leg per minute), or stride rate, which is essentially a running style that is more like "shuffle running," where the focus is on a higher turnover to overcome the shortening in the stride. High-cadence running becomes even more important during long-distance races such as the Ironman, in which the distance will add an extra level of fatigue on your legs, thereby reducing your stride length even more. By running with a lower stride rate, your second half of an Ironman will be much slower or even turn to a walk. A lot of practice is needed to develop a high stride rate because your body at first is not used to the neuromuscular pattern of firing your muscles so quickly.

Also, running at a high stride rate increases your heart rate and is aerobically taxing, so this running style works better if you haven't exhausted these components on the bike (e.g., by riding at a lower cadence). Contrary to the claims of some, it is possible to learn how to run with a faster stride rate as second nature during races. By thinking about breaking the work up into more pieces and aiming for a high stride rate in all the training runs, you will naturally learn a more efficient, triathlon-adapted stride.

Most elite runners run anywhere between 92 and 94 strides per leg per minute. I recommend 96 because it divides easily by 6, 4, and 3, meaning you can easily track the consistency of your strides per leg per minute over 10, 15, or 20 seconds at time. When tired, particularly late in an Ironman, you won't necessarily run at this rate, but by training for it and by constantly striving to hit this stride rate in training, you will naturally adopt a rate in the low to mid-90s without having to make much of a concerted effort during a race.

Using a flat treadmill and a slightly downhill gradient can help you develop a more fluid, naturally high stride rate. Both techniques enable you to run quicker than on flat land at the same aerobic stress level. Using a half- to 1-mile (.8 to 1.6 km) loop that includes a short, steeper uphill and a long, gradual downhill component, you can structure a lactate tolerance session. This is a workout meant to help an athlete handle higher loads of lactate training by training at or above current lactate threshold levels. This approach also provides the opportunity to stride it out and incorporate the mechanics of a high-speed session into the workout. By including such gravity-assisted running in the session, you develop your motor skills.

Unless you are doing a lactate tolerance session, keep treadmill sessions at a 0 percent gradient. As noted, you can train your muscles and nerves to fire at a higher rate of speed than on the road or track at the same aerobic load. This way, you train your legs to run faster for longer, sustained efforts without blowing up aerobically if you run at that pace for that duration on the road or track. You get higher-quality motor pattern training and a more effective training session this way.

## Leg Speed

Leg speed is a direct result of elasticity (the ability to "fire" the muscles quicker when running), and athletes must teach their brains how to fire their muscles quicker to improve stride rate and leg speed. Especially as we get older, we lose our natural elasticity, and repetition drills should be performed frequently to prevent running slower. More and more aging athletes are maintaining run speed. Keeping the elasticity is one of the reasons they can sustain speed. Following are a couple of my favorite running drills that will help you with elasticity.

### Marching

Lift your knee and foot and the opposite arm, as in a military march. Drive your foot down to the ground as you lift the opposite knee, foot, and arm. Move forward, alternating legs and arms. Make sure you maintain perfect posture, keeping the toes pulled up to the shin and pushing the trail foot down and back through the ground, with the hip going into full extension. Initiate movement from the glutes, and drive your elbows back as the opposite leg attacks the ground. Do three sets of 20 to 30.

## Wall Running

Stand with your left side against a wall. Place your left hand on the wall. Lift your left thigh to parallel, and lift your right heel off the ground while maintaining a straight line through the ear, shoulder, hip, knee, and ankle, and hold. Drive the left foot down and back. Quickly return to the start position by bringing the left foot toward the left hip, using a circular movement. Repeat two more times as quickly as possible and hold. Do two or three sets of five and switch sides.

## *Mobility*

Like elasticity, mobility, an increase in range of motion, is overlooked by most athletes (again, especially older athletes). To be able to run faster, your muscles need to have sufficient range of motion to allow your legs to move efficiently with less effort. The more mobile you are, the higher you can move your legs because your muscles will not be constricting the movement. You can work on increasing your mobility through dynamic stretching, myofascial release (the application of gentle pressure to the myofascial connective tissue restrictions to eliminate pain and restore motion), or running drills such as those described previously.

## *Strength and Power*

Triathlon is an endurance sport, but strength and power are required to perform at your best. With three disciplines to train for, it's difficult to find more time to concentrate on specific strength training, as everything seems geared toward building stamina and endurance. Surely all that training on its own is enough to build the strength you'll need, right? Let's look at that question differently—who doesn't think their race performances would improve if they were stronger? All things being equal, the stronger you are, the more power you're able to generate, and the faster you're able to go. It's important to understand that you're aiming to maximize your power–weight ratio, not your pure strength. Building pure strength involves increasing muscle bulk—not a good idea for endurance events such as triathlon.

The importance of power, even in endurance sports, can be seen in one simple fact. All of us can complete an Olympic-distance triathlon, but very few deliver enough power to finish in under 2 hours. So the question is not whether you have enough fuel to complete the race, but whether you can keep burning it at a high enough rate throughout the event. In addition to being crucial for power, being stronger also makes you more resilient and less susceptible to injury.

It's important to recognize that swimming, biking, and running alone don't produce overloads specific enough to generate significant strength gains. These activities are too aerobically based—you simply get tired before you start developing strength. Therefore, particularly during the off-season, it's beneficial to work on specific strength training activities, such as circuit or weight training, along with building your base fitness. Once you've developed greater strength, you can use it in your triathlon-specific training.

The off-season is the ideal time to change the emphasis of your training and incorporate strength and mobility sessions into your schedule. You will want to maintain a strength training program throughout the year to help with performance, but during the off-season you can focus more on strength when you are not swimming, biking, and running as much.

> ### ▶ Running on Fatigued Legs
>
> If you have done a triathlon, you've probably noticed how "heavy" and fatigued your legs feel when you get off the bike. For many, this feeling is still a surprise and the reason for many postrace talks: "My legs felt so heavy, I couldn't run!" If you train your body and brain to perform efficiently on fatigued legs, you will run faster and will not be surprised on race day.
>
> In many years of coaching, I have seen athletes planning a light or recovery workout the day before their key run session so they can have a high-quality workout on "fresh" legs. This has caused many athletes to get injured or at the very least sore (losing training consistency) because their muscles are too fresh, so they damage their bodies much more. Also athletes using this method rarely mimic the paces they run in a race. In a triathlon, your legs are already tight and fatigued, and the aerobic system is taxed, and they are never fresh.
>
> It is important for triathletes to build what I call an insurance policy. To reduce the chances of injury, severe muscle soreness, and training at unrealistic paces, the workout on the day before your key run session should be very muscle demanding (weight training or hill repeats on the bike at a lower cadence) so you will start your hard run already fatigued. You can also do a run session where you develop high fatigue first, then a short speed session with a focus on leg speed. For example, do a few stair repeats before 400- to 800-meter intervals on the track.
>
> Running on fatigued legs will also help you become efficient when tired, which is key for triathlon running. If you did not have the chance to do a demanding workout the day before your key run session, do a long warm-up of about 40 minutes instead; this will create a little bit of fatigue, building your "insurance policy."

For example, if you're running four times a week, swimming three times a week, and getting out on the bike twice, you should still have time for some specific strength work. These sessions could be added to the end of an easy run or swim if time is a problem. You can do a few strength exercises that focus on any areas of weakness you might have or exercises that help prevent injuries.

Also, when running speed cannot be developed much further, shifting emphasis toward leg strength instead of speed using longer, hilly runs can be a way of filling gaps that have developed in your fitness during the course of the season. Although circuits and weight training are good, you'll need some specific training to build strength. Track training and cross country or hill running are all great ways to build leg and core strength.

## *Speed*

Speed and LT (lactate tolerance) sessions are highly specific for triathlon training and need to be part of your training program, but as mentioned previously, you need to be very careful with frequency and length of intervals so you do not get injured or burned out. Speed can be developed by performing short-duration, high-intensity intervals. You can use the treadmill to control variables and to provide week-to-week performance benchmarking opportunities; on the road, use gentle downhill gradients to enable high-speed efforts at lower aerobic stress. Both will help increase range of motion, stride power, and corresponding motor skills. Keep the intervals short (30 to 45 seconds) with a long recovery, about twice the interval time. Speed work can be combined with endurance cycling sessions to more effectively train leg speed after a long bike session and to break up sluggishness of your legs.

LT sessions are race-specific efforts, with intervals of 1 to 20 minutes. The sessions should be limited to 30-45 minutes because of the high stress on the body. Avoid LT efforts without first tiring the muscles—this caps your ability to damage yourself. Sessions can be a typical negative-split effort, such as 20 minutes easy, 15 minutes at half-Ironman effort, and 10 minutes at 10K effort. A great workout that combines the speed and LT systems is to use a hilly loop to train form under duress. By running uphill hard and spiking your HR, then running with a high stride rate on a slight downhill gradient, you will have an opportunity to train a fast stride rate at a high aerobic stress load. The gentle gradient helps maintain form.

## Endurance

Endurance is one component of training that most athletes usually overemphasize. It's important to remember that endurance is also trained by your other two sports, so because of the high injury risk in running, volume should be controlled. It is recommended to do one traditional long run a week where you control the effort to avoid too much catabolic effect. You can also include short, fast efforts during the run to reduce leg sluggishness. Try to maintain your focus on a high stride rate during the entire run. To speed up your recovery, complement your long run with heavy weight training or speed-swim training later in the day (short 15- to 25-meter swim intervals with plenty of easy recovery). Strength training in the gym or the short, fast session in the pool will promote an anabolic response to balance the catabolic (breaking down muscle) damage of the long run.

## Volume and Intensity

When athletes get excited, usually after their first season, the first thought that comes to their minds is *"If I train longer and harder, I can go faster."* This statement is not totally wrong—if you *can* go harder and longer, you will get faster—but the problem is recovery. The ideal would be to train hard every day, but we all know our bodies can't recover from that level of training intensity and load, and if we train like that, we will end up crashing and burning. I believe all athletes have their own tolerance for intensity and volume; some can do more, some have to do less. I like to always err on the side of less rather than give an athlete too much and he ends up injured or burned out. Make sure you restrict the number of long runs you do a week (only one is recommended), and make sure when you're doing intervals to keep it short, maintaining the quality you have planned. "Junk miles" will not make you faster, just train you how to run slower and inefficiently.

Another important thing to remember is to pay attention to your RPE, as discussed in chapter 9 on page 119. Every day you have different fatigue levels, with many different causes, including stress, lack of sleep, too much red wine the night before, the beginning of an illness, and so on. So you cannot expect your body to react the same every day. One day, a moderate effort of 8 minutes per mile will feel more like a hard pace because of higher fatigue, but another day 6 minutes per mile could feel easy. It is best to learn how your body feels during the efforts you want and use it as the guide for your intensity.

Here are some key factors to consider when planning the volume and intensity of your run training:

### Body Type

You have probably noticed that elite runners have a very slim physique and are very light in terms of body weight. This is the ideal body type for running, allowing these athletes to do high-volume and high-intensity training. High volume and intensity are not applicable for most triathletes, who have bigger and more muscular legs and a developed upper body from swim training. Because of the impact of the foot landing on the ground, the heavier you are, the more damage you will cause your muscles and joints when performing intervals. Therefore, if you're a bit overweight or very muscular, you have to be very careful with the volume and intensity of running in your training. So if you look more like a bodybuilder, be careful with the short, high-intensity intervals or use the build (easy to fast) intervals instead.

### Biomechanics

We often see athletes running with poor form, and some of them run long and run several times a week, increasing their risk of getting injured. Running, like cycling and swimming, is a repetitive motion sport, so if you don't have proper mechanics, you will eventually injure yourself if you run too frequently or do too high a volume. The more efficient you are mechanically, the more (volume and frequency) you can run, so before you compare your training with your friend or a professional athlete, first check how efficient they look when running.

Be aware that in running, eccentric (lengthening) muscle contractions occur both in the quadriceps and the calf muscles with each step when you land. This is exaggerated, especially in the upper thigh (quadriceps muscles), during downhill running because the forces that pass through these muscles can equal three times the body weight, particularly as the foot lands on the ground. The initial contraction of the quadriceps is not quite strong enough to overcome this force; thus this muscle is stretched in an eccentric contraction for a brief instance every time either foot hits the ground. Muscles were not designed for repetitive eccentric contractions and are susceptible to damage when forced to contract this way. This explains why downhill running can be especially painful and why it takes so much longer for postrace muscle stiffness to go away after downhill races than it does after uphill or flat races.

### Background

Running background is another important factor when designing your training. If you have been running for several years, you probably have developed better movement mechanics and have trained your body to withstand the impact and eccentric load on your joints and muscles. Usually, several years of running (repetitive motion of the movement) would result in efficiency as long as you have not been injured too often in the process.

### Age

As we get older, our joints and muscles get weaker, and our ability to recover from long and hard workouts is compromised. We do not produce our hormones at the same level as when we were 20 years old, so the frequency of long and hard workouts has to be meticulously planned. The challenge for older athletes is trying to stay healthy for the important races.

### Injury History

If you have been injured in the past, you should start creating body awareness so you can read the signs your body sends to you and avoid getting injured again. If every time you do short, high-intensity intervals, for example, you get injured, well, maybe your body is telling you that type of effort is not recommended for you (even if you have done it several times before). The same idea applies to determining the volume of your long-endurance runs. If every time you run more than 90 minutes you are very sore, take a long time to recover, or even worse, get injured, you have found your limit.

Also note that you are more likely to injure yourself while running than while swimming or cycling, so you need to pay more attention to order and structure when planning the distribution of run sessions. If you're new to running, ease into it gradually. This also applies to those returning from injury. For example, an effective return from injury might be a three-runs-per-week routine alternating running and walking, gradually increasing the duration of the run component.

### Gender

In my experience in coaching, female athletes tend to recover quicker and can handle more intensity and higher training volume than males. A lot has to do with size (usually females are much lighter than males) and hormones (women's hormones allow them to recover quicker and therefore train harder and longer).

## Run Training Strategies and Workouts

Run training should be adjusted during each phase of the season to make sure you are ready for competition. In the prep phase, if you have been running, you can do three to five running workouts per week. These can be 20 to 45 minutes in duration and should be done at a low intensity, focusing on your form. If you haven't been running, start with run–walk sessions 3 days per week until you can run continuously for 20 minutes. As you move into the base phase, start doing longer-endurance runs and increase your speed work. You will be running 3 or 4 days per week. During the build phase, your volume will decrease as your intensity rises. You'll still be running 3 or 4 days per week. During the peak phase, your intensity will increase, but your volume will drop. You'll be running 2 or 3 days per week, and one of those runs should be off the bike. During the race phase, your intensity will be high, but your volume will be significantly lower. You'll be running 2 or 3 days per week, with one run off the bike. During the off-season, your goal should be to maintain your fitness by running 2 or 3 days per week or cross-training. Great cross-training activities include cross-country skiing, soccer, and hiking.

It's very important to understand that to improve your running, you need to always have three key workout sessions—strength, speed, and endurance—in your training week all year round. The following sample week incorporates all three sessions for an average age-group athlete who runs three times per week and is training for an Olympic-distance triathlon.

## Monday

Brick session: Bike strength (60 minutes) and run lactate tolerance and speed (27 minutes) immediately after the bike workout as race simulation. Run: Three sets of 3, 2, 1 minutes at 10K effort (85 to 90 percent) with 1-minute easy jog between.

## Tuesday

Long-endurance swim (45 minutes) and weight training (30 minutes).

## Wednesday

Strength session: Hill repeats (45 to 60 minutes); 10-minute easy jog as warm-up, running drills, 10 minutes easy to moderate. Find a hill that is not too steep (4 to 6 percent grade), and do three sets of 5 × 1 minute, building from moderate to hard (90 to 95 percent effort). Use 3-minute easy jogs between sets and an easy jog-down as recovery, followed by a 10-minute cool-down and regeneration (e.g., stretch, massage). Note: If you have not run much, start with two sets of 5 × 30 seconds and build to the routine just described. Swim: Recovery (30 minutes).

## Thursday

Bike lactate tolerance (race effort) (45 to 60 minutes).

## Friday

Run endurance session: Trail, treadmill, or road (45 to 75 minutes). Start very easy for the first 10 minutes, build to easy to moderate. Remember the goal is to increase your endurance, so intensity should be at 65 to 75 percent effort. As mentioned previously in this chapter, volume has to be carefully planned based on the six components (body type, biomechanics, background, injury history, gender, age). Be safe, and always start conservative and progress as you feel your body adapting to the training.

## Saturday

Day off or high-quality swim workout (45 minutes).

## Sunday

Bike endurance session: 2 to 3 hours at moderate effort.

It's important to understand that triathlon running is not the same as a running race because of the limited range of motion, fatigued muscles, taxed aerobic system, and taxed neuromuscular system. Each athlete should train differently, with corresponding intensity and volume based on what the body can tolerate. Be aware of your body, rather than the pace you're training, so you don't destroy your muscles and joints. Teach your body how to run efficiently on fatigued legs. It's the most important thing in triathlon running!

# CHAPTER 8

# Recovery and Overtraining

## Kristen Dieffenbach and Michael Kellmann

High-performance training is high stakes. From the pool deck of the local sprint series through to the iconic full Ironman, triathletes of all levels train with a unique intensity and sense of purpose. Triathletes, almost by common definition, are driven people who live to go the distance and beyond. Although the culture of "more is better" permeates many sports, the multiple elements of triathlon make high training demands and expectations even more routine. When things don't go as planned and performance suffers, athletes react poorly to the suggestion they may be doing too much. Performance disappointments are met with assumptions of personal weakness, failure, and the fear of not doing enough. Ironically, the common response is to push harder and train more, compounding an already negative cycle.

Triathlete magazines, blogs, and discussion groups routinely contain articles and threads from athletes regarding feeling burned out, concerns about overtraining, and the battle to achieve balance. Professional triathlete Mark Allen (2010), in discussing his early training methods, remarked, "Every run, even the slow ones, for at least one mile, I would try to get close to 5 minute pace. And it worked . . . sort of. I had some good races the first year or two, but I also suffered from minor injuries and was always feeling one run away from being too burned out to want to continue with my training."

In his online blog, four-time Swedish duathlon champion and Swedish Ironman record holder Clas Björling writes frequently about the toll overtraining has taken on his career, and in 2008 he posted about his need to take a full year off because of overtraining and burnout and the slow recovery process. Paula Newby-Fraser, Dave Scott, and many others have discussed their experiences with the setbacks, disappointments, and injuries related to overtraining in numerous interviews. If even elite-level athletes aren't immune, it can seem as though overtraining is a necessary evil.

Yet despite the frequent discussion of the consequences and the concern over its impact, overtraining is not as well understood as it needs to be. Although pushing hard will always carry with it the potential for both positive and negative outcomes, athletes and coaches can be empowered to greatly reduce the potential problems. Overtraining does not have to be an inevitable experience. This chapter discusses the key interactions between stress and recovery in the training process as well as the importance of considering the whole athlete, and it provides tips and suggestions for finding the optimal training balance.

# Understanding Overtraining and Recovery

Most athletes and coaches today understand, at least on some level, the risks of overtraining and the value of recovery. Unfortunately, exactly what these risks are, how they influence training and performance, and what can and cannot be done about them is not often well understood. Further, the available knowledge is not used enough to enhance training efforts as a crucial part of a healthy, balanced training equation.

The uncertainty regarding overtraining and the role it plays in optimal performance and training planning is understandable given that confusion over terminology and causes exists in the scientific literature as well. Researchers use a wide variety of terms such as *overwork, overreaching, overstraining, staleness, burnout, overfatigue,* and *short-* and *long-time overtraining* to describe the wide range of athlete experiences. Some theories isolate and emphasize hormonal, immunological, or training factors, while others take a more global or holistic approach, considering the whole athlete and the interrelationship of many elements. Further, current laboratory-based tests to evaluate overtraining are either inconclusive or impractical for routine monitoring of training and the necessary early detection. To date, sport scientists have not provided a singular definition or clear diagnosis for overtraining, and the more that is learned about the continuum and complexity of the experience, the more it is clear that a simple diagnostic tool or solution is unlikely.

Recognizing when athletes are overtrained is an important concern. In what Canadian researcher Judy Goss (1994) has called "the paradox of training," the same workouts designed to push physical limits in an effort to elicit best performances also create an optimal environment for overdoing it. Athletes and coaches anticipate and even welcome a certain amount of fatigue that accompanies hard training. However, the state of being overtrained is recognizable as an ongoing plateau in performance that does not improve with short amounts of rest and recovery. Unfortunately, it is difficult to quantify exactly how long a time and how much rest determine the difference between normal overreaching and something more troubling because of the unique individual nature of overtraining. The better coaches and athletes understand the experience and related elements, the better their chances of finding and navigating the fine line between too much and optimal preparation.

The consequences of overtraining can have a significant impact not only on performance but also on an athlete's well-being and overall quality of life. Researchers have catalogued more than 200 different symptoms in overtrained athletes. The most commonly associated warning signs associated with overtraining include depressed mood, general apathy, decreased self-esteem and performance, emotional instability, restlessness, irritability, poor sleep, weight loss, loss of appetite, increased resting heart rate, hormonal changes, and the absence of performance improvements. Athletes experiencing overtraining also often exhibit an increase in injuries, a slower injury recovery time, and an impaired immune system that can lead to problems such as upper respiratory infections (Kellmann 2002; Peterson 2003). Most of the symptoms can be recognized by coaches and athletes if they pay attention and are aware of their potential significance. However, no single symptom works as an indicator alone. It is the combination of symptoms within the context of training expectations that should raise a red flag that something is wrong.

Since the 1970s, the principles of periodization and sport science research have had an increasing impact on coaching. Coaching triathletes has evolved into a detailed science itself. Athletes run, swim, bike, and lift weights, with shifts in volume and intensity to build a proper base, develop strengths, build weaknesses, and adequately taper for peak performance following the principles of periodization. Sport science research indicates training methodologies such as monotonous training programs, more than 3 hours of training per day, failure to alternate hard and easy training days or to alternate 2 hard days followed by an easy training day, no training periodization and respective regeneration microcycles after 2 or 3 weeks of training, and lack of rest days can all contribute to the physical aspect of overtraining. Yet, even when the science of training is carefully applied and potential pitfalls such as those mentioned are avoided, overtraining may still occur, indicating there is more that needs to be considered.

In both overtraining and underrecovery, athletes see a decline in performance. However, there are key differences to note between the two. Training requires that athletes be pushed beyond their comfort zone. This overreaching causes fatigue, muscle soreness, and short-lived drops in performance, all of which are expected and necessary to elicit changes and gains. However, when prolonged overreaching slips into overtraining, a longer-term decline in performance that is harder to reverse affects the athlete both physically and psychologically. In contrast, underrecovery, the lack or absence of adequate recovery activities based on an athlete's physical and psychological needs, has been found to be a clear cause of overtraining. Although no clear, noninvasive means of determining when overreaching becomes overtraining is available, research has found that preventing underrecovery through the active and proactive enhancement of recovery can diminish overtraining. Therefore, understanding and implementing recovery enhancement into a coaching plan is an active approach to prevent overtraining among athletes.

---

### ▶ Symptoms of Overtraining

- Impaired performance
- No supercompensation in response to taper or rest
- Increased resting heart rate
- Weight loss
- Loss of appetite
- Increased vulnerability to injuries
- Hormonal changes
- Depressed mood
- General apathy
- Decreased self-esteem, emotional instability
- Restlessness, irritability
- Disturbed sleep

*Recovery* is an everyday word in training. Coaches commonly prescribe rest between intervals and talk about recovery between efforts within workouts, but what is recovery in the larger scale of overtraining and underrecovery concerns? Poor recovery, or underrecovery, is associated with poor mental and physical outcomes, including overtraining and burnout. Proper individual recovery occurs at psychological, physical, and social levels and includes both action-oriented things athletes do and the environment they are in. In 2001, researchers Kellmann and Kallus established a list of general recovery features to help coaches and athletes enhance performance and the overall sport experience. They suggest that recovery is a process that occurs over time. Like training and other stressors, recovery is cumulative and can come from multiple sources. And finally, the quality and quantity of recovery required, allowing an athlete to achieve or maintain balance, are dependent on the nature and level of stress experienced.

It can be misleading to view recovery as merely the absence of activity. Researchers Löhr and Preiser (1974) have suggested that recovery does not need to be passive relaxation activities. Depending on the nature of the situation and needs of the person, recovery can be associated with activity in several ways. Activities that provide a positive recovery or revitalization cause eustress, or positive stress (Selye 1974). The concept of positive stress helps explain how a hard training effort, while physically stressful, can simultaneously be a source of recovery, or positive eustress, for psychological stress the athlete has experienced. An analogy can also be made to the common weight-room activity of circuit training. During circuit training, an athlete alternates activities that stress different muscles while allowing previously stressed muscles to rest. Similarly, alternating activities such as training (physical stress) and learning in a classroom or work setting (mental or cognitive stress) allows for alternating recovery and can contribute to a personal sense of balance and well-being. Thus it is possible for different systems within an athlete to simultaneously work and recover during selected activities. Intentionally varying the type and nature of different sources of stimulation or stress can help facilitate other systems that are recovering, contributing to the overall balance of the whole person.

Just like training, recovery is not a one-size-fits-all proposition. Individualization of recovery is essential. Additionally, recovery flexibility, or having multiple recovery options, is important to help an athlete adjust and match his changing needs. This is particularly important for recovery activities that might be out of a person's control or that may be difficult to obtain or achieve. It is also important for athletes to have backup recovery strategies. Having alternatives can reduce the potential contributing stress an athlete may experience worrying about meeting recovery needs, a situation that obviously would only further compound the stress overload problem.

As noted, recovery comes in many forms. Typically, the types of recovery can be sorted into three categories: passive, active, and proactive. The concept of active recovery is a familiar one in the lexicon of training. Coaches frequently prescribe active recovery training sessions on light-load days, at the end of hard workouts, or at the end of a season to facilitate faster recovery. Passive recovery, perhaps the most familiar recovery concept (though less enthusiastically embraced by athletes and coaches as part of the training equation), encompasses sitting or lying quietly. Of note, passive recovery is also characterized by treatment modalities designed to facilitate recovery (e.g., massage, compression pants, hot and cold baths, steam baths, saunas). The physiological benefits of such treatments are a growing area of applied sport science, with high-performance facilities such as the U.S. Olympic Training Centers and the Australian Institute of Sport investing in recovery centers to provide athletes with access to these types of passive recovery activities.

The third category, proactive recovery, includes self-initiated activities done in anticipation of recovery needs. An athlete may engage in proactive recovery activities such as muscle relaxation and stretching as a part of her training and competition routine. These activities, embedded within the training process, diminish the accumulation of fatigue during the overall training experience, allowing more training stress adaptations to be gained. As with other recovery techniques, proactive recovery tactics are not limited to training-related applications. Taking a walk at lunch during the business day or taking time to chat with a friend are self-initiated activities that can provide a positive lift and help keep stress from accumulating.

The quantity and quality of recovery that any activity can provide are related to the situation in which it occurs. For example, sleep is widely acknowledged as a key component of physical and psychological rejuvenation. But sleeping in a noisy dorm or in a room that is too hot or too cold will provide less-than-optimal results, and the efforts to fall sleep may produce more stress. Individual assessment is an important factor in whether or not the situation is contributing negatively. To return to the sleep example, a person used to sleeping in the country may find that the street noises heard in a city hotel have a negative impact on the quality of his sleep environment, while another athlete may not even notice the noises at all.

## Balancing Stress and Recovery in Life

Laps, miles, and lifts place a physical stress on the training athlete. Although it would be nice if athletes trained in a vacuum with nothing to do but work out, the reality is always more complex. Specifically, athletes are routinely exposed to a wide variety of daily personal and environmental stressors in addition to their training load. Stress, though commonly associated with negative feelings, can come from any source—physical, psychological, or social—that places a demand on an athlete and her resources. Understanding the whole athlete and her whole experience is an important aspect for individualized training and the prevention of negative consequences related to overtraining and underrecovery.

Regardless of the source, all stressors have an impact. The amount will depend on several factors, the most important of which is how the person perceives the situation. A situation that is perceived to be stressful or draining will have a larger impact. A situation that requires time or energy to handle or that takes away from recovery activities such as quality sleep will also increase the impact. Even routine things such as the daily commute, relationships, and work duties all take a toll. The combination of life stressors and the routine changes in training intensity and volume create the cumulative stress load the athlete experiences. It is this potential source of imbalance between a person's level of stress and recovery that creates the optimal environment for overtraining.

In addition to the individual sources of stress and recovery resources, an athlete's personal approach to challenges is an important element in understanding the whole athlete. Characteristics such as optimism, resilience, hardiness, and mental toughness influence how athletes perceive the stress and recovery they experience. Optimistic people see the positive, or "glass half full," side of situations. Hardiness and mental toughness are related concepts that describe people who are inclined to see things as challenging rather than problem focused and who focus their energies on their own efforts to facilitate change. Although an athlete's natural disposition may be more or less positive, it isn't set in stone. Through practice and reinforcement, positive characteristics can be developed and strengthened.

Ultimately, understanding and valuing the whole athlete and his approach to situations provides coaches with key clues to help the athlete create the best environment for preventing overtraining and underrecovery problems. Communicating openly, asking perceptive questions, and listening carefully to athletes' responses allows coaches and the athletes themselves an opportunity to better understand recovery needs.

Ask an athlete to describe her training and the common response will be a detailed account of hours per week, miles per day, workout times, swim sets, and other related details. Ask a coach to explain an athlete's training plan and the response will be similar, with perhaps an included explanation of the various anticipated physiological responses associated with the particular phase or workout emphasis. Unfortunately, despite the integral relationship between stress and recovery demands, few athletes and coaches actively consider recovery-based activities as a part of the training plan, and even fewer regularly assess training within the broader context of life. Recovery is often assumed to occur in the spaces between workouts, without much thought to what is actually needed or how other life stressors might interfere with these activities.

Prevention of underrecovery, and as a result overtraining, necessitates that increased recovery efforts occur with increases in stress. When this doesn't happen, a negative cycle of mounting stress without repair (physical, psychological, or both) will occur. As stress levels continue to build and are met with inadequate recovery, the impact of the stress and the availability of adequate recovery continue to be compromised. A simple example can be found in the increased nightly sleep needs that coincide with training increases. All other things being equal, when an athlete increases weekly training time, nightly sleep needs will increase in response. It is the body's natural response for recovering properly. Not allowing for adequate sleep to occur as training demands increase not only affects an athlete's mood but also inhibits key physiological recovery responses that occur during proper sleep cycles—hardly a model for achieving personal best.

Just as training is made up of different types of efforts, such as long, steady endurance or short, high-intensity sprints to address issues of specificity and system development, the quality and quantity of recovery efforts need to be varied. A hard run might require recovery activities such as an easy cool-down, an ice bath, proper postrun nutrition and hydration, and a good night's sleep to optimize gains and maintain balance. A stressful day at work may benefit from the hard run as a form of recovery but may also require another form of recovery, such as being able to talk to someone or enjoying quiet time to unwind and lower the stress level. Only some of these elements are included directly in an athlete's training plan, but ultimately they are all essential for optimal performance. Both the coach and athlete must understand and account for the multiple sources of stress the athlete experiences to develop and implement appropriate recovery strategies.

## Anticipating Overtraining

All the discussions involving training, overtraining, stress, and recovery remain purely academic and without much use unless coaches and athletes have the tools they need to understand, evaluate, and apply this knowledge to the benefit of improved performance and increased enjoyment. Modern training calls on a wide variety of tools to help athletes and coaches quantify training. Variables such as distance, speed, heart rate, power, oxygen saturation, and blood lactate can all be easily and relatively inexpensively monitored. Although they provide a wealth of information for tweaking and managing training load, these measures, unfortunately, do not indicate that something is amiss until it is too late for the necessary early intervention.

First and foremost, it is crucial to acknowledge the unique individual and situation-dependent nature of all stress and recovery demands. Each athlete will have a unique experience with training and life stressors and unique recovery resources and needs; in addition, each athlete's responses and needs will differ at different points in the training season. Determining and monitoring key training and life variables and responses can help both coaches and athletes better understand the athletes' needs as well as their current overall balance status. In the long term, regular monitoring provides a wealth of information for performance assessment and accurate planning.

A sensitive recovery indicator that can be easily observed is the quality and quantity of sleep. Often overtrained athletes experience problems falling asleep at night. Circling thoughts about training progress or performance goals, muscle stiffness, or other incidents within and outside the training environment may keep athletes awake. Sometimes it takes 60 minutes or more to fall asleep. If this occurs for a longer period of time, such as several weeks, it needs to be considered as a symptom of overtraining and should be discussed with supporting experts and the coach.

Logbooks, electronic records, or old-fashioned paper and pencil are common ways for coaches and athletes to both track and share training data. Many options are available for monitoring recovery and can easily be incorporated into the training-related data that athletes already compile. Specific and nonspecific to recovery, research-based measures such as the Profile of Mood States (POMS; McNair, Lorr, and Droppleman 1971, 1992), Borg's rating of perceived exertion (RPE; Borg 1998), the Recovery-Cue (Kellmann, Patrick, Botterill, and Wilson 2002), and total quality recovery (Kenttä & Hassmén 1998, 2002) can be adapted to monitor balance status.

Another more detail-specific measure for monitoring an athlete's stress and recovery levels is the Recovery-Stress Questionnaire for Athletes (RESTQ-Sport; Kellmann and Kallus 2001). This measure looks at sport- and life-specific areas of both perceived stress and perceived levels of acquired recovery and has proven useful in monitoring an athlete's responses over time. The RESTQ-Sport has been used in various sports (e.g., triathlon, swimming, soccer, rugby) and by many nations to monitor the impact of training during the preparation camp for world championships and Olympic Games. Evaluation of the instrument shows that changes in training volume were reflected by significant changes in RESTQ-Sport scales (Kellmann 2010).

> ## ▶ Overview of the RESTQ-Sport

The RESTQ-Sport asks you to respond to a series of questions, using a six-point scale from never to always, to indicate the frequency you have done something ("I put off making decisions") or felt something ("I laughed") in the previous 3 days. You select the answers that most accurately reflect your thoughts and activities, indicating how often each statement was right in your case, in terms of performance during both competition and practice. Here are a few sample questions from the questionnaire:

*In the past (3) days/nights...*

| | never | seldom | sometimes | often | more often | very often | always |
|---|---|---|---|---|---|---|---|
| 2. I did not get enough sleep | 0 | 1 | 2 | 3 | 4 | 5 | 6 |
| 9. I felt physically relaxed | 0 | 1 | 2 | 3 | 4 | 5 | 6 |
| 28. I felt anxious or inhibited | 0 | 1 | 2 | 3 | 4 | 5 | 6 |
| 75. My body felt strong | 0 | 1 | 2 | 3 | 4 | 5 | 6 |

FIGURE 8.1    Sample RESTQ-Sport excerpt.

Adapted, by permission, from M. Kellmann and K.W. Kallus, 2001, *Recovery-Stress Questionnaire for Athletes: User manual* (Champaign, IL: Human Kinetics).

The results are created by summing your responses across 19 scales of the RESTQ-Sport. The scales fall into four categories: general stress, sport-specific stress, general recovery, and sport-specific recovery. These scale scores can be easily plotted on a graph, allowing you and your coach to watch for trends and changes in your behaviors and perceptions related to stress and recovery. Ideally, you will demonstrate a moderate to low score for stress experienced. More important, you should experience a matched or higher level of perceived recovery, which will be seen in higher recovery scale scores.

## Preventing Overtraining

Regardless of the level of competition, the consequences associated with overtraining not only have a devastating impact on hard-sought goals but also take a personal toll on athletes. Unfortunately, both professional and recreational athletes have reported experiences with overtraining. Frequently cited causes of overtraining include too much stress and pressure, too much practice and physical training, physical exhaustion and all-over soreness, boredom because of too much repetition, and poor rest or lack of proper sleep. As noted, adopting a balanced approach to training and a holistic view of the athlete can play a key role in maintaining a positive stress–recovery balance. Coaches and athletes need to be aware of both training factors and nontraining factors (e.g., work, school, travel, relationships) that contribute to an overall sense of fatigue. Further, they need to be aware of recovery opportunities and resources to ensure the athletes can strive for optimal balance.

Achieving optimal training requires an educated, self-aware, and proactive approach on both the part of the coach and the athlete. Both need to be aware of the symptoms of overtraining, have an awareness of the importance of stress–recovery balance, understand the individual athlete's needs and resources, and be able to keep the sport experience in perspective. For their part, athletes need to be honest with themselves and their coaches about stress levels, injuries, and training responses. Coaches should strive to communicate with athletes, carefully listen to the responses, and act appropriately. Further, coaches can enhance an athlete's perceived value of recovery efforts through modeling positive behaviors, making optimal recovery a part of routine training plan discussions, and designing careful individualized training.

Keeping competition fun and in perspective may be one of the most important elements for maintaining a positive stress–recovery balance. Unfortunately, it can also be one of the most challenging to implement in the current intense culture of even recreation-level events. Overemphasis on outcomes such as winning or age-group placement increases the pressure and stress associated with competition. Comparison-based outcomes are influenced by many factors outside a person's control, leaving the athlete powerless to control many facets that determine the results. For example, you have no control over which competitors show up, what direction the wind is blowing, or whether or not the small piece of unseen glass punctures a tire. Emphasizing the personal challenges that relate to the elements you do have control over, such as personal level of effort, smart implementation of a personal training plan, personal preparation, and how you handle unplanned stressors such as a flat tire, are empowering and help maintain proper perspective.

Another simple yet complex concept is recognizing what exactly recovery is and isn't. For many athletes, the concept of resting is synonymous with being lazy. Telling an athlete to take a day off can get twisted into "you can't handle it." Many endurance athletes fear the day off, and bragging about miles and days of consecutive training is a common phenomenon. Triathletes are prone to experience overtraining because of their desire to train for swimming, biking, and running at the same time. It is essential for coaches to teach and reinforce that recovery is much more than just doing nothing. Recovery is an essential active process that is the "yin" to training effort's "yang." As professional coach Hunter Allen and exercise physiology professor Dr. Andy Coggan (2010) say, fitness plus freshness is the proper equation for peak form.

Recovery encompasses a wide range of both active (e.g., light exercise, stretching) things athletes need to make time for as well as more passive elements such as quiet time to unwind and supportive relationships that athletes need to create or seek out. Coaches and their athletes should work together to brainstorm specific active and passive recovery choices and to match up the appropriate recovery to stress level combinations to ensure a healthy and productive training plan. Coaches should help athletes develop both short-term (in practice, after training) and longer-term recovery strategies. It is also important that athletes recognize and consider multiple levels and types of recovery. Ultimately, the goal of the positive recovery stress equation is always homeostasis, or balance. Be sure to keep in mind that balance is a temporary state. Once achieved, the process always starts all over again with the next training session.

In the training process, a coach is responsible for creating a personalized goal-based plan. An appropriate plan can be created only after all the information has been collected and evaluated. Understanding the complete cycle from stress through recovery creates a whole picture, allowing for optimal personalization and timely modifications. Within the process, an athlete is responsible for listening and honoring both the drive to push harder and the need to recover appropriately. Working together, a coach and athlete can use their understanding of the stress–recovery balance to reduce training frustrations, push performance to new levels, and enhance the overall sport experience.

# CHAPTER 9

# Exercise Physiology for Triathletes

## Krista Austin

Exercise physiology is the study of how systems of the human body integrate to perform work. For the purposes of this chapter, the focus is on understanding the physiology of training based on the energy systems and then applying it to the muscular and cardiorespiratory systems of the human body. In addition, this chapter covers how to monitor, evaluate, and manipulate training and describes physiological adaptations to different environments.

## Energy Systems

The ability of any athlete to sustain prolonged bouts of training or competition depends on the body's ability to generate energy. The human body can be trained so it can generate hours of muscular contraction through the energy stored within the body. Energy within the human body comes in the form of adenosine triphosphate (ATP), which is considered the universal currency of the body. Three key energy sources are available and utilized to power the production of ATP. These are creatine phosphate (CP), carbohydrate, and fat.

ATP for muscle contraction is produced by three energy systems: the immediate energy system (ATP–CP), anaerobic glycolysis (nonoxidative), and the aerobic energy system (oxidative). The first two energy systems are frequently known together as the anaerobic energy system and are able to function without the presence of oxygen ($O_2$). This energy system predominates in exercise bouts lasting up to 4 minutes. The anaerobic energy system can generate large amounts of energy very quickly; however, it is limited and provides energy for only a short period of activity. Conversely, the aerobic energy system is slower at generating energy, but it can do so for hours so that work can be sustained.

The energy systems work on a continuum, as depicted in figure 9.1. Although one energy system may be predominating, all three will work together to provide the energy needed during exercise. Energy production by each of the three systems is dependent on exercise intensity and duration. In table 9.1, the energy systems are divided based on a time continuum, and the source of energy is also provided.

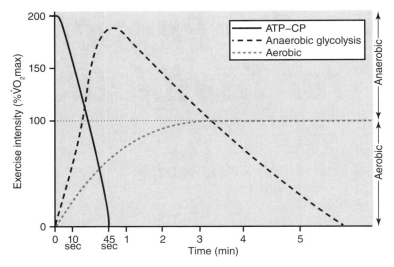

**FIGURE 9.1** **Energy systems work together to provide energy.**

Reprinted, by permission, from K. Austin and B. Seebohar, 2011, *Performance nutrition: Applying the science of nutrient timing* (Champaign, IL: Human Kinetics), 17.

**TABLE 9.1**

## Energy Systems for Activities Based on Duration

| Duration | Classification | Predominant energy supply |
|---|---|---|
| 1 sec to 10 sec | ATP–CP | ATP (in muscles) + creatine phosphate |
| 10 sec to 2 min | Anaerobic | ATP (in muscles) + creatine phosphate + muscle glycogen |
| 2 min to 4 min | Anaerobic + aerobic | Muscle glycogen + creatine phosphate + lactic acid |
| 4 min to 5.5 min | Aerobic + anaerobic | Muscle glycogen + fatty acids |
| >5.5 min | Aerobic + anaerobic | Fatty acids + muscle glycogen |

Reprinted, by permission, from K. Austin and B. Seebohar, 2011, *Performance nutrition: Applying the science of nutrient timing* (Champaign, IL: Human Kinetics), 20.

# Muscular and Cardiorespiratory Systems

The muscular system consists of the elements in a muscle cell that allow the skeletal muscle to contract and exert force. The human body requires a continuous supply of oxygen and nutrients to maintain the production of energy for its many complex functions and to sustain work during exercise. This process is facilitated by the cardiorespiratory system of the body, which consists of the heart and lungs. Together, these organs work to ensure that blood is carrying oxygen and other nutrients to active tissues (muscle, liver, and so on). This becomes especially important during exercise because oxygen and fuel are needed so the muscles of the body can continue to perform work.

Aerobic and anaerobic training lead to general adaptations of the muscular system that stimulate the cardiorespiratory system. This means the muscles provide signals for the heart and lungs. Running, swimming, and cycling provide both general and specific training adaptations. For example, all these sports give you general adaptations such as an improved heart muscle contraction rate, but it is discipline specific, meaning that swimming at a heart rate of 160 beats per minute does not prepare you to run at a heart rate of 160 beats per minute, but it did help improve general fitness. Improvements in the capacity of the muscle fibers are specific to the sport and event being participated in. This is primarily because muscle fibers learn to repeat the movements used in training. An example is the difference in muscular training that is received for the legs from running versus that of swimming. Both forms of training help develop muscle characteristics that can be utilized to train for any sport; however, running requires the right amount of ligament strength and an adaptation to the muscular and cardiorespiratory strain of bearing body weight that swimming does not. In these next sections, you will learn how muscles work, come to understand the different types of muscle, and find out how the heart and lungs adapt to training.

## Muscle Physiology

Skeletal muscle contraction is controlled by the brain through the central nervous system (CNS). The motor cortex is the area of the CNS that memorizes muscular contractions and commits them to memory. Muscles contract when messages from the CNS submit impulses to the nerves that connect to motor neurons, which directly innervate and control the muscles. The force produced from a muscular contraction is a function of the number and size of the motor neurons that are recruited and the frequency with which they are stimulated.

Force production is dependent on the type of muscle fibers recruited to perform the work. There are three primary types of muscle fibers: slow oxidative (SO), or Type I; fast oxidative glycolytic (FOG), or Type IIa; and fast glycolytic (FG), or Type IIb. Muscles are made up of all muscle fiber types. The distribution of muscle fiber type is dependent on training, genetics, and the function a muscle serves. Slow oxidative muscle fibers are associated with endurance performance and promote the production of energy through the aerobic energy system. Fast oxidative glycolytic and fast glycolytic muscle fibers are associated with strength and power performance and produce energy that is generated through glycogen and ATP–CP stored within the muscle cell. The sport of triathlon requires a significantly higher proportion of SO muscle fibers; however, it is still critical to develop the capacity of both the FOG and FG muscle fibers so that a full spectrum of energy capacity can be utilized.

Muscle fibers operate on a concept known as the sliding filament theory and are made up of many proteins. The two key proteins needed for contraction are actin and myosin. Myosin has a head-like structure, and when a muscle fiber is stimulated to contract, it binds to actin to create what is known as a muscle crossbridge. When multiple myosin heads are bound to actin, they pull one protein past another in an oar-like fashion, causing the muscle to contract. As the amount of force required by the muscle increases, more and more muscle crossbridges must be formed.

Several factors influence the number of muscle crossbridges formed and sustained during a bout of exercise. These include muscle temperature, oxygen delivery, acidity and electrical charge of the muscle, and fuel supply. Increases in muscle and whole-body temperature inhibit the ability of actin and myosin to bind and contract. In addition, the ability of the body to off-load oxygen to the muscle decreases as body temperature increases, and as a result muscle fatigue occurs. Oxygen delivery is a function of not only temperature but also the acidity of the blood and muscle.

Acidity (pH) of the blood is defined in physiology by the accumulation of hydrogen ions and lactate. The pH that can be handled during training and competition is dependent on the buffering capacity of the muscle, which is the body's ability to "soak up" and tolerate hydrogen that is produced from energy metabolism. Buffering capacity is limited by the amount of bicarbonate in the muscle. The accumulation of hydrogen is detrimental because it interferes with the ability of actin and myosin to bind. The hydrogen that is produced can be "picked up" by bicarbonate (hydrogen + bicarbonate) and converted to carbonic acid, which is immediately broken down by the body into water and carbon dioxide. Water is then recirculated into the body's system, and carbon dioxide is off-loaded at the lungs. Lactate that is produced remains in the blood and either accumulates or is used as a fuel source by the other tissues of the body. As pH continues to decline, less oxygen can be off-loaded to the muscle, more muscle fibers must be recruited to complete any exercise bout, and the amount of oxygen needed for exercise continues to increase; together, these factors will result in fatigue.

The electrical charge of a muscle is primarily maintained by two key electrolytes, sodium and potassium. Every time a muscle contracts, it is a function of the muscle's sodium and potassium levels moving through its gates and manipulating its electrical charge. A positive charge relaxes the muscle, and a negative charge contracts the muscle. The ability of a muscle to continue this process is highly dependent on the concentration of electrolytes available to it. Sodium and potassium can be significantly lost in sweat during exercise; this is why it is important that an athlete maintain fluid and electrolyte balance while in training and competition (see chapter 27 on hydration for more information). Sodium depletion through decreasing the consumption of sodium-containing foods, drinking only water, or not properly replacing electrolytes lost in sweat can lead to significant issues during prolonged exercise, including muscle cramps and thus fatigue, especially in the heat. These electrolytes are also key in assisting with muscle recovery.

The last factor in determining the number of muscle crossbridges needed to sustain work is fuel supply. Muscles require energy in the form of ATP to be available from creatine phosphate, carbohydrate, and fat sources. In the sport of triathlon, it is important that an athlete's muscles learn to predominantly derive energy from fat as a fuel source as well as from glycogen (carbohydrate) stores. As glycogen reserves become depleted, the ability to sustain muscle contraction begins to diminish, and an increased number of muscle crossbridges must be formed to continue producing the same amount of work. During competition, athletes will progressively fatigue if they lack sufficient energy supply in the form of carbohydrate, showing the importance of developing a training and competition nutrition plan that will sustain the amount of carbohydrate needed. You'll learn more about this process in chapter 26 on nutrition.

## *Cardiorespiratory Physiology*

The heart, lungs, and many blood vessels of the body form a continuous circuit that transports blood throughout the body and makes up the cardiorespiratory system. Blood consists of plasma (approximately 55 to 65 percent), leukocytes and platelets (approximately 1 percent), and red blood cells (approximately 38 to 45 percent). Red blood cells (RBCs) are the key component responsible for transporting oxygen throughout the body to working tissues. There are many RBCs in the human body, and within each RBC are approximately 250 million molecules of hemoglobin. Hemoglobin (Hb) is the protein that transports oxygen; thus it is key in providing oxygen-enriched blood to the body's tissues. An increase in blood volume through increased water, electrolyte, RBC, and hemoglobin production is a key adaptation an athlete receives from endurance training.

The lungs and other organs involved in breathing are responsible for providing oxygen-rich air and removing carbon dioxide through gas exchange. For each breath a person takes, oxygen is supplied and carbon dioxide is removed. With training, athletes adapt the muscles associated with the lungs so that breathing rate becomes more efficient. A larger amount of air is exchanged with each breath.

The response of the cardiorespiratory system to exercise training is characterized by the measures of cardiac output (CO), maximal oxygen-carrying capacity ($\dot{V}O_2max$), and the fractional percentage of maximal oxygen consumption (% $\dot{V}O_2max$) needed to perform a set workload. Cardiac output is the amount of blood pumped by the heart over a 1-minute period. It can be defined as heart rate (HR) multiplied by stroke volume (SV), where HR refers to the frequency the heart contracts and SV is the volume of blood ejected from the heart with each contraction. $\dot{V}O_2max$ is the maximal amount of oxygen the body can consume. It is found by multiplying CO by the $(a-\bar{v})O_2$ difference, which is the average difference between the oxygen content of the arterial and mixed venous blood. Oxygenated blood is supplied to the working muscles via the arterial blood vessels, and oxygen remaining in the blood once it has passed through the body is returned to the lungs via venous blood vessels.

# Effects of Training on the Muscular and Cardiorespiratory Systems

Adaptations to training require a repeated stimulus for approximately 2 to 4 weeks before the body fully takes on the stress that has been applied to the muscular and cardiorespiratory systems. Training adaptations for triathlon involve both local muscular endurance and whole-body cardiorespiratory endurance; however, it is the training performed by the muscular system that stimulates and drives adaptations of the heart and lungs. As a result, it is important that the effects of training be understood first and foremost in regard to the muscular system.

## *Training and the Muscular System*

Training can be classified based on the aerobic and anaerobic energy systems. Aerobic endurance training encompasses those adaptations that result from training at intensities at or below the anaerobic threshold (defined as the highest intensity a steady state of exercise can be maintained without significant rises in blood lactate). The intensity of training is intended to be only so high as to ensure it can be sustained for a period similar to or greater than the actual competition duration. The goal of aerobic endurance training is to help the muscles perform more efficiently through increasing and improving structural adaptations that promote the use of oxygen. This is accomplished by increasing the capacity of SO muscle fibers and potentially by converting FG fibers to FOG fibers, which improves their use of oxygen.

Four key structural adaptations can occur as a result of aerobic endurance training: (1) an increase in the number of capillaries supplying the muscle fibers, (2) an increase in muscle myoglobin content, (3) an increase in the number and size of the mitochondria in skeletal muscle, and (4) an increase in concentrations of oxidative enzymes. Capillaries are the very small blood vessels that are embedded deep within the skeletal muscle. They serve as the direct transporter of oxygen and nutrients (e.g., carbohydrate, electrolytes) and also remove carbon dioxide and metabolic by-products such as lactate and hydrogen ions. An increase in the number of capillaries that surround the muscle promotes oxygen delivery. Myoglobin is the muscle's equivalent of hemoglobin. The increase in myoglobin that occurs as a result of aerobic training improves the ability of the muscle to utilize oxygen. Myoglobin accepts the oxygen from hemoglobin and transports it to areas of the muscle that need it most. This primarily entails the oxidative pathways that exist in the mitochondria. Mitochondria are considered the powerhouse of the muscle cell. They utilize the oxygen that is delivered to create ATP through the oxidative metabolic pathways. These pathways are further enhanced by the increase in oxidative enzymes, and as a result the body is able to increase the utilization of fat as a fuel source during exercise. This boosts the amount of energy derived through aerobic metabolism and also spares muscle glycogen, both of which are critical for sustaining performance in endurance events.

Anaerobic interval training for endurance events increases the amount of energy that can be efficiently produced through anaerobic glycolysis and the ATP–CP energy systems. Interval training improves the buffering capacity of skeletal muscle and, if designed properly, improves maximal power, strength, and anaerobic capacity. This type of training, frequently referred to as high-intensity interval (HIT) training, involves repeated exercise bouts of short to moderate duration (30 seconds to 5 minutes). The training intensities associated with HIT are above the anaerobic threshold and are predominantly based on critical power outputs and paces at and above what is sustained during competition. After a period of HIT, athletes can perform the same workload with lower levels of lactate and a decreased rating of perceived exertion. In addition, higher work intensities can be sustained for longer, and the athlete also tolerates greater levels of lactate while removing lactate from the muscles at a faster rate.

The improvements in work capacity reported with HIT are a result of three key adaptations. The first key adaptation is an increase in the enzymes associated with the production of ATP through anaerobic glycolysis and the ATP–CP energy system. This allows for an improved utilization and oxidation (generating energy through oxygen-based metabolism) of carbohydrate as a fuel source. High-intensity interval training increases use of the oxidative energy pathways and decreases the amount of lactate that is spilled into the blood at a specific workload; this is a result of carbohydrate continuing through what is known as the Krebs cycle of the mitochondria to further generate ATP.

In addition to improving the oxidation of carbohydrate, the body is also capable of utilizing more carbohydrate as a result of HIT. High-intensity interval training increases the number of muscle fibers that can be recruited to do work and thus increases work capacity. As a result, higher levels of carbohydrate are utilized, and a greater amount of lactate is produced at the end of a maximal effort, thus indicating an increase in the capacity of the anaerobic energy system. The ability to tolerate high lactate levels also stimulates the development of bicarbonate. As discussed previously, bicarbonate soaks up hydrogen ions that are produced during the breakdown of carbohydrate through nonoxidative energy production. When bicarbonate levels are higher, more hydrogen ions can be removed, thereby allowing for continuous formation of a greater number of muscle crossbridges and sustainment of more forceful muscle contractions, resulting in improved performance.

Another significant benefit that comes from HIT is a decrease in the core body temperature reached during exercise. As core body temperature—the amount of heat stored by the body—increases over time, work output will begin to decrease. At a set workload, the energy cost of submaximal exercise is substantially decreased after HIT where maximal power has been improved. As a result of the improved exercise economy, the body does not accumulate heat as rapidly and muscle function is not impaired as quickly, thus resulting in a higher sustainable work output.

The development of neuromuscular patterns has also been suggested as one of the benefits of HIT. High-intensity interval training facilitates adaptations in the neuromuscular patterns that are recruited during race-pace activity. As was mentioned earlier, the brain has a region known as the motor cortex. Within this region of the brain, muscular patterns are stored along with the number of motor units required to perform them. During competition, these patterns are called upon to facilitate performance, and those muscular patterns that have been utilized the most will predominate during this time of physical stress.

Resistance training is another means of improving performance through adaptations in the muscular system. There are three key goals with this type of training. The first is to improve muscular strength as defined by the maximum force that can be generated by a muscle or group of muscles. A second goal is to improve muscular power, which is the explosive aspect of strength, by performing a specific movement at a given speed. The third goal of resistance training for endurance athletes is to improve muscular endurance. This is defined as the ability to sustain repeated muscular contractions at a fixed workload for an extended period of time. Increasing the amount of force that can be produced at a given speed, and improving the ability to sustain that force over a distance, will enhance performance because the muscles will not be as susceptible to fatigue.

## Training and the Cardiorespiratory System

Adaptations in the cardiorespiratory system are a direct result of adaptations of the skeletal muscles to the work they are performing, and in turn this stimulates the heart and lungs to adapt. The effects of training on the cardiorespiratory system are seen as increases in $\dot{V}O_2$max and cardiac output. Because of genetic factors both will eventually plateau; however, training adaptations and the economy of the cardiorespiratory system can still be significantly improved. Improvements in $\dot{V}O_2$max and cardiac output are a function of three key adaptations occurring in the body: (1) Total blood volume is increased; (2) the heart becomes stronger as a result of the work it is doing; and (3) oxygen delivery to the muscles of the body is enhanced. As a result of these adaptations, the heart is capable of more efficiently pumping larger amounts of blood to the working muscles with every contraction, and in turn oxygen is delivered and carbon dioxide, along with other by-products of metabolism, is removed more efficiently. These adaptations are described further in the following paragraphs.

The increase in total blood volume that occurs with endurance training is the result of a two-phase process. In the first, hormones stimulate an increase in total body water retention over a 10-day period, and the second is an increased production of red blood cells over an approximate 4-week period. The improvement in total blood volume benefits athletes through three different mechanisms: (1) an improved ability to regulate body temperature, as the increased water content allows for improved heat dissipation and thus an increase in sweat rate; (2) an improved efficiency and functionality of the heart muscle; and (3) an increased oxygen-carrying capacity as a result of the increased number of red blood cells.

The heart is a muscle that responds to training much like skeletal muscle. A load can be imposed on the heart by increasing the number of times it must contract or the strength with which it contracts. With repeated contraction, the heart muscle becomes stronger and more efficient, and as a result, the heart does not have to contract as frequently to perform the same amount of work. In addition, prolonged engagement in aerobic long-distance training enhances stroke volume, with a resultant reduction in resting and exercising heart rate at a specific workload. Using the formula for cardiac output (stroke volume × heart rate), it can be understood how heart rate is reduced at submaximal exercise intensities as a result of an increase in stroke volume. During maximal exercise, the increase in blood volume causes an increase in maximal cardiac output, and as a result an increase in $\dot{V}O_2$max is seen. Another benefit of a stronger heart and a larger stroke volume is a faster recovery after a hard or near-maximal bout of exercise.

The improvement in total blood volume and heart efficiency also results in an improved delivery of oxygen to the working muscles. In addition, because there is an increase in red blood cell volume, the concentration of hemoglobin is increased. This raises the oxygen-carrying capacity of the blood, and the increase in blood volume improves the transit time for supplying oxygen to working muscles. Together, these lead to improved endurance performance.

Adaptations in the lungs also facilitate the improvements in $\dot{V}O_2$max and cardiac output. With training, the lungs become more efficient and can increase the amount of oxygen supplied with each breath; as a result, ventilation is decreased. Ventilation is a function of tidal volume and the frequency of breathing (tidal volume × frequency). Tidal volume is the volume of air that is inspired or expired with each breath. The primary means for a decrease in ventilation is the increase in tidal volume, which allows for a lower frequency of breathing. The improved capacity of the lungs during exercise is an important factor in improving endurance performance.

## Assessing Your Training

Monitoring training provides a coach and athlete with a physiological snapshot of what is occurring in an athlete's body as a result of the training stimulus. The monitoring system utilized should objectively evaluate an athlete's training status and include assessment of the training load, identify the effects of a training intervention, and further serve to refine training design. Measures of adaptation to training should be taken daily and summed to provide an overall picture of the physiological changes occurring throughout the training cycle.

The key physiological predictors of triathlon performance are submaximal exercise economy and maximal velocity and power output. These predictive measures can be objectively evaluated for a triathlete through physiological measures of blood lactate, heart rate, rating of perceived exertion (RPE; see figure 9.2), and submaximal oxygen uptake. Monitoring can be accomplished through field- or laboratory-based measures depending on what an athlete and coach prefer and have access to in regard to physiological testing equipment. Regardless of whether the measures are performed in a laboratory or field setting, it is most beneficial to understand submaximal levels of work output in relation to maximal exercise capacity; thus submaximal efforts can be viewed as a relative percentage of maximal effort.

**FIGURE 9.2**

## Rating of perceived exertion (RPE) scale.

| RPE number | Breathing rate/ability to talk | Exertion |
|---|---|---|
| 1 | Resting | Very slight |
| 2 | Talking is easy | Slight |
| 3 | Talking is easy | Moderate |
| 4 | You can talk but with more effort | Somewhat hard |
| 5 | You can talk but with more effort | Hard |
| 6 | Breathing is challenged/don't want to talk | Hard |
| 7 | Breathing is challenged/don't want to talk | Very hard |
| 8 | Panting hard/conversation is difficult | Very hard |
| 9 | Panting hard/conversation is difficult | Very, very hard |
| 10 | Cannot sustain this intensity for too long | Maximal |

Reprinted, by permission, from K. Austin and B. Seebohar, 2011, *Performance nutrition: Applying the science of nutrient timing* (Champaign, IL: Human Kinetics), 30.

## *Monitoring the Training Load*

Monitoring the training load helps coaches understand how an athlete's body is tolerating the physical training being performed. Training load tells us how much work an athlete performed and how hard it was to do it. It is defined as duration multiplied by intensity (as perceived by the level of exertion). Research has shown that people can have different tolerances to the same training load. There are three potential levels or perspectives of monitoring: the athlete's, the coach's, and the sport scientist's or sports physician's view. Each has a degree of responsibility for monitoring how well an athlete is adapting to training; however, each has a different perspective on what is monitored and how it is done. The most important level is that of the athlete because she can monitor herself intrinsically on a daily basis and provide feedback and data that may inform the coach, scientist, or physician.

One of the most effective ways to monitor the training load and the athlete's responses and adaptation (positive or negative) is through the regular use of athlete-focused training journals. Both quantitative physical data and more qualitative data (feelings, moods, and emotions) should be recorded on a daily basis and reviewed regularly with coaches and assisting support staff. If introduced and monitored effectively, training journals can become a very valuable tool for raising athlete and coach awareness as well as supporting long-term athlete development and preventing overtraining.

The quantitative physiological data needed for calculating the training load can be easily assessed by monitoring either heart rate (HR) or the rating of perceived exertion (RPE) in relation to training velocity or power output. The training load can thus be defined as RPE or HR × duration (in minutes). The addition of a score from the satisfaction scale (see figure 9.3) adds a subjective psychobiological measure that includes the athlete's mental perspective on how well he believed the training session went. This is important because psychological state can significantly alter the training load. When using a satisfaction scale, the satisfaction component is added to the formula to look like this: RPE or HR × duration × satisfaction score. You can then see how your mental view played into how hard a training session seemed to be, which is very valuable to a coach or an athlete trying to understand why something just doesn't work on certain days or why it works extremely well on other days. For example, let's assume an athlete doesn't sleep well the night before a 6-hour bike session and gives it a satisfaction score of 9 because she got her butt kicked by her training partners. The next week she completes the same session but sleeps well the night before and performs well in practice; she gives this session a satisfaction score of 2. As you can see, the training load was significantly reduced from the week before, showing you how an athlete's satisfaction plays into how much she is loaded by a training session.

**FIGURE 9.3**

## Satisfaction Scale.

| 0 | Best workout ever |
|------|----------------------|
| 1-2 | Very satisfied |
| 3-4 | Fairly satisfied |
| 5-6 | Neither |
| 7-8 | Fairly dissatisfied |
| 9 | Very dissatisfied |
| 10 | Worst workout imaginable |

Adapted, by permission, from K. Austin and B. Seebohar, 2011, *Performance nutrition: Applying the science of nutrient timing* (Champaign, IL: Human Kinetics), 33.

An example of a calculated training load utilizing RPE and a score from the satisfaction scale can be seen in table 9.2; an additional example utilizing HR is provided in table 9.3.

**TABLE 9.2**

## Calculating Training Load Using RPE and a Satisfaction Score

| Day | RPE | Satisfaction | Duration (min) | Training load |
|-----|-----|--------------|----------------|---------------|
| Sunday | 2 | 1 | 45 | 90 |
| Monday | 9 | 5 | 60 | 2,700 |
| Tuesday | 4 | 3 | 90 | 1,080 |
| Wednesday | 3 | 2 | 30 | 180 |
| Thursday | 7 | 1 | 45 | 315 |
| Friday | 2 | 1 | 45 | 90 |
| Saturday | 3 | 1 | 120 | 360 |

**TABLE 9.3**

## Calculating Training Load Using Average HR and a Satisfaction Score

| Day | HR (divided by 100) | Satisfaction | Duration (min) | Training load |
|-----|---------------------|--------------|----------------|---------------|
| Sunday | 1.1 | 1 | 45 | 49.5 |
| Monday | 1.9 | 5 | 60 | 570 |
| Tuesday | 1.35 | 3 | 90 | 364.5 |
| Wednesday | 1.20 | 2 | 30 | 72 |
| Thursday | 1.60 | 1 | 45 | 72 |
| Friday | 1.05 | 1 | 45 | 47.25 |
| Saturday | 1.15 | 1 | 120 | 138 |

Another key aspect of monitoring training is recovery. The primary measures that can be monitored to examine adaptation to training are the number of hours an athlete sleeps, the quality of the sleep, and a total quality recovery score (TQR; figure 9.4). The amount and quality of sleep an athlete achieves are two of the greatest predictors of recovery and how well he can handle the training load. TQR was developed around the RPE scale to emphasize the relationship that must exist between recovery and the difficulty of a training session. The goal is to understand the athlete's ability to recover from different types of training sessions. If he recovers very well from a 1-mile repeat

### FIGURE 9.4

## Total quality recovery scale.

| 0 | No recovery |
|------|---------------------|
| 1 | Extremely bad recovery |
| 2-3 | Very bad recovery |
| 4 | Bad recovery |
| 5 | Recovery OK |
| 6-7 | Good recovery |
| 8 | Very good recovery |
| 9-10 | Extremely good recovery |

Adapted, by permission, from K. Austin and B. Seebohar, 2011, *Performance nutrition: Applying the science of nutrient timing* (Champaign, IL: Human Kinetics), 33.

session where the RPE is 9 out of 10 but not from a 200-meter repeat session with the same RPE, it tells us he will require more recovery after those training days, and so usually a coach or athlete training himself will allow more time in between hard training sessions. TQR also indicates the type of training sessions where the athlete has to be more proactive at recovery and make it a priority. According to the principle of supercompensation, the greater a training stimulus, the more recovery will be needed. When recovery is monitored closely along with the training load, the negative effects of a high training stimulus can be prevented. Athletes who recover adequately are able to tolerate the training load, whereas athletes who have limited or no recovery cannot tolerate a high training load. If an athlete recovers from training, the body can adapt, and he can then move forward with training.

Monitoring the training load along with an athlete's satisfaction with training and ability to recover can be a valuable process, but it often takes patience and reflection to understand what it all means. The training load should be examined in relation to the performance gains obtained from training underneath the total load and the loads tolerated at various intensities, with the goal of understanding how much of a load is necessary for subsequent training cycles to produce similar improvements. When examining the training load and the types of training used to achieve the load, a coach or athlete must consider how this form of training was tolerated psychologically and how well an athlete recovered in appropriate amounts of time considering the way training was designed and delivered. Over time, the goal is to find patterns of loading that result in the best physiological and psychological rewards and to avoid training styles that result in poor training tolerance and adaptation.

Criterion workouts and training courses are two of the best and simplest ways to monitor adaptations to training. Measures of blood lactate, HR, and RPE can be monitored during these training sessions to provide objective and subjective feedback regarding training. Criterion workouts and training courses typically involve completing (or attempting to complete) a set number of repetitions or covering a distance in a given amount of time. This may include choosing to perform a long-course swim session at race pace (e.g., 4 × 1K at pace identified) or finding a 10-mile (16 km) loop to run and evaluating how well training is going based on how quickly you run it. Recovery times between repetitions are usually manipulated, either shortened or lengthened, based on how fit you are. As you get fitter, you should be able to shorten recovery times, and if you are away from training for a long period, more recovery is given so you can complete the work.

# ▶ Physiological Adaptations to Training in Extreme Temperatures

Triathletes attempting to train at altitude or in very hot or cold temperatures should be aware of important changes in the cardiorespiratory and muscular systems that occur in these environments. A hot environment will increase the strain of work by raising core body and muscle temperature and the heart rate associated with a given work intensity. The sweat rate is higher, and the potential for dehydration increases as the body attempts to dissipate heat.

Successfully competing in the heat requires acclimatization, or the physiological adaptations that improve work tolerance after a chronic change in environment. When first arriving in a hot environment, it is best to train in the cooler parts of the day and to slowly increase the amount of training volume done in the heat of the day that best mimics competition. Once the body has adapted to low-intensity training volumes, acclimatization can be furthered by introducing sessions that require intensity. Acclimatization to a hot environment is first marked by decreases in HR and RPE during a training bout, then by an increase in sweat rate to help maintain a lower core body temperature. The timeline for these adaptations can be seen in figure 9.5

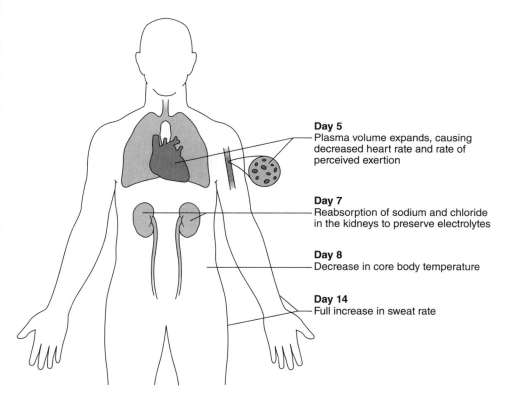

**Day 5**
Plasma volume expands, causing decreased heart rate and rate of perceived exertion

**Day 7**
Reabsorption of sodium and chloride in the kidneys to preserve electrolytes

**Day 8**
Decrease in core body temperature

**Day 14**
Full increase in sweat rate

**FIGURE 9.5**    **Adaptations that occur in the body as a result of heat acclimatization.**

Reprinted, by permission, from K. Austin and B. Seebohar, 2011, *Performance nutrition: Applying the science of nutrient timing* (Champaign, IL: Human Kinetics), 147.

*(continued)*

*(continued)*

Athletes who train and compete in cold environments must focus on maintaining core body temperature. This requires dressing appropriately (and not removing too much clothing during training or competition) and ensuring adequate fuel and fluid intake. The loss of too much body heat can result in hypothermia, which alters the physiological systems of the body. When hypothermia begins, the ability to produce muscular contractions is significantly reduced, and work output will begin to decline. As hypothermia continues, core body temperature will decline to dangerous levels, with a further decrease in the quality of work output. Indicators of hypothermia include a rapidly declining HR and increased shivering as the body attempts to maintain its temperature through muscular contractions. Adaptations to the cold can be seen in figure 9.6.

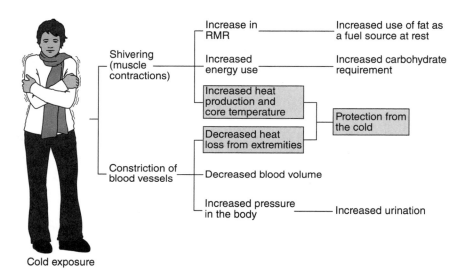

**FIGURE 9.6** **Physical and metabolic reactions to cold.**

Reprinted, by permission, from K. Austin and B. Seebohar, 2011, *Performance nutrition: Applying the science of nutrient timing* (Champaign, IL: Human Kinetics), 33.

## Manipulating the Training Load

Designing training is never an easy task. Each athlete is a unique person and requires an individualized plan that will optimize training stress. The key to manipulating the training load is variation of the three key stressors (frequency, intensity, and volume) and periodization of the energy systems while following basic yet important principles of training.

Any training program should progressively increase the training load in a manner that promotes a high quality of work. For most athletes, the most effective way to increase the training load is by using the step method. This method increases the training load through the manipulation of one variable every week for a period of 2 or 3 weeks. A week of regeneration in which the training load is significantly reduced should then follow before any further increases in training load occur.

Increasing the training load is first accomplished by establishing the frequency at which training will take place. Once this has been established, the volume of training is increased to the point desired, and then increases in training intensity should follow. Volume and intensity of training should not be increased simultaneously. Training volume is the total duration of time spent in training or the number of miles or kilometers run, bike, or swum over a period of time (usually a week; however, most athletes calculate total volume for a training period as well). Training intensity is how hard the athlete works. It typically is expressed as a percentage out of 100 percent. For example, an athlete completes a session at 80 percent of maximal effort. The other way to describe intensity is based on pace. For example, an athlete completes a 50-mile (80 km) bike training session at a pace she is targeting for the 112 (180 km) miles of an Ironman bike. Volume should be increased by no more than 10 percent at a time and can be manipulated by increasing the duration of a training session, the number of repetitions performed, or the distance or duration of a repetition. The intensity of training can be manipulated by increasing velocity, power output, and the number of repetitions and decreasing the rest interval between repetitions.

Periodization is the key to ensuring training load is manipulated appropriately. Periodization can be defined as the structuring of a training program to produce optimal performance at a given time. It is critical that the energy systems be structured appropriately to ensure that an athlete has a solid aerobic foundation and does not increase fitness too rapidly or train too intensely for a prolonged time, which can lead to overtraining. Periodization of training is traditionally divided into three phases that may be repeated several times throughout the year depending on the number of identified competitions:

- Preparatory
- Competitive
- Transition

The preparatory phase is further divided into general and sport-specific speed and power development. The energy system components of these phases are divided into the following eight elements during a training cycle: active recovery, general endurance, aerobic endurance, lactate threshold, aerobic interval, anaerobic power, anaerobic tolerance, and maintenance. An example of a single training cycle based on a traditional plan for periodization of the energy systems is provided in figure 9.7. Although it is important to always be tapping into some aspect of each energy system, the focus of training should always predominate.

Successful periodization of the energy systems requires that specific principles of training be applied to each athlete. There are four key principles that should be incorporated into periodization: progressive overload, individualization, specificity, and reversibility. The proper integration of these principles should lead to higher levels of performance for athletes of all capabilities.

Progressive overload is an intentional increase in training volume or intensity to create a training adaptation that will improve performance. For short periods, athletes can handle an increase in stress that taxes their maximal work capacity. For a muscle to build strength, it must be gradually stressed by working against a load greater than what it is used to, and in order to increase endurance, muscles must work for a longer time or at a higher intensity than what they are accustomed to performing.

FIGURE 9.7

## Traditional Periodization of the Energy Systems.

| Preparatory | | | | | | Competitive | Transition |
|---|---|---|---|---|---|---|---|
| *General preparation* | | | | *Specific preparation* | | Maintenance | Active recovery/rest |
| General endurance | Aerobic endurance | Lactate threshold | Aerobic interval | Anaerobic power | Anaerobic tolerance | | |
| • Development of training volume<br>• Overall cardiorespiratory development<br>• Development of muscular endurance<br>• Initializing the neuromuscular aspects of muscle recruitment<br>• Building the athlete's base of strength<br>• Development of the psychology of training and competition as well as the mind's cognitive ability to perform prolonged and high-volume work<br>• Development of fundamental skills and abilities, with emphasis on technical components necessary to improve sport-specific endurance in the later stages of the training program | • Development of oxygen supply and utilization<br>• Aerobic work performed at a more intense level in order to prepare for intensities associated with sport-specific work<br>• Steady-state cardiorespiratory and muscular stimulus that will transition into distance-specific endurance | • Development of high levels of aerobic power under significant levels of lactic acid<br>• Psychological development of pain tolerance/threshold | • Development of the ability to uptake and transport oxygen and tolerate high levels of lactate<br>• Development of specific endurance at and above competition power levels<br>• Progressive elevation of intensity from moderate to medium-fast speeds within one training session | • Development of power levels at maximal and submaximal levels for progressively longer distances or periods of time<br>• Development of ability to perform high levels of power without oxygen<br>• Development of maximal muscular recruitment | • Development of peak fitness through the production of power and energy in the absence of oxygen<br>• Recovery periods are shortened during interval training<br>• Race-specific muscular patterns are developed<br>• Maximal development of the central nervous system | | |

Various methods have been examined in regard to imposing an increase in training load. The three primary methods that have been documented include a linear and continuous method, a step method, and a method known as flat loading.

The linear and continuous method involves athletes continuously training at workloads that are higher than those normally encountered. There is not an intentional unloading until after the season is completed. The step approach, which was described earlier, allows for a progressive increased loading, with a phase of unloading that also allows the athlete to adapt and regenerate. Flat loading places the highest volume and intensity an athlete can tolerate in the first 3 weeks of a training cycle and is followed by a week of unloading for regeneration and relaxation. It is intended only for experienced national and international athletes and should be used only after the general endurance phase of the preparatory cycle. Regardless of the loading method utilized, the key to successfully adapting the body to any training demand is recovery that in turn allows for regeneration. Incorporating the regeneration period into the training cycle is important to remove both the physiological and psychological fatigue that has accumulated during the period of overload.

The principle of individualization refers to designing training based on each athlete's physical capabilities, utilizing his strengths and improving his weaknesses in a progressive manner so he does not ever limit his strengths. This aspect of training should integrate the objective use of physiological assessment measures as well as the subjective understanding a coach has from working with an athlete. In the sport of triathlon, it must also take into account the differences in an athlete's physical build and the sport discipline he is most suited for and has a background competing in. For example, an athlete who enters triathlon and is built with broad shoulders and a significant amount of upper body musculature from swimming and competing in flat-water kayaking will need to train at a different run volume and intensity than an athlete who comes from a running background. In the same sense, because of a lack of upper body strength and musculature, the amount of swim training a runner will be capable of performing will determine how much swim volume and intensity he can handle. Placing both of these athletes on the same training program will push them past their tolerance level in a nonprogressive manner and will only result in injury and a poor quality of training.

The principle of specificity refers to training athletes toward the relevant elements of what will be necessary for successful performance. This includes designing training to match the volume and intensity of competition as well as preparing an athlete for things such as the strategy she will need to use in racing each of the sport disciplines and the environment she may have to compete in. For example, if an athlete must learn to take repeated attacks during the cycling component of the race and then come off the bike to run above her lactate threshold for the first part of the run, this should be progressively incorporated into the training cycle to mimic the specificity of the race.

Reversibility is the training principle that refers to the gradual loss of work capacity as a result of decreases in training frequency, intensity, or volume. Periodization should be designed to provide an athlete with regeneration periods where there is little or no physical activity; although rest and recovery are important, these time periods should never be so long that there is a significant loss in physical fitness. The loss of physical work capacity is known as detraining. Significant decreases in physiological work capacity occur after approximately 2 weeks of inactivity; thus it is recommended that no more than a 2-week regeneration period be incorporated into the training plan.

Air pressure is reduced at altitude, which means less oxygen is taken in with every breath of air. This results in hypoxia (the rate of oxygen supply cannot meet the oxygen used by the body). The initial reaction of the body is depicted in figure 9.8. Endurance athletes intentionally travel or live at altitude to improve oxidative capacity and increase the RBCs and Hb available to transport oxygen to the exercising muscles. Training at altitude can also improve the body's ability to utilize fat as a fuel source and the muscles' ability to buffer lactic acid.

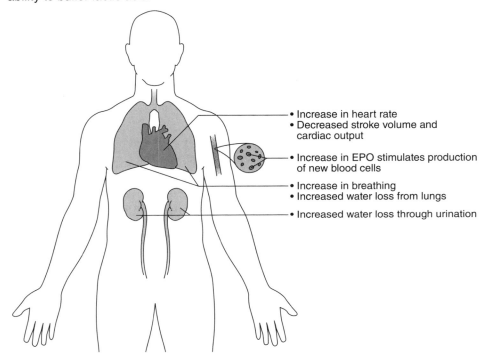

• Increase in heart rate
• Decreased stroke volume and cardiac output

• Increase in EPO stimulates production of new blood cells

• Increase in breathing
• Increased water loss from lungs

• Increased water loss through urination

**FIGURE 9.8** **Adaptations occurring as a result of altitude exposure.**

Reprinted, by permission, from K. Austin and B. Seebohar, 2011, *Performance nutrition: Applying the science of nutrient timing* (Champaign, IL: Human Kinetics), 33.

There are several different approaches to altitude training; the two most promising are living high, training low and living high, training high and low. These allow an athlete to successfully maintain training quality, which is key for optimal performance. Aerobic work capacity begins to significantly decrease at 4,900 feet (1,500 m), and despite acclimatization, an athlete's maximal work capacity will not be the same as at sea level; thus the quality of HIT and aerobic training sessions is compromised at altitude.

Using the live high, train low approach, athletes live for the majority of the day at altitude (above 4,900 feet and no higher than 9,800 feet, or 3,000 meters). The athlete trains at or below 4,000 feet (1,200 m) and ideally as close to sea level as possible. Utilizing the live high, train high and low approach, athletes complete low-intensity training sessions at altitude and train low for any sessions that are of a high intensity or prolonged aerobic effort at a critical race intensity (i.e., long threshold training sessions that are relative to race intensity).

Another option is simulated altitude systems, which allow an athlete to live at altitude without leaving the comforts of home. Most athletes prefer to stay close to family and friends, and many cannot afford the time away from work to train at altitude. Simulated altitude training systems also allow an athlete to perform low-intensity training in a hypoxic environment by breathing reduced-oxygen air through a mask.

Physiology provides an explanation for how the body's muscular and cardiorespiratory systems adapt to training. As a result, it is the basis for every aspect of training, whether it be strength training, tapering for competition, or even choosing tactics for an-open water race. Physiology is also critical in understanding the response to training in different environments. Monitoring the body's response to a training plan is a key component for refining training design regardless of the level an athlete competes at. Periodization and the implementation of key training principles will provide a structured plan for long-term development in the sport of triathlon.

# CHAPTER 10

# The Art and Science of Tapering

## Iñigo Mujika and Yann Le Meur

The most important goal for coaches and triathletes is to increase the physical, technical, and psychological abilities of the athletes to the highest possible levels and to develop a precisely controlled training program to ensure that maximal performance is attained at the right moment of the season (i.e., at each point of a major triathlon competition). In many competitive endurance events such as triathlon, these top performances are often associated with a marked reduction in the training load undertaken by the athletes during the days before the competition. This period, known as the taper, has been defined as "a progressive, nonlinear reduction of the training load during a variable amount of time that is intended to reduce physiological and psychological stress of daily training and optimize sport performance" (Mujika and Padilla 2003).

In this perspective, the taper is of paramount importance to a triathlete's performance and the outcome of the event. However, in this training phase coaches are the most insecure about the best training strategies for each individual triathlete, as they rely almost exclusively on a trial-and-error approach. Indeed, only recently have sport scientists increased their understanding of the relationships between the reduction of the training load before a competition and the associated performance changes.

A comprehensive and integrated analysis of the available scientific literature on tapering allows us to make a contribution to the optimization of tapering programs for triathletes. Although we acknowledge that designing training and tapering programs remains an art rather than a science, this chapter intends to establish the scientific bases for the precompetition tapering strategies in triathlon. We hope the following information will help individual triathletes, coaches, and sport scientists in their goal of achieving the optimal training mix during the taper, leading to more peak performances at the expected time of the season. Because the taper is also dependent on removal or minimization of the triathlete's habitual stressors, permitting physiological systems to replenish or further enhance their capabilities, this chapter also addresses recovery strategies and acclimatization to stressful environments before competition.

# Managing the Training Load During the Taper

The training load, or training stimulus, in a competitive sport such as triathlon can be described as a combination of training intensity, volume, and frequency (Wenger and Bell 1986). This training load is markedly reduced during the taper in an attempt to reduce accumulated fatigue, but reduced training should not be detrimental to training-induced adaptations. An insufficient training stimulus could result in a partial loss of training-induced anatomical, physiological, and performance adaptations, also known as detraining (Mujika and Padilla 2000). Therefore, triathletes and their coaches must determine the extent to which the training load can be reduced at the expense of the training components while retaining or even improving adaptations. A meta-analysis conducted by Bosquet et al. (2007) combined the results of tapering studies on highly trained athletes to establish the scientific bases for successfully reducing precompetition training loads to achieve peak performances at the desired point of the season. Although most of the studies were conducted on single activities (e.g., swimming, cycling, or running), they are certainly relevant for triathletes. Bosquet et al. assessed the effects of altering components of the taper on performance. The dependent variable analyzed was the performance change during the taper, whereas the independent variables included reductions in training intensity, volume, and frequency; taper pattern; and taper duration.

## Training Reduction

Overall, performance remains stable or drops slightly when training intensity is reduced, whereas it improves substantially when intensity is maintained or increased. Therefore, the training load of triathletes should not be reduced at the expense of training intensity during a taper (Bosquet et al. 2007).

With regard to training volume, several investigations have shown that this training component can be markedly reduced without a risk of losing training-induced adaptations or hampering performance. For instance, Hickson et al. (1982) reported that subjects trained in either cycling or treadmill running for 10 weeks retained most of their physiological and endurance performance adaptations during 15 subsequent weeks of reduced training, during which the volume of the sessions was diminished by as much as two-thirds. Studying highly trained middle-distance runners, both Shepley et al. (1992) and Mujika et al. (2000) reported better physiological and performance outcomes with low-volume than with moderate-volume tapers. Bosquet et al. (2007) determined through their meta-analysis that performance improvement during the taper was highly sensitive to the reduction in training volume. These researchers determined that maximal performance gains are obtained with a total reduction in training volume of 41 to 60 percent of pretaper value and that such a reduction should be achieved by decreasing the duration of the training sessions rather than decreasing the frequency of training. This finding suggests that triathletes would maximize taper-associated benefits by roughly dividing their training volume by half.

According to Bosquet et al. (2007), decreasing training frequency (i.e., the number of weekly training sessions) has not been shown to significantly improve performance. However, the decrease in training frequency interacts with other training variables, particularly training volume and intensity, which makes it difficult to isolate the precise effect of a reduction in training frequency on performance. Although further investigations are required, this result suggests that triathletes would benefit from maintaining a similar number of training sessions per week during the taper.

## Pattern of the Taper

Mujika and Padilla (2003) identify three types of taper patterns: (1) linear taper, in which the training load is progressively reduced by a similar amount each day; (2) exponential taper, characterized by a large initial reduction of the training load followed by a leveling off of the training load; and (3) step taper, which is also referred to as reduced training and is characterized by a sudden constant reduction of the training load (see figure 10.1).

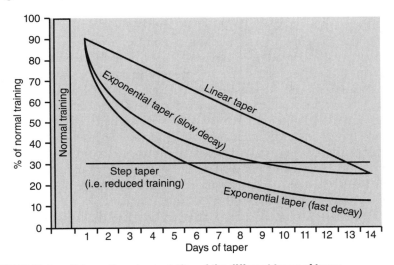

**FIGURE 10.1** **Schematic representation of the different types of taper.**
Reprinted, by permission, from I. Mujika and S. Padilla, 2003, "Scientific bases for precompetition tapering strategies," *Medicine & Science in Sports & Exercise* 35(7): 1182-1187.

The majority of available studies used a progressive decrease of the training load. The studies of Banister, Carter, and Zarkadas (1999) and Bosquet et al. (2007) reported bigger performance improvements after a progressive taper (i.e., linear or exponential) when compared with a step taper. Nevertheless, Bosquet et al. (2007) were not able to address the effect of the kind of progressive taper on performance. Recommendations rely on the work of Banister et al. (1999) with triathletes, who suggest that a fast decay, which implied a lower training volume, was more beneficial to cycling and running performance than a slow decay of the training load. Thomas, Mujika, and Busso (2009) recently reported that the taper may be optimized by increasing the training load by 20 to 30 percent during the final 3 days of the taper, by allowing additional adaptations without compromising the removal of fatigue.

## Duration of the Taper

Bosquet et al. (2007) found a dose–response relationship between the duration of the taper and the performance improvement. A taper duration of 8 to 14 days seems to represent the borderline between the positive influence of fatigue disappearance and the negative influence of detraining on performance. Performance improvements can also be expected after 1-, 3-, or 4-week tapers. However, negative results may be experienced by some triathletes. This interindividual variability in the optimal taper duration has already been highlighted by some mathematical modeling studies (Mujika, Busso, et al. 1996; Thomas and Busso 2005). Differences in the physiological and psychological adaptations to reduced training (Mujika, Busso, et al. 1996; Mujika, Chatard, et al. 1996; Mujika, Padilla, and Pyne 2002), as well as the use of an overload intervention (i.e., a voluntary increase in the fatigue level of the athlete) in the weeks before the taper (Thomas and Busso 2005), are some of the variables that can account for this variability.

Recent mathematical modeling simulations suggest that the training performed in the lead-up to the taper greatly influences the optimal individual duration of the taper. A 20 percent increase over normal training during 28 days before the taper requires a step-load reduction of around 65 percent during 3 weeks, instead of 2 weeks when no overload training is performed. A progressive taper requires a smaller load reduction over a longer duration than a step taper, whatever the pretaper training. The impact of the pretaper training on the duration of the optimal taper seems obvious in regard to the reduction of the accumulated fatigue. Overload training before the taper causes a greater stress and needs a longer recovery time. Nevertheless, the more severe training loads could make adaptations peak at a higher level (Thomas, Mujika, and Busso 2008). In other words, greater training volume, intensity, or both before the taper would allow bigger performance gains but would also demand a reduction of the training load over a longer taper.

This hypothesis was strengthened by Coutts, Slattery, and Wallace (2007), who compared physiological, biochemical, and psychological markers of overreaching in well-trained triathletes after either 4 weeks of overload training and a 2-week taper or 4 weeks of normal training and a similar taper. Overreaching was diagnosed in the intensified training group after the 4 weeks of overload training, with a worsened (–3.7 percent) 3-kilometer (1.9 mile) running time-trial performance. In contrast, a gain in performance (+3.0 percent) was observed in the normal training group during the same period. During the taper, gains (+7.0 percent) in 3-km running time-trial performance were observed in the intensified training group. These findings suggest that a 2-week taper was enough for the intensified training group to recover and experience a positive training adaptation. Nevertheless, there was no difference in performance improvement between both training groups, suggesting that the length of the taper for the intensified group was not sufficient to allow for full recovery. Future work should compare different strategies for the implementation of physical training load in preparation for triathlon competition.

Millet et al. (2005) used mathematical modeling to describe the relationships between training loads and anxiety and perceived fatigue as a new method for assessing the effects of training on the psychological status of athletes, in this case four professional triathletes. The time for self-perceived fatigue to return to its baseline level was 15 days, which was close to the time modeled by previous researchers as optimal for tapering (Busso et al. 2002; Busso, Candau, and Lacour 1994; Fitz-Clarke, Morton, and Banister 1991). Millet et al. concluded that a simple questionnaire to assess anxiety and perceived fatigue could be used to adjust the optimal duration of tapering in triathlon.

Taken together, these results suggest that, in general, the optimal taper duration in triathlon is 2 weeks, even though positive performance outcomes can occur with both shorter and longer tapers. Testing different taper durations (from 1 to 4 weeks) while using a training log will help triathletes determine their own optimal taper duration.

Although the data on swimming, cycling, and running were insufficient in the meta-analysis conducted by Bosquet et al. (2007) to provide specific recommendations for each sport, it was possible to identify some trends that may help optimize taper in triathlon. The first, indisputable one is the need to maintain training intensity, whatever the mode of locomotion. Substantial small to moderate improvements were indeed achieved only when training intensity was not decreased during the taper in swimming, cycling, and running. Although a 41 to 60 percent decrease in training volume seems to be optimal in swimming, Bosquet et al. (2007) were not able to find a similar cutoff value in cycling and running, the optimal decrease being somewhere between 21 and 60 percent. A period of 8 to 14 days seems to represent the optimal taper duration in cycling and running. It should be noted, however, that significant improvements can be expected from longer taper durations in swimming, but the number of cycling and running subjects for such durations was insufficient to test this hypothesis with adequate statistical power ($n = 10$ in running and 0 in cycling for tapers lasting 15 to 21 days and 22 days or more). Finally, there is limited evidence indicating that cyclists seem to respond particularly well to step tapers in which training frequency is reduced (Bosquet et al. 2007).

Maintaining training intensity is absolutely necessary to retain and enhance training-induced adaptations during tapering in triathlon, but it is obvious that reductions in other training variables should allow for sufficient recovery to optimize performance. Lowering training volume appears to induce positive physiological, psychological, and performance adaptations in highly trained triathletes. A safe bet in terms of training volume reduction would be 41 to 60 percent, but performance benefits could be attained with somewhat smaller or bigger volumes. A final increase of 20 to 30 percent of the training load during the last 3 days before the triathlon race may be beneficial.

High training frequencies (greater than 80 percent) seem to be necessary to avoid detraining and "loss of feel" in highly trained triathletes. Conversely, training-induced adaptations can be readily maintained with very low training frequencies in moderately trained athletes (30 to 50 percent).

The optimal duration of the taper is not known. Indeed, positive physiological and performance adaptations can be expected as a result of tapers lasting 4 to 28 days, yet the negative effects of complete inactivity are readily apparent in athletes. When we are unsure about the individual adaptation profile of a particular triathlete (this is what determines the optimal taper duration), 2 weeks seems to be a suit-all taper duration. This period may be beneficially increased to 4 weeks if a temporary increase of about 20 percent over the normal training load is planned during the month preceding the taper. Testing different taper methods while using a training log may also help a triathlete determine his own optimal training strategy during the precompetition period.

# Enhancing Recovery During the Taper

Achieving an appropriate balance between training stress and recovery is important in maximizing performance in triathlon. The cumulative effects of training-induced fatigue must be reduced during the weeks immediately preceding competition, and a wide range of recovery modalities can be used as an integral part of the taper to help optimize performance (see chapter 8 for more information). Long-lasting fatigue experienced during the taper in endurance sports such as triathlon may be related to exercise-induced muscle injury, delayed-onset muscle soreness (DOMS) (Cheung, Hume, and Maxwell 2003), or an imbalance of the autonomic nervous system (Garet et al. 2004; Pichot et al. 2000). This section discusses interventions likely to improve recovery processes.

## Reduce Muscular Fatigue

Many studies examining the efficacy of recovery modalities have focused on exercise-induced muscle damage, usually associated with DOMS, a sensation of pain or discomfort occurring 1 or 2 days postexercise. Although the underlying mechanism is not well understood, full recovery of strength and power after a training session that causes DOMS may take several days (Cheung, Hume, and Maxwell 2003). Therefore, its occurrence may be detrimental to an ongoing training program. Modalities that enhance the rate of recovery from DOMS and exercise-induced muscle damage may enhance the beneficial effects of the taper for triathletes.

### Massage

Massage therapy is a commonly used recovery treatment after eccentric exercise that resulted in DOMS. Weber, Servedio, and Woodall (1994) investigated the effects of massage, aerobic exercise, microcurrent stimulation, and passive recovery on force deficits after eccentric exercise. None of the treatment modalities had any significant effects on soreness, maximal isometric contraction, and peak torque production. Hilbert, Sforzo, and Swensen (2003) reported no effect of massage administered 2 hours after a bout of eccentric exercise on peak torque produced by the hamstring muscle; however, muscle soreness ratings were decreased 48 hours postexercise. Farr et al. (2002) also reported no effect of 30 minutes of leg massage on muscle strength in healthy males, although soreness and tenderness ratings were lower 48 hours postexercise. However, a significant improvement in vertical jump performance was reported after high-intensity exercise in female college athletes (Mancinelli et al. 2006).

Although the outcome measures of a wide range of massage techniques have been studied, very few investigations have examined the effect of massage on sport performance. However, some evidence suggests that massage after eccentric exercise may reduce muscle soreness (Weerapong, Hume, and Kolt 2005). Moraska (2007) showed that the training level of the therapist influences the effectiveness of massage after a 10-kilometer (6 mile) race. Many studies investigating massage and its relevance to recovery examined the mechanisms of massage, and thus there is slightly more research in this area compared with performance. Interestingly, recent research (Jakeman, Byrne, and Eston 2010) reported that a combined treatment of 30 minutes of manual massage and 12 hours of lower limb compression (i.e., wearing compressive clothing) significantly moderated perceived soreness at 48 and 72 hours after plyometric exercise in comparison with passive recovery or compression alone.

### Compression Garments

Clothing with specific compressive qualities is becoming increasingly popular, especially as competition approaches, and studies have shown improved performance and recovery after exercise-induced damage (Ali, Caine, and Snow 2007; Kraemer et al. 2001; Trenell et al. 2006). The use of lower limb compression for athletes derives from research in clinical settings showing positive effects of compression after trauma or some chronic diseases. Bringard et al. (2006) observed positive effects of calf compression on calf muscle oxygenation and venous pooling in resting positions, while Hirai, Iwata, and Hayakawa (2002) reported reduced foot edema in patients with varicose veins. These effects can be attributed to the alteration in hemodynamics resulting from the application of compression (Ibegbuna et al. 2003). Studies investigating whether these effects are transferable to athletic populations found some encouraging results (Ali, Caine, and Snow 2007; Bringard, Perrey, and Belluye 2006), but other research did not (French et al. 2008; Trenell et al. 2006). The positive effect reported by some studies may be associated with the ability of compression to moderate the formation of edema and accelerate muscle recovery.

Compression has also been suggested to offer mechanical support to the muscle, allowing faster recovery after damaging exercise (Kraemer et al. 2001). Kraemer et al. speculated that a dynamic casting effect caused by compression may promote stable alignment of muscle fibers and attenuate the inflammatory response. This would, therefore, reduce both the magnitude of muscle damage and recovery time after injury. Although further research is required to test these hypotheses, triathletes could be encouraged to use lower limb compression during the taper, notably when engaged in long-haul travel.

## Rebound of the Autonomic Nervous System

Triathletes usually endure very severe training loads that induce both adaptive effects and stress reactions. The high frequency of the stimuli imposed ensures that these adaptive effects are cumulative. Unfortunately, incomplete recovery from frequent training can make the stress-related side effects cumulative as well. One key aspect of the stress response is decreased activity of the autonomic nervous system (ANS), which regulates the basic visceral (organ) processes needed for the maintenance of normal bodily functions. Garet et al. (2004) reported that the reduction of ANS activity during intensive training was correlated with the loss in performance of seven well-trained swimmers, and the rebound in ANS activity during tapering paralleled the gain in performance. In this perspective, one of the main goals of recovery during the taper would be to increase the magnitude of ANS reactivation (Garet et al. 2004).

Several recovery methods enhance autonomic tone, including nutrition strategies (promoting fruits and vegetables with a low glycemic index), massage (Weerapong, Hume, and Kolt 2005), and cold-water immersion of the whole body or face (Al Haddad et al. 2010; Buchheit et al. 2009). Nevertheless, the most important factor determining ANS reactivation seems to be sleep duration and quality. Maximizing sleep in a dark, calm, relaxing, and fresh atmosphere is essential during the week preceding the race for optimal performance (Halson 2008). A warm shower may help initiate sleep. Naps may also be planned by the triathlete at the beginning of the afternoon but should not last more than 30 minutes to prevent a lethargic state during the remainder of the day (Reilly et al. 2006).

The main aim of the taper is to reduce the negative physiological and psychological impact of daily training (i.e., accumulated fatigue), although further improvements in the positive consequences of training (i.e., fitness gains) can also be achieved. In this perspective, particular attention should be given during the taper to recovery strategies, which may help induce parasympathetic reactivation (sleep, hydrotherapy, massage) and reduce muscle fatigue (massage, compression garments).

# Managing Nutrition and Hydration During the Taper

For triathletes, maintaining a good nutrition and hydration status remains critical for successful participation in competition. Starting a race with a poor hydration status or low glycogen stores directly endangers the performance level of athletes engaged in long-duration events, such as triathlons. Triathletes need to adopt both nutrition and hydration strategies during the precompetition period to maximize the taper-associated benefits.

## *Ensure Good Hydration Status*

Environmental heat stress can challenge the limits of a triathlete's cardiovascular and temperature regulation systems, body fluid balance, and performance. Evaporative sweating is the principal means of heat loss in warm to hot environments where sweat losses frequently exceed fluid intakes. When dehydration exceeds 3 percent of total body water (2 percent of body mass), then aerobic performance may be consistently impaired independent of and additive to heat stress. Dehydration augments hyperthermia and plasma volume reductions, which combine to accentuate cardiovascular strain and reduce $\dot{V}O_2max$ (Cheuvront et al. 2010). Casa et al. (2010) showed that a small decrement in hydration status (body mass loss of 2.3 percent) at the start of a 12-kilometer (7.5 mile) race impaired physiological function and performance while running in the heat. This finding highlights that adequate hydration during the taper, especially during the 48 hours preceding a triathlon competition, is crucial for ensuring that work capacity is not diminished at the beginning of the race.

Urine color is an inexpensive and reliable indicator of hydration status (Armstrong et al. 1994). Normal urine color is described as light yellow, whereas moderate and severe dehydration are associated with a dark yellow and brownish-green color, respectively. Although urine color tends to underestimate the level of hydration, and it may be misleading if a large amount of fluid is consumed rapidly, it provides a valid means for triathletes to self-assess hydration level, notably during the taper period.

## *Favor Glycogen Resynthesis*

Energy metabolism can be altered during a taper. Reductions in the training load in favor of rest and recovery lower a triathlete's daily energy expenditure, potentially affecting energy balance and body composition. Triathletes should therefore pay special attention to their energy intake during the taper to avoid energy imbalance and undesirable changes in body composition. To the best of our knowledge, no scientific reports are available on the nutrition pattern of triathletes undergoing a taper characterized by light daily training loads. Some studies indicate that training-load alterations are not necessarily accompanied by matched changes in dietary habits, and this has a direct impact on athletes' body composition (Almeras et al. 1997; Mujika, Chaouachi, and Chamari 2010). It is therefore advisable for triathletes to take into account training schedules and loads, which can vary dramatically between peak training and the taper. In this context, triathletes need to be educated to match their energy and macronutrient intakes to their training loads.

Wilson and Wilson (2008) suggest not only matching energy intake to energy expenditure but also doing carbohydrate loading during this precompetition period to optimize muscle glycogen storage. Although adequate muscle glycogen stores may be achieved by 24 to 36 hours of high carbohydrate intake for sprint-distance triathlons (Pitsiladis, Duignan, and Maughan 1996; Sherman et al. 1981), longer carbohydrate loading in preparation for short- to long-distance triathlons is beneficial (Burke, Millet, and Tarnopolsky 2007). In a study examining energy balance of 10 male and 8 female triathletes participating in an Ironman event, Kimber et al. (2002) demonstrated a relatively high rate of energy expenditure in relation to energy intake in both female and male triathletes. Since energy intake was calculated to provide approximately 40 percent of total energy expenditure, endogenous fuel stores were estimated to supply more than half the energy expended during the Ironman. This finding illustrates the importance of consuming a high-carbohydrate diet before long-distance triathlons to maximize endogenous fuel stores.

Nutrition strategies should be implemented in two phases: (1) to match reduced energy expenditure in the first phase of the taper and (2) to induce a supercompensation of the glycogen stores during the second phase of the taper. Walker et al. (2000) reported that cyclists increased their performance during a time-to-fatigue exercise performed at 80 percent $\dot{V}O_2$max in response to a high-carbohydrate diet (approximately 78 percent carbohydrate) compared with a moderate-carbohydrate diet (approximately 48 percent carbohydrate) followed during the last 4 days of the taper. Interestingly, Sherman et al. (1981) showed that no glycogen-depleting period of exercise is needed to induce such supercompensation in well-trained runners undergoing 3 days of high carbohydrate intake during the taper. If a two-phase taper is planned (increase of the training load during the final days before competition), this strategy of matching energy intake to energy expenditure plus carbohydrate loading may be particularly beneficial (Mujika, Chaouachi, and Chamari 2010).

Developing an adequate hydration strategy during the taper is crucial for triathletes to ensure good hydration status at the start of the race. Paying attention to morning urine color, which should be light yellow, is a practical solution for reaching this goal. Carbohydrate-loading strategies are recommended during race preparation to help triathletes cross the finish line matching their potential. For the well-trained competitor, this may be as simple as tapering exercise over the final days and ensuring daily carbohydrate intakes of 10 to 12 grams per kilogram of body mass over the 36 to 48 hours before a race (i.e., if your body mass is 70 kilograms, or 165 pounds, your daily carbohydrate intake should range between 700 and 840 grams). It is not absolutely necessary to undertake a depletion phase before carbohydrate loading.

# Addressing Other Details Related to Tapering

A taper targets the removal or minimization of a triathlete's habitual stressors, permitting physiological systems to replenish their capabilities or even undergo supercompensation. There is very little scientific information regarding the possible interactions of environmental variables on tapering processes in athletes, whether the stressor is heat, cold, or altitude. Experimental work on the additive effects of altitude on climatic stress and travel fatigue or jet lag is lacking (Pyne, Mujika, and Reilly 2009). This gap in knowledge is largely due to the enormous difficulties in addressing these problems adequately in experimental designs, as well as the challenges facing researchers in the field in controlling the many variables involved. Nevertheless, the likely effects of environmental factors must be considered in a systematic way when tapering is prescribed within a triathlete's annual plan.

## Stress of Travel

International travel is an essential part of the lives of elite triathletes both for competition and training. It is also becoming increasingly common among recreational triathletes, particularly those who participate in long-distance events. Long-distance travel is associated with a group of transient negative effects, collectively referred to as travel fatigue, that result from anxiety about the journey, changes in daily routine, and dehydration due to time spent in the dry air of the aircraft cabin. Travel fatigue lasts for only a day or so, but for those who fly across several time zones, there are longer-lasting difficulties associated with jet lag. The problems of jet lag can last for more than a week if the flight crosses 10 time zones or more, and performance can suffer. Knowledge of the properties of the body clock clarifies the cause of the difficulties (an unadjusted body clock) and forms the basis of using light in the new time zone to adjust the body clock (Waterhouse, Reilly, et al. 2007).

The timescale for adjustment of the body clock can be incorporated into the taper when competition requires travel across multiple meridians. It is logical to allow sufficient time for the triathlete to adjust completely to the new time zone before competing (Waterhouse, Reilly, et al. 2007). The period of readjustment might constitute a part of the lowered training volume integral to the taper. Since training in the morning is not advocated after traveling eastward, allowance should be made for the timing of training over the first few days so that a phase delay rather than the desired phase advance is not erroneously promoted (Reilly, Waterhouse, and Edwards 2005). There also seems little point in training hard at home before leaving, since arriving tired at the airport of departure may delay adjustment later (Waterhouse et al. 2003). Similarly, attempting to shift the phase of the body clock in the required direction before departure is counterproductive because performance (and hence training quality) may be disrupted by this strategy (Reilly and Maskell 1989).

Tapering should proceed as planned in the company of jet lag even if the interactions between body clock disturbances and the recovery processes associated with tapering have not been fully delineated. Although quality of sleep is an essential component of recovery, napping at an inappropriate time of day when adjusting to a new time zone may delay resynchronization (Minors and Waterhouse 1981), but in certain circumstances a short nap of about 30 minutes can be restorative (Waterhouse, Atkinson, et al. 2007). Suppression of immune responses is more likely to be linked with sleep disruption than with jet lag per se (Reilly and Waterhouse 2007). Therefore, readjustment of the body clock should be harmonized with the moderations of training during the taper. Triathletes, coaches, and support staff should implement strategies to minimize the effects of travel stress before departure, during long-haul international travel, and upon arrival at the destination.

## Heat Acclimatization

Most triathlon competitions take place during summer and in warm environmental conditions, and exercising in the heat can lead to serious performance decrements. Because heat acclimatization seems to be the most effective strategy to limit the deleterious effects of heat on performance, triathletes need to take this into account to optimize the benefits of the taper. Tapering in hot conditions before competition is compatible with the 7 to 14 days' reduction in training volume advocated when encountering heat stress. The increased glycogen utilization associated with exercise in the heat should be compensated for by the reduced training load—both intensity and duration (Armstrong 2006). Athletes should be acclimatized to the heat, otherwise performance in the forthcoming competition might be compromised.

Regular exposure to hot environments results in a number of physiological adaptations that reduce the negative effects associated with exercise in the heat. These adaptations include decreased core body temperature at rest, decreased heart rate during exercise, increased sweat rate and sweat sensitivity, decreased sodium losses in sweat and urine, and expanded plasma volume (Armstrong and Maresh 1991). The effect of acclimatization on plasma volume is extremely important in terms of cardiovascular stability as it allows for a greater stroke volume and a lowering of the heart rate (Pandolf 1998).

The process of acclimatization to exercise in the heat begins within a few days, and full adaptation takes 1 to 2 weeks for most people (Wendt, van Loon, and Lichtenbelt 2007). It is clear that the systems of the human body adapt at varying rates to successive days of heat exposure. The early adaptations during heat acclimatization primarily include improved control of cardiovascular function through an expansion of plasma volume and a reduction in heart rate. An increase in sweat rate and cutaneous vasodilation is seen during the later stages of heat acclimatization (Armstrong and Maresh 1991). Triathletes exhibit many of the characteristics of heat-acclimatized people and are therefore thought to be partially adapted; however, full adaptation is not seen until at least a week is spent training in the heat (Pandolf 1998). It is not necessary to train every day in the heat; exercising in the heat every 3rd day for 30 days results in the same degree of acclimatization as exercising every day for 10 days (Fein, Haymes, and Buskirk 1975).

Because maintenance of an elevated core body temperature and stimulation of sweating appear to be the critical stimuli for optimal heat acclimatization, strenuous interval training or continuous exercise should be performed at an intensity exceeding 50 percent of the maximal oxygen uptake (Armstrong and Maresh 1991). There is evidence that exercise bouts of about 100 minutes are most effective for the induction of heat acclimatization, and there is no advantage in spending longer periods exercising in the heat (Lind and Bass 1963).

Unfortunately, heat acclimatization is a transient process and will gradually disappear if not maintained by repeated exercise in the heat. It appears that the first physiological adaptations to occur during heat acclimatization are also the first to be lost (Armstrong and Maresh 1991). There is considerable variability concerning the rate of decay of heat acclimatization; some researchers report significant losses of heat acclimatization in less than a week, whereas others show that acclimatization responses are fairly well maintained for up to a month. In general, most studies show that dry-heat acclimatization is better retained than humid-heat acclimatization and that high levels of aerobic fitness are also associated with a greater retention of heat acclimatization (Pandolf 1998).

## *Altitude*

At altitude, $\dot{V}O_2$max is reduced according to the prevailing ambient pressure. An immediate consequence is that the exercise intensity or power output at a given relative aerobic load is decreased. In the first few days at altitude, a respiratory alkalosis (increased respiration which elevates the blood pH) occurs because of the increased ventilatory response to hypoxic (lack of oxygen) conditions. This condition is normally self-limiting due to a gradual renal compensation, meaning the kidneys can regulate the blood pH. Athletes in training camps at altitude resorts recognize that an initial reduction in training load is imperative at altitude as acclimatization begins. The extra hydration requirements due to the dry ambient air and the initial increased urination, combined with plasma volume changes (Rusko, Tikkanen, and Peltonen 2004), increased utilization of carbohydrate as a substrate for exercise (Butterfield et al. 1992), and tendency for sleep apnea (Pedlar et al. 2005), run counter to the benefits of tapering. In this instance, the reduced training load would not substitute for a taper. There is the added risk of illness because of decreased immunoreactivity associated with exposure to altitude (Rusko, Tikkanen, and Peltonen 2004). Maximal cardiac output may also be reduced in the course of a typical 14- to 21-day sojourn at altitude as a result of the impairment in training quality. Altitude training camps should therefore be lodged strategically in the annual plan to avoid unwanted, if unknown, interactions with environmental variables.

Many elite-level athletes use altitude training for conditioning purposes. For example, it is accepted as good practice among elite swimmers and rowing squads preparing for Olympic competition despite an absence of compelling evidence of its effectiveness. There remains a question as to the timing of the return to sea level for best effects, an issue relatively neglected by researchers in the field, with a few exceptions (Ingjer and Myhre 1992). Three phases have been observed by coaches (Millet et al. 2010). So far, however, these are not fully supported by scientific evidence and are therefore under debate:

1. A positive phase observed *during the first 2 to 4 days*, but not in all athletes.
2. A phase of progressive reestablishment of sea-level training volume and intensity, *2 to 4 days after the return to sea level*. The probability of good performance is reduced. This decrease in performance fitness might be related to the altered energy cost and loss of the neuromuscular adaptations induced by training at altitude.

**3.** A third phase, *15 to 21 days after return to sea level*, is characterized by a plateau in fitness. It is optimal to delay competition until this third phase, although some triathletes may reach their peak performance during the first phase. Improvement in energy cost and loss of the neuromuscular adaptations after several days at sea level, in conjunction with the further increase in oxygen transport and delayed ventilatatory benefits of altitude training, may explain this third phase.

In this context, a period of lowered training is observed before competing after altitude training, which constitutes a form of tapering. The extent of the benefits, as well as the variation between athletes, has not been adequately explored. Future investigations are required.

## Multiple Peaking

Most experimental and observation research on tapering has been conducted in the context of singular sports events (Pyne, Mujika, and Reilly 2009). Triathletes competing in sprint- and short-distance competitions, however, sometimes have reduced opportunities to taper because of the repetition of the races during the competitive period (e.g., seven World Championship Series races between the end of March and the beginning of September in 2010). Peaking for major competitions each month (even every other week) usually poses the problem of choosing between recovering from the previous competition and rebuilding fitness or maintaining intensive training and capitalizing on adaptations acquired during the previous training cycle. Both approaches can be valid, and the choice should depend on the level of fatigue triathletes present after a race (or a series of competitions) and the time frame between the last triathlon and the next one. Additional research is required to examine the taper in the context of multiple peaking. Nevertheless, some guidelines could be addressed.

- Optimized taper periods associated with a large training volume reduction (approximately 50 percent) over a prolonged period (approximately 2 weeks) should be scheduled two or three times per year. Additional taper periods may be detrimental for performance improvement by minimizing the total time of the normal heavy training load, which is essential to induce training adaptations.

- Prioritizing a limited number of races each season (e.g., two or three major events) seems to be a good solution for planning the taper periods in the competitive season. Altitude camps may be adequately programmed before these competitions.

- A sufficient training block lasting at least 2 months should be planned between two major objectives to allow for appropriate recovery, training, and taper phases.

- Only short-duration tapers (4 to 7 days) should be programmed before minor events, paying special attention to recovery (nutrition, hydration, sleep, massage, hydrotherapy, compression garments). Because of the likely persistence of training-induced fatigue despite such short tapers, triathletes should be aware that this strategy may sometimes lead to below-optimal performances.

- Because the recovery period after minor competitions (associated with nonoptimal taper) should be as short as possible to allow a quick restoration of the training load, long-haul travel should be avoided.

The taper is a key element of a triathlete's physical preparation in the weeks before a competition. Since the early 1990s, there has been substantial research interest in the taper and its importance in transitioning athletes from the preparatory to competitive phase of the season. Physiological and performance adaptations can be optimized during periods of taper preceding triathlon competitions by means of significant reduction in training volume, moderate reduction in training frequency, and maintenance of training intensity. Particular attention given to nutrition, hydration, and recovery strategies during the preevent taper may help maximize its associated positive effects. In this context, tapering strategies may be associated with a competition performance improvement of about 3 percent (usual range is .5 to 6.0 percent).

Future progress in sport science will play an important part in refining existing and developing tapering methodologies. These developments should involve a combination of research and practical experience of coaches and triathletes, experimental and observational research, and elegant mathematical models to refine our understanding of the physiological and performance elements of the taper.

# PART II

# Technique

# CHAPTER 11

# Bike-Handling Techniques From the Pros

### Kurt Perham

Ask most triathletes about their bike training, and you will hear about long rides or intervals. Sometimes, they'll tell you about the occasional group session or brick. Now, if you ask them how many times they practice their bike *driving* skills, it would be rare to find that many do. To this point, triathletes have a bad reputation for their inability to corner, handle the bike in tight confines, and hold their lines.

For many athletes, it can be hard to stress the importance of *why* they should practice the act of driving the bike. Their mentality is that if it doesn't hurt or feel like work, then the gains will be minimal. This is not true! Moving a bicycle around a set course requires both physiology and physics. Most athletes understand the physiology, the work we produce with our human engines. They know terms such as *watts*, *heart rate*, and *cadence*.

Physics comes into the equation in the form of drag. There are four types of drag that slow down a bicycle and rider: mechanical resistance, rolling resistance, gravity, and aerodynamic drag. Mechanical resistance comes from drivetrain friction (gears, chain, bearings, and so on). Next up is rolling resistance, in the form of energy needed to make your round, highly inflated tire "contour" to the road and then return to a round shape; this is expressed as Crr. Gravity comes into play as the combined rider and bicycle weight is "lifted" up hills using watts (physiology). Finally, aerodynamic drag is wind resistance against the rider and bicycle; this is expressed as CdA.

Now you might ask, "What do these four forms of drag have to do with me driving my bicycle?" The answer lies mostly in that final component of drag, wind resistance. If you are proficient driving the bicycle in a fairly aerodynamic position that is still comfortable enough for you to corner well, avoid other riders or road hazards, and use your momentum in different terrain, it will yield a faster overall bike split. This is the ultimate goal.

This chapter covers aspects of bike fitting and mounting as well as cycling skills for the road and for race day that you can incorporate into your annual training. These skills will allow you to drive your bike faster, not just push harder on the pedals.

# Bike Fitting and Mounting

Bike fit is key in that the athlete is the engine in the equation, and small changes in the mechanics of the human movements can affect power output, comfort, and risk of injury. The first step in a great bike fit is to find a reputable shop that sells triathlon-specific bicycles. Look for accreditations from Serotta or F.I.S.T. as a starting point. Speak with the salesperson, and explain your race plans and what your primary riding will be. Explain your past cycling experience and any limiters you might have (e.g., injury, lack of flexibility).

A good triathlon bike fit has elements of comfort, aerodynamics, and power output, without any of these diluting the other. Each is a key variable. You should not be too stretched out or overly compressed. You should be able to rest on the aero extensions, with most of your torso supported by your skeletal structure. Your hands should rest at the end of the extensions, just where the shifters start. If you have to make a drastic movement to shift, then the extensions are too long or the reach to the aero pads is incorrect. Seat height should fall so your leg is extended approximately 145 to 155 degrees at the bottom of the pedal stroke. When a plumb line is dropped from the bony protrusion just below the knee, it should intersect just in front of the pedal spindle. These are just a few baseline fit coordinates; it is not in the scope of this chapter to fully address all the possible fit scenarios that might arise. Seek out a reputable bike fitter or professional bike shop in your area, and you will be on your way to a great bike position.

Once you have a properly fitting bike, you need to know how to get on and off of it quickly, also known as a "flying" mount and dismount or cyclo-cross mount and dismount. Let's start with getting off the bike, the dismount. For most athletes, this is easier to master, so it is the first thing to practice. The goal is to safely get off the bike while losing as little momentum as possible as you near the dismount line at transition number two (T2).

> *Perfect the flying-mount early in your pro career. The five seconds you lose could be the difference between making the pack and riding solo!*
>
> —*Sara McLarty*

Knowing where the dismount line is important (this is part of your warm-up protocol, I hope!). Approximately 500 yards or meters from the line, you will want to start getting your feet out of your cycling shoes. Reach down and unstrap the right shoe, and place your foot on top of the shoe. Then pedal two or three revolutions, bringing the left pedal to the top of the stroke. Unstrap the left shoe and remove your foot; rest it on top of the shoe. Continue to pedal with your feet on top of your shoes until approximately 30 to 50 yards or meters before the line. At this point you will coast and bring the left pedal to the 6 o'clock position and be standing on this foot. Now swing your right leg around behind the seat, placing it just behind the left leg (which you are now weighting). When you are 10 feet (3 m) from the line, feather the brakes and hop off, landing on your right foot and moving straight into a run. Jog the bike to your transition rack by the seat, and you're ready to make the change to running shoes for the final leg of the race.

> *To enter T2 at the front of the group, unstrap your shoes and take your feet out early. Be comfortable riding with your feet on top and be aggressive the last half mile to get back to the front while everyone else is unstrapping.*
>
> —Sara McLarty

For most athletes, the dismount is less daunting than the mount. But you have to get on the bike, so let's break it down and get comfortable with it. First, you need to decide on a critical component. Do you leave your shoes clipped into the pedals, or do you slip them on in T1 and run in them to the mount line? This is a tough question and one I struggle with annually in my own racing. In most cases, if the run to the mount line is not far, I have found putting shoes on and running to the mount line yields the fastest overall T1 and initial bike speed. The reason is once you are comfortable with the fast (flying) mount, if your shoes are already on, you can clip in and accelerate away quickly. If the number of athletes leaving T1 is high and you are fumbling around trying to get your shoes on (and worst-case scenario, you fall over), then it is a net loss . . . and the goal is for a fast triathlon time, not just a fast T1 time. If you choose to have your shoes on the bike, make sure you are comfortable running to the mount line, then pedaling with your feet on top of your shoes until you are up to speed, and then getting into the shoes and strapping them. For athletes racing ITU draft-legal events, the shoes on the pedals and getting into them on the fly is always the best decision. This is covered in more detail in chapter 17.

Back to the actual mount. Hopefully in your prerace warm-up, you scouted out the mount line and surrounding area, letting you select the optimal gear to get up to speed straightaway and making you aware of any debris or road hazards to avoid. As you leave T1, you will be pushing your bike by the saddle or stem and guiding it to the line. As you pass the line, you want to grab both sides of the base bar and swing your legs around behind the saddle and rear wheel in a single, fluid movement. You are not so much jumping as you are "flicking" your legs around the bike. Imagine your legs in a slight V pattern while executing this. Now, here comes the landing. This is where folks have concern. You don't actually land directly on your normal "sit area" but more on the very inside of your right thigh (assuming you are running with the bike on your right side). Left-handed folks would land on the opposite side. Then you make a very slight adjustment of your hips and slide into your normal sit position on the bike. At this point the right foot is starting to clip into the right (forward) pedal; you then pedal half a revolution and clip into the left pedal. You are now ready to accelerate away.

## Skills for the Road

Once you are comfortable getting on and off the bike, you must be able to ride in a straight line at any speed while moving through the basic operations of driving. You will also need to carry your momentum around corners in a quick and safe way, no matter the conditions. One of the best ways to practice this is to do some low-speed drills in a safe environment. Your local park or an empty industrial area works great for this. For some of these drills, you will want to recruit a training partner.

> *Staying in the drops during corners lowers your center of gravity and increases your chances of staying upright. Also, I find that the best way to avoid crashes in a pack is not to look at the rider just ahead of you but several riders ahead so you can anticipate problems before they reach you.*
>
> *—Joe Umphenour*

## Riding in a Straight Line

Riding in a straight line sounds like a simple thing to do, but for a newer cyclist it can be quite challenging. It all starts with a comfortable and appropriate position on the bicycle; without this, you will have a hard time relaxing and allowing the bike to track straight. Straight-line stability drills are best done in a striped parking lot or industrial park on a weekend. Find a straight painted line, and ride along it at varying speeds. The goal is to stay on the paint as long as you can. Mix it up by doing this drill while pedaling and coasting. Practice turning off of the line and then coming back onto it and quickly regaining your stability. Pick a few landmarks in the distance, and focus on them instead of staring down at the painted line. Repeat 5 to 10 times or until you feel comfortable doing this at various speeds.

> *To practice riding in a straight line, try following the white line on the road. Also, work on single-leg drills to smooth out your pedal stroke and limit the motion of the upper body.*
>
> *—Sarah Haskins*

### Look Back

This drill can be done on grass or in an empty parking lot. The act of looking back for another cyclist can often cause you to swerve in the direction you look. To practice this, find some short grass with a line of trees to use as a guide or an empty parking lot with some painted lines. While pedaling with your hands on the base bars, rotate your head around, acting as if you are looking behind you for a riding partner or to check if the road is clear. Continue to pedal, and try to relax your upper body so that input from the movement of your head does not cause the bike to swerve. Perform this for only 1 or 2 seconds, and then return to your normal line of sight. Continue to pedal easily throughout this skill development. The goal is to stay on your initial trajectory throughout the drill. Practice rotating to both sides.

### Elbow Bump

To perform this drill, you will need a riding partner. Although most nondraft triathlons are individual events, there are times when you are in close quarters with other athletes, and incidental contact does happen. It is important to know what this feels like and that you can still control your bicycle when it happens. Start by riding in a straight line, on grass as close to your partner as you can; you'll be making light contact with your partner during the drill. With your hands on the base bar to prevent your handlebars from hooking, stick your elbows out and ride 80 to 160 feet (25 to 50 m) while knocking elbows. You can use your elbows as bumpers, letting them absorb the brunt of the impact. After a set distance, swing off and ride away.

## Shoulder Bump

This drill is a progression of the elbow bump. You want to get even closer to your partner and bump shoulders as you ride along. Again, relax your hands on the base bar, and continue to pedal throughout the drill. Do four to six light bumps on each side, and then pedal away.

## *Maneuvering Aid Stations*

One of the more dangerous places to be on a bike in any triathlon is the aid station. There tends to be a large number of crashes in these areas at most major events. The cause has to do with many riders changing speed suddenly as they try to retrieve bottles or other nutrition needs from the aid station workers. If you ever watch pro cyclists, you'll notice they speed through the feed zones without slowing, even while surrounded by 150-plus other cyclists. A lot of this has to do with their ability to reach out and grab their feed bags (musettes) or extra bottles, all while driving in a straight line with one hand on the bars.

*If you find yourself falling, keep your hands on the handlebars. Try avoid putting your hands and arms out to catch yourself because this can more easily lead to broken bones. Practice falling and rolling on grass so that it becomes second nature.*

*—Joe Umphenour*

## Object Pickup

One of the best ways to get comfortable with reaching out while driving is to do an object pickup drill. This is a great drill for new cyclists because it is very easy to add a progression by changing the size of the object or where it is placed. Again, the park is a great place to practice this, but you will not need a partner. For the first run-through, start by putting a water bottle on a park bench. Ride toward the bench at a slow but steady pace, and as you approach the bench, remove your hand from the base bar and grab the bottle as you pedal by. Practice on both sides.

To add difficulty, simply put the bottle in a different location, maybe someplace higher, or even on the ground. The goal is to not make a sharp swerve with the bike as you are grabbing the bottle, then to resume pedaling and get up to speed as seamlessly as possible.

*In a training session, practice picking up a bottle from the ground or from a helpful training friend as you are riding by. This will help you become comfortable once you are in the race situation.*

*—Sarah Haskins*

## *Cornering on the Bike*

You also need to think about actually driving the bike and some of the more dynamic movements you have to make while racing around a course. One of the areas where athletes lose speed is in corners. These athletes lack the knowledge and the confidence to navigate a corner while slowing only slightly and letting their momentum carry them through safely and back up to racing speeds.

There are a few methods of steering a bicycle at race speed. The most common are the lean and the steer. Many variables affect which method you use including road conditions, turn location, entrance speed, and number of other athletes near you as you approach the corner. I will touch on each and how you might practice them.

> *Remember to shift your bike while keeping a higher cadence in order to prevent dropping your chain. Also, be one or two steps ahead on the bike course, and shift your bike into the appropriate gear before you head into a corner. You don't want to stand out of a corner either spinning without pressure on the pedals or mashing the gears.*
>
> *—Sarah Haskins*

### Lean

The lean is the version most cyclists know and use in higher-speed conditions. This involves leaning the bicycle into the corner as needed, based on the radius of the curve and the speed at which you enter the corner. You will be leaning, but at a slightly lesser angle than the bicycle. For many athletes in mass-start triathlons or other multisport events, the safest method is to pedal normally until you are approximately 70 to 100 yards or meters from the apex of the corner (the center point of the radius, usually). At this point, you will decide if you need to coast or brake before entering the corner. If you need to apply the brakes, do so gradually, and remember your front brake provides most of the power to slow the bicycle. More advanced athletes will remain on the aero extensions (if a nondrafting event), while beginner athletes might sit up and drive from the base bar.

Just as you enter the corner, pedal half a revolution so your outside foot is at the 6 o'clock position, and apply pressure with it toward the ground. This "pushes" the tires down and helps settle the bike. Keep your body equally balanced between the front and back tires. Lean your bike and then your body in sync as needed, and continue to push on that outside foot. Now let the bike roll. (When you brake hard in the corner, you tend to *throw* the mass of your body forward, and this unsettles the bike and can cause the wheels to come off your chosen line.) As soon as you are clear of the corner, start to straighten the bike, and you can pedal away safely, hopefully without losing too much momentum.

### Steer

Once you have mastered the lean and feel comfortable doing it, you need to work on the next progression: the steer. If you have practiced the lean, you will notice a few things. First, you don't actually turn the handlebars much (or thus the front wheel), and second, you are really moving through the corner on a small contact patch of the tire on the outside edge of the tread. This tends to be the preferred method for higher speeds or dry conditions.

When the situation calls for it, you will need to steer the bicycle through the corner. This varies slightly from the method used for the lean. You will set up much the same, but the major difference is that the speed will be lower (think 180-degree turnaround or rain-soaked corner). So, you will start to brake earlier and most definitely will be driving from the base bar (or hoods for a road bike). The outside pedal is still weighted. Now, as you approach the apex of the corner, you will turn the front wheel as needed based on approach speed and radius of the corner. Here is where it gets a little tricky! You will still lean through the corner, but mainly your body is leaning into the apex and the bike is staying more upright. This is not an extreme body lean—think more of "leading" the bicycle a bit. The goal is to keep the bike more upright and thus keep a larger contact patch of the tire on the road. Once you have rounded the corner, you straighten the body and bring the front wheel back in line and pedal away.

*A good skill to practice at low speed in the grass with a few friends is bumping each other from the sides or brushing their rear wheels with your front wheel. This will help you become accustomed to contact between riders so you react calmly to it when it happens in a race.*

—*Joe Umphenour*

## Shifting

One of the most frequent questions asked by new athletes is "When do I shift?" This is a tough question to answer. There isn't really a right or wrong time, just the optimal time. A modern racing bicycle has between 18 and 30 available gears and the mechanisms to shift through those gears at the flip of a lever or the push of a button.

The terrain and a rider's output (watts) will dictate when the shift should happen. It's best not to overthink the simple act of shifting, but you should be aware of a few things *not* to do. First, avoid the cross chain; this is the gearing when the chain is on the biggest (outside) chain ring in the front and the biggest (inside) cog in the rear. A modern bicycle will operate just fine in this gear combination, but it adds undue stress to the drivetrain, and especially the chain itself, increasing wear. The simplest solution is to shift down to the inner chain ring in the front and then shift down two or three cogs in the rear and find a suitable gear ratio with a much better chain line.

The next scenario that is best to avoid is a drastic shift in multiple gears while pedaling under heavy load. Usually when you see an athlete drop a chain off of the front chain ring, it is when he has tried to make a quick multiple-gear change under load; the derailleur tension cannot compensate for the rapid change in chain position, and the chain can drop off the chain ring, falling into the bottom bracket area or toward the outside of the big chain ring. This comes down to the issue of course knowledge, as this situation usually arises when you are caught off guard by a steep climb or sharp curve. It is not always convenient to arrive early or the day before an event, so you have to use your best judgment when navigating the course if the terrain is new to you. The safer option is to be in too easy a gear and keep your cadence a few rpm above your self-selected range, as it is always easier to drop to a harder gear than it is to try to force the chain up the cassette to a very easy gear.

The question also comes up regarding the correct rpm, or cadence, to maintain. Cadence is a very individual metric. Some athletes "mash" the big gears, and others are "spinners" who ride at a very high cadence. In many instances, these athletes get around the course quickly *and* are still able to run well off the bike. Experience has shown that the sweet spot in cadence likely falls from the high 70s to the low 100s, with most folks falling very near 90 rpm. For more info on the optimal cadence, see chapter 12.

*While racing in triathlon, I mentally check my cadence every 5 miles [8 km] on the bike. It is important to keep a higher cadence while on the bike to lessen muscular fatigue before heading out onto the run course. If you slow your cadence down too much, it can greatly affect your run performance.*

*—Sarah Haskins*

## Braking

Most of this chapter is spent covering topics to make you go *faster* on the bicycle. But the truth is, sometimes proper braking will yield overall faster bike splits. It's important for an athlete to understand when to brake (such as before a tight turn) and then accelerate out of the turn. It is also important for the athlete to know how to brake downhill, feather the front brake, and apply consistent pressure on the back brake with your weight shifted back. Remember, momentum on a bicycle is hard to get but easy to keep, so if a rider is smart with her application of brakes at strategic times, she will lose less overall speed and maybe avoid a worst-case scenario—a crash.

Earlier in the chapter, potentially hazardous aid stations were mentioned to emphasize the importance of proper bike handling. Here is a possible scenario. Picture this: You are 30 miles (48 km) into your Iron-distance bike leg, and you slow to retrieve a bottle of sports drink from the aid station. Just then the athlete in front of you slams on his brakes, and you run straight into him, sending you careening. Your day could be over. Don't let this happen to you! When approaching aid stations, come off of your aero extensions and ride on the base bar, covering your brakes with a single finger on the lever. Look for a volunteer down the line a bit, and make your way toward her while feathering the brakes. Note: Most aid stations are set up on the right side of the road, and you will be reaching with that hand for the bottle (or other nutrition), thus you are covering the front brake. Continue to look for other athletes, and drag that front brake a bit to scrub speed; grab the bottle on the fly, and ease yourself back into the course properly. If stowing the bottle in a rear mount behind the seat carrier, take caution in doing so, and try to get clear of the aid station and back up to speed. Most important, pay attention and be prepared to take evasive action if needed.

*There are two important things to remember when participating in a rotating pace line. First, as you drop to the back after a pull at the front, stay close to the side of the riders behind you. This allows them to continue drafting off you as they move forward. And, second, do not dramatically accelerate your speed when you move to the front. This will cause gaps in the group and slow the overall pace.*

*—Sara McLarty*

> ## ▶ Special Considerations for Draft-Legal Racing
>
> When triathlon was added to the 2000 Sydney Olympic Games, a new version of the sport was also introduced: draft-legal triathlon. For draft-legal races, the swim and run remained the same as for other Olympic-distance races (1,500 meters and 10K, respectively). The bicycle leg was changed to allow riders to stay together in packs, with riders shielded behind lead riders, similar to stand-alone bicycle racing. This changed the whole dynamic of international-level racing. In these events, the athletes ride a road-racing bicycle (often with small aero extensions), and they are allowed to draft off one another. This type of racing adds a dimension of speed and danger, as large "draft packs" can be riding in close quarters at nearly 30 miles per hour (48 km/h). Bike-driving skills are at a premium for sure!
>
> An ITU (International Triathlon Union) athlete will need to be well versed in all the skills. Being able to handle your bike is even more important in such tight confines because one bad decision can take down dozens of riders. For athletes looking to step up to an ITU draft-legal event, the best thing to do is search out some local experienced ITU athletes or road-cycling racers. They will be quick to teach you the basics of pack riding, thus speeding the learning curve. Let's cover some of the basic concepts of draft-legal cycling.
>
> Drafting is an art, and a good cyclist can save 40-plus percent in energy by sitting on the wheel of the cyclist in front of her. The key is to be only inches behind the front athlete's rear wheel, all the while trusting her to navigate around any road hazards such as potholes, traffic barriers, and islands. When a number of athletes are executing this well, it is called a pace line—and it is a thing of beauty. This skill gets tricky when an athlete (or group of athletes) is faced with strong winds. These winds will invariability lead to a crosswind situation, and you will need to know how to echelon. In an echelon, a group of athletes staggers across the road, thus slightly shielding each subsequent athlete from the full force of the wind. When this happens, there tends to be an unspoken rule about each athlete taking his "pull." When the front rider has ridden at the front for anywhere from 5 to 120 seconds, he will swing off by continuing to pedal and easing to one side of the road, dropping down the shielded side of the staggers and moving into the last position on the group. This can be a critical situation in a race. If a group of riders is aware that the wind has changed, they can create an echelon quickly and create a separation in the group that could affect the outcome of the race in a matter of minutes.
>
> Athletes racing in ITU events will need to reinforce these skills before taking the course for their first events.

I have discussed many criteria that outline some basic skills of good bike drivers, many of which were drill and repetition based. As I wrap up this section, I will cover a few fun and less structured ways to work on improving your ability to drive a bicycle throughout your multisport career.

*The worst place to be in a large cycling pack is at the back. Stay in the front third of the group to avoid most crashes, minimize being gapped around corners, and to counter any break-away attempts.*

*—Sara McLarty*

Cyclo-cross! This is one of my favorite ways for triathletes to improve their bike skills. Cross, as it is sometimes called, is an event raced in the fall and winter on a closed circuit of approximately 2 miles (3 km) with a mix of grass, fields, pavement, and barriers. The cyclo-cross bicycle looks similar to a road-racing machine with the exception of a wider cantilever-style brake setup and different tires with a knobby profile. Throughout most courses, small wood barriers that are approximately 16 inches (40 cm) tall are used to force the athlete to dismount and run for sections of the track. Cross is raced in all conditions, including mud, rain, snow, and ice. This puts a premium on bike handling and control in slick and unpredictable conditions.

Group rides are another great way to speed the learning curve a bit. Once you are comfortable riding in close confines, seek out a welcoming local group ride and join up. The beauty of a good group ride is that most feature a mix of abilities and fitness levels. Ask around to find out who the more seasoned riders are. Ask lots of questions regarding road etiquette and how the dynamics of the group work. You will usually get some great info from the veterans, and your comfort level riding in tight confines will improve quickly.

Last, check into borrowing or renting a mountain bike. On a single mountain bike ride on your local trail network, you can address several bike-handling skills. Mounting and dismounting, choosing a good line and sticking to it, staying loose and agile on the bike, leaning, and steering form the basis of a good mountain biker. You might even like it and search out an Xterra mountain bike triathlon for your next event.

So next time you plan your training season, make sure to add a focus period of bike skills and drills, all while focusing on *driving* the bike faster, not just doing the work to make yourself more fit.

# CHAPTER 12

# Setting the Perfect Cadence and Stride Rate

## Jackie Dowdeswell

You probably mostly hear cadence referred to when talking about the bike, and in this context it is revolutions per minute, or rpm (i.e., the number of pedal strokes you make in 1 minute). However, cadence is also relevant to running, where it is also known as stride rate. Similar to the bike, this refers to the number of steps you make in 1 minute.

When measuring cadence, there are gadgets available to keep things simple and easy. Many bike computers have cadence monitors, and bike GPS units may come with the option of an add-on cadence sensor. For the run, you can use a metronome or tempo trainer, which both beep at an interval you set, to help monitor cadence. These gadgets are useful, yes, but they aren't absolutely necessary if you have the ability to count (however, when fatigued this ability might be impaired). For bike or run cadence, you can just time yourself for 15 seconds and simply count your number of pedal strokes or steps. Then, multiply this number by 4 for your number per minute. For both the bike and the run, you will soon get a "feel" for what your cadence is. Having similar bike and run cadences makes transitioning from bike to run easier to do. As it happens, the optimal cadences you should be aiming for on the bike is 80 to 100 rpm and 180 steps per minute for the run. Regardless of how you have ridden the bike leg of your race, use the last mile or so to start spinning with a lower gear and higher cadence, as you learned in the previous chapter.

This chapter covers cadence for both the bike and run—from what the ideals are to how you should train to achieve these ideals and when you should diverge from them. Also covered is how pacing links into maintaining these "perfect" cadences.

> ▶ **Efficiency and Economy:**
> **What Are They, and What's the Difference?**

Throughout this chapter, efficiency is mentioned multiple times relating to both the bike and run because a perfect cadence is efficient. However, the term *economy* is also used, particularly in relation to running. There is some confusion about what these mean, and the terms are often used (incorrectly) interchangeably. Overall, improving efficiency will improve economy, which will allow you to go farther or faster at your given level of fitness.

Economy is the amount of oxygen consumed relative to weight and speed. For example, two bikers may use different amounts of oxygen per kilogram per minute to maintain the same speed. The one who uses the lesser amount is said to be more economical. (Think of a gas-guzzling car versus one that isn't a gas-guzzler.) Ultimately, if you improve your economy of motion (the amount of oxygen you use for a movement), then you will be wasting less energy (oxygen consumption) and will be able to go farther or faster using the same amount of oxygen—both in training and in races.

Efficiency is one of the factors that contribute to economy. Efficiency is usually used as a looser term to describe how your body makes use of its energy mechanically to produce its output (your running or biking speed). Technically it can be measured as a ratio by comparing the amount of energy consumed to produce a given amount of energy (work), but it is not necessary to go into that sort of detail here.

# Bike Cadence

For an endurance sport such as triathlon, regardless of the distance of the race you're training for, you want to be the most efficient on the bike—that is, to make sure you use your available energy in the best way possible to go farther or faster or both given your current level of fitness. Technique is key for improving efficiency on the bike, and cadence is one important element of cycling efficiency. Good technique, including cadence, is also one of the keys to minimizing injury. Knowing what cadence you should aim for and then how to practice and train with it is an important part of bike and triathlon training.

## Setting Your Perfect Cadence

Your cadence is directly related to which gear you select. Selecting a gear that results in your cadence being 80 to 100 rpm is optimal for triathletes. To do this usually necessitates choosing an easy (low) gear to allow high rpm and is often referred to as "spinning."

A cadence of 80 to 100 is the most efficient range for triathletes because it results in less muscle fatigue and less stress on the cardiovascular system compared with pushing a harder gear at a lower rpm. A good analogy for understanding this is to compare it with weightlifting—it is much easier to lift a 1-pound (.5 kg) weight 100 times than it is to lift a 50-pound (25 kg) weight twice.

Pedaling with a cadence less than 70 rpm (known as "mashing") will result in quicker fatigue and more cardiovascular stress, and it also increases the risk of injury, particularly of the knees because cycling with lower cadences places a lot of stress on these joints. This does not mean you should never use lower cadences—every workout has a purpose, and the purpose of some workouts may involve lower gears (see Training Your Bike Cadence on page 162). The 80 to 100 guide is for normal cycling when not doing some other cadence-specific training within a workout.

## Improving Your Bike Efficiency With Cadence

To improve your cadence takes practice. The preparation and early base training phases are great times to work on all aspects of technique, and cadence is an important one of those. However, cadence work and skills can continue throughout your season.

If you are not used to pedaling with a cadence as high as 80 to 100 rpm, then you may find that your effort seems high for the speed you are going. Like any new skill, there is an adaptation period, and so if this is new to you, it is a good reason to start work on it early in your season. It is well worth persevering for the long-term benefits. The more you practice your desired movement, the better your nervous system becomes at producing this movement by activating the correct muscle patterns to produce it, and the easier it will become. There are of course many "pure" cyclists who have a natural, normal cadence in excess of 100 rpm. If you find your natural or comfortable cadence is in excess of 100 rpm, that isn't necessarily a bad thing. However, for triathletes the 80 to 100 rpm range is considered optimal, particularly because they have to run after they get off the bike.

There are various skills and drills you can do to practice increasing and maintaining your bike cadence (some examples you may like to try are included later). For general riding, the following would be a sensible progression:

1. Get comfortable pedaling with a cadence in the range of 80 to 100 rpm on flat terrain or on an indoor trainer.

2. Go out and find constantly changing terrain, and learn to change your gears as often as needed to keep your cadence within the 80 to 100 rpm range, regardless of incline or decline (although see notes on steep hills in the next section). Learn to think ahead so you are anticipating what gears you need to change to in order to maintain this cadence. Another variation is cycling in different weather conditions. Be able to maintain your cadence even when cycling into a strong headwind and while cycling with a tailwind.

3. As you progress through your training and are able to do these first two exercises, then you can start to practice using more of your muscle power to maintain this ideal cadence range rather than constantly changing gears.

## Maintaining Bike Cadence on Hills

Although it is reasonably straightforward to practice and maintain cadence while pedaling along a flat route, the reality is you will usually encounter a variety of hills, big and small, not only in day-to-day training but also in races. Knowing how to ride hills, not just to get to the top of them but to do so in the most efficient, nonfatiguing way, is another important part of bike training for triathlon. Maintaining a cadence in the ideal range can help with this.

## Biking Uphill

For most hills, especially long ones, it is far more efficient to use your gears to shift to lower (easier) gears and maintain your cadence by spinning up the hills within your normal cadence range (hopefully 80 to 100 rpm). There will occasionally be hills that are just far too long or too steep for you to maintain this cadence. You will have to let your cadence drop, but generally aim to get it back within range as soon as you can so as not to overly fatigue your muscles.

Apart from those times on particularly long or steep hills where your cadence decreases by necessity rather than choice, there may be the occasional situation when lower cadence could be used beneficially, albeit for short periods only. An example is on long or steep hills when you feel the need to stand. Standing for a few seconds can break the monotony of a long climb. In a close short-distance race such as a sprint-distance triathlon, standing can also be used for a quick burst of power up a hill or to put space between you and nearby competitors. Generally, though, you should try to remain seated to maintain efficiency and to save your muscles for the run after your bike. Pure cyclists use standing a lot more, but they do not need to run off the bike. Standing requires more power and so necessitates recruitment of more fast-twitch muscle fibers—the ones that fatigue quickly and recover slowly. Although cycle racers may be able to push through to the end of a race, triathletes have to run afterward, so it is important to save these fibers for late in the run when you may need to recruit them as you fatigue. If you do feel the need to stand, then make sure you anticipate this and change gears accordingly (higher gear for standing).

You may find that the most efficient way to climb is to be in the lower part of your comfortable cadence range for climbing, even if you prefer the higher part of this range when spinning on flat terrain. This again takes practice to find what works best for you. Keep your cadence high right up to and over the top of the hill until gravity starts working with you rather than against you. With time and practice, you will learn to feel and anticipate your cadence changing as you climb, so use your gears and effort to maintain it. The key of course to learning these skills and making them automatic is to practice.

As you learn and practice, you may like to use tools such as a bike cadence monitor, a heart rate monitor, a power meter, or perceived exertion (see page 119 in chapter 9 for more information about the rating of perceived exertion, or RPE). For example, if your cadence is dropping as you go up a hill, or even if you are managing to maintain your cadence but your effort is increasing (as shown by heart rate, power, or perceived exertion), or even if your cadence is increasing at a summit, these tools can be effective to remind you when to change gears—both into a lower gear when climbing or into a higher gear when descending. Try not to rely too much on these gadgets, though—as you learn and practice, try to change gears by feel, with the gadgets just as checks.

## Biking Downhill

When going downhill, whether you pedal or not depends on several factors such as the steepness of the hill and how much recovery you need from biking up the hill. If the downhill slope is not that steep, then you may find you can keep pedaling. Similar to uphill, you should aim to keep your cadence in the optimal 80 to 100 rpm range, although hopefully it will feel easier than when you were going uphill. However, you may find that you need to or would prefer to coast for a while to recover from the effort of going uphill. Alternatively, you can choose a very easy gear and "spin" your legs at 80 to 100 rpm at a very easy effort as an active recovery. If you are a more experienced triathlete racing shorter-distance triathlons (such as sprint-distance triathlons), then you could keep your effort high on downhill slopes by changing to higher gears and continuing to push yourself.

For steeper hills, the time to stop pedaling and coast is when you can gain more speed holding a tightly tucked aero position on your bike than you can with pedaling. If you continue pedaling at this point, you're just wasting energy because you would be going that speed without pedaling anyway. You also don't want to get to the point where your legs spin around so fast that you end up "bouncing" in the saddle while pedaling. This is not only a waste of energy but also unsafe from a stability point of view, particularly at the higher speeds you will likely be achieving down a hill.

A quick but important safety note: Never let yourself go so fast down a hill that you feel out of control or your bike gets a speed wobble. Always feel confident that you are in control, and always feel confident that you will be able to brake if necessary. Of course road safety is another area altogether, but when you are going downhill at these increased speeds, it is necessary to be extra aware of your surroundings and traffic patterns, regardless of whether in training or in a race.

## Maintaining Bike Cadence While Managing Pace

Although you should be aiming to keep your cadence in the ideal range, the gears you select to do this will depend on the overall effort you are maintaining. Triathlons by their nature are endurance events, and your overall effort or pace should be guided by the distance of your race, the purpose of your workout, your fitness, and your overall racing goals.

As a general guide while racing, even for shorter events you should minimize the time (if any) you spend above your anaerobic (lactate) threshold, which is the point where your anaerobic energy system becomes dominant. You should be able to feel this as your breathing becomes labored and your effort unsustainable. This level of effort is extremely fatiguing; the energy systems and muscle patterns used are slow to recover, and they are best saved for a last burst at the end of a race if used at all. Even if you do not have a coach providing you with a race plan, you should have researched or ridden the course and thought about how you intend to ride it. You should know whether to expect hills or flat terrain, how many, how steep, what part of the course, and so on so you are not only prepared on race day but also able to simulate the race course in training as part of your preparation.

The effort you plan will be dependent on length of race, experience, fitness, and goals. For example, an experienced sprint-distance triathlete will likely aim for an effort just below his anaerobic threshold for the entire race, whereas a first-time Ironman-distance triathlete may aim to stay at a comfortable endurance-effort pace for the whole race. Whether you train and race by feel (your perceived exertion, or RPE, as discussed in chapter 9), heart rate, or power, use your gears to remain as far as you can in your ideal cadence range and to maintain your cadence on varied terrain or in wind while keeping your effort at your planned intensity, which may include easy recovery rides to efforts in excess of anaerobic threshold. The exception to this of course is when the purpose of the workout is deliberately higher or lower cadence, as discussed in the next section on higher- and lower-cadence training.

## Training Your Bike Cadence

Although most of your training should be done within your ideal cadence range, training should also incorporate both higher and lower cadences as explained here. Higher cadence refers to a cadence above the normal range of 80 to 100 rpm (e.g., spinning at a cadence in excess of 100 rpm). Conversely, lower cadence refers to a cadence below the normal range (e.g., maintaining a cadence of 60 to 70 rpm).

### Higher-Cadence Work

Higher-cadence work should initially take place early in the season, such as the preparation and early base periods, often as part of skill and technique development. Early in the season, and if you are new to this type of training, you should keep the effort and gears fairly easy—although if you are completely new to higher-cadence work, you may find the initial effort of just achieving the higher cadences seems challenging. As you progress through your season or if you are more experienced, then you can work on maintaining these cadences with increased effort and intensity by using higher (harder) gears. Drills such as spin-ups or intervals can be done throughout the year.

### Spin-Ups

Spin-ups are good to do during a recovery week or several times during an endurance ride. To do these, increase your cadence over a certain period of time to maximum. To know if you are at your maximum, keep increasing cadence until you are starting to bounce in the saddle. Back off slightly (so you are no longer bouncing), hold for the remaining time, then ease off and recover completely before the next one. Relax and try to make it feel effortless. An example is six to eight 30-second spin-ups with 4 minutes and 30 seconds of recovery in between. Don't forget to include a warm-up and cool-down before and after.

### Intervals

There are numerous ways of incorporating high-cadence work into any workout, thus creating interval work. All you need to do is focus on maintaining a high cadence for a certain amount of time. This can be for very specific periods of higher than normal cadence, or you can just monitor it while you are out riding. Examples include the following:

- Six to eight sets of 30-second sprints, aiming to keep your cadence above 100 rpm
- Several sets of 2 to 5 minutes at a cadence above 100 rpm, a 2-minute recovery above 80 rpm, another 1 to 2 minutes at a cadence above 110 rpm, and then a 2-minute recovery above 80 rpm
- A 10- to 30-minute spin in an easy gear right at the top of your normal comfortable range (the aim being to shift your comfort range upward by getting used to it)

You could also practice higher-cadence work during your warm-up by setting targets for yourself (e.g., to keep cadence above 80 or 90 rpm, since you're using easier gears).

## Lower-Cadence Work

In triathlon racing, you should minimize the amount of time you need a lower cadence, so lower-cadence work is not particularly specific to triathlon training. For this reason, although lower-cadence training does have its uses, it is best done early in the season. As you get nearer your racing season, the relevance of lower-cadence training decreases, and you should be focusing on other aspects of cycle training (e.g., threshold workouts at higher cadences).

Nevertheless, benefits of lower-cadence training include the following:

- Increased range of cadences at which you can pedal comfortably. Although hopefully you will not often need the lower cadence, it is still a good skill to have—for example, on a tough hill where you have run out of gears (of course, there could be an entire chapter devoted to gear selection for your race course).
- Increased leg strength if force on the bike is one of your limiters. Lower-cadence interval work is a good leg strengthener, but bear in mind the specificity of triathlon racing, and do this type of training early on in your season.
- Improved muscular endurance through hilly terrain riding (allowing your cadence to drop on hills is a good way to improve muscular endurance).

For any ride that includes lower-cadence work, it is important to warm up thoroughly first for 20 to 40 minutes. Then, a good example of low-cadence training is multiple sets of 3 to 10 minutes at a lower cadence (e.g., 65 to 70 rpm), with easy spinning recovery in between, starting with fewer repetitions and lower interval times and working up gradually. When completing lower-cadence work, you can allow your cadence to drop into the 60s, but do not go below this level because it puts excessive load on your knees, which increases the risk of injury or inflammation. Also, lower-cadence work while on a trainer or using hills outside should be done primarily while remaining seated—specific to triathlon racing where you should remain seated as much as possible.

# Run Cadence

Just as for cycling, regardless of the distance of the race you are training for, you want your run cadence, or stride rate, to be as efficient as possible. This is particularly important in the triathlon, where the run is usually last and is therefore going to use your remaining energy.

Technique is again key to improving efficiency and minimizing injury. Running form is something you should be constantly working on, and you'll learn more about running form in terms of body position and breathing in the next chapter. However, here we'll talk specifically about form as it pertains to setting your perfect cadence (or stride rate).

## *Setting Your Run Cadence*

In addition to stride rate, stride length is another factor that determines how fast you run. Stride length is the distance you cover with each step. To increase your speed, you need to increase your stride rate, your stride length, or both. Changing one of these usually changes the other. The best way to run faster (at a given level of effort) is to increase your run cadence while maintaining or even decreasing your stride length. Increasing cadence is a more economical way to increase speed than increasing stride length, and some of the reasons why are explained next. As you learned at the beginning of this chapter, the more economical you are, the faster you can run at any given effort.

Run cadence will vary from person to person depending on size (in particular leg length) and running ability. It is easier to move a short leg faster than a long leg, but the long one covers more distance with each step. Of course there are always exceptions, but generally top-class runners and triathletes run with cadences in excess of 180 steps per minute, regardless of their height. Getting technical for a few moments, some of the reasons for this are as follows:

- The longer your foot is in contact with the ground on each stride, the more time there is for the stored elastic energy to dissipate, and so less energy is returned on your *elastic recoil response*. This results in your muscles having to contract more forcefully for the same overall effect. To benefit from elastic recoil response, you want your foot in contact with the ground for the least amount of time per stride. For a given pace, longer strides mean more contact time with the ground—for this given pace it is beneficial to keep contact time short by reducing stride length and increasing cadence. Tall runners (longer leg length) take strides proportionally shorter to their leg length to do this compared with shorter runners (shorter leg lengths).

- A longer stride requires more *vertical displacement*, which is the height your body moves from the surface it is running on. To visualize this, imagine throwing a baseball 20 feet (65 m) or 50 feet (165 m)—the shorter the distance, the flatter you can throw. Good running form shows minimal vertical displacement. A more forceful contraction is required to overcome vertical displacement—energy that would be better used moving forward.

- In both these cases, longer strides necessitate more forceful contraction of the muscles. This will result in muscle fatigue earlier than if contracting them with less force and more frequently (remember, lifting a 1-pound weight 100 times is easier than lifting a 50-pound weight twice). This is due in part to the need to use your fast-twitch (forceful but not good endurance) muscle fibers to top up on the force needed, whereas at lower forces your slow-twitch endurance muscles can primarily cope with the load.

Many age-group runners have a cadence significantly slower than 180 steps per minute. Overstriding is often a main contributor to this. This common running problem can lead to injury and is uneconomical—if your foot lands in front of your body (your center of gravity), then it acts as a brake. To take your next step, you have to use energy to move your body (center of gravity) over your outstretched foot.

Generally, most age-groupers can benefit their running by increasing their cadence until it reaches around 180 or more. If you are shorter, you may more easily get slightly in excess of this. If you are particularly tall, then you might find you can only get to a few steps fewer than this.

## Improving Run Efficiency With Cadence

Working on good overall running form—in particular, by paying attention to where your foot lands in relation to your body to eliminate overstriding—often results in a higher cadence. Your foot should land beneath your center of gravity (easiest to visualize as beneath your hips). You may also find that a very slight lean forward (from the ankles, not the waist) helps increase cadence (body position for good running form is discussed in more detail in the next chapter).

You must teach your body to run at a faster cadence—the nerves and muscles need to get used to firing and contracting or relaxing at a faster rate. The best time to focus on increasing running cadence is early season and during recovery and endurance runs throughout your season. Early season is best because it gives you time to ingrain new good habits. Also, at first you will likely feel you are taking "baby steps" and running slower than you are used to for a given effort. This is temporary. Higher cadence is a skill that has to be learned—old habits are hard to break. Your speed will return and your effort will go back to your normal expectations over the next months. Persevere and you will be rewarded long term with better form, increased speed, and reduced chance of injuries.

## Maintaining Run Cadence on Hills

As discussed earlier for bike cadence, it is easier to practice and maintain cadence, or stride rate, while training on flat terrain, but in reality you will likely need to run up and down hills. Using an ideal cadence together with good running form can make running hills less exhausting.

### Running Uphill

When running uphill, ideally you would like to maintain your speed. The simplest and most efficient way to do this is by shortening your stride slightly and increasing your cadence slightly. Of course for some hills, maintaining speed will not be practical or possible. You should still aim to maintain or even increase your cadence even though this will mean shortening your stride. This will result in optimal speed while minimizing muscular fatigue.

### Running Downhill

The most important factor when running downhill is to make sure you stay in control. Within that, use gravity and good running form to help you get down the hill. You should be able to maintain your cadence. If it is a steep downhill, you may need to shorten your stride to maintain control and cadence. For many downhills, you may find that your stride length will increase as you maintain your cadence. Let it do this naturally while maintaining good form.

## Maintaining Cadence While Managing Pace

Managing your pace (sometimes called running speed) or effort (sometimes called intensity) is very important for running success, both in training and racing triathlons. When referring to pace, many people think of going faster or slower (i.e., increasing or decreasing your running pace). However, you should really be managing your effort for most training because many things out of your control can affect your pace even with a constant effort, such as terrain and weather conditions. Just as for cycling, run pace or effort required for a specific race or workout is dependent on variables such as length of race, purpose of workout, fitness, and goals.

An ideal cadence of around 180 steps per minute can be maintained regardless of terrain or effort required for a particular workout or race. It is important to learn to run at different paces (speeds) or efforts and not just gravitate to one pace or effort, which many age-groupers do because they think they are getting a good workout. You can't expect to improve your running speed if you never run at faster paces. On the opposite side of the pace spectrum, you can't expect to perform your key workouts to the best of your ability if you haven't taken recovery runs at an easy enough pace or effort. This is where the benefit of a structured training program (or use of a coach) will come in to maximize personal potential and minimize performance stagnation.

## Training Your Run Cadence

Training your cadence usually means training to increase or maintain a higher cadence, aiming toward the ideal of 180 steps per minute or more. If you want to run at a particular cadence, then you have to teach your body to run at that cadence. The nerves and muscles need to get used to firing and contracting or relaxing at that specific rate. So to increase your running cadence, you need to practice. Many running drills can help with this, and some are explained here.

### Strides

Strides are short bursts of running at an increased pace or speed. They can (and should) be used throughout your training season and are also good to do in the warm-up before races. Strides are purely technique based to teach your nerves and muscles to fire and contract faster. They are not designed to fatigue and should be performed with perfect form, with full recovery in between (walking or easy jogging). Pace should not be all-out but approximately your 5K race pace, one where you can aim for quick turnover of your feet and maintain perfect form. Ideally, sprints should be done on a very slightly downhill or flat terrain. An example is four to eight 20-to 30-second strides either within or at the end of a workout, with an easy jog back to the starting point as recovery.

### Downhill Running

Downhill runs are similar to strides but are performed on a moderate (less than 8 percent) slope. For these you should allow gravity to pull you down, working on making your feet keep up with a fast turnover. Keep good running form—slightly leaning forward to allow gravity to assist (if you lean back you are working against gravity). An example is four to eight 30-second sessions of downhill running, with easy recovery of a couple of minutes in between (e.g., walk back up to the top).

## Accelerations

Accelerations are another speed activity that requires high cadence. They are short bursts of running where you gradually increase your pace (speed). This teaches your body to run efficiently at faster speeds than you are used to, using short distances and a fast foot turnover. Choose a distance of approximately 100 yards or meters, and gradually build your speed throughout, with a full recovery between accelerations (e.g., an easy jog or walk to get your breathing and heart rate back down and under control, to what they were before the acceleration). Like strides, these are not designed to fatigue and can be done year round. An example is four to eight 100-meter accelerations, walking back to the start as recovery.

## Cadence Monitoring

You can set a cadence monitor (e.g., metronome or tempo trainer) to beep at a specific cadence and then aim to keep your stride in line with the beeps. To use this tool effectively, first find your current cadence by counting a few times, and then gradually over the next weeks or months, increase your cadence by setting the monitor at successively higher cadences (e.g., increasing two steps per minute per week). Take your time so as not to put undue stress on your body—it may take several seasons to increase your cadence to your desired level.

## Cadence Counting

Counting your cadence on runs is easy to do, and all you need is a watch. If you know your cadence, you can work on increasing or maintaining it. Simply count your strides (of either your left foot or right foot) for 15 seconds at various points on your run, and multiply by 4 for a cadence per minute per foot. For example, if you do 23 left foot strikes in 15 seconds, that is 92 per minute per foot, which equates to 184 per minute total for both feet; this is a good cadence to maintain.

## Running in Place

Running in place while monitoring cadence is a good way to get used to the feel of a higher cadence. Running in place is as simple as it sounds—you move your legs as if you were running, but you don't move forward. In this position you can increase your cadence without the added energy required to move your body forward. A clock or watch in front of you (rather than looking at your wrist as you would if running normally) is also a good way to monitor and increase your cadence without disrupting your running form for an even better feel. If you have enough room, you can try moving a short distance forward to see if you can maintain that cadence. Remember, you don't need to run in place for long to get the benefit; just a few minutes is sufficient. Once you have gotten the feel of a higher cadence, pay attention to making sure your good running form is also maintained.

## Skipping

Most people can think back to childhood when they first discovered how to skip. If you need a reminder, to skip you take a step with one foot, then a hop on the same foot, before taking a step with the other foot, followed by a hop—so there is a double impact for each foot as you move forward. Skipping can help increase the intensity of your recoil response and calf muscle contraction and also train your neuromuscular system to fire quickly. You can combine this drill with other drills (e.g., by skipping back to the start after every stride on a strides workout). An example is four to eight sets of skipping 10 times on each leg, walking back to the start as recovery.

## Running Barefoot on Grass

Run barefoot on grass for 30 seconds to 1 minute several times, and you will find not only that you run with a lighter step but also that your cadence will probably naturally increase. This happens because running barefoot without the support of running shoes lets your body run more naturally, where you land on your forefoot, often resulting in a higher cadence. Without the cushion of a running shoe to protect your feet, you will also find that you land more lightly. An added benefit is it strengthens your feet because you learn to use your foot muscles, which get lazy when always supported by a shoe. Do not be tempted to do too much of this, particularly to start with, because it takes your body a while to get used to. Just focus on how it feels, and run barefoot for a minute or two before a run, then put your shoes on and go for your planned run, trying to re-create the feeling and cadence during your warm-up.

You have learned in this chapter that an ideal cadence is important for both cycling and running. Cadence is a key element of efficient technique for both cycling and running, resulting in minimizing fatigue and reducing chances of injury—both vital for an endurance sport such as triathlon. The ideal cadence is in the range of 80 to 100 rpm for the bike and at or above 180 steps per minute for running, regardless of terrain or workout effort (the exception being a workout set purposely out of these ranges). These cadences are often higher than inexperienced or age-group triathletes are used to.

Improving cadence takes practice, and it can take many years to become completely natural. There are many drills to help achieve an ideal cadence, and these can be integrated into training plans throughout any training and racing season. It is well worth persevering with practice to achieve these ideal cadences for long-term benefits. Be patient and you will be rewarded with faster speeds and reduced chance of injury.

# CHAPTER 13

# Assessing Your Running Form

## Jess Manning

Throughout your running career, your running form will change and evolve, and so will your understanding of what constitutes good form. Just like most areas of any sport, running included, in order to properly ascertain something as a whole, it must be broken down into various parts, and this chapter addresses the parts of running that make up your form. You may have heard many of these areas mentioned by a variety of sources: from coaches to fellow athletes to the "really cool" running guy you saw on TV.

The first piece of advice, however, is that you should take these parts and put them into one big pot, mix it up, and from that, come up with what works best for you. Everyone's running form is different, and we have all probably seen athletes who have surprised us by running as fast or as well as they did in spite of how they were running. Ask yourself this: Are you running the speeds as well as you are in spite of your form, and thus limiting your results, or are you simply getting the most out of your abilities by running the way that feels "right" to you, and thus the most efficient with the best outcome? To take it one step further and simplify, would changing your running form help or hurt you?

One thing that is constant is that most running technique improvements can benefit almost everyone. Professional athletes do drills and skills training every day. The major difference between running and the other two disciplines in triathlon as far as proper form goes is that you can get by with a lot more technique issues in the run and still find a certain degree of success. I have listened to and been trained by some of the most advanced and knowledgeable running coaches in the world, and they have looked at and dissected the form of some of the top athletes in the world, and many times have not been impressed with their running form. It is like someone telling Michael Phelps that his stroke needs improvement. So here is the bottom line: The most important part of assessing your running should be whether it feels right.

Now, on to assessing the parts of your running form. This assessment starts at the very top and works all the way down to the most obvious, your feet.

# Head, Neck, and Eye Position

In relation to your head, neck, and eyes, begin by asking yourself, "What am I looking at when I run?" If the answer is "a lot of things," you may need to change it up a bit. Although the scenery is one of the reasons many athletes enjoy running, proper head position plays a key role in what the rest of the body is doing. It may not be as noticeable when you are running outside, but have you ever tried to turn around even just a little bit on a treadmill? How about attempting to shoot a sideways glance in a different direction than you were running? Disaster! Many athletes have the scars to prove it. It's almost impossible to have your head or eyes looking in a different direction and stay on the treadmill (safely). Your head tells the body where to go, and your eyes often tell your head.

Now, why is this important? The number one reason is safety. Some of the same reasons it is unsafe to run with your head turned on the treadmill apply here. You might be setting yourself up for several opportunities to get injured if you are not looking where you are going. The second reason, and most important for running form, is alignment. You need to keep your head in line with the rest of your body. World-renowned running coach Bobby McGee refers to this as being "connected and stacked." You should keep all the parts of your upper body in line and move them as a single unit in harmony. The goal is to keep your head relaxed but steady and your eyes focused on the close horizon.

# Breathing

Breathing is next for the mere fact it is connected to the head as well as the torso. There are varied opinions when it comes to breathing and technique, but the one constant you will hear from any running expert is this: You have to breathe! Now all kidding aside, it's important to make sure you are receiving the right amount (volume) of oxygen at the right times (frequency). We have a tendency to want to breathe faster when we exercise for obvious reasons, but this does not necessarily mean we are getting the oxygen we need in the most efficient manner.

Breathing should be even and deep, almost relaxing. Understand that the speeds at which you run ultimately dictate how frequently you take in oxygen, and your ability to slow down your intake frequency can help keep your heart rate down. There are many schools of thought on this, but since the goal of breathing is to take in the most oxygen when you need it, the best way to take in the highest volume of oxygen the fastest is to breathe through your mouth. Pay attention to making sure you do not always breathe on the same-side footfall every time. Believe it or not, this can actually encourage repetitive-use injuries. Take every opportunity you can to change up small details in your form throughout your longer runs. This can make sure you are evenly distributing the loads and stresses of each discipline to help you stay injury free.

# Shoulders

The shoulders are one of the easiest problem areas to spot and to correct. Go for a long run with a group, or look at the last couple of miles of any race, and you are sure to see athletes of all shapes and sizes with their shoulders up to their ears. It seems that as we fatigue we begin to tense up, and this leads to overcompensation through holding the shoulders well above the needed or recommended location. Think about your shoulder location, and be aware of it the next time you run. Are your shoulders loose and relaxed? Stressed out and overtightened shoulders radiate throughout the rest of your body greater than almost anything else. The first place a person goes to help you relax is your shoulders. Coincidence? Highly unlikely. Try to keep them as comfortably low as possible. This will in turn allow the rest of your upper body muscles to follow suit.

# Arms

Arm position is one of the most important and contested areas of form. In fact, it also may be the area that has the widest range of differences between runners. Some runners attempt to keep their arms tucked very close to the point that it almost looks as if they are trying to punch themselves in the face. Other runners look as if they have lost complete control of their upper limbs altogether. As with the other areas discussed, the optimal location is a neutral position. Arms should remain relaxed and tension free. They should not cross over your midline (the imaginary vertical line down the center of the front of the body) as they move front to back.

Picture the control arms on the wheel of a train. They move backward and forward in perfect synchronization and harmony. Always point your arms toward the desired direction of travel: forward. The rule of thumb is this: Your arms are really along for the ride. They are there to assist when necessary and to help with the balance and harmony of your stride. Try not to run with your arms. Rather, allow them to move freely, and call on them only when necessary.

# Core

The core of any athlete is one of the most important areas of focus, if not the most important. This section of your body is pivotal not just for your running form but also for the form of all the disciplines in triathlon. All major movements from top to bottom should originate from this part of your body. Because of the importance of this area, it can be the quickest to unravel. When you are running, think about your core and what it is doing. Is it loose and moving all over the place? Or is it rock hard and tightened up as if you are in a plank hold? Again, the goal is moderation. Ideally, you want a firmly held position from which the rest of your running form can radiate and find strength.

One of the quickest areas to fail in runners is their core section. Do a quick core check on yourself when you run to see where you stand. However, do not attempt to make your core do something it is not trained to do. If you hold your core super tight and rigid when it is not trained to do so, you will fatigue at an alarming rate. Keep your core as firm as you are comfortable to aid in your overall upper body positioning, and incorporate as much core training as possible in your training schedule for continued improvement.

# Hips

When you run, one of the biggest areas where you waste energy and lose efficiency is your vertical rise. This means the "bounce" in your step. At a recent marathon, one runner was estimated to have traveled more than three times the height of the Empire State Building vertically over the course of the 26.2 miles. In contrast, the runner who won the event that day traveled only one time the distance. This should help you understand why you should check to see how much you bounce when you run.

Keeping bounce to a minimum means saved effort, and that means efficiency, which can equal speed and endurance. Keeping your bounce to a minimum is covered further in the section on legs. Additionally, you are looking for your hips to stay in alignment with the rest of your upper body. If you allow your hips to lag behind the rest of your torso or stand too upright in comparison to your torso, you may be losing you forward momentum either out the back or the front of your stride.

Try to envision that you have a stack of empty boxes in your hands, and you are going to attempt to throw them all at once. The only way you can do this is to use the bottom box in the stack to help propel the upper boxes forward as well. You need to keep those boxes stacked on top of each other to allow them to work together. If they fall out of alignment, or if you try to move too quickly, the bottom box will fly forward or backward while the other boxes fall to the ground. This bottom box is your hips. Try to focus on keeping everything else above it, on top of it. As mentioned later in the section on legs, your forward lean will play a large role in how efficiently you run. This concept of staying aligned will come easier as you find the proper lean for your running style.

# Hands

Ask yourself this question: When you run, what are your hands doing? Are they clinched together tightly? Are they loose and floppy or maybe open but rigid as if you could snap a salute on command? With any luck you answered no to all these questions. More than likely, though, you may need to sharpen your focus in this area. Your hands help with the circulation of your limbs, which helps with the rest of your body. If you clinch your hands up tightly, you are restricting this circulation and overworking the rest of your upper body. The result is that you are not only vascularly restricting yourself but also fatiguing your hands at a quicker rate than necessary. Fatigued muscles do not perform at their best, plain and simple. This makes the need to run as easily as possible paramount.

Remember, you may need your hands to help you on the hills or at the sprint finish of your events. So rest and relax them as often as you can. The ideal position for your hands is loosely closed. This means they are closed but not clinched. As you are running, open them on occasion and shake them out.

# Legs and Stride

When I refer to your stride (or gait), I am typically referring to the distance between your feet and legs when you run. Take a stride forward and then pause. Where did you land?

## ▶ Selecting the Correct Running Shoe

There are several rules of thumb when choosing a running shoe. And although there may be numerous outside influences telling you that one brand or another will make you faster, keep in mind that this decision is one of the most important and should be made with care.

### Determine what type of shoe you need.

First, when trying to figure out what type of running shoe you need, ask yourself a few questions: What are the shoes for? There is a shoe for every type of situation or event that you can think of, so decide if you are looking for one that will hopefully do it all or for multiple shoes for different distances and conditions. Next, what type of runner are you? Typically, beginners and many distance runners use a more stability-based shoe, whereas more advanced and faster runners often lean toward a lighter or flat racing shoe.

### Locate a running store that performs foot and running analysis.

This is really important in your quest to determine whether you are wearing the right shoe, not only from a functional standpoint but also from a comfort standpoint. The best shoes in the world will not help you if they hurt your feet. Additionally, many running stores will even let you go for a stroll around the block on surfaces similar to what you might have in an event. This is a great benefit because most of the triathlons out there are not on carpet.

### Choose for function, not fashion.

This is probably one of the most common offenses, and it's made not just by the ladies (sorry fellas!). We have all done it. We walk into a store and see a shoe that catches our eye. Now although it is very important that you like how they look, make sure the function of the shoe fits your needs.

### Start with more stability than you think you need.

This is a tricky area for many runners. We hear the word *stability*, and we automatically think either comfort or safety shoes. Neither is the truth, actually. As you run, your body has to adjust and adapt to the force and physical demands of the training. As your running improves, you will find that the need for a more supportive shoe may diminish. Do not be afraid to go to a lighter shoe because this will be faster, but take your time working into one. Whereas the downside of wearing too much shoe may be a slower time, the comparison to the injuries that can come from running in too little of a shoe really is not even a comparison at all.

### Buy multiple pairs as often as your budget permits.

Just like our bodies, shoes need to be allowed to recover—from sweat that accumulates and from the pounding on the pavement. It is a good idea to not use the same pair every single day. This will make your shoes last longer as well. Another point worth noting is that trying to get your feet used to different types of shoes can be a great training tool. It encourages you to run "with your feet" as opposed to relying on the footwear for the outcome.

*(continued)*

*(continued)*

**Wear what works.**

One final and important note: Try different brands. Do not claim loyalty to a certain brand name and then limit yourself to running only in that type of shoe. I have coached many athletes who swore they had "insert brand name" feet. Sure we all have favorite athletes and brands we love, but although you may be able to force your body into a particular triathlon suit and get by with just a bit of discomfort, shoving your feet into a running shoe that isn't right for you may be the quickest way to injury. All feet are different, and until you are paid to wear a certain manufacturer, you should focus on what feels right for you and what the professionals recommend for your foot style.

Where was your leg in relation to your body? Make sure you are attempting to land with your feet under your torso, not in front of you. Try to avoid overdoing your heel kick or the lift of your knee. Remember, the goal is efficiency, and extra wasted movements will only be counterproductive. High knees and butt-kickers are wonderful drills; they should not, however, be running styles. Fast turnover requires that you get your feet on and back off the ground as quickly as possible. So if you add extra time by bringing your knees high, and your feet to your backside, you have essentially slowed down your cadence, all for the sake of making it look as if you are flying for the finish line photo. The best runners look efficient, not fast. When you watch a marathon on television, how often do you think *They don't look that fast*, only to find out they are running 5:05 splits? They make it look easy because they are running properly. Keep your focus on efficiency of stride, not how it looks.

Another important detail is your forward lean. Good running lets you use gravity as opposed to working against it. Maintaining a slight forward lean will enhance your forward propulsion and momentum. Another item of note is that the focus of your turnover should be on "catching" yourself with your legs. The best way to minimize the vertical rise described earlier is to develop optimal leg strength to keep you from having to bounce yourself up to move forward.

# Feet

In terms of running form, your foot position will be one of the trickiest to ascertain by yourself. Besides its being extremely difficult to look down at your feet while running from any angle, it is also hard to accurately tell what happens in that split second when your foot is on the ground. One great way to tell what your feet do is to check out the bottom of your shoes. Where are they worn out? If you see a lot of worn-off sole in the heel area, you may be a heel striker. You can also look for uneven wear to see if you have any unbalanced areas of your foot strike as well as if you pronate or supinate. Another, and probably the best, way is to have yourself filmed. (This of course applies to the rest of your gait as well, but in particular to this part of your form.) Most good coaches offer this service and have found it to be an invaluable training tool in helping athletes understand the biomechanics of their form.

If you do not work with a coach (you should!), you can also head to your local specialty running store. Most of the good locations offer a video service done on a treadmill to aid them and you in the selection of your shoes. Although the clip may be short, and you will not have the opportunity to play it back a hundred times on your computer in super slow motion, it is a start. Pay close attention to what your foot does. How do you land? Do you land on your heels or toes? Maybe right in the middle? Do your ankles roll out (supinate) or in (pronate)

There are a couple of things to keep in mind when you review the video. Time on the ground is time not moving forward. It's almost like driving around with the parking brake on. So, you want to try to keep that to a minimum. Landing on your heels requires you to roll forward to your toes (often creating a double tap, heel then toe). Also, you are looking for a neutral, solid foot strike, with minimal back-and-forth movement after you land. A brief note about the cadence of your run: When I use the term *cadence*, I am referring to the frequency of your stride. Ideally this rate will fall somewhere around 180 strides per minute. Take the opportunity to count this in your own stride. Quicker turnover will provide you with the most efficient stride. It will also make you less injury prone by helping you stay off your heels and keeping your landing point beneath your body where it belongs.

The information in this chapter is by no means everything you need to know. The hope is, however, that it will help you become a more informed runner, and as such, a smarter and maybe even faster triathlete. Many agree that the race is won and lost on the run. This possibly makes the run the most important discipline of the three. Assessing your form could be the difference in not just where you finish in the race, but if you finish at all. Proper running form helps you not only from a performance and results standpoint but also from a career longevity standpoint. Proper form gives you the best chance of having a career that is as injury free as possible.

Now that you've assessed your form, what do you do with the information? Well, if you take one piece of advice away from this chapter, please take this one: Relax! Most of the errors in running form revolve around being too tense and uptight. Don't get overwhelmed by all the information or try to make changes all at once. As you do in any other discipline, set aside portions of your training session to review form. Utilize drills, coaches, and fellow runners. Do not get frustrated! As stated at the beginning of the chapter, running form evolves over the years. I've had the opportunity to run 12 marathons and 3 Ironman events so far, and my form has changed and improved with each one. It will not come all at once. So, whether you are training for your 1st or 50th event, follow these basic steps and you're headed for a successful competition and, more important, a great time and a long-running multisport career!

# CHAPTER 14

# Improving Your Transitions

## Graham Wilson and Mathew Wilson

Most triathletes spend the majority of their training hours on the three disciplines of the sport; few spend sufficient time practicing the actual mechanics of transitions and preparing for the subsequent segment while still competing in either the swim or bike portion. Therefore, the aim of this chapter is to discuss what some have called the fourth discipline of triathlon—transitions—including how to minimize the amount of time spent in T1 and T2 and how, from an exercise physiology aspect, to improve overall triathlon performance by taking advantage of recent advancements in pacing and drafting strategies across all disciplines.

## Transitions

Various studies have shown that the transition from one event of the race to another has important implications for physiological and kinematic (movement of the body) measures that affect both perceived effort and performance in the remaining events. One study found that athletes do not bike or run as economically after swimming and do not run as economically after the bike segment. Part of this lack of economy may in fact be due to an athlete's inadequate technical ability or fitness level, which in turn leads to an increased metabolic load. This, then, emphasizes the need for transition training between each discipline and specific physiological training that will help triathletes switch between disciplines quickly and more efficiently—thus biking faster out of T1 and running faster out of T2.

### Transition Layout

One of the key factors in having a successful transition experience is knowing the layout of the transition area, including its entry and exit points, and also the layout of your own equipment. Many triathletes bring far too much baggage into the area and clutter it up, not only for themselves but also for those sharing the rack, so bring only what you will be using during the actual race. You should also note that in accordance with USAT rules, you "own" only the piece of real estate where your wheel touches the ground, so do not spread your equipment in too large an area.

Most athletes rack their bikes by the seat so the front wheel is touching the ground. This can make for a faster exit from the bike rack than, say, if the bike is racked by the brake levers, which makes it more difficult to remove. Most races have a single transition area, so according to USAT rules, athletes must return their bikes to their assigned positions on the bike rack, and failure to do so may result in a penalty.

Remember that others will be in close proximity to you, and thus you should be considerate and keep your equipment in a tight and logical order. Lay your equipment out in reverse order, meaning the items that are farthest away are those you will be putting on last. For example, if you are looking down at the ground from farthest away to nearest, you would lay out your gear next to your bike in the following order:

1. Running shoes with lace locks or similar
2. Hat or visor
3. Socks (although many think they can race without them, the time spent putting them on for the run may be well spent rather than getting a blister)
4. Bike shoes (see later section on cyclo-cross mount and dismount)
5. Race number, which is usually attached to an elastic race belt so it's easy to put on (check with the race director on local rules because some require you to wear your race number on the bike and some only for the run segment; if you have to wear it on the bike, in order to stop it flapping so much in the breeze, scrunch it up and wrinkle the whole race number, then spread it out and attach it to your race belt to limit the "sail effect" behind you)
6. Helmet and sunglasses, which may be on the ground or hanging on the front of your bike, but remember your helmet must be on and securely fastened before you leave the transition area; if you do not fasten your helmet before mounting your bike (outside the transition area), you could be disqualified

It is worthwhile to lay out your kit the same way for every race and have a set routine of what you put on first so you have less to think about in the heat of the race.

## Swim to Bike Transition (T1)

It is well known that swimming has an impact on subsequent cycling performance, with some studies demonstrating that overall cycling performance may be hindered by short-duration, high-intensity swimming, such as a sprint triathlon when the distance is much shorter (usually 750-meter swim, 20K bike, and 5K run), thus many athletes try to swim this leg much faster than normal. One method of countering the detrimental impact of high-intensity swimming is drafting.

Drafting is the act of swimming very close behind or at hip level to another swimmer. It reduces passive drag, thus decreasing the effort to swim the same distance. Also drafting usually improves stroke economy and efficiency, therefore potentially improving the subsequent cycling performance. To take maximal advantage of drafting, swimming behind another triathlete at a distance up to 1.5 feet (.5 m) back from the toes is the most advantageous; in lateral drafting—in kayaking this is termed "catching the bow wave"—a swimmer's head can be level with another swimmer's hips. You would do this when there isn't physical room to get behind another swimmer's toes or there are other athletes all around you, preventing you from moving.

Also, many triathletes are aware of terms such as *blood pooling* and *orthostatic intolerance* but don't actually know what they are. Orthostatic intolerance is characterized by impaired balance, dizziness, blurred vision, or even partial or complete loss of consciousness. This may occur postswim in athletes with normal blood pressure because of gravitational stress and the removal of the muscle pump. In fact, one study showed that severe dizziness after swimming when exiting the water and standing up for the transition section is a common occurrence for many triathletes, but it is more prevalent in highly trained endurance athletes. If this happens to you frequently, you should seek medical advice. However, the good news is that most athletes who get checked out by their doctors discover that severe dizziness is usually benign.

To counteract the effect of gravity and maintain blood pressure and venous return, one study suggests continuing to keep moving rather than stopping abruptly. This is especially important when removing the wetsuit upon exiting the water, stopping to walk up wet steps or noncarpeted transitions, bending down to put on cycling shoes, and so on. One way to offset dizziness as you leave the swim is to start utilizing the muscular pump by working the calf muscles as soon as possible, meaning you should take short steps at a higher cadence than normal as you make your way to the transition. Ultimately, this will improve your ability to maintain venous return and blood pressure,

---

### ▶ Starts

It would be remiss if we did not touch on what for many triathletes is the most challenging skill—the swim start, especially if it is in open water and the waves are rolling into the beach.

Perhaps the biggest mistake most triathletes make is what we term *overseeding*—starting too near the front in a wave start and thus enduring a great deal of body contact in the first several hundred meters, as faster swimmers go over, under, or around them. Holding back a few seconds at the start of the wave allows many of the faster swimmers to go ahead, giving slower swimmers more open water to have a clean and contact-free swim without giving up too much time.

Another matter to consider is swim pace. Many triathletes go off too hard in the first couple of hundred meters and suffer for this later in the swim and even the race. So ensure your start pace is something you can keep up for the whole swim portion, or even consider a slightly slower race pace at first until you get comfortable in the water, and then start cranking it up. It is better to start a bit slower and finish fast rather than the other way round.

Perhaps the only way to replicate the swim start is to practice it. In a pool, several triathletes in a single lane can all start off at the same time, making race-like body contact, even to the point of pulling each other back and pushing each other under the water. This practice will never be the same as a race, but it will give you a feeling of what it is like and how you will react to the body contact.

Finally, please remember you are doing a triathlon, so pace yourself for the whole distance and don't leave your bike in the water or your run on the bike—intelligent pacing will win every time.

maintain mental concentration through the transition, and execute pacing strategies for the start of the cycling discipline—thus going faster out of T1.

## Bike to Run Transition (T2)

A debate exists regarding the metabolic cost of running at the end of a triathlon compared with running the same distance in isolation. However, the vast majority of research suggests that high-intensity cycling will have a detrimental effect on subsequent running performance, with the effects dependent on the fitness level of the triathlete; the greatest decreases in performance are observed in recreational triathletes, and minimal effects are seen in elite triathletes.

To offset the impact of cycling on running performance, researchers have come up with a few practical strategies; see Bentley et al. (2008) for further details. In summary, triathletes may be able to improve running performance by (1) drafting behind as many athletes as is practical (in draft-legal events); (2) adopting a cycling cadence of between 80-100 rpm (note, however, that cadence is a very personal matter—just consider the cycling cadence of Lance Armstrong (above 110 rpm for several hours at a time), for example—but many in triathlon will find a slightly higher cadence is acceptable); and (3) concentrating on reducing the effort during the final minutes of the cycling stage to prepare for the run. Points 2 and 3 really strike home for many coaches and physiologists. Pro cyclists will of course state the physiological benefits of spinning at greater than 110 rpm, but all too often, triathletes will trash themselves on the last 5K of the cycling discipline when coming in for the home stretch. However, the global performance time of a triathlon is *the* most important aspect, not the bike time. As such, establishing optimal pacing strategies for the start of the bike, the end of the bike, and the start of the run is an individual task and should be done in training on a regular basis. To put it as simply as possible: Don't leave your run on the bike! And spinning is better than crunching big gears.

To emphasize this point, various studies tried to determine the best pacing strategy during the initial phase of an Olympic-distance triathlon for highly trained triathletes. Ten male triathletes completed a 10K control run at free pace as well as three individual time-trial triathlons in a randomized order. In the time trials, the swimming and cycling speeds imposed were identical to the first triathlon performed, and the first run kilometer was done alternately 5 percent faster, 5 percent slower, and 10 percent slower than in the control run. The triathletes were instructed to finish the remaining 9 kilometers (5.6 miles) as quickly as possible at a self-selected pace. The 5 percent slower run resulted in a significantly faster overall 10K performance than the 5 percent faster and 10 percent slower runs, respectively ($p < .05$). Of note, the 5 percent faster strategy resulted in higher values for oxygen uptake, ventilation, heart rate, and blood lactate at the end of the first kilometer than the two other conditions. After 5 and 9.5 kilometers, these values were higher for the 5 percent slower run ($p < .05$).

This excellent and well-controlled study demonstrates that contrary to popular belief, running slower during the first kilometer of an Olympic-distance triathlon may actually improve overall 10K performance. With the recent advances in global positioning system (GPS) watches, split times and distances are easily available for triathletes to take advantage of even if no distance markers are provided during the triathlon. This technology is best used only if the triathlete has previously established performance standards for that particular event. Thus, for these data to be most effective, the triathlete must know what split time equals 5 percent slower than his maximal effort.

# Transition Practice Workouts

Very few studies have investigated the physiological effects of multiple swim–bike–run sessions during training and their impact on total performance. One study of 6 weeks of multicycle run training compared with normal isolation training found that this type of training did not produce a greater improvement in bike–run performance versus normal isolation training, but it did induce significant improvement in the bike–run transition. Clearly this is an understudied aspect of triathlon performance, although British Olympic coaches have focused on this area since the early 2000s. (Mat Wilson, one of the coauthors of this chapter, was one of those coaches.) The six swim–bike and bike–run sessions provided next were extensively used by the 2000 and 2004 British Olympic squads.

## Swim to Bike Workouts

Three sample swim to bike sessions are provided in this section. The prime objective of these sessions is to enable you to bike faster out of the swim in an effort to reduce overall bike time. Typically, these sessions should be conducted in the preparatory phase of your training cycle.

All swim to bike sessions require a pool, your race bike, and a bike trainer. Set up the bike and bike trainer about 10 yards or meters from the poolside, with a large towel on the floor next to the bike for drying yourself. The equipment layout is exactly as you would normally do it in a race. At the end of each set, take the time to lay out your equipment again as if it were a proper T1 setup—but keep the time to the absolute minimum.

When you perform the following swim to bike workouts, first warm up as you normally would for a speed-based session. A proper warm-up increases heart rate, breathing rate, and the flow of blood to the muscles to prepare the body for increasingly vigorous activity. This means you should include some tempo work, and as you near the end of your warm-up, increase the pace slightly. In addition, using a heart rate monitor for these sessions is not recommended, as the chest strap may become dislodged in the water and distract you from the prime purpose of the session, which is to increase your speed out of the water and onto the bike.

Before performing these sessions, it is necessary to know your benchmark times for the swim and bike distances, so before you enter this phase of your training, conduct time-trial sessions for the 200-meter, 400-meter, and 800-meter swim and time-trial sessions for the 2K, 4K, and 8K cycle. The times recorded will become your benchmarks to measure consistency throughout the session and to measure your overall improvement.

## Swim to Bike Session 1: Maximal Intensity

Maximal intensity, sometimes called *steady state*, is the level of effort you can maintain for the full duration of the whole session. The aim of this maximal intensity session is for you to push yourself as hard as possible in each set as close as you can to your maximal time-trial effort. The objective is for you to become aware of what your body will feel like coming out of the swim so you can then become as economical as possible, thus training the mind and body.

Do your usual warm-up, and then do five sets of the following: 200-meter swim immediately followed by a 2K cycle at greater than 100 rpm. The total number of transitions for the session is nine, and the total distance covered is 1 kilometer for the swim and 10 kilometers for the bike. This is a short overall session, but, as mentioned, each set is conducted at your best sustainable speed for the whole session. To get maximum benefit, do not take a rest between sets. During the first set of 200-meter swimming and 2K cycling, you must try to equal the established fastest time-trial times you conducted before, with the aim of maintaining this performance.

Clearly many triathletes will slow as the session continues, and you should record your fatigue as a percentage time increase. As you progress, you should notice an overall reduction of fatigue, seen as improved and maintained performance times. When you get stronger, you can increase the number of sets if you choose. Be careful of doing too many, though, because this is a very taxing session, and recovery will be much longer than normal, thus affecting the rest of your training modules.

## Swim to Bike Session 2: Lactate Tolerance

Lactate tolerance training will help you recover more quickly from bursts of speed and power, and while triathletes should try to minimize this type of effort in a race, it is inevitable that you will need to increase power on the bike or run harder on a hill to pass other runners. By training properly, you can push your lactate tolerance up to a higher heart rate. Since LT is the point where significant amounts of lactate start to accumulate in the blood, improving your ability to clear lactate means you can ride harder before you reach LT. By training slightly below LT, you train your body to convert lactate to fuel for the slow-twitch muscles, thus clearing lactate from the bloodstream. The most effective training to raise LT is relatively long efforts just below LT, with only partial recovery between each effort. Starting the next hard interval before lactate is fully cleared continues the training stimulus to remove lactate.

Do your usual warm-up, and then do two sets of the following: 400-meter swim and 4K cycle at greater than 95 rpm. This is followed by four sets of the following: 200-meter swim and 2K cycle at greater than 90 rpm. The total number of transitions for the session is eleven, and the total distance covered is 1,600 meters for the swim and 16 kilometers for the bike.

To get the most benefit from this session, there should be no rest between sets, and all swim and cycle reps must be within 10 percent of your fastest established time-trial times, with the aim of maintaining this performance. Again, record your fatigue as a percentage time increase. You can measure your overall improvement by noticing a reduction of fatigue, seen as improved and maintained performance times. This session can be physically uncomfortable and mentally taxing for many because it requires you to maintain your concentration for a long time and because it is very tiring in a progressive manner. Once you feel OK with this session, you can increase the effort by either adding more sets or adding the following: 1 × 800-meter swim and 8K cycle at greater than 100 rpm to the beginning of the set.

## Swim to Bike Session 3: Aerobic Development

Aerobic development is important because the more work you do aerobically, meaning with oxygen, then generally the more efficient you become. As an added bonus, aerobic work trains the body to break down and use stored fat for energy (fat is a primary source of fuel for the aerobic energy system). Another benefit of aerobic development is an increase in heart stroke volume, which means more blood pumping oxygen to the muscles. As most triathletes tend to train and race aerobically, it is useful to include an aerobic development session to increase your ability to be economical and efficient while exercising.

Do your usual warm-up, and then do two sets of the following: 800-meter swim and 8K bike at greater than 100 rpm. The total number of transitions for the session is three, and the total distance covered is 1,600 meters for the swim and 16 kilometers for the bike.

Again, no rest should be taken between sets. You should record negative split times, with the second set being within 5 percent of the fastest of your established time-trial times. This can be a long, tiring session with what may appear to be very little progression. However, by working on aerobic development, you are building a stronger base to work from. Because it can be tiring, this session should be completed once or twice per month only. Thus a reduction of fatigue by improving performance time is the main goal.

## Bike to Run Workouts

Three sample bike to run sessions are provided in this section. Each session trains you to run faster off the bike, something many athletes struggle with, certainly in the first mile or two. The key to these bike to run sessions is using correct running posture (not leaning too far forward in the first kilometer), opening running gait, and keeping mental focus and concentration at maximal heart rates. Clearly you need to keep an eye on heart rate, but again the prime focus should be on time splits and limiting fatigue through session progression, thus ensuring you are running at your best speed during this segment of the race.

All bike to run sessions require a mag trainer and a running track (not a treadmill if possible, although this may be your only option in the winter depending on where you live). Set the mag trainer up next to the running track, with full race equipment laid out as per your usual setup.

Warm up adequately before beginning. Because the sessions involve a higher heart rate, add some speed elements to your warm-up while being careful of injury. Before performing these sessions, it is necessary to know your benchmark times for the bike and run distances, so before you enter this phase of your training, conduct time-trial sessions for the 2K, 4K, and 8K cycle and time-trial sessions for the 400-meter, 800-meter, and 1K run. The times recorded will become your benchmarks to measure consistency throughout the session and to measure your overall improvement.

### Bike to Run Session 1: Maximal Intensity

As mentioned in the previous swim to bike maximal intensity session, maximal intensity is the level of effort you can maintain for the full duration of the whole session, and the aim of this session is for you to push yourself as hard as possible in each set as close as you can to your maximal time-trial effort. This session includes 10 sets of 400-meter running and 2K cycling at greater than 100 rpm. The total number of transitions for this session is 19, and the total distance covered is 4 kilometers for the run and 20 kilometers for the bike.

Lay out your running gear as if it were a race so you will have the added benefit of ensuring your logistics for the transition are correct. One noticeable difference this time is that you must take a 2-minute rest between sets to reset transition equipment, hydrate, and so on, and the first run and cycle set must be equivalent to your fastest established time-trial times. The primary aim of this set is consistency of time and effort. As previously stated, you will slow (in some cases by a lot), but you must record your fatigue as a percentage time increase.

If each set is completed to your maximal intensity, there is a good chance this session could be the hardest you will ever do. Also, because this set can be very taxing, it may be conducted in your base phase but most likely will have a bigger impact in your build phase.

## Bike to Run Session 2: Lactate Tolerance

As mentioned in the previous swim to bike lactate tolerance session, lactate tolerance training will help you recover more quickly from bursts of speed and power, and while triathletes should try to minimize this type of effort, it is inevitable that you will need to increase power at some point during the race. This session includes three sets of 800-meter running and 4K cycling at greater than 95 rpm followed by four sets of 400-meter running and 2K cycling at greater than 100 rpm. The total number of transitions for this session is 13, and the total distance covered is 4 kilometers for the run and 20 kilometers for the bike.

To maintain consistency of effort throughout the session, take 3 minutes' rest between sets so you have time to set up your T2, hydrate, and so on. All run and cycle reps must be within 10 percent of your fastest established time-trial times, with the aim of maintaining this performance. Again note your fatigue factor. You can monitor your progress by feeling a reduction of fatigue for the same time or better, and once you reach this stage you can add a complete set to the whole session.

## Bike to Run Session 3: Aerobic Development

As mentioned in the previous swim to bike aerobic development session, aerobic development is important because the more work you do aerobically, meaning with oxygen, then generally the more efficient you become. As most triathletes tend to train and race aerobically, it is useful to include an aerobic development session to increase your ability to be economical and efficient while exercising. This session includes four sets of 1K running and 8K cycling at greater than 100 rpm. The total number of transitions for this session is seven, and the total distance covered is 4 kilometers for the run and a whopping 32 kilometers for the bike.

A full 5-minute rest must be taken between sets, and your heart rate should drop rapidly during this rest phase (to do this, you may wish to walk the track very slowly). Once again, you must try to get negative split times, with the third and fourth sets being within 10 percent of your fastest established time-trial times. A reduction of fatigue by improving performance time is your main goal. This is a very tough session mentally and physically, with little progression. The mental focus required during the longer sets is vital to success because so many times during a race we find ourselves admiring the scenery and perhaps slowing down. You should enjoy your sessions but remember why you are there—to try to get faster. This is the longest of the sets listed, and because it is so tough, it is recommend that you complete this session once or twice per month only. Also, this session is best conducted in your preparatory (base) phase.

For any action that is repeatable, you can devise a process around it. By practicing some of the sets outlined in this chapter, you will be playing in the world of specificity—each workout is specifically designed to help you become faster in triathlon. You will not only become faster in and out of transitions but also should be able to bike faster out of the swim and run faster off the bike.

The key to real success, however, is ensuring you know how your body reacts to the intensity of racing for the full duration of the race and to structure certain aspects of your training to replicate those stresses. If you are a wonderful swimmer and can come out with a good lead only to lose it on the bike or run, then perhaps your training focus needs to be realigned—the same goes if you are a strong biker or runner. Pacing is paramount for overall success. Yes, use your natural talent for each discipline, but be conscious of the overall effort needed to finish well. Your racing should be the culmination of good rehearsal and preparation—you have to occasionally feel discomfort in training to know how hard you can push in racing, so there is an element of truth in "no pain, no gain"—you have to know your limits but feel the burn every so often.

# CHAPTER 15

# Troubleshooting Your Freestyle

## Ian Murray

There are plenty of signs that tell you when your swim is lacking. Perhaps every lap is a struggle, or swimming faster or farther seems impossible. Maybe panic sets in during a race, or you see other swimmers glide by you easily and often. Knowing there are areas to improve is one thing; knowing how to fix them is another. Swimming is a technique sport, much like golf, tennis, alpine skiing, and many others where skill trumps strength. The density of water—nearly one thousand times thicker than air—demands a technical approach to swimming. For lower-level and intermediate swimmers, fitness is usually not what limits their swim ability. It is lack of proper technique that slows them down. Even for advanced swimmers, a small technical change brings immediate results that might take weeks or even months to acquire through mindless training. In this chapter, the focus is on reducing drag and *then* creating propulsion. It is vital to approach the list of skills in order so you master each skill before moving on to the next, empowering you to troubleshoot your freestyle swim.

## Reducing Drag

Many triathletes wisely invest in aerodynamic technology for their cycling equipment to save seconds off their bike splits but foolishly ignore areas of drag in their swim, where *minutes* can be saved through simple changes. In reducing drag, the number one issue is a level body. The next priority is how the arms and hands enter the water and extend forward in front of the body. The final priority is the kick.

### Level Body

The number one priority when trying to reduce drag is to have a level body position at the surface of the water. This means the back of your swim cap, the back of your suit, and your heels are all very near the surface. That level body position is obtained and maintained through balance, *not* through kicking harder. No amount of strength or struggle will overcome body drag. The resistance of water, as it attacks the chest, abdomen, hips, and thighs, will always be greater than any force you generate against it.

There are three tools a swimmer can use to get level: head position, lead-arm depth, and pressure on the upper torso. The head should be deep enough in the water so that only a small patch of swim cap is exposed to the air, so deep that a thin film of water washes over the back of the cap. When the head is in the correct position, there will be no wrinkles in the skin at the back of the neck, the eyes will gaze *straight down* at the pool bottom below, and the crown of the head will be pointing directly at the end of the lane. When the lead arm is at the proper depth at full extension, the fingers will be 2 to 4 inches (5 to 10 cm) below the surface of the water. The arm should enter the water on a trajectory that takes it straight to that depth as opposed to entering shallow, just skimming the surface of the water and settling to that depth.

The idea of pressure on the upper torso can be the most elusive and confusing. Imagine that your torso (hips to shoulders) is full of air, all hollowed out and inflated like a balloon. Your lungs provide balloon-like buoyancy in this part of the body, so by pressing down or leaning on your collarbones, the front of the body will sink deeper into the water. The hips and legs will then automatically rise up. The human body acts in water as a seesaw acts on a playground; when one end goes down, the other end goes up. By blending the three tools—head depth, arm depth, and pressure—you can find level balance at the surface of the water and reduce body drag.

## Clean Entry and Extension

The points of entry and extension are the next items to assess. The entry is when the hand enters the water. The extension is when it reaches out to its longest length. In a clean entry, the hand enters the water with little splash, and the arm achieves full extension with few air bubbles. This type of entry maximizes forward thrust while also minimizing drag.

The most common problem in this area is the dreaded crossover, which occurs when a swimmer's entry point is too close to the top of the head, and the hand and forearm travel across the center line of the body during extension. This wastes energy by sending the body side to side rather than forward. A crossover also creates drag by allowing the water to take hold of a larger area (the side of the forearm from elbow to pinkie finger) than it would if the arm entered and extended straight ahead. Crossovers are rarely symmetrical; one arm often wanders errantly to a greater degree than the other. When solving this problem, swim with the mantra of "enter wide, extend wide." A swimmer will move a body part a millimeter and feel as if it's been adjusted a mile, so the remedy requires an exaggerated feeling of width to approach an accurate result. The exaggeration might have you feeling as if you are entering and extending at 10 o'clock and 2 o'clock. After several focused swims, that oddly wide feeling will lessen.

Another area to analyze is the position of the elbow at full extension. Confirm that the elbow is straight and locked out, with no elbow dip. One of the laws of swimming is that no matter where your arm is in the stroke cycle (recovery, entry, extension, catch, arm sweep, finish), the fingers are always below the wrist and the wrist is always below the elbow. At complete extension this law is nearly broken; the fingers are only slightly below the wrist, and the wrist is nearly even with the elbow. If the elbow dips below the wrist and the hand appears to scoop upward at full extension, a swimmer gets a double whammy. First, there is the problem of drag. An elbow that has dropped below the wrist and fingers at full extension creates drag from the enlarged surface area of the raised forearm. Much like Diana Ross and the Supremes doing "Stop! In the Name of Love," that arm is projected forward in a fashion perfect for mid-1960s choreography but horrendous in the water. Second, there is a delay in the catch. This will be covered later in this chapter in the section on propulsion.

Also note: The wrist and fingers need to be flat and straight as they enter and extend so that no unnecessary drag is created from other joints. Swimmers often unknowingly allow the wrist to soften and fingers to bend, and all the corners created are immediately attacked by the dreaded enemy, drag. Think of your hand as a knife that will slice into and through the water. It should enter flat as if you were slipping it through the mail slot of a door.

Only the details remain, including a classic hot-button topic for new swimmers that simply has to be noted. The question of fingers—should they be spread or together? Most recent studies suggest that the best position of the fingers (in terms of spacing and cupping) is as they fall in their own natural resting posture. This speaks to an important overall element of swimming: relaxation. Great swimming can be done with little effort. Tension causes greater stress, elevated heart rate, and faster fatigue, so you must remain relaxed as you swim. Water has the ability to cradle a balanced body and hold it at the surface. Relaxation also minimizes muscle cramping. During the recovery phase of each stroke, relaxation is vital. Let the shoulder muscles lift only the elbow high into the air, and let the forearm, wrist, hand, and fingers dangle down like overcooked linguine.

## Legs

Observe your legs first through the perspective of drag. Imagine there is a tube around the largest part of your body: the chest or the hips. The kick must remain small, tight, and within that tube. Anything that strays outside the tube during the swim is drag.

---

### ▶ Managing Breathing During the Swim

The obvious and immediate challenge with swimming is that you can't simply inhale and exhale as you can on the bike or while running. The exchange of breath requires some thought, planning, and coordination with the rotation of the arms and body. A regular and steady breath will reduce anxiety and improve performance.

Swim with a steady rhythm to your breath. This will require you to exhale in the water. There isn't time to exhale and inhale when the mouth is out of the water, so you must inhale at the surface and exhale when your face is submerged. You can choose to breathe out through your nose, your mouth, or a combination of both. With higher effort, the gas exchange rate is increased. Mouth breathing then becomes the more efficient function. Also, there is value in the ability to breathe on both the right and left sides of your body (bilateral breathing). During faster-paced swims and races, however, you will tend to breathe more often to fulfill your oxygen needs, thus on the same side (unilateral breathing).

If you recall, a level body is priority one in swimming, and like a seesaw, when one end goes up, the other end goes down. Check to make sure you are not lifting your head out of the water as you breathe; this may cause the hips and legs to sink momentarily and create drag. As you turn to breathe, think of turning the crown of the head down and lifting the chin up for air.

If your kick is too wide, then your calves, shins, and feet creep outside that boundary and slow you down. Many runners and cyclists come into triathlon with the habit and mind-set of using lots of knee angle for motion. A swimmer's kick should stem more from the hips, with only a slight amount of knee articulation. There is often a cause and effect attached to a wide kick: If the arm sweep (the pull of the arm as it moves past the chest and abdomen) crosses too far under the body, it can cause an overrotation of the entire body. A splayed kick is often a counterbalance to that overrotation.

# Creating Propulsion

Only after you have eliminated as much drag as humanly possible can you begin focusing on increasing propulsion. As with the section on reducing drag: the biggest, most valuable elements of swimming faster are stated first.

## *Core Power*

In humans, great power never comes from the limbs alone. The body's true power source is its center of mass: the hips. A superior golf swing and tennis forehand are not generated from just the arms; they are powered by the hips. A karate punch, fastball, and javelin throw all originate from the body's core. This is true for swimming as well. When a swimmer lies dead flat in the water and pulls herself forward with arms alone, there is no potential for power, no possibility for speed. A powerful swim is generated from the body rolling like a log, pivoting on its long axis. The power is maximized when all parts of the torso—shoulders down to hips—move together and that core movement is timed perfectly to *both* the arm entry and the pull.

The degree of rotation changes slightly with the pace of the swim. A warm-up or cool-down pace involves slightly more rotation. The body tips up on its side a bit more and glides there a bit longer as a slower arm moves forward through the recovery phase. On the other hand, a 50-meter all-out sprint has far less body rotation—not flat but certainly not as much as in the warm-up. Swim speed comes from arm turnover, and, as the arm and hand exit the water and rush forward through recovery, too much rotation can actually hinder the process. Check to make sure you have some rotation in your swim in order to access the core power but not so much rotation that you are hindering your potential for faster turnover and, therefore, a faster swim.

## *Timing*

Timing refers to the position of the arms at the moment of the body's core rotation. When timing is at its best, the body's core is powering both the pull and the entry to their maximum potential. There are two ways to mess this up. The more common way is to pull too early. In this scenario, the pull is happening at the same time as the recovery. The arm pulling has started too early, is moving independently, and is not connected to any of the critical core body power. To correct this, the lead arm must remain out front, in full extension for a moment longer, as it waits for the recovery arm to advance forward. Think of stretching the extension farther forward, reaching out as if you are trying to touch the pool wall at the end of your lane.

The other, less common mistake is to pull too late. In this scenario the lead arm remains out front, fully extended even after the recovery arm has entered and extended. The hip power has been completely spent by this time, and the pulling arm, moving too late, is once again detached from the core power source. In this case, make sure the lead arm gets active and begins the pull as the recovery arm passes by your ear on its way to entering the water.

Once corrected, both the arm entering the water and the arm pulling through the water will be attached to that valuable power generated from the body's rotation. It may help to imagine your swim as a four-cylinder engine: The two primary cylinders are your hips, and they always fire together and cannot be separated. The third cylinder is your entry arm, and you want the two hip cylinders to fire at the moment the entry fingers touch the water so that the hips drive that arm forward into the water. Now, the last cylinder, the pull, needs to be attached to this engine. The pulling arm should still be out in front of you, having lowered only a few inches from where it was positioned at full extension. Then the two hip cylinders are firing in a manner that maximizes the entry arm and the greatest amount of the pull. That's hitting on all four cylinders.

Many of the skills identified in this chapter are fairly simple elements that have one correct position and a sense of finality once fixed. That's not the case with timing. You'll likely find a spot where hips and arms are working well together at one pace, but then you'll just want to swim faster. Faster swimming comes from faster arm turnover. This means timing must be learned again at the new, faster pace. This continues over and over through many different speeds until you reach an all-out sprint. Be patient with the process, and remain mentally present during your swims. Be aware of your body and head position as well as your arms and focus on your stroke so that you can be aware of how you feel while you are swimming. Keep tuned into your swim so that you can identify areas of weakness to work on that will ultimately help you become a faster swimmer. Focus will expedite your improvement. Timing is challenged by another element of the swim stroke, the catch.

## *Catch*

The catch is the moment of the swim stroke after the lead arm obtains full extension and before the pull. Here you have the opportunity to get the best grip on the water. A swim without a catch results in a straight arm pull. When the arm pull is straight, the arm is pressing down on the water and moving the body up a bit into the air. The result is a body that bobs up and down across the pool with each stroke. When a catch is employed, the arm is moving the body forward through the water and not up and down. To activate your catch, think about lifting the elbow toward the surface of the water and letting your fingers drop down toward the bottom of the pool the instant before you pull. The old adage of "reaching over a barrel" is still a great cue to get the desired arm shape. A more modern term is evolving: EVF, or early vertical forearm. Avoid the common flaw of bending the wrist; a superior catch comes from the elbow so that you are "holding" the water with the maximum surface area: forearm, palm, and fingers.

In the section on reducing drag earlier in this chapter, I discuss the drag resulting from an elbow that dips at full extension. This error also reduces propulsion: When the elbow dips below the wrist at full extension, a high-quality catch is virtually impossible to achieve. The arm extension must be flawless so that the elbow can quickly and easily lift to gain purchase on the water for the catch. Also, in the section on timing, I mention how the catch complicates the pursuit of a well-timed stroke. If you find that both your timing and catch need work, master timing first. It is far easier to add better shape to the lead arm for an improved catch once good timing has been locked into muscle memory.

## Pull

The pull is a critical aspect of the swim stroke. The priority is to maintain the widest surface area of your hand during the entire pull phase, which keeps the pull flat against the water like a paddle. If the hand rotates sideways, it begins to slip through the water with less effectiveness.

An ongoing debate in swimming centers around the best path for the pull to follow. One school of thought is that a deliberate S curve should be added to the pull so that it sweeps to the inside a bit at the beginning and then sweeps outside a bit toward the end. The basic idea is that the hand and forearm should constantly chase still water. The other school of thought is that the pull should be straight backward with no curve at all—as if you were paddling a surfboard and were restricted in your lateral motion by the rails of the bulky board. Your pull should be somewhere in the middle of these two philosophies. Adding intentional curves to your stroke isn't necessary, nor is it necessary to deliberately resist them. Because of the body's rotation during the stroke, a natural, moderate curve is added to the pull. Let that be your goal.

An effective catch and pull rely on a combination of muscular fitness including speed, endurance, power, and strength. One of the key principles of training is specificity: The most specific form of exercise for swimming is *swimming*. To enhance this activity, a small portion of your swim workouts can be done with a moderately sized paddle. Apply the principle of specificity in the gym as well: A seated pull-down exercise can be modified to become a standing swim-specific pull-down that more closely mimics the catch and pull used in the water.

## Kick

Previously, in the segment on timing, the focus was on the hips and hands working together. The kinetic chain of events actually includes the legs as well. Most triathletes who enter the sport with a rich history in bike or run, but very little swim background, place too much emphasis on the kick. An overactive kick can be a problem in two possible ways: (1) If a swimmer's kick is working too fast and too furious, it is likely out of sync with the body's rotation and working against each stroke. (2) The muscles that power a strong kick are some of the largest muscles in the body, and they demand oxygen. An overactive kick elevates heart rate, and the return on the kicking investment is not all that great.

An athlete can swim fast with just a light kick. That kick, however, has to be timed to effectively rotate the core during each stroke. Try this progression: Start by swimming with legs that are absolutely relaxed. Let them naturally and slightly separate in response to the body's rotation. Once the rhythm of that natural separation is established, begin to add only the slightest assistance, a "thump" to enhance the natural movement of the legs. This single beat will enhance the body's rotation and add a dynamic quality to that stroke. Then, attach that thump to each stroke. Later, for more speed, you can add additional kicks between each of the essential thumps.

Swimming is a skill sport, and the density of the water demands precision. The quickest results will come with complete focus on the issue you've selected. That may mean swimming smaller distances at a slower pace with longer rest to create greater mental concentration and more accurate movements. It is said the average human requires ten thousand precise repetitions before muscle memory can "own" the motion. You can expect to reduce that number as you increase your mental presence. Swim for accuracy, and remember it's not practice that makes perfect in swimming, it's *perfect* practice that makes perfect.

# PART III

# Competitive Strategy

# CHAPTER 16

# Open-Water Race Tactics

## Sara McLarty

Open-water swimming is one of the scariest parts of a triathlon. The murky water; the other competitors; and the lack of lanes, walls, and lines to follow can intimidate even the most fearless competitor. Using the knowledge provided by experienced athletes and coaches can make the first leg of a triathlon more enjoyable and full of success. This chapter covers many aspects of open-water swimming, including training, the start, drafting, transitioning to the bike, and much more, all developed through countless races, learned after making many mistakes, and resulting in a lot of success.

## Open-Water and Pool Training

Most triathlon swims take place in the open water, and for a good race performance, open-water training sessions are essential in the weeks before your event. But before diving into the nearest lake or ocean, take a few precautions for your personal safety:

- Wear a brightly colored cap to be visible to other swimmers, lifeguards, and boats.
- Tell someone where you are going and how far you are swimming.
- Swim in a group with other athletes, or have someone stay close by in a boat.
- Check with the local authorities to receive permission to swim in the open water.
- Stay alert, and be aware of your surroundings at all times.

Also, open-water swimming can help you practice in ways that more closely resemble a race course. Create a practice course using buoys made out of brightly colored plastic jugs tied to a weight or natural landmarks that are tall and easily observable. Use these open-water swims to practice sighting and turning at the buoys. When swimming with other athletes, practice drafting, passing, and dealing with the chaos that occurs at the start and at turn buoys. Learn how to quickly find the strap and unzip your wetsuit while jogging out of the water. Find open water that closely mimics an upcoming race environment to get comfortable with the water conditions (e.g., colder temperatures to practice with a full-body wetsuit).

Although open-water training is necessary as you get closer to race time, most swim training for triathlons takes place in a pool. Most athletes feel more comfortable training in the safety of a pool and enjoy participating with swim groups at local aquatic centers. The best pool is of standard length, such as 50 meters, 25 meters, or 25 yards, and is set up for lap swimming. Small or kidney-shaped backyard pools found as added amenities at homes and hotels may do in a pinch, but an actual lap pool, designed for swimming, is a far superior place to train. Even so, the safe and clear conditions of swim training in a pool do not fully prepare you for the situations that arise in open-water events. Lap pools offer clear water, lane markers, and lines on the bottom of the pool, while open-water courses are usually murky, and directional buoys are few and far between. The following drills are open-water specific and can be used in the pool to help prepare you for some of the open-water conditions you will encounter.

- *Tarzan*. Just like any other muscle, the neck needs to be prepared for sighting countless times during the race. This drill simply requires you to swim freestyle with your head out of the water. The body's position changes when your head is lifted out of the water. This activity teaches you to arch your back and kick hard to keep your feet near the surface.

- *Turning at the T*. This activity is a great way to simulate the continuous swimming of open-water events. Instead of swimming all the way to the wall, turn or flip 2 or 3 meters before the wall. This removes the small break you receive at each wall and can make any long swim feel more challenging.

- *Draft pack*. Several swimmers in the pool can simulate the feeling of drafting other swimmers during a race. Swimmers can practice positioning themselves behind the lead swimmer and learn how to not touch their feet with every stroke. After each 100, the lead swimmer should move to the back of the pack so the group is continually rotating.

- *Recovery stroke*. Learn to swim another stroke, such as backstroke or breaststroke, to feel more comfortable in the water. Back and breast strokes are good *safety strokes* you can switch to when you are feeling tired during an open-water swim or when you are having trouble locating a course buoy. Practice these strokes in the pool, and use them to keep moving forward during a long swim instead of hanging on the wall to rest.

## Dryland Preparations Before a Race

To gain as much information about the race and to be able to use that information to your advantage tactically, you should first learn the rules front and back as they apply to the race you are participating in. Also, take time to assess the water and scout the swim course before the start of the race. Many events open the course for practice a day before the race so that athletes can use this time to get to know specifics about the water and weather conditions in addition to the course. With limited time on race morning, the details picked up during a practice swim can provide good data during the race.

## Learn the Rules

Knowing and understanding the race rules as they apply to the swim leg of a triathlon is an invaluable tool. Rules that describe legal speedsuits and wetsuit thickness are constantly being reviewed and updated with advancements in technology. Ironman and 70.3 events generally follow USA Triathlon rules, but several technical rules and penalty enforcements have been relaxed. Be aware of the changes from one race to another.

The USAT rules that apply to the swimming leg of a triathlon are very straightforward. Swimmers may use any stroke for forward moment. Goggles and masks are permitted, but artificial propulsion devices (e.g., fins, paddles) are not allowed. A swimmer must complete the entire course and swim around all required buoys. Swim caps that are provided by the race management must be worn at the start of the race. According to Section 4.2, a swimmer may use the bottom to make forward progress. This allows athletes to stand and rest or dolphin dive through shallow water and underneath waves. Swimmers may touch or hold onto buoys and boats; however, they cannot use these objects to make forward progress. The general USAT rules of sportsmanship, conduct, and abandonment of equipment also apply to the swim course.

For more information and the most updated rules, see the following:

- USA Triathlon competitive rules at www.usatriathlon.org
- USA Triathlon's list of approved speedsuits and skinsuits at www.usatriathlon.org
- USA Triathlon's 2013 wetsuit rule FAQ at www.usatriathlon.org
- Ironman and 70.3 rules and FAQ at www.ironman.com
- ITU events competition rules at www.triathlon.org

## Assess the Water

Know as much about the water conditions as possible before race morning. Most practice swims are held during afternoon hours. The water and weather conditions can be very different in the early-morning hours, so talk with the locals and question the lifeguards about conditions at race time. Ask about typical wind speeds, wave conditions, current and tidal flows, and water quality. If there is no local knowledge available, perform a float test during the practice swim. Lie on the surface, and make note of the direction and speed you are drifting in order to detect water-flow currents or strong surface winds. When you are racing perpendicular to the current direction, make necessary adjustments to your directional heading to prevent being swept past a turn buoy. A shorter line can be swum between buoys by compensating for currents during the race. For example, if the ocean current is moving south, position yourself to start as far north on the beach as possible. This will allow you to use the flow of the current to get to the first turn buoy much easier and faster.

Pay attention to the quality of the water, and know that this can have serious effects on the outcome of your race. In saltwater events, be diligent about not swallowing or drinking an excess amount of water. Consuming too much seawater can lead to dehydration as the body tries to balance internal sodium levels. Also, be aware of the weather reports when racing in freshwater events. A recent rain can wash foreign substances into the water, which can lead to high levels of bacteria. Taking precautions, such as having antibiotics on hand, is not uncommon among elite triathletes who swim in foreign countries on a regular basis.

Races will continue as scheduled during a light rain shower but be postponed or canceled in the case of extreme downpours and lightning. Check online for rain dates and the organization's policy on weather-canceled events. Before signing up for any event, research the typical weather patterns on the race date, and prepare yourself for the worst-case scenario. Pack clear and metallic goggles to be ready for dark and light weather conditions on race morning.

## *Scout the Course*

Every athlete should learn the shape and direction of the swim course. Determine if you should stay to the left or the right side of the buoys. Memorize the total number of buoys in each direction, and note if the color and shape of the turn buoys are different. This is especially important when different-length courses are marked at the same time. For example, take a look at figure 16.1. This is a common setup for an event with a 750-meter and a 1.5K swim course. This course-within-a-course design allows the event directors to maximize the number of buoys they have at their disposal, but it can create some confusion for the athletes.

Athletes competing on the 750-meter course should be aware that they make a turn at the first buoy. Mistakes are easily made when an athlete does not make this turn because she sees another buoy in the distance. The second turn on the 750-meter course is after the swimmers pass three red buoys. The 1.5K course has triangle-turn buoys. These are important buoys, and some races will use buoys of different shapes or colors to mark the turns. An athlete on the 1.5K course needs to know that the red buoys are not part of his course.

Use the bright daylight hours during a practice swim to pick out high landmarks that can be sighted during the race. When you are surrounded by other swimmers or in choppy and wavy conditions, the buoys and finish chute are not always visible. Find something such as a building, tree, or radio antenna that is directly in line with the course. Use these landmarks for general sighting to stay on course. Also check the bottom surface at the start and finish areas, and make note of the degree of slope from shore. Practice run-ins, and count the number of steps from the starting line into knee-deep water. Then count the number of dolphin dives to waist-deep water. Use these numbers during the race as a general guide when the visual conditions are not perfect.

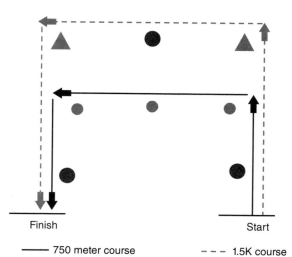

Finish          Start

——— 750 meter course          – – – 1.5K course

**FIGURE 16.1** **Sample swim course set up for multiple-distance races.**

▶ **Benefits of a Prerace Warm-Up**

To prevent cold and stiff muscles at the beginning of the race, a warm-up is necessary. Spend enough time in the water to activate muscles and increase heart rate. Athletes who take a long time to get activated should arrive early to benefit from the greatest amount of time in the water. In addition, water that is very cold can be shocking to the nervous system and cause panic and shortness of breath. In this situation, use any opportunity to get in the water before the race starts and adapt to the cold. This can reduce panic, shock, and pain at the start of the race. A prerace swim in cold water also provides an opportunity for the body to heat a layer of water between the skin and wetsuit, keeping you warm during the race.

However, triathletes may not be able to warm up in the water, depending on venue rules that prohibit people in the water (e.g., Florida 70.3); whether athletes have access to the water (e.g., Escape from Alcatraz); or poor time management by an athlete. Also a good prerace warm-up can be negated if an athlete becomes chilled while waiting for the race to start. In many cases, the early-morning air temperature will be much cooler than during the race, so staying dry can also mean staying warm. To ensure this, toss a cheap pair of thick socks and mittens into a prerace bag. These items can be worn on the beach and discarded before the start.

If a warm-up in the water is not an option, stretch cords or resistance bands are a great item to include in a prerace bag. Tie each end into a loop around a tree or pole, or grasp the tubing in each hand, and perform a few minutes of light dryland swimming movements. The resistance provided by the elastic band allows the arm and shoulder muscles to activate and warm up.

Also, a sufficient amount of running, cycling, yoga, or any activity that will raise the heart rate and increase blood flow can be substituted for swimming.

## Start

The start of a triathlon is the most chaotic moment of multisport. With a well-planned strategy, any triathlete can create an advantage for himself before the gun is fired. The simplest way is by choosing a starting position.

Take a look at figure 16.2. The shortest path from the starting line to the first buoy is the straight line A. Many athletes crowd into this position, assuming it is the fastest path to get to the first turn buoy. If starting line B is 50 meters wide, a simple calculation of Pythagorean's theorem shows that line C is only 403 meters. The time it takes to cover a distance of 3 meters in open water is insignificant when the hazards avoided by starting away from the crowd are considered. Although an outside starting position has advantages, weaker swimmers will benefit less. The shortest line, A, will always provide a strong drafting area that is created by the large crowd of swimmers racing to the buoy. However, novice athletes and others not comfortable with the high-contact zones should start to the outside for a more pleasant experience.

The outside starting position can also be utilized when there is a current in the water. If the water is running north, as in figure 16.2, a swimmer starting on the southern edge of starting line B is least likely to be carried past the first turn buoy. When the race is very crowded or there is no beneficial starting position, choose a position based on the

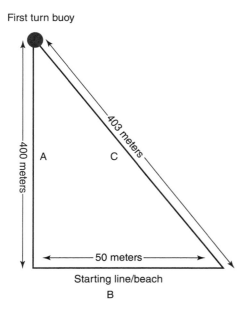

First turn buoy

403 meters

A    C

400 meters

50 meters

Starting line/beach

B

**FIGURE 16.2** **Maximize your starting position by choosing the smartest line to the first turn buoy.**

location of other athletes. Create an instant drafting position by lining up next to a slightly stronger swimmer. Follow the bubbles trailing behind the lead swimmers as soon as the race starts.

Many triathlons start on land, with a short run into the water. This is referred to as a beach start. The simple rule of thumb for a beach start is to run normally into the water. When you reach the water, lift your legs and feet up in a high-stepping run until the water is over your knees. In most situations, you can launch into your first dolphin dive when the water is above your knees (be sure to verify the slope of the ground *before* the start of the race). Dolphin-dive until the water is about waist high, and then begin swimming.

In an open-water start, the swimmers are all in the water and can begin swimming when the start is signaled. When a 30-second warning is announced, or if the start is imminent, put your body into a horizontal position on the surface of the water, but keep your head raised. Scull lightly with your hands, and kick lightly with your feet to maintain a stationary position at the line. When the race starts, drop your head into the water, and immediately start kicking and swimming forward.

Also, many elite athletes will have the opportunity to dive off a pontoon or stationary pier to start a triathlon. These starts are designed to give each athlete an equal position on the course. Success at this kind of start is based on reaction time, leg power, underwater kicking and breakout efficiency, and starting speed in the water. Basically, these are the same principles that apply to a start from the diving blocks into a pool. Coaching and training should be modeled similar to that of a competitive swimmer.

# Triathlon Swim Tactics

Triathletes have adopted many methods of moving through the open water quickly and efficiently. Some things, such as dolphin dives, have been adapted from lifeguards in action, while other tactics, such as drafting other competitors, are tricks that open-water swimmers have been doing for many years. Triathlon events take place in all types of bodies of water and conditions, so athletes must learn how to maneuver and stay competitive. The following are some very common tactics you can employ in almost any type of triathlon competition.

## *Dolphin Dives*

Dolphin dives are a quick and efficient way to move through shallow water and maneuver through breaking waves. They are named as such because the athletes look like dolphins when they dive underwater and then pop up and arc over the surface.

Start by practicing in water that is deep enough to cover your knees but does not come above your waist. Jump forward with your arms outstretched in front of your face and dive down toward the bottom. When your hands come in contact with the ground, dig your fingers into the soil, and use this leverage to pull your body forward through your arms. Grabbing the sand when diving under a powerful wave will keep you from being swept backward by the undercurrent. Then, use your feet to push off the bottom and launch your body forward along the surface of the water. Don't forget to look forward and breathe between every dive. Bring your arms around like the recovery of a butterfly stroke, and then dive toward the bottom again. Water deeper than waist high is not efficient for dolphin diving because the momentum of pushing off the bottom and flying over the surface of the water does not carry you all the way to the bottom.

Remember, however, that when doing dolphin dives, safety is of utmost importance. Always lead with your hands and arms to prevent injuries caused by hitting the ground with your face or head. Open water can have little to no visibility, so sandbars, rocks, or other unknown objects can be lying just under the surface.

## Sighting

There are no lane markers or lines on the bottom in open water. Staying on course and swimming from one buoy to the next depends on how well each athlete can maintain a straight line in the water. *Sighting* is the term used to describe when an athlete lifts her head to look for the buoys and other landmarks while swimming. There are many ways to sight the course markers (e.g., taking a few strokes of breaststroke), but most of these methods reduce speed and efficiency in the water.

In calm water, you should lift only your eyes and nose out of the water to look forward. After sighting, turn your head to the side for a breath and continue swimming. You can sight a couple of times in quick succession to recognize and memorize the position of the buoys and other swimmers. If the immediate area is clear, and waves and current aren't a factor, swim without sighting for a while to let you maintain an efficient stroke, resulting in a faster swim with less energy used for unnecessary sighting. In rough water, ocean waves, or other unsatisfactory conditions, however, you should sight often to maintain the most direct line between buoys. Use the same method as described previously, but lift your head higher to sight over small, choppy waves. In large ocean waves, feel the rhythm and swells in the water, and plan to sight on top of the wave to catch the best view of the course.

A swimmer is most efficient while maintaining a horizontal body position, but when the head is lifted to sight for a buoy or landmark, the swimmer is forced out of this position. When sighting, arch your back and kick extra hard to compensate for lifting your head out of the water. It is easier to return to a horizontal body position if the abdomen drops than if the legs and feet sink.

## Drafting

According to a study published in 2008 (Silva et al.), a swimmer on the feet of another can experience between 16 and 45 percent less drag through the water. This is very significant over distances such as 2.4 miles (3.8 km), but it has a direct impact on all open-water swimming events. Drafting can allow an athlete to finish a swim in the same time with less effort expended, or it can help a swimmer finish faster by using the same effort.

The hardest part of drafting is knowing whom to draft. Athletes who continually compete against the same people will figure out whose feet they should be following. When racing an unknown crowd, it is best to start at your own pace. As the crowd thins out after the start, settle in behind someone and draft for a while. If you think the pace is too slow, move to the side, swim ahead, and look for different feet to draft. Drafting etiquette, though, is to not touch the feet of the lead swimmer. This not only irritates the swimmer but can also slow him down. Excessive feet tapping can also lead to angry retaliations by the lead swimmer. When drafting, swim with a very wide arm entry at the front of the stroke. This will place your hands on either side of the lead swimmer's feet.

Another type of drafting, called *shorting*, is where an athlete drafts on the hip, which is another beneficial location. A drafting athlete can ride the wave of another swimmer by positioning her head next to the lead swimmer's hip. No contact is necessary between athletes. It is easier to sight when drafting in this position because the lead swimmer is not blocking the drafting swimmer's view. An athlete in the shorting position can quickly swim over the hips of the lead athlete to change positions or swim in a different direction. Changing sides is common when drafting in a choppy or wavy course. The shorting athlete can use other swimmers as a wall to reduce the chop and battering from waves on the upwind side.

When drafting, remember you should never rely on another athlete to swim the correct course or take the shortest path between buoys. Every triathlete should sight the course to prevent misdirection, even when following the bubbles of another athlete.

## Buoy Turns

Turn buoys are one of the most chaotic places in a triathlon or open-water swim. Packs of swimmers get backed up trying to take the shortest and most direct line. As a result, many people get pushed underwater, have their goggles knocked off, or experience some other form of unfriendly contact.

To escape the chaos, a swimmer can choose to swim a slightly longer route to the outside of the melee. This is a good choice for faster swimmers, timid swimmers, and smaller athletes. In most cases the excess distance swum is insignificant, but some races are so large and crowded that swimming to the outside of the group can be a poor decision. In this case, the shortest and smartest decision is to stay close to the buoy. Take short strokes with a high cadence when navigating through the chaos near a buoy. Long strokes are usually impossible, and quick strokes will keep you on top of the water and moving forward.

## Pacing

With no pace clocks or marked distances, properly pacing an open-water swim can be a challenge. Any experienced triathlete knows that responding incorrectly to the natural adrenaline burst at the start of a race can lead to a poor overall swim. Learning how to pace begins long before race day arrives, and every swim practice is important training for a successful open-water swim.

Pacing in open water can become simple by listening to your body and associating an effort level with a speed. During practice, label personal swimming speeds with an effort level similar to the rating of perceived exertion (RPE) scale you learned about in chapter 9:

- *Level 1 (RPE 1-3)*—I can swim at this effort for an hour.
- *Level 2 (RPE 4-6)*—I can swim at this effort for 30 minutes.
- *Level 3 (RPE 7-8)*—I can swim at this effort for 10 minutes.
- *Level 4 (RPE 9)*—I can swim at this effort for 5 minutes.
- *Level 5 (RPE 10)*—I can swim at this effort for 60 seconds.

You should associate each effort level with an internal feeling so you can recognize that level without any outside data. For example, you might associate moving from level 2 to level 3 with a need to breathe more often. Other personal cues that can be easily perceived are heart rate, kicking tempo, and muscle sensation. Use your personal swimming effort levels to map out a plan for a successful open-water swim. By recognizing personal cues in the race, you can adjust your effort level to swim at the same levels you have been training in practice.

## Finish

Depending on the length of the course, athletes are typically in the water between 10 minutes and 2 hours during the swim leg of a triathlon. During this time, your body adjusts to a horizontal position. The legs are kept in a relatively straight position with minimal movement, especially with a wetsuit providing flotation. As a result, when you reach the swim exit, you can have trouble standing and moving in a vertical position. To prepare for the quick transition from swimming to standing and running, use the last 200 to 400 meters of the swim course to help your body adjust. Start by increasing the kick to warm up the leg muscles. A few small breaststroke kicks are helpful to loosen up the quadriceps and provide a light flexion stretch to the ankles and calves.

Many athletes experience a spike in heart rate during the swim exit. Prepare for this spike by kicking more and building to a higher effort level during the last 100 meters. Getting the blood moving in the lower extremities and increasing heart rate is the first step. The second step is to swim as far as possible into the shallow water. It is inefficient to try to walk or wade through deep water, and dolphin diving is dangerous because the ground slants upward. By swimming until your hands scrape the bottom, you can stand up in very shallow water and immediately start running.

Training harder is not the only way to a faster and more successful open-water swim. Learning from your mistakes, watching experienced athletes, and using a few commonsense tips can turn a choppy, cold, and overcrowded race into an enjoyable and successful experience. The little details from an event are the first to fade from your memory. Whether or not you are satisfied with your results at the finish line, jot down a couple of notes after each race. After the endorphins, adrenaline, and muscle soreness have faded, take a look at your postrace notes. Find little places where improvements can be made. Address these changes during practice so they become automatic and natural. Talk with other triathletes, and share personal stories of failures and successes in the journey to leading the pack out of the water.

# CHAPTER 17

# Strategies for Drafting and Nondrafting Races

## Scott Schnitzspahn

Riding a bike may seem pretty simple considering most of us learned the basic skill of riding as a youth. Through training, though, we can become even more skilled and efficient in pedaling, cornering, and maintaining an aerodynamic and powerful position on the bike.

However, going fast in a triathlon cycling leg requires more than just being well conditioned and having proficient skills—you must also be tactically smart. Nondrafting triathlon races, the most common for amateur athletes, do not allow athletes to ride close behind another rider and gain an aerodynamic benefit. In these races, an even-paced effort over the race course is the best tactic. With proper pacing, an athlete should reach the end of the bike leg with adequate energy left for the run, but a fast time recorded on the bike will aid the overall race time (and finish place).

In draft-legal racing, drafting behind another rider is allowed. This racing format is not just for professionals anymore but also for aspiring Olympians in races for the youth elite (13 to 15 years old in the United States), junior (16 to 19 years old), and under 23 divisions, and even a few races for age-group (amateur) athletes. The tactics in draft-legal racing differ drastically, as athletes must react to each other according to their strengths and weaknesses to get to the end of the bike leg in a position to maximize their race-finish placing, regardless of overall finishing time.

## Nondrafting Races

As mentioned, traditional triathlon rules prohibit riding in close enough proximity to other riders to gain an advantage through drafting, which means being shielded from the wind by another rider. However, by effectively maneuvering your bike around other riders, you can have a smooth and fast individual race.

Once aboard your bike and into your pedals, take a position in your lane according to the rules of your race. The majority of races will have you riding in the direction of automobile traffic, and just like when driving a car, you should stay to the right unless passing. Along the right-hand side of the road is often a painted white line. If you can comfortably ride this line, it can sometimes offer a smoother surface than the road and reduce your rolling resistance slightly where the tires meet the tarmac, resulting in a slightly faster speed depending on the surface of the road. Keep your head up, though, to look for riders who may be riding slower than you that you will need to pass.

The pass in nondrafting triathlon is where tactics come into play. Passes must be made quickly and intentionally or the passing rider risks being in the draft of the rider he is passing for too long and gaining an advantage that can result in a time penalty. According to USA Triathlon age-group rules, once a rider is within 7 meters of the leading edge of the front wheel (approximately three bike lengths) of the rider in front of him, he is drafting. But the rules do allow for some time to cross the draft of another rider legally. USA Triathlon rules state that passes must be made within 15 seconds of entering the draft zone. A strong rider who is making his way through the field should pass others by riding straight up behind the rider to be passed and entering his draft zone, progressing up to a few meters behind the rider he is passing (see figure 17.1), and then moving to the side and completing the pass. This brief respite from the wind can temporarily increase your speed or decrease the amount of work required to maintain your speed. If you are able to leapfrog from rider to rider, continually passing others, you can essentially be legally drafting for a large portion of the race. In addition, when you are being passed by faster riders, you can also use their temporary draft as they accelerate away from you. Again, rules stipulate that you must immediately exit the draft zone of another rider, but those few seconds can be helpful, and multiple occasions of saving a few seconds can add up over the course and leave you more fresh for the run.

Riders should be aware of wind direction and barriers to the wind as well, such as buildings, trees, or vehicle barriers that might provide a moment or two of shelter from the wind, and use these moments to gain free time on the course by riding closer to the wind-shielding object and accelerating slightly.

Corners also provide a tactical opportunity in the race. Being the first into a corner allows you to choose the speed and path (or line) that is fastest for you. If you enter a corner behind a less skilled rider, you may be forced to slow down to avoid a collision or alter your course through the turn, losing time. Ideally, make your passes well before the corner so you can choose your best line. Sprinting to pass someone too close to a corner just means you'll need to brake harder than you wanted to avoid taking the turn too fast. This wastes effort and will cost you momentum that you could otherwise carry out of the turn and down the next straightaway. Saving energy and being smooth on the bike course through smart tactics of legal drafting and managing other riders through corners can leave you with more energy for a fast run.

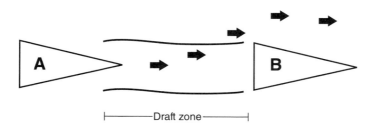

**FIGURE 17.1**    **Rider A passes rider B through the draft zone, gaining time.**

# Drafting Races

In draft-legal racing, practiced at the Olympic Games, international elite races, and junior development events, riding in the draft of another cyclist is allowed and, in fact, encouraged. A draft-legal race is much more tactical in nature, as riders jockey for position in a rolling chess match much like a bike race.

The primary difference between a bike race and a triathlon is what happens at the very end of this game of aerodynamic chess. In a bike race, riders strategize to put themselves in a position to contend for the final sprint and win the race as the bikes cross the finish line. In a triathlon, the finish line of the cycling portion is the dismount line, where the stage for the run is set. Both are similar, though, in that the goal is to approach the finish line with an advantage over the other opponents and enough energy in reserve for the final effort at the end of the race, whether that be a mad sprint to the finish line or a switch to the run leg of a triathlon. The strategy that each athlete employs throughout the race will depend on her individual strengths and weaknesses compared with the strengths and weaknesses of her opponents.

## *Moving Within the Pack*

Because the bike leg of a draft-legal triathlon has been described as a game of chess, please consider the road as the chess board and the riders as the chess pieces. Each rider, just like each chess piece, has a specific set of skills, or "moves." If you have ever played chess, you will recognize the following pieces and their analogous riders.

### *Pawns*

The pawn in chess is the worker, present in large numbers. Pawns have limited mobility, able to move only one square on the chess board at a turn in only the forward direction, unless overtaking an opposing piece, when they are allowed to move diagonally. Most packs of riders have a large number of pawns in them as well. These riders are content to sit in their positions in the pack, occasionally moving slowly forward in the pack to briefly take a turn at the front before being overtaken by other riders. Just as in chess, pawns serve the purpose of protecting the more valuable pieces on the board (athletes with the ability to win the race) and make occasional attacks to the more vulnerable pieces (making the cycle leg harder on their teammates' competitors).

### *Rooks and Bishops*

The rook and bishop are able to move in a straight (rook) or diagonal (bishop) direction for as many spaces as the board is clear of other pieces. The riders who are rooks and bishops have the strength to move very quickly past the pawns from the back of the pack and straight to (or off of) the front of a pack. Rooks and bishops don't have a lot of technical skill, but they are very strong and make aggressive offensive moves.

### *Knights*

In chess, the knight can move two squares in a horizontal or vertical direction and then one square at a 90-degree angle. This piece cannot cover as much ground in one turn as a rook or bishop, but it has the ability to go around corners in tactical offensive or defensive moves. Knights are the riders in a race who may not be the strongest of the bunch, but they have the technical ability to move easily within the pack, take corners quickly and easily, and use very little energy.

### King

The king, although the most valuable piece in a chess game since its capture ends the game, is really quite weak and vulnerable to attack. Although the king can move in any direction, it can move only one square of the board at a time, meaning it must use all the other pieces on the board to hide behind and move only to stay out of trouble. On the bike, the king is usually very skilled, but he can be weak compared with the other riders, so he will do everything he can to stay in the protection of the pack, riding as easily as possible and hoping to get to the end of the ride with as much energy as he can. In bike racing, kings are the specialist sprinters who, if they can get to the finish line with the front group, can win the race with their devastating sprint ability. In triathlon, the few very best runners are the kings. They hide in the pack on the bike, conserving as much energy as possible for the upcoming run, where they can move to the front of the field and break the tape first with their dominant running ability.

### Queen

The queen moves like both a rook and a bishop, able to cover many squares of the board at a time in any direction. The queen can't change direction like a knight, but the ability to move around the board with ease makes it the most valuable offensive and defensive piece on the board. The queen is the perfect partner to the king, as the queen can protect the king or strike quickly against the opposing player's defenses. The queen is usually the piece that ends the day for the opposing king. In a race, the queen is the all-arounder, the athlete who can launch an attack, cover moves by other riders, move easily in the pack, and protect her teammate who might be the runner or sprinter on her team who needs to get to the finish line fresh and still in the game.

Now that you know the chess pieces on the board and their skills and tendencies, I'm sure you can quickly name elite triathletes, teammates, or training partners who match these descriptions. In a race, if you know what chess pieces are on the road and where they are positioned as well as what kind of chess piece you are, you'll be able to make better tactical decisions for your own benefit and that of your teammates.

## Transition 1 (T1)

After the chaos of the first stage of a triathlon—the swim—all the athletes enter the first transition area, get their bikes, and frantically dash onto the bike course. The first 400 yards or meters of the bike course can determine the outcome of the race as the athletes scramble to form up into various packs, finding other riders to work with in an effort not to be caught without a partner to share the work by taking turns drafting off each other. They also fight to close gaps in front of them so that the pack they end up in is as close to the front of the race as possible, before the "chess moves" begin. A slow transition can mean the difference between making the front pack and being in contention for a medal at the end of the race, or being stuck in the purgatory of a large chase pack that crawls around the course, unable to organize a proper chase, sealing the fate of all who are caught in it.

If you are not a strong swimmer or the shuffle in the first transition leaves you out of the front pack, or breakaway (which I talk about in the next section), you may be out in no-man's land at the start of the ride. Immediately out of transition you have a choice: Ride as hard as you can to catch the front pack or the group immediately in front of you, or sit up and wait for a pack of riders coming from behind. If you know who is in front of you and who is behind and the ratio of "chess pieces" among them, you can make an informed decision about the piece you are. Otherwise, 9 times out of 10, the best answer is to ride as hard as you can until the various groups form in the first lap, taking note of who you are passing and who is getting a free ride on your wheel and vice versa. Once in a group, take the time to recover by sitting in the draft of other riders, cycling in an easy gear, and taking in water or other nutrition.

The most common mistake that triathletes in draft-legal races make at this crucial time is to immediately begin putting on their shoes after mounting their bikes out of T1. Riders should keep their heads up and ride through the initial chaos on the road, waiting to put on their shoes until they are up to speed and in a group or, at the least, on another rider's wheel getting a strong draft.

## Breakaway and Front Pack

After the swim and T1, the leaders of the race onto the bike course form up into the breakaway (a small group of approximately 10 riders or fewer) or the front pack (the first large group of approximately 10 or more riders).

A small breakaway group off the front is ideal for those who compose this group because of the physical and psychological advantages. Physically, a smaller group is able to take tight turns quicker and negotiate a technical course more efficiently than a large group of riders in the chase group. The "accordion effect" causes a large group of riders to slow down as they negotiate a turn or obstacle and bunch up and then stretch out as the front of the group accelerates away and the back of the group has to wait for those in front of them to pick up the pace. A long accordion compresses and extends much slower than a short accordion, as does a pack of riders.

Psychologically, a small group off the front knows that if they work together and are successful, they will share in the spoils of victory among them, and thus most of the group are motivated to work hard. In large groups, many of the riders believe they can benefit from the group and adopt a parasitic role, happy to let others do the work for them. Usually there are more parasites than workers in these groups, and the large group becomes unmotivated very quickly, slowing down and benefiting the breakaway even more.

If you find yourself in the breakaway or front pack, you must quickly assess the other athletes in the group and ascertain the "chess piece" that each member of the group represents. If a group is small, usually between four and eight riders, and is made up mostly of rooks and bishops, the group has a very strong chance of being successful and getting away from the other athletes in the race and should begin work immediately to extend their slim advantage. If the group is mostly pawns and kings, they won't have the strength to stay away from the bishops, rooks, and queens quickly hunting them down from behind.

If you find yourself in a small group of bishops, rooks, and queens, jump in and get to work. Expect a very hard ride with a great reward for your effort at the end. The first step for a group like this is to establish a tight formation, adjusted in shape to make the best use of the prevailing winds on the course. Usually the fastest is a straight line, with athletes taking turns at the front slicing the wind and providing a draft for the other riders in their wake. Each rider should adopt a low aerodynamic position, with the lead rider in the line using his aerobars if he has them and the riders behind with hands on their lowest handlebar position ("the drops") and a finger on the brake/shift lever. Elbows should be bent to make backs flat and heads low. This low position not only creates a bullet shape to move fast through the air but also lowers the rider's center of gravity for fast cornering.

Once the line is formed, each athlete will take a "pull" at the front and then move over to allow another rider to take a pull in short intervals. Usually 5 to 15 seconds works best depending on the group size and individual strengths of the riders. Stronger riders or riders in smaller groups can take longer pulls. After taking her pull, the lead rider will flick her elbow out to the side, signaling the next rider in line that she will be moving slightly to the side of any crosswind and allowing the line to proceed alongside her. The former leader will ease her effort ever so slightly as she moves over and allows the line to pass, providing the riders who are passing a slight shielding from the crosswind in addition to the aerodynamic benefit of having a rider in front of them (see figure 17.2). Once at the back of the line, the former leader increases her pace slightly and rejoins the line at the back. A helpful gesture is for the last rider in the line to let the former leader know she has reached the back with a hand gesture, short word or two, or even a grunt, as that may be all that is possible with the hard effort the breakaway requires.

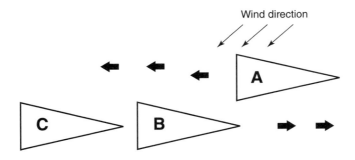

**FIGURE 17.2**　**Rider A finishes her pull and moves toward the direction of the wind, easing off her effort to allow riders B and C to pass her before taking her position at the back of the line.**

The key to this group's success is that every athlete shares the work and that the group moves smoothly, with no rapid accelerations or decelerations. Often a rider will get excited when he takes the lead position in line and increases his pace. In turn, the other riders must also accelerate to stay together. This causes the group to fatigue faster from the repeated hard efforts and to be less aerodynamic as large gaps open between the riders. These surges can sabotage a group and cause a loss of time to the chasers and in most cases should be avoided. There are exceptions to every rule, though, and a poorly functioning group can be a great tactic, as will be described later.

## Sitting In

Although the ideal front pack contains bishops, rooks, and queens, if you find yourself in a front group of kings and pawns, you might as well become a pawn yourself. To become a pawn, you need to "sit in," meaning get in the draft of another pawn, and wait for the next group of riders to join you and change the dynamics in the group. These types of athletes will not be strong enough to stay away from the chasers no matter how hard they try. Also, if all the kings of the race, the best runners in the field, are in the lead group, they will immediately realize it and reduce their cycling efforts because they all will want to stay as fresh as possible for the duel on foot that lies ahead. The kings will want their queens and other henchmen to join their group to protect them and get them to the end of the game either equal with their opposing kings or with a slight advantage, but rarely will they try to push the cycle leg without help.

## Slowing the Front Pack

Now, if you are not a king but rather a pawn or other chess piece in the race and find yourself in a lead pack that has a chance at success because of the number of bishops, rooks, and queens in the group, you can help your king (who is behind in the chase pack) by staying in the front group and disrupting their efforts. To slow down your lead group and increase the chances of the chase pack's catching up, you have a number of options depending on your skill set.

One way to slow a pack down is to actually ride faster, just at the wrong times. As described earlier, taking pulls at the front that are too hard with sudden accelerations causes the group to string out, making the trailing riders sprint to close the nonaerodynamic gaps (see figure 17.3). Once they have sprinted to catch your wheel, ease off your effort, and now they will have to brake to avoid running into you, or they will have to come around you and take the lead themselves. Although hard efforts to slow the pack seem counterintuitive and may actually cause a temporary increase in the overall pace of the group, consistently bad moves in the group will wear out the other riders and ultimately slow the pack down. At a minimum, the cyclists' legs will be more tired for the run than if the group had been riding a steady pace. You will not win any popularity contests within your group of riders with this tactic, so be prepared for a tongue lashing at best, and if they are smart, they will try to drop you at worst.

Another way to slow the group is to purposely ride a little slower than the group wants to go. This can be done by taking weaker pulls; going more slowly than necessary through turns; and allowing gaps to slowly open up between you and the riders in front of you that must be closed by the riders behind you, who have to accelerate and come around you. Again, your pack mates won't be particularly pleased with you, so

**FIGURE 17.3**    **Rider A surges to open up a gap between him and the other riders.**

be ready to sprint back on to the group repeatedly as your disruptions are countered by hard accelerations designed to drop you from the group.

## Dropping Riders From Your Pack

As a strong rider in a group of other strong riders, you will want the group to work together and have each member carry her fair share of the load. However, often there will be a "passenger" or two on your train who intends only to go along for the ride. If these passengers are pawns or riders who are simply not strong enough to contribute, and you know you or your king can outrun them, there is no harm in letting them sit in the back and get a free ride in the draft of the group. Encourage them to stay out of the way and not disrupt the smooth, strong pace of your group, though. If a passenger starts slowing you down by employing some of the tactics just described, or if she is a strong runner who is saving her energy by hiding at the back of your group, then it's time to drop this passenger from your train.

To drop a rider from your pack, you and the other riders in your group will need to coordinate your efforts to wear out the passenger until he can no longer stay with you or deem it not worth the effort. If he is taking a pull at the front now and then, you can start by having the strongest rider of the group position himself immediately behind the targeted passenger when he takes his pull. Once he is a little fatigued from his effort at the front and has pulled off to allow the strongest rider to take his turn, the group can accelerate rapidly behind the strongest rider's effort at the front (see figure 17.4). The sudden acceleration combined with the fatigue from just taking a pull should catch the passenger off guard and make it difficult for him to get back into the draft of the group that is now accelerating up the road in front of him. To make it even more challenging for the passenger, the strong lead rider should move the pack across the road away from the passenger, isolating him in the wind by himself. A few of these efforts should cause the passenger to drop off, or at least get him to stay away from the front of the group where he isn't helpful.

Once the passenger has resigned himself to a seat at the back of the train, it will be a little more difficult to drop him off, and a rider may even need to be sacrificed to take the passenger off with him. A simple tactic is to have the rider immediately in front of the passenger suddenly move out of the draft of the pack and accelerate up the

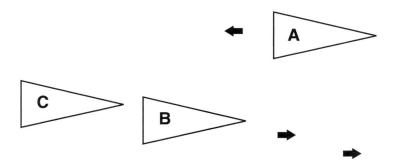

**FIGURE 17.4**    **After "the passenger" (rider A) takes his pull, the strongest rider of the group (rider B) pulls hard and takes the rest of the group away from rider A in an attempt to drop him.**

road, leaving a gap in front of the passenger and eliminating his draft. The passenger will need to accelerate and expend energy to get back into the draft on his own or be dropped. Recognizing this tactic, the pack should allow the rider who just "attacked" the passenger to get easily back into the pack and recover in the draft. If repeated efforts to cut the passenger loose by attacking him haven't worked, a sacrifice may be required.

A rider who is working for her teammate in the pack can sacrifice herself and try to take the passenger off the back of the group with her. This tactic again calls for the passenger to be at or near the back of the group. Ideally, a rider who is strong enough to chase back on to the group alone will sacrifice herself as the antagonist to drop off the passenger and then get back on to the group on her own effort. The antagonist again positions herself immediately in front of the passenger, but this time instead of attacking, simply rides a little slower than the pack and allows a gap to open up in front of her (see figure 17.5). The passenger now is in "check" (to continue the chess analogy) and must make a decision—accelerate around the rider in front of her and try to regain the group or stay on the wheel of the rider in front of her and watch the pack ride away. If the passenger chases the group, the rider who allowed the gap to open up simply gets in the draft of the passenger and gets a free ride back to the group in order to try again or gets to witness the implosion of the passenger chasing the pack in vain. Ideally, once the antagonist realizes the passenger cannot regain the pack by herself, she can attack the passenger from behind by riding across the road and getting separation, leaving the passenger to fend for herself and sprinting back into the group.

**FIGURE 17.5**    Once "the passenger" (rider A) has taken her place at the back, "the antagonist" (rider C) allows a gap to open up between them and the rider just ahead. The passenger must now decide to stay in the draft of the antagonist or go around her to close the gap and get back in the draft of rider B.

## Chase Pack

The chase pack or packs in a draft-legal triathlon work in a similar way to the front pack or breakaway, but there are a lot more chess pieces to figure out and manipulate. Depending on who is in the lead pack or breakaway, the chase pack may want to chase and catch the leaders or let them tire out all by themselves.

If a chase is required because of dangerous runners being in the lead pack, the same principles apply. The chase needs a consistently strong effort, with little disruption to the pace. The group must communicate to keep the pace high and smooth and relegate the passengers to the back of the train. Although weaker riders can be dropped from a well-organized chase pack, dropping off passengers can be much harder in a larger chase pack. The kings in the group should hide from the wind and be protected by their pawns, who will look out for road hazards and lead their runners safely around the course within the pack, being mindful of what is happening at the front of the race.

## *All Together*

Often times, especially on flatter and less technical bike courses, the packs will come together and form a large pack, or peloton, of riders with all the chess pieces represented. Once this happens, each rider needs to make a lot of decisions. Although everyone wants to save energy for the run, some riders will recognize that they need to break away from the group if they want to factor in the medals. Positioning within the pack is important. There is a saying that goes "The front third of the pack makes it happen. The middle third of the pack watches it happen. The back third of the pack asks what happened."

Smart riders who need a breakaway will watch for the opportunity when their main competitors for the run are out of position and back in the pack and unable to respond to their moves. They will stay up front to respond to other riders' attacks and try to join them in a breakaway or wait until the right moment to launch their own attack.

Flat races can be very exciting if the pack is aggressive and attacks are common. The biggest mistake many attackers make is giving up too soon. Many times a rider will make a strong move away from the pack and establish separation between himself and the chasers in the group and then look back within a few pedal strokes to assess his progress. If there are even a few riders chasing him, often the attacker will give up his effort and return to the group, and the pace slows again until the next attack. The lulls in the pace of the group after an attacker is caught can be prime opportunities for a counterattack, so riders should always be on their guard when the pace slows too much.

Attackers will be more successful if they fully commit to their tactic and go hard for at least 30 seconds. Usually there will be a strong initial chase from behind by the stronger riders, but somewhere near the front of this chase will be a weak link, a rider who can't maintain the effort for more than a few seconds. When that weaker rider "cracks," the gap will open up and the breakaway will go. Solo attacks are almost never successful in triathlon, so a small group off the front is exactly what an attacker should want. If you attack, commit fully to your effort until the elastic snaps and you are away with some other strong riders who can assist you in your aggressive and possibly race-changing move.

However, "false attacks" can also be very useful in trying to lull your competitors into a false sense of security. If you attack the group repeatedly but give up early and allow yourself to be caught a few times, the group will begin to believe you are not worth chasing. When you finally commit to your attack, you may be able to more easily get away with a compatriot or two.

Timing your attack properly is important as well. If you are trying to get away with a few other strong riders, wait until just before they take a pull to attack. This will ensure they are fresh and fully ready to join you in your efforts. If you attack when a strong rider has just finished his pull at the front, he most likely won't have the energy to go with you.

## *Head to Head*

If you do get into a small breakaway, either off the swim or from a large main pack, the first task is to get a comfortable gap from the pack. Encourage your group, communicate, and work together for everyone's benefit. However, once that gap is established, you must be smart in your tactics to win the race.

If you find yourself in a head-to-head competition with another or a few athletes, with a large enough gap over the rest of the field that you know the winner of the race will come from your group, you'll need to establish who is the best runner in your duel. If you are favored on the run, simply do your fair share of the work, or even a little more, knowing you can beat your rivals, and contribute to holding off the field. If your rivals are stronger on the run, you must make them work, keeping yourself as fresh as possible while still maintaining the gap over the rest of the field.

The passenger scenarios described earlier can be used in your tactical maneuvers. Simply slowing down while in front will force your competitors to work harder to come around you or lose time to the group. If they take more of their fair share, you can sit in and stay fresh for the run. If they slow as well and refuse to lead, or play games with you by slowing when leading as well, you can attack them and try to gain an advantage going into the run, or at least wear them out chasing you. The ultimate scenario is a two-on-one or three-on-one situation, where multiple athletes act as a team and use the passenger scenarios to drop off or exhaust the best runner of the small group.

## Transition 2 (T2)

In draft-legal racing, the medals are usually decided by a few seconds or less. Positioning as you enter the second transition from bike to run is key to winning medals. Whether you are in a breakaway, front pack, chase pack, or large main pack, being first out of transition gives you a head start on the run.

The most challenging situation tactically and technically for draft-legal racing comes within the final kilometer of the bike course as riders remove their feet from their cycling shoes and jockey for position at the end of the ride to be the first of their group into transition. Similar to a bike race as riders move forward for the final sprint, riders who have been sitting on as passengers suddenly appear at the front of the pack looking for an advantage over the other athletes in their group who have been doing all the work. Because riders are fatigued from the swim and bike, unsafe risks are often taken. Riders must be aggressive to ensure a good position at the dismount line but weigh the risks against their safety and running abilities. A strong runner may choose to stay out of the melee and safely ride in at the back of the field, but if another strong runner who is her equal chooses to be aggressive and gets a few seconds' advantage at the end of the bike, the difference in the race can be made.

## Getting to the Front

Typically, as the pack approaches the finish line, riders move forward from the back to the front around the outsides of the group (see figure 17.6). If you are attentive and act decisively, you can jump into this movement on a strong rider's wheel and get a free ride to the front. Be careful not to move erratically and cut off another rider, causing a crash. If you are a strong rider, get out of your shoes early and move forward around the group when others are slowing to remove their shoes. The trick if you are not the best bike handler or strongest rider is to time your move properly so you don't go too

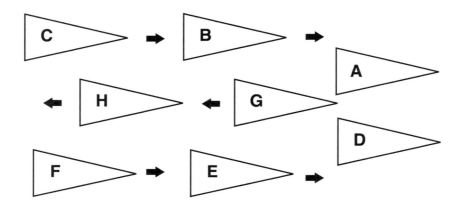

**FIGURE 17.6** **The typical flow of the pack as the end of the bike leg approaches. Riders A, B, and C are moving up on the left side, while riders D, E, and F move up on the right side. Riders G and H are boxed in and forced to move backward through the pack.**

soon and get sucked to the back before the dismount line or wait too long and miss the current moving forward after the strong riders have established themselves at the front.

Once you have made it to the front of the group as the line is approaching, the challenge is to hold your position and not get pulled back down through the middle of the pack as more riders move up around the outside. One tactic to maintain status at the front is to take an outer position at the front of the pack, forcing riders from the back to go up on your inside. This way you can stay out of the scrum, not get boxed in, and hopefully be first off the bike.

Whether you are racing in draft-legal or nondrafting triathlon races, strategy and tactics will play a key role in determining your success. Be sure to know your strengths and weaknesses (and those of your competitors in draft-legal events), and practice the skills and "chess moves" that will lead to a personal record or victory for you or a teammate.

# CHAPTER 18

# Performance Tips for Any Distance

## Michael Ricci

When it comes to triathlon training, there are a few broad topics that can be helpful in your quest for improvement and efficiency. In today's world of trying to do too much, we often lose our ability to focus on what's important, dial it in, and execute the correct game plan. To have the correct plan, you must recognize and then be able to correct any limitations. I have strongly believed for many years that in order to get faster it's a matter of doing harder work, not more work, and by that I mean quality over quantity.

## Recognizing Limitations

As an athlete, it's important to recognize your limitations and start the training season off slowly. You will want to build up your training volume and intensity gradually. Athletes tend to push themselves with unnecessary volumes at inappropriate times, which isn't beneficial for positive performance outcomes.

Winter is a time for most of us to start getting back into shape and rev up our fitness for the season ahead. It's very early in the training cycle, and you are months away from your biggest race of the year. This time of year many athletes plan a schedule that is usually too intense with too much volume. Instead of getting fit, many of these athletes miss workouts and end up with inconsistent weeks. What they should be doing is trying to maintain consistency in their training week after week. Here's what a typical overenthusiastic triathlete's training week may tend to look like:

- *Monday, Wednesday, and Friday*: organized group swim at high intensity and weight training at high intensity
- *Tuesday and Thursday*: spin class at high intensity
- *Tuesday, Friday, and Sunday*: running
- *Saturday*: long spin class at high intensity or a group ride with significant work
- *Sunday*: group run, with a lot of hard running

At this pace, after about 3 weeks, the athlete ends up with a cold, can't work out, and all her so-called fitness is gone. Does this sound familiar? If so, then how exactly do you change such a pattern of self-abuse? There are actually two critical steps in creating a more productive weekly plan:

- *Step 1*: Create a schedule around the hard/easy concept, where after every hard day, an easy day or an easy 36 hours follow. If you are deeply fatigued, you can take two easy days or a complete day off. Sounds easy enough, but athletes have a tendency to overdo it. Trust me, I have been there!

- *Step 2*: Apply the repeatability factor (i.e., how many days in a row can you repeat what you are doing?). Even though you are training day after day, it doesn't have to be all low intensity—and it shouldn't be. You can add some higher intensity aerobic workouts, some faster swims, and some strides on the run. It all comes down to asking yourself whether you could repeat the same workout tomorrow. If you can't, then you should back off.

Here's an example of two athletes and how different their training plans are: John and Bob both attend the same spin class on Thursday. It's a 90-minute grinder, and the teacher is one of those in-your-face instructors who yells at you for not maxing your heart rate. Bob is all about getting the most out of his 90 minutes. He hammers himself into the ground, his heart rate is through the roof, and that night he is sore and can't even sleep. As a matter of fact, he can't get his workout in on Friday or Saturday because he is so wiped out. He goes out to run on Sunday, but it's at a slow pace, and he thinks, *Wow, I really pushed myself on Thursday. I'm getting more fit.*

John, on the other hand, knows he has to recover for Friday night's organized group swim, and he still has the group ride on Saturday. He has ensured that his training plan has purpose and that he knows what needs to be done. Because of this, he caps his heart rate at five beats over the top of zone 2, which is where 85 percent of his training should be targeted. John goes high into his aerobic zone and even bumps his heart rate into zone 3, which is more of a tempo effort, on some of the climbs, but he quickly recovers. After the spin session, he is still ready to face his other workouts later in the week.

Let's assume this same scenario takes place over 6 weeks, as these athletes are working on their build phase, with John hitting most if not all of his workouts and Bob missing three workouts a week. Who do you think is going to be more fit? Bob, who blows himself up whenever he can work out, or John who rarely misses a workout and just keeps grinding the workouts out, week after week, month after the month? Your money should be on John because his consistency over time will keep his aerobic base and fitness level growing. When it comes time to add some race-specific workouts, his body will be ready to absorb those harder efforts because he has built the foundation to do so. His ability to be smart enough to know how hard he can go each day, week in and week out, will allow him to keep repeating his training cycle without any major hiccups. Bob, on the other hand, is in trouble, and his improvement has stagnated for another season. Of course he will wonder why. After all, he pushes himself very hard in that spin class, and he can get his heart rate very high. He just can't seem to put in any consistent weeks of training.

So, to get the most out of your training and the time you spend doing it, here's what a triathlete's typical week of training should really look like:

- *Monday, Wednesday, and Friday*: masters swim where Monday is hard, Wednesday is easy, and Friday is pacing
- *Monday and Friday*: weight training with high reps and low weight
- *Tuesday and Thursday*: spin class where Tuesday is cadence and form work and Thursday focuses on big-gear strength and low cadence while keeping the heart rate down
- *Saturday*: long spin class or a group ride (keep the heart rate down, well below the top of zone 2) and run for 30 to 60 minutes after the bike
- *Tuesday, Wednesday, Friday, and Sunday*: running where Tuesday is an easy run for 30 minutes; Wednesday is a long run of 75 minutes or greater, keeping the heart rate in zone 2, not above; and Friday is an aerobic day, where the athlete keeps the effort easy. Sunday is going to be another long run of 75 minutes or greater.

# Strengthen Your Weaknesses

It's not uncommon to hear a triathlete talk about how she is very strong in one or two events but seems to be weak in the third. The question becomes, how do we change this pattern? How do we take the swim from being a weakness to something respectable? How do we do the same for our bike or run events if they are our weakness? It's not easy to do, but it's possible. In my early 20s, I worked in a big city, took the train to work every day, and trained for triathlon about 6 hours per week. Even in this less-than-perfect training environment, I was able to improve my fitness and my weakest link. From this experience I learned about something called *sport rotation*. Although I found this training theory by accident—because the weather dictated my training schedule—it worked for me. Riding my bike outside in the winter months wasn't an option. Swimming year-round with a master's program was out because I had to drive 30 minutes each way to get there. Time was a limiting factor for me.

Taking a closer look at some of the world's best endurance athletes, we see that they usually run or swim twice per day. Even cyclists ride for a few hours, refuel, and ride some more. When these athletes train, they are focusing on one sport at a time. If you have the desire to get better, you should think about implementing sport rotation in your season. Letting your body focus on one event at a time will help it adapt more quickly and improve technique and endurance. If you continue training the way you are now and you aren't improving, then what do you have to lose by trying this approach?

If you are interested in using sport rotation (some coaches call such programs run camps, swim camps, or bike camps), then my suggestion is to focus on one sport for 3 weeks, take an easy week, and then repeat the cycle. If you focus on one sport for 2 months, then a complete rotation would take 6 months. After 6 months you can return to a more balanced approach. If you live in a part of the world where you have all four seasons, let the seasons dictate your schedule. It would look something like this: Around November 1, you start your run focus. By early January you would start your swim focus, and by early March you would be starting your bike focus. You don't have to make it that rigid—everyone has off weeks, colds in the winter, and life that gets in the way of training. It happens.

To set up a sport rotation cycle, first look at your training in terms of time and frequency. You want 50 to 75 percent of your training time to be focused on that sport.

Let's take running, for example: If you currently run 3 days a week, work yourself up to 5 or 6 days per week, even if that 5th or 6th day is only a 15- or 20-minute run. This employs the component of frequency, and it will help you run better the more you are on your feet. In the other two sports, you would still train two times per week (e.g., one drill session in the pool and on the bike plus an endurance set for each as well). Since the focus is on the running, the nonrunning workouts are just maintenance or skills sessions (drills).

After a 2-month cycle, switch to swimming, working at a higher frequency by increasing your time in the pool. During this swimming focus, you would train running and cycling two times per week, with the focus on drills and endurance. Then, when you move into the cycling phase, cycling becomes the focus, and the goal for the other sports is to maintain fitness gains and continue to work on skills and endurance.

Most important, become a runner during your run focus. Run with people who are better than you. Watch how they train. Swim with the swimmers during your swim focus. Become a fish. Watch the fast swimmers swim. Watch their form and see what you can learn. On the bike, become a cyclist during your focus months. Ride with a group. Learn bike-handling skills. Learn to ride in a pack. During these focus months you can learn a lot, you can improve a lot, and you can take your fitness levels to places you haven't been before. Don't become a slave to training. Use these ideas as a guideline, but not the end-all for your training. I have tried this approach with many athletes, and even in situations where we did only a 3-week block of focused training, there was improvement. So, if you really want to improve that weakest link, spend some time focusing on it, and in a few weeks, you may just turn a weakness into a strength.

# Increase Your Strength

One of the great parts about being a triathlon coach is being able to brag about how your athletes improve. I take as much pride in my athletes' success as in my own. We have seen quite a few athletes improve over the years, and in this section I wanted to touch on how these athletes got faster without doing mega volume or months of base-building work. Once athletes are experienced enough, they can do without the mega base mileage. I firmly believe that at least 6 weeks of base work is important no matter what your experience level is. After that, though, I like to see some harder work brought into the training program.

Dr. Max Testa is considered one of the best cycling coaches in the world. I had the pleasure of listening to him present at my USAT Level III Coaching Certification class in 2005. Dr. Testa made quite an impression on me, and I walked away with the tenet that "strength equals speed" etched into my mind. The stronger you are, the faster you will race. The stronger you are, the more watts you can push on the bike, the faster you can run up a hill, and the faster you can swim. Getting stronger requires doing more hard work than you are currently doing and improving your aerobic base, or zone 2 speed. Note: I did not say work harder, but do more hard work. There is a big difference there.

Taking this point even further, it's helpful to see what strength coaches think about strength and endurance. Mike Boyle is the premier strength and conditioning coach in this country and maybe the world. Alwyn Cosgrove is an Olympic-level strength coach of triathletes, boxers, soccer players, and others. It is Alwyn's belief that maximal strength levels should be achieved before endurance or energy system development.

Says Cosgrove (2005), "If we haven't built up appreciable levels of power, speed or strength, then what the hell are we trying to endure? A low level of power? A low level of speed?" Conditioning coach Mike Boyle once pointed out that "It is significantly easier to get an explosive athlete in shape than it is to make an in-shape athlete explosive. The first will take weeks; the second may take years."

Does that make any buzzers go off in your head? If you don't have speed and you go out on a long ride, what are you learning to endure? Riding slowly? Riding at a low level of power? Do you see how riding long, slow miles at 16 miles per hour (26 km/h) is only going to make you good at . . . riding at 16 miles per hour? For example, wouldn't you rather build your base speed up to 20-plus miles per hour (32+ km/h) in training so that when you add endurance you can do your long rides at 19 to 20 miles per hour (31 to 32 km/h)? Even better yet, learning to push 400 watts in training will make pushing 200 watts *much* easier. A 200-watt average in an Ironman race such as Arizona or Florida will net a 160-pound (73 kg) triathlete a 5:15 bike split. Being stronger means going faster.

Let's look at a real-life example of this: Starting in 1989 and continuing for the next 6 years, Mark Allen dominated the Ironman World Championship. He raced Olympic-distance races all the way up until August, when he would start his endurance training for Hawaii. He did this for many years. Racing and training hard for months let him build up his strength and speed so that when he added his endurance, the speed was already there. As Mike Boyle says, "It is significantly easier to get an explosive athlete in shape"—and here was our future Ironman world champ racing his butt off (becoming explosive) to win Olympic-distance races *before* he started his training for long-distance racing. Boyle continues, "The first will take weeks; the second may take years." Exactly! If this athlete already has the speed, all he has to do is add some longer-distance training and then he is ready to race long and fast. By the way, this same athlete also won the 1989 ITU World Championships after Ironman Hawaii. So, it wasn't as if he was racing Olympic-distance races just to race them.

I give many of my athletes up to 6 weeks off from any structured training after their final race of the season. They are free to do whatever they want in this time. When they come back onto the program, we usually give them a few easy weeks to get used to the training again, and then we'll start off with a little bit of hard stuff. This may mean a short tempo run of 10 minutes or even some short threshold efforts on the bike.

If you work hard all season to peak for a race, then take a month off, then spend 4 months building a base, what have you done besides having gone backward with your training? For every month you take off from training, it takes about twice as long to get back those losses. So if you take 1 month off from training, it will take you 2 months to get your fitness back.

Athletes work so hard to make improvements, so why let it all go to waste and let all that strength and power disappear? I am all for time away from training, and in no way am I advocating hammering your body 52 weeks a year; what I am saying is that if you want to go fast you need to get strong, stay strong, and work on getting stronger. Riding and running long and slow for months will make you neither stronger nor faster. Training with a plan and a purpose will get you stronger and faster. After all, if you need proof of this theory, you can look at our athletes' results, year after year. If you want to get faster, forgo the endless hours of low aerobic training and add some harder work to your early-season training.

# Individualize Your Training

The most commonly asked question of any triathlon coach is "How do I get faster?" Pretty simple question but there is no simple answer, unfortunately. My typical reply is "How much time do you have to train? And what are your strengths and weaknesses?" These two factors will determine how the training should be structured. So much is made of intervals, tempo workouts, using new equipment guaranteed to make you faster, and so on. What it really comes down to is the basics: how much time you have to train and what you do with that time. As my former coach, Rick Niles, says, "It's not how *much* you train, but *how* you train." That is one of the most important things to remember in setting up your training plan.

In 2008 I took the head coaching position with the University of Colorado triathlon team. This is a team steeped in history and success. Ten national titles in 12 years led to a 5-year drought of watching other teams walk away with the big prize. The team was stuck in the old-school way of training, which was lots of volume, not much swimming (twice per week), and hardly any race-specific workouts. During my first week, I added $\dot{V}O_2$ workouts, time trials, and more swim workouts. Gone were the long rides and runs without structure. In their place were shorter, harder rides; lots of climbing on the bike; weekly run workouts at goal-race pace; and running off the bike twice per week.

One of the senior members of the team came up to me after the first month and said, "Mike, what you are doing is completely different from what we've been doing the last few years. We usually do a bunch of long slow distance and then add in the fast stuff before nationals." Without trying to sound pompous, I replied, "I understand that. But if what you've been doing hasn't been working, maybe we need to flip things upside down and see if we can't shake out a different result." I didn't know if it was going to work, and I was pretty nervous it might not, but I was going to give it my best effort. As I viewed it, we didn't have anything to lose. It took 18 solid months of training like this and a little psychological warfare with some of my resistant charges before CU was able to recapture the title of "champions."

One of the first things I did with my team was ask the athletes to fill out and return an athlete profile, with such information as best times for 5K and 10K runs, best swim times, best bike times, their favorite sport to train, how many times a week they train in each sport, and so on. I wanted a profile of each athlete so I could help everyone as best I could and create a schedule specific to them and their strengths and weaknesses.

The following matrix (see figure 18.1) came about from that season. It was something that helped me realize how easy it is to individualize training based on only a few factors:

- There are only so many hours in a week to train.
- Every athlete has a weakness.
- Every athlete has a strength.
- It takes at least four sessions per week to see improvement, as two or three sessions per week is more along maintenance work.

FIGURE 18.1

## Triathlon Training Matrix.

| Hours of training | Limiter | Strength | # of swims per week | # of hours: SWIM | # of bikes per week | # of hours: BIKE | # of runs per week | # of hours: RUN | # of weight sessions per week | # of hours: WEIGHTS | Total workouts | Total hours |
|---|---|---|---|---|---|---|---|---|---|---|---|---|
| 0 | Swim | Run | 5 | 4 | 3 | 3 | 2 | 2 | 2 | 1.5 | 12 | 10.5 |
| 10 | Swim | Bike | 5 | 4 | 2 | 2 | 3 | 2.5 | 2 | 1.5 | 12 | 10 |
| 10 | Bike | Swim | 2 | 2 | 5 | 5 | 3 | 2 | 2 | 1 | 12 | 10 |
| 10 | Bike | Run | 2 | 2 | 5 | 5 | 3 | 2 | 2 | 1 | 12 | 10 |
| 10 | Run | Swim | 2 | 2 | 2 | 2 | 4 | 4 | 2 | 2 | 10 | 10 |
| 10 | Run | Bike | 2 | 2 | 2 | 2 | 4 | 4 | 2 | 2 | 10 | 10 |
| 10-12 | Swim | Run | 5 | 4 | 3 | 3 | 3 | 3 | 2 | 1.5 | 13 | 11.5 |
| 10-12 | Swim | Bike | 5 | 4 | 2 | 2 | 3 | 3.5 | 2 | 1.5 | 12 | 11 |
| 10-12 | Bike | Swim | 2 | 2 | 5 | 6 | 3 | 3 | 2 | 1 | 12 | 12 |
| 10-12 | Bike | Run | 3 | 2.5 | 5 | 6 | 3 | 3 | 2 | 1 | 13 | 12.5 |
| 10-12 | Run | Swim | 2 | 2 | 3 | 3 | 4 | 5 | 2 | 2 | 11 | 12 |
| 10-12 | Run | Bike | 3 | 3 | 3 | 3 | 4 | 4 | 2 | 2 | 12 | 12 |
| 14-15 | Swim | Run | 6 | 5 | 4 | 5 | 4 | 3 | 2 | 1.5 | 16 | 14.5 |
| 14-15 | Swim | Bike | 6 | 6 | 3 | 4 | 4 | 3 | 2 | 1.5 | 15 | 14.5 |
| 14-15 | Bike | Swim | 3 | 3 | 5 | 7 | 3 | 3 | 2 | 1 | 13 | 14 |
| 14-15 | Bike | Run | 3 | 3 | 5 | 7 | 3 | 3 | 2 | 1 | 13 | 14 |
| 14-15 | Run | Swim | 3 | 3 | 3 | 4 | 5 | 6 | 2 | 1 | 13 | 14 |
| 14-15 | Run | Bike | 3 | 3 | 3 | 4 | 5 | 6 | 2 | 1 | 13 | 14 |
| 16+ | Swim | Run | 6 | 6 | 4 | 6 | 4 | 3 | 2 | 1.5 | 16 | 16.5 |
| 16+ | Swim | Bike | 6 | 6 | 3 | 4.5 | 4 | 4.5 | 2 | 1.5 | 15 | 16.5 |
| 16+ | Bike | Swim | 3 | 3 | 5 | 8 | 3 | 4 | 2 | 1 | 13 | 16 |
| 16+ | Bike | Run | 3 | 4 | 5 | 8 | 3 | 3 | 2 | 1 | 13 | 16 |
| 16+ | Run | Swim | 3 | 3 | 3 | 5.5 | 5 | 6.5 | 2 | 1 | 13 | 16 |

In the matrix, the strength is listed as well as the weakest sport, and from there you'll know how to break up the week in terms of how many times you should train in each sport (frequency) and duration (volume). Before using this matrix, ask yourself the following key questions:

- How much time do I have to train?
- What is my strength?
- What is my weakness?

We typically focus our training around this matrix until about 12 weeks from the A race of the season. This gives our athletes more than enough time to get into race shape with race-specific workouts and race-specific efforts. But don't get too caught up in trying to hit every hour, every week. What you are striving for is consistency. If you are a weak swimmer and need to work on swimming, then get in the water four or five times per week. There is no shortcut for hard work. Hard work doesn't mean you have to "go hard" all the time. Hard work is defined by doing the work, week in and week out. I'll repeat it again: You don't need to hammer all the time to be working hard. You just need to be consistent with getting the workouts in. The key to success in anything, be it work, training, or life, is consistency.

If you gain only one thing from this chapter, I hope it is how to organize your training and how to make your workouts count rather than full of wasted miles and tons of volume. Sometimes in coaching we call this high-volume strategy "checking the box," meaning you didn't want to do the workout, you didn't enjoy it, but you got it done, and you've "checked the box." The problem with this type of training is it's mentally draining and often doesn't serve a specific purpose.

I promise that if you can create a training plan that is based on the hard/easy concept, considers the repeatability factor, addresses weaknesses, and has strength work sprinkled throughout, you'll have an effective plan that will lead you to improvement in a safe and timely fashion. These are concepts I've used for more than two decades of coaching and racing, and year after year with athletes of all abilities I see the proven results time and again.

# CHAPTER 19

# Mental Strategies for Training and Racing

## *Barb Lindquist*

In sport there are athletes who have risen above their potential in stressful situations. Similarly, there are talented athletes expected to win who crumble under the pressure. These racers could have been at their peak of physical training, and yet their success or failure was a result of what was going on in the mind. Every athlete, from newbie triathlete to Olympian, knows from firsthand experience that the mind can help or hinder race performance.

Likewise, most good athletes can tell you what time they expect to do in a race, based on their training, but their mental state may keep them from racing the times they know they can do. On the other hand, the great athletes are the ones who are not limited by their training results. Their mental state allows them to do, on race day, things that could not be predicted from their training. The goal of this chapter is to shed light on areas of thinking that could make that good athlete a great one, even a champion.

Champions make success look easy and natural. And yet, champions realize that success doesn't just happen by chance or because they are talented physically. Success requires planning and preparation, including mental preparation. Champions see their races as they want them to unfold before the race even happens, and yet they are unflappable when a race doesn't follow the ideal script. They work toward creating the positive mental environment for that champion performance to be fulfilled.

Champions realize that little things add up to separate the good from the truly great. Practicing mental strategies for race day is one of the biggest little things an athlete can do. It is one of those little things that is hard to quantify in a logbook, and yet an hour a week of mental preparation can far outweigh the benefits of riding the bike another hour. By self-evaluating your current mental skills—the strengths and the weaknesses—and then learning what mental tools are available to strengthen those weaknesses, you will be ready to practice these skills so that on race day, a champion can emerge.

# Evaluating Your Mental Skills

The first place to start, as with any training program, is to evaluate your current status in regard to the mental aspect of racing. Looking at past races, honestly evaluate your areas of vulnerability. These are reoccurring patterns of when and where the mind is susceptible to being a limiter to the physical performance. Does the same situation (e.g., hills, when you are in the lead) trigger similar patterns race after race such as negative self-talk, doubt, or lack of focus? If so, these patterns are holding you back and need attention.

The evaluation should include each of the key race points listed here:

- *The week before the race*: What situations trigger positive feelings of excitement, negative thoughts, nervousness, or questioning of purpose?
- *On the starting line*: When standing next to your competitor? When seeing all those fit bodies? When thinking about the washing machine you will enter soon?
- *During the swim*: First 5 minutes of the swim? When getting swum over by competitors? When getting tired? When leading the race? When you can't see the buoy?
- *Transitions*: When you can't find your bike? When fumbling with skills? When your supporters are watching?
- *On the bike*: First 5 minutes of the bike? On the hills? In a headwind? When getting passed? When it is hard to pass racers because of a crowded course? When leading the race? When your legs feel tired? When it is hot? When you get assessed a penalty?
- *On the run*: First 5 minutes out of transition? When your legs feel heavy? When it is hot? When leading? On the hills? When getting passed? When you want to walk?

After you have answered these questions about the mental thought processes going on at specific parts of the race, you need to evaluate whether the thoughts were negative or positive. They were negative if they held you back from reaching full physical performance. The thoughts were positive if they empowered you to reach beyond what training had predicted. The mental skills strategies in the next section will give you tools to change a negative thought to a positive one.

Barb's self-evaluation early in her triathlon career: When I was a swimmer in college my senior year, I began to swim out of the fear of failure. My self-worth was wrapped up in how I swam. If I swam well, I felt good about myself. When I swam poorly, I felt bad about myself. I identified that pattern before I became a professional triathlete and overcame it by defining my purpose and working on self-talk so that I would not race out of fear, but out of excitement. Specifically in races, like many triathletes, I dreaded the start of the swim. Being a distance swimmer, pure speed was not a strength. I identified my thoughts on the starting line as a weakness, so I addressed them with affirmations, imagery, and goal setting. On the bike, my mind would start to wander in a 40K. This was an area of vulnerability, especially in the second half of the bike. I used imagery to keep me in the moment. In draft-legal events, I was not confident in bike tactics, so I used visualization to give me confidence for all tactical scenarios. And lastly, for years I thought of myself as "the swimmer," then "the swimmer/cyclist," but I was always told I wasn't "a runner." And I believed it. So much negative self-talk came in during the run when I was tired, especially on hills, or when I could see competitors chasing down my lead. I recognized I needed to believe I was a runner, and I used affirmations, visualization, and imagery to allow my mind to carry me beyond the limit of my physical skills.

# Employing Mental Skills Strategies

Just as an athlete has a physiological purpose behind each workout, an athlete also needs a mental training purpose behind key workouts in order to strengthen the positive connection between the mind and body. Here, four techniques to enhance mental strength—goal setting, visualization, affirmations, and imagery—are described, including examples related to the self-evaluation discussed in the previous section.

## Goal Setting

Goals are the targets to which an athlete directs his efforts. Outcome goals, such as winning a race or a specific course time, themselves motivate an athlete if they are specific, measurable, challenging, and realistic. The purpose of race goals is to create action steps in training that power the athlete toward the desired race outcome.

Setting race goals in triathlon can be tricky. Our sport is not like swimming or track in that the field of play is not always consistent. For example, a goal might be to break 1 hour on the bike split at the local triathlon in August. This outcome goal is specific and measurable, challenging and realistic (last year's split was 1:03), but outside factors can come into play such as rainy weather, high winds, or a flat tire. Outcome goals can be dangerous on their own because outcomes are not completely under an athlete's control. However, mental changes are, so setting goals for mental changes that might power you to the outcome goals is a better way to go. Examples of mental goals in the race include staying relaxed and confident at the swim start by using deep-breathing exercises and affirmations, being mentally focused in the second half of the bike by staying in the moment, sticking to your race plan even if other athletes go out too fast, and utilizing mental skills at key points in the race. These mental goals are all under your control and, if reached, will increase the probability that the outcome goal is reached as well.

As a distance swimmer, getting out fast in the swim was a struggle. I used the goal of being the first swimmer to the first buoy as a way to change my mental approach. I became more aggressive at the swim start, and with that goal in mind, it kept me focused when I was being hit by other racers in the swim. Even though I was not always the first swimmer to the first buoy, the mental change accomplished the same purpose.

## Visualization

Visualization is seeing a race performance before it happens. It is creating a movie of success using the imagination in order to mentally rehearse the perfect performance. Using all the senses, not just the visual, magnifies the strength of this mental strategy.

When visualizing a race, it is best to have a clear mind and be in a quiet environment absent of distractions. Seeing the movie from the angle of a camera mounted on your head gives you the true vantage point for experiencing the future race performance. This vantage point will fully focus you on being in the moment rather than seeing the big picture of how the race unfolds, much of which is out of your control and is distracting anyway.

Visualization reinforces success, so it is important to experience how you want the race to be. That said, visualization can also be used to go over plan B, C, and D. What will you do if your goggles get knocked crooked on your face, or if you need to change a flat? Visualization can help you get out of these unpredictable situations and mentally back into the race, something champions do so well. Although it is important to experience the not-so-ideal race scenarios, you always wants to finish a visualization session having completed the perfect race. Rewinding the tape back to before the contingency plan went into action allows you to continue with your ideal race.

> I used visualization all the time for transitions, especially if I had been to the race venue before. I would see myself exit the water, run to where my bike is (counting racks if need be), perform T1 feeling smooth and powerful like a ballerina, hear the crowds roar, then move onto the perfect bike mount. I also used visualization in bike-pack scenarios that my coach and I would discuss. I would see the different scenarios unfold and how I would cover attacks, create my own attacks, and ride smart. After visualizing the many bike scenarios, I would finish off with how I wanted the bike to pan out if I were in complete control.

## Affirmations

Negative self-talk is the chatter that goes on in the mind, telling an athlete he is not good enough, he can't do it, and that success is doubtful. No single factor is more devastating to an athlete's performance than negative self-talk. Through self-evaluation an athlete can identify trends of what is said and when it is said in the mind. When the destructive talk rears its ugly head in the heat of battle, it is too much of a challenge for the athlete to think, *No, don't say that*, or *La-la-la, I'm not listening*. The athlete is too fatigued to fight that battle during a race. What is possible, though, is for the athlete to proactively create positive affirmations to replace the negative self-talk. If the athlete already knows the mind will say, *You are just a swimmer shuffling on land*, the athlete can create a positive affirmation well before the race, practice it, and then in the race replace the negative chatter with *I'm a runner!* And not just replace it once, but use it as a mantra, repeating it so the negative talk has no room to come back in a mind filled with positive thoughts. Importantly, the athlete does not actually have to believe the affirmation to make these magical words work.

Creating affirmations can be a fun and creative process. Here are a few guidelines to help make them most effective:

- Use first person, such as "I thrive on challenges thrown my way."
- Use present infinitive tense, meaning it is happening now and into the future, such as "The first buoy is mine."
- Make affirmations short and snappy, something that is easy to repeat, especially

with the rhythm of breathing in a race, such as "I'm a runner," which is four syllables, perfect for four foot strikes.

■ Replace and update affirmations to keep them fresh.

> Affirmations were the single biggest transformation in the mental aspect of my racing. When I would start to lose focus in the swim, I targeted getting the most out of each arm stroke by thinking, *I am long and strong.* When my legs fatigued on the bike, I would think, *My legs are like steel pistons, smooth and strong.* In the second half of the run I thought, *The longer I go the stronger I get.*

## Imagery

Imagery is a set of mental pictures used to create a positive image affecting an athlete's mind and body. Pictures can be powerful. As humans, we remember scenes from films or from our past much easier than we remember words. Imagery is that snapshot picture that creates a feeling in the athlete, whether it be a feeling of calm before the race or of power up a hill. To find what imagery works for you, ask what pictures illicit the feelings you want to have at certain points in a race. At the race start, for example, do you want to radiate quiet confidence? Perhaps the image of a lightly rolling sea, which can turn from calm to dynamic in an instant when the gun goes off, is the picture you want to focus on. Do you want to keep the leg turnover up at the end of the run? Perhaps creating a picture of running on hot coals will keep you focused on fast feet.

> Running hills was a weakness of mine. One year while racing in Australia, the America's Cup sailing race was going on. I saw the grinders use their huge arms to turn the handles powerfully and quickly on the winch drum in order to pull in the sails. I created the image that at the top of each hill was a grinder, and as I started climbing the hill, a rope was attached to my waist, and the grinder would pull me up. Another time I used the imagery of balloons attached to my knees to help lift my legs as I ran up the hills.

# Practicing Mental Skills

The ultimate objective is to practice the mental strategies listed in the previous section in order to finalize a mental racing plan. An athlete would not try a new nutrition strategy on race day and should not try new mental strategies, either. Mental strategies must be practiced in key sessions during training.

Practice of mental skills in training sessions will test which skills are most helpful in certain situations and will give an athlete confidence in the race. If there is one takeaway lesson to this chapter, it is that just as you have a training plan in place, so too must you have a mental plan to practice. As with any skill, mental skills training initially takes time to master, but once the groundwork is laid, using mental skills will come naturally to you. And it is fun! It is similar to working on running technique, for example. At first you may spend extra time on drills. Ultimately with practice the new technique comes naturally. The same is true for mental skills practice. Following are suggestions for practicing.

### Goal Setting

- Write down an outcome goal for your next race. Determine three mental goals that will bring you closer to reaching that outcome goal. Last, write how and when you will practice those mental goals in each week leading up to the race.
- Share your goals with someone in order to keep you accountable.

### Visualization

- Set aside three 10-minute sessions each week to visualize your race. Make one of these sessions a time to visualize race situations that are not in your A plan.
- Visualize your transition skills at a specific venue before the race.
- Visualize an ideal race morning, starting from the time you wake up until the gun goes off.

### Affirmations

- Create two or three affirmations for each vulnerability area identified in the self-evaluation. In a key workout corresponding to a trigger for negative self-talk, pick one affirmation to practice. Repeat the other affirmations in other key workouts so that by the time the race arrives, you have picked which affirmations work for you.
- Create a list of affirmations for general areas of vulnerability in the week before the key triathlon. When negative talk, self-doubt, or nervousness arises, repeat the affirmations.

### Imagery

- Identify the picture of yourself that you see when thinking about your areas of vulnerability. Next think of an opposite strong picture you want to see in order to give you the positive feeling to overcome the situation. Use your imagination, let the mind wander, and be creative as to what this picture looks like. After creating images, practice bringing them up in key workouts.
- Practice controlling your level of excitement using imagery. Pick an image that raises your level of readiness, and also pick an image that calms you down. In training, practice using the first picture to get you excited for a key workout where perhaps you are struggling to get fired up, and practice using the second picture to help control and relax you when you are getting too nervous for a training session.

You can also use a combination of affirmations with the other mental strategies:

- Practice combining both imagery and affirmations in workouts. For example, with the image of running hills with balloons attached to the knees, the affirmation could be "My legs are light as they drive up the hill."
- Practice combining both visualization and affirmations. While seeing the race in your mind, hear the affirmations you will use.
- Practice combining both goal setting and affirmations. For the goal of being the first to the first buoy try "The first buoy is mine."

As a final note on practice, there is a trend in younger athletes of listening to music during every training session. Music moves us, it motivates us, it is wonderful. But music also makes athletes mentally lazy, allowing them to zone out and keeping them from using mental skills. Caution needs to be taken in how often music is used in training, especially since it is illegal for athletes to listen to music in races.

Employing the previously listed skills in practice is a key element of racing success. Additionally, the following sections offer helpful tips for race week, race morning, and the race itself that can reduce energy-wasting stress and maximize race-day performance.

## Week of the Race

This is the week for you to solidify the race plan and corresponding mental strategies you will employ in the race to bring out a superhuman race performance. The starting point for this is having a race plan: a written description of what you will do on race day. Prepare it a week before the race, and then review it daily throughout race week.

Writing down the strategies so you can review them will help you focus on what you can control. Writing them down and sharing them with someone also makes the plan more real. And last, recording the plan creates a record for the postrace evaluation and for future races. Here are some common items to consider including in your plan.

- What equipment and clothing will you use if on race day there is high wind, rain, snow, heat, cold, bright sun, or an overcast sky?
- What time will you get out of bed on race morning?
- What will you eat and drink for the prerace meal? When will you eat it?
- On race morning, what time will you arrive at the race venue?
- How will you set up your transition area?
- What sport nutrition products (if any) will you take in during the race?
- How will you gauge and regulate intensity on the bike? Will you use a rating of perceived exertion (RPE), heart rate, or power?
- Regardless of what tool you use, what will be your goal intensity? Will it vary during the race?
- How will you react if passed by other riders?
- How will you efficiently and quickly transition both in T1 and T2?

Also, during race week, things will come up that are out of your control. The boss may throw an extra project on your plate. A child may get sick. You may hyperanalyze every feeling in a workout and start to worry when you don't feel just right. Although these factors may be out of your control, how you deal with them is not. Learning to roll with the punches of outside factors while addressing details that can be controlled will allow you to remain focused and calm.

Details that are under your control include packing; pack your things early, using checklists so you don't pack too much or forget last-minute items. When you know details about the course, the prerace meetings, directions from hotel to race site, and so on, it can instill confidence and alleviate stress. Stress wastes energy and takes focus from the race. The body does not know the difference between mental stress and physical stress.

## Morning of the Race

Writing down a morning timeline gives you something to focus on, something to control. The timeline should include logistics such as wake-up time, traveling to the race, warm-up, and food to be eaten.

A comment needs to be made about prerace mode and personality types. When some athletes get nervous, they are chatty or outgoing, and some can be downright obnoxious. Other athletes close up and get introspective when they are in prerace mode. Both are OK if the athlete is being true to her personality. An introspective athlete should not feel she needs to be talkative, even if she is setting up transition next to someone being the life of the party.

Racing should be viewed as a celebration of the wonder of the body in motion. Creating a moment of quiet for a deep breath to be thankful helps center and relax an athlete. Remembering the journey and saying affirmations can start you off on the right foot.

## The Race

The more practice you have creating a mental strategy for racing, the more the positive thinking will flow naturally from the inside mind to the outside physical results. Be patient with yourself, realizing it takes time and continual practice for mental skills to become second nature.

By staying in the moment, not thinking about what just happened or what will happen, you can focus on what you can control. Maximizing each arm stroke, each pedal stroke, and each foot strike with a positive mind-set will give you the best performance possible. Thinking about what your competitors are doing, the weather, or anything else out of your control only drains your energy.

Planning and practice have been the theme up to this point. Champions realize it is a rare day to be enjoyed when a race goes completely as planned. Champions are, above all, adaptable. Although they enjoy and savor the winning performance that went according to plan, they thrive on being thrown challenges within a race, challenges that allow them to rise above a normal, predictable human performance to accomplish something truly remarkable. Challenges allow athletes to grow and learn lessons about their character that reach far beyond triathlon. Each race is an adventure. When racing is viewed with this excitement and wonder, and yet rooted in preparation, an athlete is prepared to take that leap into the unknown realm beyond his potential.

Two of the best races in my career came from races that didn't go according to plan. In one nondrafting race, during the swim I felt absolutely rotten, even though I was right with the leader. The negative thought came in, saying, *It is going to be a long day.* I then replaced it with a positive affirmation I had practiced in swim workouts: *I am too good of a swimmer to let a little thing like how I feel affect how I race.* I went on to have an amazing race, winning the biggest prize purse of my career. In another draft-legal race, my swimmer group out of the water disintegrated. I wound up in the main pack with a bunch of runners. On the bike the negative thought crept in: *Rats, this was my race to win, I am so fit and now it is a runner's race.* It took me half a lap on the bike to bring up one of my affirmations: *I thrive on challenges!* I thought, *When have I ever run with fresh legs off the bike to see just how fast I could run?* I had visualized head-to-head run racing, knowing at some point I would be in that situation. I started to get excited about the run possibilities. I wound up outrunning all the runners and won the race. Both races had challenges that I had to adapt to, and the mental training I had practiced allowed me to stay focused in the race when my ideal race plan fell through.

## After the Race

Just as an athlete evaluates the race from a training point of view, so too should an athlete evaluate his mental strategy. After a race, assess whether the mental strategies you used on areas of vulnerability allowed you to perform above your level of training or if any new weaknesses revealed themselves. Identifying what worked and what didn't is the first step of fine-tuning a mental strategy for future races. That said, sometimes a mental strategy that worked at one race will not work in the next race. It is an ever-evolving process. If the race was great, the feeling of success should be captured into an image to pull up in a future race. Recalling a success can be used as future motivation. After a race you can rewrite your mental strategy and then set up a training plan to execute it before the next race.

---

### ▶ Dealing With Fear

Many athletes race with fear—fear of failure, fear of success, fear of what others may think, fear of taking risks out of their comfort zone. To overcome fear, the first step is to say "so what" to the "what ifs." Address each fear by identifying the worst-case scenario of that fear. Ignoring the fear won't make it go away. A monster hiding under the bed is best fought by turning on the light and facing it, only to discover it's not so scary after all.

What is the worst that can happen if you fail in a race? What does failure look like? Some athletes think "dying in a race" is failure. Of course an athlete doesn't really die. She just took a risk out of her comfort zone and learned the limit of how hard to push for her fitness level. Is failure not finishing a race? Certainly something was learned to make the athlete better prepared for the next event, so it really wasn't a failure after all. What is the worst that can happen regarding what others think of an athlete's performance? Will other people love the athlete less or think less of him? Someone who truly cares for the racer won't love or respect him less or more depending on the race outcome. The antidote to fear is confidence, a confidence that the athlete is adequately prepared not only physically but also mentally through structured practice of both.

---

It is more fun and rewarding to race for a specific purpose outside of ourselves. Reaching goals is great. Winning races is wonderful. But there are countless reasons why triathletes train and race beyond these personal goals: in memory of someone close to them; to lose excess weight so they are healthier for their families; to inspire other Moms to do a triathlon; to raise money for a cause close to the heart; or simply to foster community with others who love to swim, bike, and run. When we race for something bigger than ourselves, our sacrificial, mindful purpose empowers the body beyond normal levels.

# CHAPTER 20

# Traveling for Competition

## Joe Umphenour

Traveling to a triathlon can seem somewhat daunting because of all the logistics it involves. It doesn't seem as easy as throwing everything into a car and driving an hour or two to a race site on the morning of the competition. Preparing for a race in an entirely different region requires good planning ahead of time. Also, since flights are the most common method of travel, you must be aware that flying can be a bit disorienting to the body, as can the sensations you feel once you have landed, so you must take steps and plan ahead in order to feel the best you can for the race. When flying, you are also limited in what you can bring, so you need to plan well and pack only the essentials. Packing your bicycle is another challenge because you not only have to safely pack it into a bike box, you also need to learn how to disassemble and assemble it. Over the years, I've learned the essentials of race travel and shortcuts that will make your trip the best experience it can be.

## Preparing for Travel

All trips start with a purpose. You should focus on what your priorities are for your travel. Is it all about the race itself, or do you want this to be a family vacation, with the race being just one of the things on the agenda? Next, you should set a timeline for when you want to arrive at and depart from your destination. Be sure you don't overextend yourself as you travel. Your body will be under some extra stress because it is in a new place, so it is good to remember some of your triathlon skills: Keep it simple, and look ahead to the next step rather than the entire getaway. By all means, check the race website for important information to plan for, such as race meetings, course walk-throughs, when to turn in bikes and equipment before the race, and when you can pick them up afterward.

Also do a little research about the city you are traveling to. Find out what the climate is like at that time of year. Learn what kind of cuisine is most prevalent. Learn the time difference between here and there. This type of information will give you ideas as to what kind of clothing to pack, how far ahead to fly into the area, and whether or not you should be bringing extra provisions so you have some familiar food in your belly on race day. If you are traveling to a foreign country, be sure your passport is up to date. You should also find out what the visa requirements are and how far in advance you may need to start the process of getting one. Considering extra insurance is not a bad idea, since many countries have a different system of health care than you are used to.

When you have your timeline, start making reservations. It's a good idea to start with race accommodations first because you want to have your choice of location and price. Race directors will usually arrange for host hotels that have either a prime location or a discounted price for athletes. Although being in a hotel close to the race site or expo can be convenient, getting a room away from the bustle can be less stressful and may be a better option if you are traveling with your family. But remember what your priorities are. If you are there to race, choose what's best for your race.

Plan on arriving at least 2 days ahead for domestic races and 4 days for international destinations. The extra days are for building your bike early enough so you have some time to fix any issues that may have arisen during transport and for doing your prerace meetings and preparation. The additional days for overseas travel are for adapting to the time change and because solving unforeseen puzzles always takes longer in foreign countries.

# Packing for the Trip

Packing for your triathlon adventure is a lot like packing for any vacation except you have to pack for three sports in addition to taking normal items. Thankfully, most of your activities will be centered on those three sports, so it will be easier to choose what stays and what goes. Personal gear can be kept to a minimum to make room for your race gear. Packing your bike might seem like a formidable challenge, but by planning ahead, it can be the least stressful part of the trip.

## Personal Items

Packing your bag is not as difficult as it might seem if you concentrate on bringing the least that you can and pieces that are multifunctional (e.g., two pairs of quick-dry undergarments and socks can be washed and worn several times and also cut down on bulk). Realize that you won't be seeing the same people too often, so you don't need a different outfit for each day. Buy smaller travel-size items for your toiletries and for your essential personal care items such as curling irons or hairdryers. Be sure you have researched the local voltage, and bring a voltage converter and plug adapter if needed. There are also excellent packing cubes on the market that minimize bulk and help organize. Remember to leave room for the race shirt in your bag; you might consider making that the shirt you wear home on the plane as your badge of honor, especially since it may be the only clean shirt you have left.

## Race Gear

Packing your race gear is something you have probably already prepared for. It is a good idea to have a checklist of race gear for your races anyway. For travel, use the same list but pare it down a bit (see Race Gear Checklist). Bring the things that are essential, and leave the things that would be nice to have at home. Instead of that big jacket for race morning, use your cycling arm warmers, leg warmers, and windbreaker to keep you warm before the race. Besides, they are much easier to pack down and can be used during the race if it's cooler than expected. Travel-size versions of baby powder and race lube also reduce the overall size of your pack. The gear bag normally goes in the bike case, but consider putting essential specific gear such as your race uniform, goggles, racing flats, and bike shoes into your carry-on. If the bike case doesn't make it to your destination in time for the race, you can always salvage the weekend by borrowing or renting a bike, and you will still have equipment that is specific to you and your body. Although the bike may feel different, you will be using familiar gear that is important to your race.

---

## Race Gear Checklist

| | | |
|---|---|---|
| _____ Swim goggles | _____ Bike helmet | _____ Knee warmers |
| _____ Race uniform | _____ Cycling glasses | _____ Windbreaker |
| _____ Wetsuit | _____ Running shoes | _____ Running gloves or liners |
| _____ Bodyglide | _____ Running hat or visor | _____ Warm hat |
| _____ Bike shoes | _____ Race belt | _____ Spare laces for shoes |
| _____ Baby powder | _____ Sunblock | _____ Extra gels |
| _____ Rubber bands | _____ Arm warmers | |

---

If you have already done your homework on the local food choices, you can compare what you can expect to find versus what you typically consume before a race. Your race-morning meal is something that won't change, so plan on bringing what works well for you. Instant cereals, teas, or coffees can be made in your room with an inexpensive hot pot. The American athletes going to the Beijing Olympics in 2008 were all given a small one for this very purpose. Bringing an easily portable favorite comfort food can be a good way to ease stress in a new place. Voltage adapters are important for some countries because frying your appliance on race morning can put a crimp in your routine.

## Bike

You've got your suitcase packed, your race-gear bag stuffed, and your dietary needs prepared for. But before you are ready to go, you have your largest piece of equipment to stow safely for the trip: your bike.

### Shipping Your Bike

Shipping bicycles economically has become harder and harder to do over the last 20 years. Costs have easily doubled and in some cases tripled because of rising fuel costs and airlines constantly looking for additional income sources. So, when you look for a bike case, you have two choices: something heavier, very sturdy, and tough that will take a beating with no harm to your bike or something smaller and lighter that isn't as protective.

Hard cases are very sturdy and can handle most anything thrown at them, but you pay extra when you need to ship them. Domestic airlines will charge extra if your box is more than 62 linear inches (height + length + depth) (157 linear cm) or more than 50 pounds (23 kg). Many international airlines will drop the weight limit to 42 pounds (19 kg), especially on inter-European flights. They will not accept packed bike boxes that weigh more than 70 pounds (32 kg). Shipping on the ground domestically costs less, but you need to give yourself up to a week of lead time to get your bike there on time. Cost is contingent on the same principles as the airlines, so it is a good idea to find out ahead of time where price cutoffs are for certain weights and linear lengths. For these reasons, soft cases have become a more popular choice. If small and packed lightly enough, soft cases can sometimes avoid the excess-weight fees. If proper precautions are taken, they can be just as safe as a hard case. In the end, it comes down to a personal choice.

Domestic shipping can be an easy way to go if you don't mind being away from your race bike the week before the race. Most companies have a return service that allows you to prepay both the outbound and return trips. Once you are ready to send your bike back after the race, you simply affix the return tag on the bike case and schedule a pickup. To keep costs down, it is cheaper to ship business to business since it is a part of their usual deliveries. Send it to and from the race hotel or a local bike shop. Most won't mind if you call ahead of time.

Also, since your bike case is your biggest piece of luggage, be aware that you can stuff a lot into it. Wetsuits make a great extra bit of padding for your bike (often stored in that plastic bag from your last race), as do training shoes. Be mindful, though, of how much weight you are adding. Make sure to keep it under 50 pounds (23 kg) total so you don't have to pay for excess weight. An easy way to keep track is to know how much the case and your bike weigh and to weigh whatever else you are putting in on your bathroom scale. Some travel companies have a hand scale for this purpose.

## Maintenance Tune-Up and Disassembly of Your Bike

About 2 to 4 weeks before you leave, take your bike to a shop and have them do a maintenance tune-up. Be sure they check the condition of brake and derailleur cables, the chain, wear on the race tires, and anything else you might want to upgrade for the race. It's always a good idea to give yourself this much lead time so you have time to break in any new parts and give yourself piece of mind.

Also, before you travel, you'll need to learn how to disassemble certain parts of the bike so you can fit it into your bike case. Going to a bike maintenance course is a good place to start, but you'll probably need to learn it yourself since all bikes are different. The basic parts you will need to remove or loosen are the seatpost, the pedals, the wheels, and the handlebars. Additionally, removing the rear derailleur can prevent damage to it or the derailleur hanger, even in a hard case. If you have integrated aerobars, you may have to remove the whole assembly from the steerer tube. Finding out these twists and practicing ahead will save you time and stress when you pack for the trip.

When disassembling your bike, first get a small nylon bag big enough to hold the tools you will need to take your bike apart, your wheel skewers, your pedals, and perhaps a little chain oil (make sure this is inside two plastic bags, as containers tend to leak in cargo holds because of pressure changes). The only tools you will need are a set of hex wrenches or a multitool and perhaps a crescent wrench for your pedals if they don't use a hex wrench. To protect your bicycle frame from impacts, go to a larger hardware store and pick up 9 feet (3 m) of pipe insulation. You will be cutting this down to fit later on. Also buy a roll of little Velcro straps that you will use later to tie down the insulation. This is easier and more reusable than duct tape.

When taking the bicycle apart, there are some important things to do before you touch a single bolt. Measure the distance from the top of your seat to the center of the crank bolt. This is your seat height, which is good to know so that, if necessary, you can set up your bike or any spare bike with your proper length so it doesn't affect your cycling. Once you have recorded this, mark the seatpost at the point where it enters the bike with a white or gray permanent marker or electrical tape. You should also do this with any other adjustable or removable piece so you know exactly how far to insert it back into its socket. This will make reassembly much easier and create the exact same riding setup that you have trained on and become used to. Any changes to these measurements during a race can decrease your performance drastically.

For the disassembly, step one is to shift your chain onto the big ring to prevent the chainring teeth from being damaged or damaging your bike case. Then take off the pedals. Use either a hex key on the end of the spindle or a crescent or pedal wrench where it meets the crank. To loosen, it's clockwise on the left side of the bike and counterclockwise on the right side of the bike. Once the pedals and any associated washers are off, put them in a separate plastic bag to keep them from getting other things greasy.

Be sure your seatpost is marked with the correct height before you remove it, loosening the bolts with a hex wrench. Cut a length of pipe insulation to cover the length of the seatpost and fasten with Velcro straps. Take your front wheel off, putting the skewer into the parts bag with your pedals. Cut lengths of insulation that fit each individual tube on the front part your frame, including the forks. Strap each length down with one of the Velcro straps.

Two problem areas when bikes are packed are the rear triangle and the forks. If they are not reinforced, they could be crushed, even in the most sturdy bike case. To solve this, get either a pair of old hubs or two threaded bolts that are long enough to fit between the dropouts, with two sets of wingnuts on either end. Once you take the wheels off, you can use your quick releases on the old hubs and secure them on the front forks and the rear triangle, with the bike chain resting on the freehub in the rear.

When you have the rear wheel off, continue to cut pipe insulation to fit all the tubes on the rear of the bike. The more you can cover, the more protected your bike will be. Realize that when you fly, security will go through your bike case, moving some things around. The pipe insulation helps ensure that your bike will still be safe from loose objects moving around in your case.

Opening your bike case when you arrive and finding that the rear derailleur hanger has been bent or broken during transport is not the way you want to start your race weekend. This is easily prevented by removing the rear derailleur from the hanger with a hex wrench. Once it is separated from the frame, lash it and the chain to the chainstay so it doesn't get twisted. It is also a good idea to get a spare derailleur hanger just in case yours gets damaged. The shop you bought the bike from should be able to get one for you from the manufacturer.

The final bit of disassembly is removing the handlebars from the stem. If you have a stem with a removable faceplate where the handlebars clamp onto the stem, this is as simple as loosening all the clamp bolts, removing the bars, and then replacing the faceplate and tightening down the screws so they don't get lost. You may also have to loosen the stem bolts that clamp onto the steerer tube so you can turn the stem toward the frame so it fits into a smaller case.

Integrated aero bars are a little different. Your first step is loosening the bolts clamping the stem onto the steerer tube. Then you loosen the bolt on the very top of the stem and remove it and the top cap. Be aware of how the spacers are set up above and below the stem before you gently lift it off the steerer tube. Insert an old stem or shim onto the steerer tube, and replace the spacers on top and the top cap and bolt. This will prevent the fork from shaking loose during travel and spreading bearings around your bike case.

Fold the handlebar assembly down parallel with your bike frame. You may need to loosen brake cables to allow for a snugger fit in smaller cases. Having the aerobars pointed downward and lashed to the bike with Velcro straps prevents them from bouncing against the frame. This is the point where you can add additional bits of pipe insulation on parts that are not protected.

You are now ready to put your bike in the bike case. This may take a couple of tries to get the fit just right, especially the first time. Once you have a good fit, tie down the bike securely to the case at one or two spots so it won't get damaged bouncing around inside the case. Most cases have tie-downs built in, typically around the bottom bracket, and some even have a quick release to hold the front fork securely to the case. If you are using a cardboard bike box, then the best way to keep the bike secure is to use your wetsuit, gear bag, training shoes, or even wadded-up newspaper to act as a buffer between the bike and the box.

The wheels typically go in after the bike, on either side of a soft case or on top of the frame, separated by a layer of thick foam. A wheel cover can be zipped around the wheels to provide additional protection. Then fit in your bicycle pump, but don't ship $CO_2$ cartridges you might use for your race because they are prohibited on aircraft, even in checked bags. You should be able to find them at the race expo or a nearby bike shop. Why your pump? The airlines ask that you deflate your tires before the flight, and it's one less thing you have to try to find before the race.

## Ensuring Low-Stress Travel

Now that your bike and all your bags are packed correctly, it's time to start your triathlon adventure. Always allow yourself extra time at the airport if your bike is accompanying you on the flight. Have your carry-on packed with whatever comfort food or entertainment you need to sustain you. Look at the flight as an opportunity to do whatever you want. It is one of the few times when you have no errands to run, no phones to answer, and no chores to do. This is your chance to read that book or those magazines you just haven't had time to get to. Just completely relax, and let everything else fall by the wayside.

Also, when en route, there are easy ways to prevent you from catching a bug and to be more comfortable on the plane. Bring a little bottle of hand sanitizer to use before your meals. Stay hydrated by drinking plenty of fluids, and even adding a drink mix that has extra vitamin C won't hurt. The practice of putting a triple antibiotic inside your nose to prevent illness or dryness has its supporters and detractors. Most doctors agree that putting petroleum-based products in your nose isn't the best idea since they are absorbed so quickly through the sinus membranes and into the bloodstream. A simple saline nasal spray is a good solution for a dry nose. Bring a moisturizing hand or body lotion to keep your skin comfortable in the dry air of the cabin.

Jet lag is created by many factors all coming together at the same time. First, your body's inner clock is at odds with the time at your new destination. Second, your body is at odds with itself after been cooped up in a plane for many hours and in a dry environment. There are easy ways to fight these. Some believe that you should start shifting your sleep–wake cycle to match that of your destination several days before departure, changing at the rate of one hour per day. Some places are so far away that a shift of more than 6 hours may not be realistic.

Once on the plane, begin adjusting to the time zone of your destination by resetting your watch at the beginning of your flight. You are no longer at home when you step on the plane anyway. Plan to sleep on the plane when it is nighttime at your destination. Eye masks and noise-canceling headphones or earplugs can help reduce light and noise. Taking melatonin, a naturally occurring chemical in the brain, will help convince your body it's time to sleep. Do your best to stay awake on the plane when it is daytime at your destination. This is a good time to catch up on your reading or indulge yourself with a double feature on the video system. The air on planes is extremely dry, so drink plenty of water, which is why it is a good idea to bring drink mixes to make it more tasty. Stay away from alcohol and caffeine because they increase dehydration. Move often on the flight during waking hours: Stretch or walk down the aisles. This will also help keep you awake.

When traveling east, most flights that cross the Atlantic leave later in the day so you have a morning arrival the next day on the other side of the ocean. This will make it easier to fall asleep on the plane. Once you get there, though, do everything in your power not to fall asleep during the day. It will disrupt everything until you get on your new time. Traveling west across the Pacific is easier on the body since most flights leave in the afternoon or evening and land the next evening. Sleep the first part of the flight, then stay awake the rest of the flight. Your reward will be a blissful first night's sleep at your destination. Another trick of the trade is to wear compression socks on all your flights. This will reduce swelling, aiding in the recovery time after a flight.

Also, dealing with the possibility of a radical difference in climate from what you're used to is very important when you race. You can start preparing for a race locale's climate weeks before you leave by adjusting your clothing layers. If you are traveling to a warmer climate, wear more clothing to increase your temperature. If you are going to race in a colder climate, wear thinner clothing. Try to avoid overdoing it either way and risking heat stroke or hypothermia. With the adjustment to a warmer climate, be sure you are drinking more.

## Arriving at Your Destination

Once you arrive, reassemble your bike as soon as possible; follow the instructions described in the previous section, but in reverse order. When you put the rear derailleur back on, be sure the stop screw near the mounting bolt fits behind the tab on the derailleur hanger. Make sure all systems are working, and everything is in one piece. If not, you have some lead time to solve the issue before the race.

Remember to drink to stay hydrated, get in a good meal, and even add extra salt to your food to help your body replace what has been lost. If you have time, go for a short, easy run or ride to help begin the recovery from your flight. This is also an opportunity to get the lay of the land and find out where everything is. To help make it an easy run or ride, bring along your small point-and-shoot camera, and take some pictures while you take in the sights.

Try not to get too caught up in the excitement of a new place before your race. The most important night of sleep and most important meal are two nights before your race. The night before is never as restful because you're focused on the race the next morning, so getting a lot of rest two nights before will help offset that. Save anything different from your usual dietary routine until after the race. Remember the mantra: Avoid trying anything new during and *before* your race.

In addition, race morning will go much easier if you pack your backpack the evening before so all you need to do is put on your race clothing and go. Strap your bike pump to the back of your pack so you can make sure your tires are still up to their race pressure. Go for an easy 10-minute jog as soon as you get up to wake up your body and its systems. Have a light breakfast to give your body a little fuel, but keep in mind that you should have your last solid "real" food 3 hours before to give your stomach time to process it. Since you've already scouted out the area during your easy runs, it will be easy for you to go to the race site and prepare yourself for an awesome race. Finish knowing you have done your best, and look forward to enjoying the rest of your travel adventure.

Being able to journey to different parts of the country and the world, while incorporating an activity you enjoy, is having your cake and eating it too. You can have the best of both worlds by preparing for your trip the same way you practice and prepare for your race. Be aware of the differences between your normal routines at home and what small changes you will need to make when you travel to a new locale. Learn to be your own bike mechanic to ease transporting your bike. Take care of yourself before, during, and after your race so your triathlon travel adventures will become some of the best experiences you will ever have. Happy and safe travels!

# PART IV

# The Triathlon Lifestyle

# CHAPTER 21

# Fitting Triathlon Into Busy Lives

## Linda Cleveland

For most working adults, trying to incorporate triathlon training into your schedule can be stressful. You want to give your best at the office and spend meaningful time with your family and friends, but you also love to train and race. How do you find time for yourself while nurturing relationships and growing your career? If you are a parent, you know it is especially difficult to find time to stay fit, let alone train enough to make improvements or to prepare for a long-distance event. I'd like to share some of the recommendations I've used myself and have learned from research and speaking with others.

## Training and Your Schedule

Everyone has different schedules. Whether you go to school, stay at home with your kids, work outside the house, work at home, or are retired, you will need to find a time to train that works best for your home and employment situation. If you like to get up early to train before your day starts, then maybe early-morning workouts are best for you. If you're not a morning person but do best exercising during your lunch break, then maybe a midday workout is right for you. If you would rather work out at the end of the day to relieve stress and unwind, then maybe a workout before or after dinner fits your lifestyle the best. Whatever time works best for you, try to make it a part of your schedule, and it will eventually become a part of your lifestyle.

### Early-Morning Workouts

Do you have the option of working a flexible schedule? If your boss is willing to let you go in an hour late to the office if you stay an hour later, then you have time to get up early for a high-quality training session before work. If you are a student who likes to squeeze in a workout before class, or your first class isn't until late morning, then early-morning training is perfect for you. If you have kids, then you know that day care, doctor's appointments, playdates, and illnesses can make your day-to-day schedule unpredictable. Many parents find it easier to get up very early before their children wake to ride on the trainer or run on the treadmill before the craziness of the day begins. You know how hectic life can be, and projects at work or sick kids can change your schedule at a moment's notice. You have several choices for where you can do those early-morning training sessions, including going to the gym or pool, training outside, or training inside at home.

Many pools, gyms, and YMCAs offer early-morning masters swim practices. Committing to meeting your friends at the pool a few days a week for training might be the perfect way to motivate yourself to get out of bed and into the water. If you have friends waiting for you, you're more likely to get up and go work out so you don't let them down. Make sure you commit to meeting a friend or fellow training partner there so you aren't tempted to sleep in and bail on the workout. You can probably find an early-morning spin class to take as well, which is especially great during the winter when riding outside isn't realistic.

In the summer, it's usually light out by 5:00 a.m., so you could get out for a 2-hour ride or 90-minute run before heading to the office. Again, maybe you have a dedicated training partner, coach, or athlete you can meet once a week for an early workout. Do you have dogs? My dogs love to get up early and go for a run with me. It's great for them, and I feel safer in the Colorado mountains having them along with me. Who says your training partner has to be a person? A great way to get some mileage in is to ride your bike to work or run to work. If you're going to bike to work, you can either carry a commuter bag with your clothes for the day or leave some clothes at your office for the week so you have something to change into once you get there. If you are going to run to work, you can plan ahead by bringing extra clothes for the days you are running in. If you are running home, it's easy to bring your running gear and then just change after work to run home.

In the winter you can use that trainer you bought to get a good ride in before the sun even comes up. Trainers don't take up a lot of space and can be set up just about anywhere—in the basement, in the garage, or in front of the TV. For those of you who want to catch up on some reading or the news, you can easily watch TV or read the newspaper or a book while riding on the trainer. Treadmills are great too, although they take up more space and cost a bit more. You can get your run in without worrying about icy roads, slippery sidewalks, and darkness.

## *Midday Workouts*

If you're not exactly a morning person but dread the thought of training after a long day with the kids, at the office, at school, or of whatever your day is filled with, then a lunchtime workout is probably perfect for you.

For example, the staff at my office are extremely lucky. We are located close to running and biking trails and have locker rooms and showers on site, which makes working out at lunchtime a great option. We work with a lot of people who are training for triathlons, running races, cycling races, and so on and enjoy the opportunity to work out with a buddy or group of people during our lunch break. Sometimes the best meetings are held while running with a coworker. It's a chance to get out and clear your head and come back refreshed and more focused for the afternoon. You might be lucky enough to work for a company that has an on-site fitness center or at least a place for you to change clothes for a lunchtime workout. If you don't have the luxury of an on-site gym or showers, you can always get creative by bringing supplies and cleaning up in the bathroom sink.

Organizing group workouts at lunch is a great way to promote fitness and health for all employees. Studies have shown that the healthier employees are by working out and eating well, the less work they miss and therefore the more productive they are. If your schedule is swamped with meetings and other obligations, you might want to block out an hour at lunch so that when people are scheduling meetings, they can see on your calendar that you are not available. Other people take an hour to go out to lunch, so why not use your break to work out?

## Evening Workouts

Does the thought of getting up at 5:00 a.m. just not appeal to you? Some people would rather do their training at night, after work or school. You will likely need a trainer or treadmill at your house or access to a gym, especially during the winter. During the summer, it stays light out late, so you can ride or run for a few hours in the evening (or, if you rode your bike or ran to work, you'll be able to do the same for your commute home). If you don't have a family, then you can probably get your training in right after work. However, if you have kids, you know that evenings are when you actually get to spend time with them. We will discuss training and your family a little later.

Another option is to get into the office earlier a few days a week so you can do some longer workouts in the afternoon. Just a word of caution: It's really easy to get wrapped up in a project or meeting and not leave the office on time, which then defeats the whole point of going in early to get a longer training session done later in the day. Another way to balance leaving a bit earlier in the day is to catch up on e-mails or other projects later in the evening after you've done your training, had dinner, and put the kids to bed.

# Time Management

The key to any successful training program is having a manageable training plan and sticking to it. Most triathletes are type A and therefore good time managers, but we could all use a little help once in a while. Whether you are getting back in shape after having a baby, training for your first sprint race, or getting ready for your sixth Ironman, you need a plan to manage your time. Here are a few ways to better manage your time:

### Hire a Coach

Consider hiring a triathlon coach or personal trainer to structure your training plans for you. A coach should be able to help you get the most out of the time you do have for training (information about what to look for in a coach can be found in chapter 23).

### Create a Schedule

With the help of your family, you can create a family schedule on the kitchen calendar that includes the days you are taking spin classes or training after work and the kids' soccer and swim practices. This way, everyone will know who is expected to take care of the kids and dinner that day. A favorite treat of my husband's is to offer to pick up a pizza on the evening he will be arriving home late. It's one less thing to worry about, and I can focus on spending time with our child.

## ▶ Training When You Travel

Does your job require you to travel a lot? We all know that traveling messes up our sleeping, eating, and training patterns. However, there are several things you can do while on the road to stay fit. Before you book your hotel room, make sure there is an on-site fitness center. That way, if you have to get up early or work out after a long day of meetings, you can still do so in a safe environment. Most hotel fitness centers have a treadmill, bike, elliptical machine, and weights, so it's easy to get in a bike, run, or strength training session. You can take stretch bands with you and do some simple exercises in your hotel room. If the hotel has an indoor pool, you might even be able to swim a few laps. If you like to run, then have your coach develop a training block that focuses on running while you are on the road. There is usually a break between a day of meetings and dinner, so give yourself an hour to unwind and squeeze a training session in. You can also look at booking your flights so you can go for a run or ride early in the morning before heading to the airport. It might mean you have to get up earlier, but then if you have flight delays or don't reach your destination at the time you planned, you've at least had a chance to work out.

Following are a few travel-friendly exercises you can do in your hotel room using stretch bands. Remember that stretch bands come in various levels of resistance, so choose a band that is challenging yet movable.

### Seated Row

Sit with the band wrapped around your feet and crossed. Hold the ends of the band, one in each hand (see figure 21.1a). Pull your shoulder blades straight back (see figure 21.1b), and slowly release back to starting position. Start by doing two sets of 15 repetitions, with 20 seconds' rest between each set.

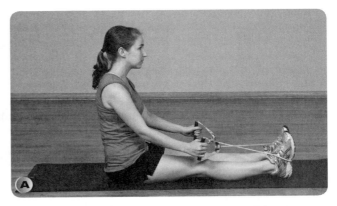

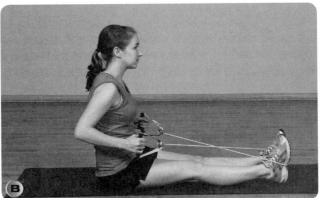

FIGURE 21.1　Seated row.

FIGURE 21.2    One-arm raise.

## One-Arm Raise

Stand with the band under both feet, and hold the ends of the band, one in each hand. One arm at a time and with the top of your hand facing the ceiling, pull up on the band until you reach shoulder height (see figure 21.2), and slowly release back down. Start by doing two sets of 15 repetitions, with 20 seconds' rest between each set.

## Biceps Curl

Stand with the band under both feet, and hold the ends of the band, one in each hand (see figure 21.3a). One arm at a time and with your palm facing the ceiling, pull up on the band until your hand reaches your shoulder (see figure 21.3b), and slowly release back down. Start by doing two sets of 15 repetitions with each arm, with 20 seconds' rest between each set.

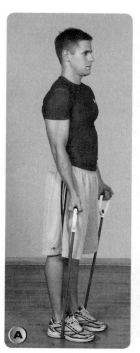

FIGURE 21.3    Biceps curl.

(continued)

FIGURE 21.4    **Triceps extension.**

## Triceps Extension

Stand (or sit) and hold the band behind your head. One hand should be holding the band near the base of the neck, and the other should be holding the band near the small of the back (see figure 21.4a). Extend your top hand straight up (see figure 21.4b), and slowly lower back down. Start by doing two sets of 15 repetitions with each arm, with 20 seconds' rest between each set.

## Chest Press

Lie down with the band under your back, holding one end of the band in each hand (see figure 21.5a). You may need to wrap the ends of the band around your wrists in order to gain adequate tension. Push your arms up and together until your hands meet over the center of your chest (see figure 21.5b), and then slowly lower back down. Start by doing two sets of 15 repetitions, with 20 seconds' rest between each set.

FIGURE 21.5    **Chest press.**

You can also easily do many other common exercises such as squats, lunges, leg lifts, push-ups, and curl-ups or sit-ups in your hotel while you are traveling. It is advisable to check your hotel fitness center to maximize benefits while you are away from home.

### Share the Load

In many families, both parents are training and racing for triathlons or other races, so you have to be careful to give each person equal time to train. For example, I am much more of a morning exerciser than my husband is. I am willing to get up at 5:00 a.m. to work out while my husband takes care of the dogs and gets ready for the day. He is much more of an afternoon or evening exerciser, so while I get our child after day care, he will go ride his bike or go for a run. If we both need to get our training sessions in before work, one of us will stay in the house and ride the trainer while our child sleeps, and the other one will get to go outside. We then trade off a day or two each week, depending on our schedules.

### Take Advantage of Weekends and Downtime

Weekends are also great for trading off days. Is there a Saturday ride that you really like to do each week? If so, maybe you can suggest that you will train on Saturday mornings but take Sunday off completely so your significant other can train in the morning, and then you can have some family time together later in the day. Another great use of weekends or evenings, if your children are still young enough to take naps or go to bed early, is to do your workouts while they are napping. This might require you to train indoors, but it's better than not being able to do anything. As for me, I have never ridden the trainer as much as I do now that I have a child. It's super convenient, and I can get a great session in while my child sleeps.

### Involve Your Kids

As your children get older, you might consider getting a bike trailer and pulling them along. It's a great workout for you, and kids love to get outside in the fresh air. You can also use a baby jogger and take your child with you for a run. You have to wait until the baby is strong enough to hold up his head (ask your pediatrician), but then you are set until he outgrows the jogger (or he gets too heavy and you have a hard time pushing him). It's an incredible workout and, especially for new moms, a great way to get back into pre-baby shape. Once your child is too big for the jogger and the trailer, hopefully she will be riding her own bike. This is a great time to go for family bike rides together, or have your child bike beside you while you run. If your kids are old enough, they may want to swim, bike, and run with you, which is a great way to help them live an active lifestyle.

### Get a Babysitter

There are times when you are training for a longer-distance race when you might need to get in more than an hour workout. You might consider hiring a babysitter for a few hours a weekend to give you the extra time to train. You can also get creative and share a babysitter with another tri-mom, tri-dad, or tri-family and do your workouts together. The kids get a playdate and have fun, and you have to find only one sitter. You could also offer to switch off weekends of watching each other's kids so you aren't paying anyone. This can also be done with your own spouse, as mentioned earlier. Grandparents, trusted neighbors, and family friends also make great babysitters. Grandma and Grandpa are often happy to spend a day with their grandchildren while you and your spouse go on a bike-riding date. They get to enjoy time with the kids, and you and your significant other get to train as you did before you had kids. The key is to schedule sessions that work for your family and still allow you time to see them. That means many of you Ironman athletes will have to be out the door by 5:00 a.m. to get that long bike ride in so you can spend time with your family the rest of the day.

Time management is key to sticking to your training schedule. The easier it is for you to set aside time for training by using the previously mentioned strategies, the better chances you have of meeting your training and racing goals. It's important to be flexible and realize that even the best planning and scheduling will not always work. It's not always easy, and life has a way of getting in the way sometimes, but if you can manage your time effectively and stick to your plan, you'll have a much better chance of success.

# Support Network

With all this talk of training, have I forgotten that you might have a family, friends, and job or school commitments? No, I realize you are a parent, spouse, partner, friend, employee, or student first, and then an athlete. Your kids, family, school, and job should come before your training. And no triathlete achieves success without a really good support network.

The first thing you need to do is share your goals with your significant other. For example, if you want to do your first half Ironman next year, you need to get the support of your family because of the time commitment involved. So, what if your significant other doesn't participate in triathlons or doesn't want to train as you do, but you really need her support to achieve your personal goal? Well, you could incorporate your races into family vacations. You can choose races that are in family-friendly locations and take the whole family on a trip. Disney is popular with kids, and who isn't ready for a week on the Big Island of Hawaii? Closer to home, Xterra races are known for being in camping-friendly areas, so pack up the tent and take the whole family. Yes, there is some pressure on you to qualify for certain events, but how great would it be to show your kids that all the training you do results in a cool family vacation for them?

When enlisting support from your significant other, it would be good to include the sacrifices you are willing to make for the family as well. For example, you'll take the kids every Sunday afternoon so your partner can have some free time, or you'll make dinner an extra night per week to relieve the burden on your spouse. You'll also want to be prepared with a plan and schedule to present to the family to show how it can all work. This is where you've done your homework ahead of time and lined up a few babysitters and the grandparents to help out. Get creative in how you manage all the training and family responsibilities. I've had an Ironman athlete tell me he sets up his bike trainer at his kid's soccer practice so he can watch while getting in a training session, eliciting some weird looks from other parents.

Also, believe it or not, you may be able to get support from your kids. Fitness centers that offer on-site babysitting and fun activities for children while you train are a great way to expose younger kids to fitness and a healthy lifestyle. This might spark their interest in other sports as well, and the more sports your children want to try, the more balanced they will be as athletes. Also, many of the races you enter will have a kids' event the day before the adult race, so you can get your kids not only excited about their own race but also involved in your training as well. You can sign your kids up for swimming lessons so they can learn to swim, or let them join a local swimming team. Some YMCAs and community centers offer youth-based triathlon programs. It's a fantastic way for your kids to learn more about triathlon skills, get exercise, and be a part of a team. Even if your kids aren't old enough to join a triathlon or swim team, they can help you track your workouts and come out to watch you race. Older kids will have a great time creating signs that say "Go Mom" or "My dad is a triathlete." It will also be extremely rewarding to complete a race after having a baby. The sense of accomplishment of having a goal and sticking to it and knowing you have been able to balance all of life's demands will be well worth it.

---

### ▶ Balancing the Role of Mother and Athlete

Maintaining fitness while balancing a career and a family can cause a lot of parents additional stress, especially women. Family and social pressure to be the primary caregiver, cook, and housekeeper can sometimes prevent women from believing they are able to take time for themselves to exercise. If you are a new mother—or if you don't have kids yet but are planning to some day—and you are an athlete, you'll want to read on for some advice on how to keep your athlete identity while adding "mother" to your resume.

Studies show that exercise helps relieve stress, and there is nothing more stressful than having children. Yes, kids are wonderful, and once you get the hang of caring for them, they add great joy to your life. However, babies with sporadic sleep and eating patterns can really throw even the most calm, relaxed mother out of her comfort zone. In addition, many mothers have to work full time outside of the home (and often struggle with guilt about leaving their children in the care of someone else all day). It's not surprising that many female athletes wonder whether they will ever regain their fitness and get back to racing at some point. It is possible; it just takes a lot of what we've already discussed, including time management and a support network.

Are you wondering how you will continue to train with your new addition? While the kids are still young, you can utilize the baby jogger, bike trailer, indoor trainer, and treadmill as discussed earlier. You will also be surprised how many people are willing to watch your baby while you go for a short swim or other workout at the gym. You can also sign up for mommy-and-me exercise classes that incorporate your child into a workout. As the kids get older, you will be setting a great example by incorporating activity into your day and encouraging them to do the same. This is where the family bike rides and having your child bike alongside you while you run come in. You are bringing them with you, so there is no guilt about leaving them behind to train. And about that guilt: It is OK to leave your child with a trusted adult, husband, or grandparent so you can get a little "me" time. You are not being selfish—you need some sanity as well. Exercising improves your mood, and the happier you are, the more enjoyable it will be for your kids to be around you.

---

The purpose of this chapter is to give you some ideas of how to balance your family and work life with your triathlon training. The keys are to become a great time manager, have a good support network, be flexible with your training, include your children, and lead by example. It's important to realize that even a busy working professional can still find time for family, training and racing, and living a healthy lifestyle. Triathlon offers a great way to be a fitter and happier person, so embrace the opportunities to train and race when you can.

# CHAPTER 22

# Choosing the Ideal Gear

## Timothy Carlson

From the first triathlon held in San Diego's Mission Bay on September 25, 1974, through the very first Hawaii Ironman held in February 1978, there was no standard of equipment for this new sport that combined swim, bike, and run. This might have been the very best thing for the long-term growth of triathlon.

Whereas cycling, swimming, and running had long traditions and carefully crafted technical rules, the first triathlons were spontaneous, improvisational happenings that drew an eclectic group of can-do athletes seeking an informal challenge. Those first events offered simple rules and welcomed a run-in-what-ya-brung, can-do attitude. "In the long run, that absence of predefined triathlon gear set the stage for a spirit of innovation that pervades the sport today," says two-time Ironman winner and technical expert Jordan Rapp (personal communication).

The sport offered a clean slate and became famous as the sport of early adopters—smart athletes eager to seek out and use the latest in technological innovation. Sometimes, triathlon pioneers led the way. Other times, they helped tweak and refine the original innovations. And always, triathletes just found the best stuff in other areas and put it to good use.

## Technological Milestones Key to Triathlon Development

Although one of the attractions of triathlons from the beginning was the thrill of meeting the challenge of various distances, from Ironman to sprint, the sport would not have reached its current state of worldwide popularity without some key inventions that made it more accessible to the ordinary human. When Dan Empfield developed the swim-specific wetsuit that not only guarded against hypothermia but also offered built-in buoyancy, it opened the gates for weak-swimming beginners to survive in oceans and windswept lakes.

Electrolyte-replacement sports drinks and energy gels not only helped elite triathletes go faster but also made it possible for athletes of modest talents to take on heroic training distances and finish long races without fear of collapse. Heart rate monitors and cycling power meters offered biofeedback that helped pinpoint optimal training intensities, giving triathletes at all levels a higher rate of success that kept them in the game. And given triathlon's primary focus on nondrafting cycling, the efficient seat angle of triathlon-specific bikes and aerobars and aero wheels were energy-saving, speed-enhancing tools that made the sport more comfortable, faster, and more fun. Taken as a whole, it seems likely that without those new products, triathlon's gateway would have been far narrower, and swim–bike–run would still be a cult activity for the few.

### Triathlon Bikes

While sponsoring competitors in his wetsuits, Quintana Roo owner Dan Empfield noticed that women had a hard time getting a good fit on bikes equipped with the new aerobars, which made the frame too long from the bottom bracket to the front axle. Inspired by his initial desire to help level the gender gap in bike design, Empfield found himself rethinking bike design from the ground up for triathlon time-trial riding. "I was riding with Boone Lennon's aero bars and it occurred to me that the fastest thing about the bike was the aero bars," he told Jason Sumner of *Inside Triathlon* (2007a). "So instead of aero bars being a component of the frame, why not build a frame that optimized the bars?" To make everything fit, Empfield decided to shrink the whole bike proportionately, using 26-inch (650 mm, or 650c) wheels fore and aft.

While racing himself, Empfield found the Scott DH bars uncomfortable, and he thought the saddles needed to be farther forward than on road bikes. In 1988, Empfield decided to steepen the seat angle. His first effort, the Quintana Roo Superform, had an 80-degree seat angle, which he later reduced to 78 degrees. Ray Browning debuted the Superform with a dominant victory at Ironman New Zealand, putting 30 minutes on cofavorites Scott Tinley and Richard Wells.

### Aerobars

In 1987, ski equipment designer and bike racer Boone Lennon adapted and improved on the first wide-grip aerobars made by Richard Bryne for use by Chris Elliott in the 1984 Race Across America and improved by 1986 RAAM winner Pete Penseyres, who added armrests with handholds on a platform in front of the handlebars. Lennon's version made the most difference in speed, putting the rider in the flat-back, narrow-shoulder aerodynamic tuck position of a downhill ski racer. Lennon patented his aerobar design and sold it to Scott USA. In 1988, Profile put big money into marketing and sponsored top triathlon pros such as Mike Pigg, and sales took off. In 1989 Greg LeMond used Scott aerobars for his last-day time-trial heroics and came from behind to win the Tour de France by 8 seconds.

### Affordable Disc Wheels

Although companies such as JDisc developed inexpensive plastic wheel covers to fit over normal bicycle wheels and improve aerodynamics, it took innovative designer Steve Hed of Minnesota to take space-age materials such as carbon fiber and turn them into affordable and fast time-trial weapons. When Italian Francesco Moser broke cycling's 1-hour time-trial world record in 1984, Hed thought the $6,000 price tag on the wheel was bad for the sport. "I was worried about the rich doing too well," said Hed, who then proceeded to tinker with different designs and materials, fashioning his first disc wheel for $395 (2007a). Hed sold his bike shop to launch a bicycle wheel business and created a first mold by hand. He built the first deep-dish carbon wheel and followed with a variety of dish wheels of normal depth that have remained a standard of the cycling and triathlon world for 20 years.

### Triathlon-Specific Wetsuits

In 1987, bike racer and triathlete Dan Empfield saw Scott Tinley was using a thick, bulky, constricting surfing wetsuit on bone-chilling days and still matched his warm-water, nonwetsuit swim times. "I reasoned that if you produced a wetsuit that had swim-specific characteristics, you could actually make it easier for people to swim in cold water without the wetsuit being a detriment," said Empfield (2007b). When surf wetsuit manufacturer Victory allowed Empfield to putter around their factory in Huntington Beach, he came up with a winning formula: Thinner, more flexible material in the shoulder. A smooth, hydrodynamic exterior and thicker material in strategic areas to improve flotation and correct poor body position. Ease of exit and a closed neck so no water flowed into the body. When he tried out that prototype suit, Empfield told Sumner (2007b), "I swam 100 yards and was 7 seconds faster than I would have been without the suit. Right then I knew what I would be doing for the next 10 years." Empfield's Quintana Roo wetsuits encouraged countless newcomers to join the sport by making life comfortable in cold water and also making everyone, especially swim slugs, faster. Furthermore, the world-record-smashing Fastskin swimsuits that dominated the Beijing Olympics—and were subsequently outlawed—operated on the basic principles of the triathlon wetsuit.

### Cycling Power Meters

In 1986, the SRM [Schoberer Rad Messtechnik] Training System made it possible to measure power in watts while cycling on roads and not just in the lab. Before founding SRM, medical engineer Ulrich Schoberer spent years thinking up ways to measure an athlete's power output on the pedals. Once Schoberer devised a special bottom bracket that could measure power at the point where output occurs, constant development has made it possible to record a complete record of power output versus speed, distance, and heart rate throughout the ride. The cycling power meter became popular in the late 1990s when word got out that Lance Armstrong used it as a key element of his training and racing. Since then the power meter has become an essential tool for elite cyclists and triathletes.

### Heart Rate Monitors

In 1978, the Finnish company Polar Electro Oy developed their first heart rate monitor with a cable-connected chest belt. By 1984, Polar had developed a small monitor worn like a watch on the wrist with a transmitter attached to the chest. This groundbreaking model gave an accurate heart rate measure that worked in real-life training conditions, thus revolutionizing training and fitness assessment. From 1984 on, triathletes and their coaches were among the very first to use this valuable new tool, which offered unmatched precision in determining the most efficient aerobic and anaerobic training levels.

### Endurance Sports Drinks

In the mid-1960s, Dr. Robert Cade developed a drink he called Gatorade to counteract dehydration in the University of Florida football team. Gatorade was bought in 1967 by

Stokely-Van Camp and immediately marketed nationwide. In 1969, San Diego marathon runner and trained biochemist Bill Gookin tinkered with the Gatorade concept to make a drink that more closely matched the concentrations of glucose and ions (sodium and potassium) lost in exercise to the actual concentrations found in the fluids and blood of fit runners. He also added magnesium and vitamin C and took care to find the right pH to avoid gastric distress. His brew, called Gookinaid (now Hydralyte), was used by the San Diego Track Club at the first triathlon in 1974 and by Ironman Hawaii in 1981; it provided a crucial step in the refinement and development of the modern electrolyte-replacement drinks critical for triathlon's endurance athletes.

### Energy Gels

In the early 1980s, Dr. Tim Noakes, a famed sport physiologist from the University of Cape Town, developed a long-chain carbohydrate polymer that had a lower osmolality, which meant that higher concentrations of water and energy could be absorbed by the body during intense exercise. After some trials, Noakes and Leppin devised the ideal form—concentrated liquid in plastic. From that, it was packaged in rip-open plastic similar to fast-food ketchup packets. Soon, innovative triathletes were ordering the Leppin Squeezy. By the mid-1990s, Brian Maxwell's partner at PowerBar, UC Berkeley PhD in biophysics and medical physics William Vaughan, further advanced the energy gel formula with his groundbreaking Gu energy gel.

Although these key innovations helped launch the sport, the sheer volume and intensity of change have just kept on accelerating into the 21st century, with new materials and high-tech, digital concepts rocketing the triathlon envelope into orbit in a constant technical revolution.

# Choosing Gear for Your Skill Level

Even if you had an endless cash flow, it would not make sense to breeze into a high-end triathlon store and buy the Ferrari of bikes, NASA-level heart rate monitors and power meters, super-slick aerodynamic helmets, complex reinforced running shoes, and all the advanced gear the sport has developed for its most accomplished and experienced practitioners. First of all, triathlon equipment at all levels offers so many choices and answers so many comfort and performance questions that starting off with some basic, safe, and reasonably serviceable swim, bike, and run gear gives everyone the opportunity to discover just what is important to them—as well as fits the wallet.

One of the wonderful things about triathlon is that the sport offers thrills and emotions during the most humble first-time race that are often just as great as the exultation experienced by an Ironman winner. And it would be a shame to discourage anyone from experiencing his first triathlon by making him think he has to keep up with the demographic elite just to try it out. A first triathlon can be done with a few well-worn items found in the garage and in the old clothes bin, and it's arguably a better way to start. But as the beginner evolves into an intermediate and then to an expert and elite athlete, the fine equipment the sport has produced becomes an increasingly reasonable and worthwhile investment.

# *Beginners*

Maybe you saw the NBC Ironman broadcast or the Olympic triathlon. Maybe you saw bikes whizzing by at a small local sprint triathlon, or an army of swimmers, bikers, and runners invading a big-city triathlon. And once you saw the smiles and exuberance at the finish, you had an inexplicable urge to join the parade. No matter, the spark caught fire, and you were determined to join the estimated quarter million active triathletes in the United States—or at least put your toe in the water. So what kind of stuff do you need, and where do you get it?

You might be stunned to hear that some studies in a demographic analysis of the triathlon market claim that the median income of a triathlete is in six figures and that the mythical average triathlete spends from $2,000 to $5,000 a year on equipment, much of it bright, shiny, exotic, jewel-like, high-tech gear. So what about starving students or hard-working family men and women on a tight budget who want to give triathlon a try? Not a problem. Actually, a survey of the 135,000 members of USA Triathlon (2009) showed that the average active triathlete spent about $150 a year on swimming equipment, roughly $350 a year on cycling equipment (excluding bicycles), and $200 a year on running equipment.

For starters, once you find a small short-distance local triathlon that is not sold out well ahead of time, you can satisfy your impulse quickly and barely dent your wallet. If you are blissfully immune to status or performance anxiety, the core joy and exhilaration are to be had without the trimmings. There are two skill sets you cannot do without—you must know how to swim and ride a bike. Beyond that, the bar is low. If the water is not too cold, you *can* do a triathlon in surfer board shorts; old sneakers; a rusty, mud-streaked mountain bike; a well-worn softball T-shirt; and, of course, your U.S. CPSC–approved bicycle helmet, which is a USA Triathlon safety requirement. But if you want to arrive at your first start line reasonably well equipped for the challenge, there are many options. First off, do not go on a spending spree for your first race. Until you've trained a while and raced a few times, you will not know what you really want or need.

Thanks to the growth of the sport and the Internet, there are many ways to find out about local races. Perhaps the best way is to join a triathlon club in your hometown. Race size ranges from a few dozen like-minded souls to 1,000 to 3,000 in the well-established clubs in the biggest cities. If you are lucky enough to live in one of these major cities, established triathlon clubs are a great source of information (and coaching) as well as a great source of used equipment because members are constantly turning over excellent bikes. Another resource is the triathlon forums. The largest, Slowtwitch.com, has more than 14,000 knowledgeable forum contributors who share expertise and advice on any legitimate questions posed. For the face-to-face, personal touch, established cycling shops and multisport and triathlon shops are great. Although all are happy to sell you equipment, almost all of them will offer good basic advice knowing that if they steer you right, you will come back. In addition, eBay, classifieds, and triathlon shops offer used gear, and some have rentals.

## Swim Gear for Beginners

For the sprint triathlons held in warm water with a distance of 200 to 500 meters, you can consider thrashing through the swim in a bathing suit or bike shorts. For many triathlons, the water will be 70 degrees Fahrenheit (21 degrees Celsius) or less, and a triathlon wetsuit is a very good idea both for flotation and warmth. Although the best wetsuits cost from $450 to $650, you can rent a good one from a local triathlon shop for $25 to $60 for one race. Some very good Internet sites offer excellent wetsuit rentals for $45 with convenient FedEx and UPS delivery. They also sell used wetsuits for anywhere from $50 to $150. If you are lucky enough to have a triathlete neighbor your size, you could borrow one as well. No-sleeve models (Farmer Johns) are good if the water is relatively warm because they are easier to take off, but they take on water and make you work harder. If the water is 66 degrees Fahrenheit (19 degrees Celsius) or below and the swim is half a mile (800 m) or longer, a full-length wetsuit is worth the trouble. Most of all, said famed triathlon coach Joe Friel in a telephone conversation, "Find out what you like and don't like about the wetsuits you try out before buying one."

Although you may swim without goggles, the cost–benefit ratio of buying a pair, which may cost between $12 and $35, is very good. Why? There can be a lot of turbulence on the swim, and you won't have to close your eyes, especially in saltwater, if you are wearing goggles. In addition, they are a great aid for navigating around the buoys and keeping your eyes from stinging in heavily chlorinated pools. But try on all the brands in the store, because goggle fit varies widely from person to person and from brand to brand.

## Bike Gear for Beginners

Although you can do a triathlon on a bike that has been gathering dust in your garage or is borrowed from a neighbor, you can rent or buy a well-maintained used triathlon bike for a reasonable fee. But before you pull the trigger, said Ironman pro Jordan Rapp in a telephone conversation, "Get a fit first. Don't buy a bike first and then try to make it fit." For the beginner, the best strategy is to find a bike shop or a triathlon or multisport store and have a qualified mechanic measure you to determine what size bike frame you will need. With rentals and used bikes, you will likely have to start with just the basics—a rough fit measuring your height and inseam. Larger folks, say a 6-foot, 5-inch (196 cm) man with a 35-inch (89 cm) inseam, would generally take a 60 to 62 cm frame (23.6 in to 24.4 in). A 5-foot, 10-inch (178 cm) man with a 32-inch (81 cm) inseam would probably take a 55 to 56 cm (21.6 in to 22 in) frame. A 5-foot (152 cm) woman with a 29-inch (74 cm) inseam might take a 42 to 44 cm (16.5 in to 17.3 in) frame. After your first triathlon, a more thorough, careful bike fit by qualified personnel such as a certified Retul fitter; or a technician at a sports medicine lab such as the Boulder Center for Sports Medicine; or a well-regarded, trained, and certified bike fitter at a triathlon store will be worth every penny in high function and injury avoidance.

In terms of used bikes, veteran age-group triathletes recommend buying anything from "a $50 beater," which would likely be a steel frame with inexpensive toe clips with straps ($15 to $17 new) on the pedals (so you can keep it simple and use running shoes on both bike and run) up to a basic $500 road or triathlon bike with an aluminum frame that includes clip-on aerobars, decent clip-in pedals, and basic hard cycling shoes. "Don't buy a new bike," Joe Friel advised in a telephone conversation. "Wait a year for a better bike." When buying a used bike, said Xlab USA boss, Nytro Multisport Technology founder, and triathlon equipment guru to the stars Craig Turner in a phone conversation, "Watch out for worn derailleurs and bottom brackets. Check for crisp shifting and vertical movement in the bottom bracket. Also look all over the frame for cracks, especially around the base of the seatpost." Of course, it is better if the seller will let you take the bike to a local bike shop to offer an expert appraisal.

In the triathlon bike-rental market, most major cities have well-equipped stores. In one popular Washington DC triathlon store, the 1-day race fee is $50 for a standard road bike with clip-on aerobars, $75 for a carbon frame, and $100 for a carbon bike with top-of-the-line components and built-in aerobars; the fee for a weekend rental to allow practice and adaptation before the race is $125 to $150. If you are traveling to one of your first races, note that a $150 weekend rental of a well-maintained bike would be no more expensive than many fees airlines charge for a bike box.

Although a simple race cyclometer (a speedometer and odometer on a bicycle) that gives speed and distance figures may be of some pacing help, a first-time triathlete can do without. It is probably better to focus on the road ahead to avoid first-race crashes into potholes or other competitors. If you do not already have a lot of miles on your bike in the aero position, it might be better to forgo attempting the flat-back tucked position in a race. Also, even for sprint races, it is advisable to have bike bottles of your favorite electrolyte-replacement drinks in cages on the frame. But save the fuel belt with bandolier-style holders for squeeze bottles of Gu and drinks on the run for later, longer races.

## Run Gear for Beginners

Beginners may not need much in the way of run gear and accessories for a first-time sprint race finishing off with a 5K. Odds are, at least one-third of beginner triathletes have running experience and possess current running shoes. Also, in a sprint triathlon, even the raw beginner might benefit from simple transition strategies—if only to reduce the stress. That's why inexpensive toe clips on the pedals—allowing the competitor to keep the same run shoes through the bike and run—are a good first-race choice. For beginners who insist on trying out the more advanced clip-in pedals with hard-shell bike shoes, the switch to running shoes can be made smoother by using run shoes with elastic laces or, if the triathlete has old-school tendencies, using lace locks on standard laces.

Also in sprint races, it is advisable to wear either a running- or triathlon-specific singlet with triathlon or bike shorts through the swim, bike, and run. Or else wear Speedo-style bathing suits throughout rather than spending long minutes changing from one specialized piece of clothing to the next. For those beginners absolutely certain they will stick with the sport, the one-piece and two-piece tri-suits ($80 to $160) are rugged, aerodynamic, stylish, colorful, and functional—if not absolutely necessary.

Although a running cap and sunglasses may be de rigueur for Olympic-distance and longer events, they are optional for a sprint and may be ignored in the interest of simplicity. The place where sunglasses might be of greatest value is on the bike to prevent dirt or dust from catching in your eyes while charging along at 20 to 25 miles per hour (32 to 40 km/h). But that function does *not* require $150 to $250 sport eyewear. One piece of triathlon equipment that is not optional is waterproof sun block.

## *Intermediates*

Odds are the new triathlete had a great time in her first few triathlons with borrowed, rented, or used gear. And this triathlete is often hooked and wants to give the sport her best shot for a year or more. But it is likely that the bike and those shorts and sneakers were a wee bit uncomfortable. And this now committed triathlon enthusiast wants to see how good she can be. So what are the smartest, most effective, and somewhat reasonably affordable pieces of equipment she should acquire?

When contemplating buying a more extensive list of better equipment to carry you through a full season or more of triathlon, a longer-term budgeting strategy might be of value. First of all, you can start by selling your $500 used bike for close to what you paid for it and get half what you paid for your first wetsuit. Then, when the cost of middle-range triathlon bikes and other equipment looms large, think of it as depreciating over 2 or 3 years. If the initial investment is too much, spread out these purchases over a year or 18 months, and make them in order of greatest necessity. If you can't own all the stuff you'd like, a membership in a triathlon club might allow some pooling of race-day equipment.

According to a survey of coaches, shop owners, tech writers, and athletes, there is a rough logical order to second-stage triathlon equipment purchases.

## Swim Gear for Intermediates

Although the list of swim accessories for the intermediate triathlete may not be as long or as expensive as that of the bike, the increased mastery of the swim pays almost as big a dividend. Not all swim expenditures come under the equipment category, but they are all related. The first priority is to join a masters swim program in your area. The second priority is to pay for a few private sessions with a top-notch instructor to fine-tune your stroke mechanics. Along with this coaching, an increasingly dedicated triathlete should buy swim fins and a pull buoy for workout drills. Dryland training and warm-up exercises travel well with simple and effective 10-foot (3 m) rubber stretch cords. And the improving triathlete should probably try out a few new models of swim goggles to see if there is a better fit. Finally, if you sense your fast-improving swim technique has plateaued—and you have room in your budget—you may consider one of the elite $450 to $650 wetsuits with super-smooth and fast rubber.

## Bike Gear for Intermediates

Intermediate triathletes may want to start searching for a better bike. When you are searching to buy, first get a fit in the shop. If you have the money, a more complete fit by experts that may cost from $80 to $250 will indeed pay off in the long run in preventing injury, increasing speed, and finding ease of use. At this stage, it might also pay to look at the USA Triathlon member survey to see what brands of bikes and components are favored. Almost all modern bikes meet a standard of performance and quality, so knowing the most popular brands may be a useful shortcut to making your decision. If your overriding goal is to do half-Ironman and Ironman events, looking at the Ironman Hawaii bike check survey will also offer a good idea of what bikes work well—triathletes are a pretty discriminating bunch.

If your bike budget is $500 to $1,000, your choices will likely be limited to aluminum-frame road bikes with basic components. For $1,000 to $1,500, many excellent road bikes have aluminum frames with decent components such as the popular smooth-shifting Shimano 105, with clip-on aerobars, a decent cyclometer, and a choice of pedals that includes the lollipop-shaped Speedplay clip-ins ($185) or the wide-based Look pedals, which will be fitted to contact with hard-shell bike shoes to give power to the up and down stroke. If you must keep closer to the $1,000 mark, you won't be buying aero wheels for a while and will do your training and racing with standard spoke wheels on regular tires with tubes. One other hint: If you are contemplating climbing a lot of steep hills and you are not as strong as Alberto Contador or Chris Lieto, you would do well to ask your bike shop to install climbing gearing for roughly $125 to $200.

For $1,500 to $3,000, which is the higher end of what is considered a middle-range bike, many more options open up. This price range may include triathlon-specific bikes with aerodynamic 78-degree seat angles and integrated aerobars with bar-end shifters. Perhaps more significant for many, it will also include carbon-fiber frames, which are lighter and offer far more shock absorption than aluminum frames, thereby encouraging more long-distance riding. This price point may also include race-quality components such as the Shimano DuraAce or Campagnolo shifters.

At this price point, it is assumed you have trained regularly on the bike and are improving, so better-quality race tires such as Continental, Vittoria, or Michelin might well be part of the package. If you have reached the point of qualifying for USAT national events or ITU World Championships, you could also contemplate buying a rear disc wheel or other deep-dish carbon wheels, which start out at $400 a pair for good used ones and go up to $2,500 for top-of-the-line Zipp, Hed, or other wheels. In addition, Xlab makes very aerodynamically beneficial water bottle frames mounted behind the seat.

Another aerodynamic tip: To avoid the weight and aerodynamic negatives of an air pump mounted on the frame, $CO_2$ cartridges for fixing a flat are a good idea.

Also, at faster speeds and in closer competitions, cycling headgear starts to make a significant difference. Once you are competitive and willing to pay more for helmets, the choice is between composite helmets with large ventilation channels to cool the head such as the Giro, Bell, and Specialized models versus the purely aerodynamic models, which are up to 2 percent faster but have no ventilation and so are hotter and increase hydration risk. Because triathlon is a total energy equation, those minutes gained with hot helmets can lead to a net loss if they affect the run.

At the intermediate level, scientific coaching is effective and appropriate—whether a local hands-on coach or Internet coaching. At minimum, a simple heart rate monitor without the ability to record splits or other data can be of great help and costs around $80 to $120. For more complete data such as splits and average heart rates for the workout and even GPS and altitude figures, Polar, Timex, and Garmin make great HRMs from $120 up to $450. Some coaches swear by power meters for the bike, which can range from $300 for indirect-measurement versions to full-on $4,000 CycleOps PowerTap and SRM DuraAce models.

Also, for winter weather, days when it's really too cold to ride outdoors, everything from $120 wind trainers to full-on CompuTrainers can help you keep up with your training. CompuTrainers have changing pedaling resistance made to mimic synchronized video versions of famed triathlon venues. They sell for about $1,200 and offer an accurate way to measure power output as well as maintain fitness on icy winter days.

## Run Gear for Intermediates

Once you have established a regular running workout schedule, you may consider buying a wider range of advanced run gear.

Start with shoes. With the advancement of barefoot running—or more conservatively, the popularity of minimal running footwear—it may be time to carefully explore the concept by checking out the growing popularity of the Newton shoe or the minimalist offerings of big companies such as Nike, Asics, and Saucony. Although many of these are not far from the long-established lightweight race shoes, there may be something to be said for the theory that wearing shoes with minimal cushioning may lead to a lighter foot strike and a more natural stride that is both faster and healthier. But this approach should be made only with the guidance of a running coach. And remember, if you prefer the heavily cushioned versions, thousands of runners and triathletes use them.

Another tactic that has worked for some triathletes is the use of tall compression socks, which make rough and tough elite runners look a little like English school boys and girls. The theory is that the socks keep the blood from pooling lower in the legs on long runs—and many elites swear by them. Also, especially if you are branching out and considering longer events such as half and full Ironmans, a fuel belt that holds both water bottles and bandolier-style holsters of Gu will be very helpful in training and racing. For racing, the one- and two-piece triathlon suits are water resistant, wick off all the sweat that long runs incite, are hydrodynamic in the water and aerodynamic on the bike, and look great. These suits range in cost from $75 to $175.

Now that you have established a regular, long-term running regimen, you will also want to record values such as heart rate, mileage, altitude, and running cadence, either by pen in an old-fashioned training notebook or on your computer in a training program or your own self-fashioned spreadsheet. The higher-end heart rate monitors such as the Garmin, Polar, or Ironman Timex models can save that data as well as multiple laps and splits and calculate overall, average, and range of splits matched with heart rates. And some measure air temperature and altitude and even estimate calorie consumption.

If you have a run coach, he will almost assuredly have a video camera to analyze your stride. However, if you are recording much of your data on your computer, having a small video camera or flip cam—both available for $100 to $350—could be helpful for recording your running stride throughout the season to track your form's evolution. This also becomes much more practical if you are working with an online coach who can look at your videos and then lend his experienced and well-trained eye to analyze your form and help you keep your technique on the right track.

## Experts

An expert status implies that a triathlete has experience, proven talent with championship aspirations, and money or sponsors willing to help her. If we were talking about auto racing, it would be the open or unlimited class. More modestly talented amateurs could also opt for some of these products.

### High-Performance Triathlon Bike

A lot of high performance can be had from triathlon bikes costing up to $3,000, including state-of-the-art aerodynamics. But right now the biggest change in bike frame shaping, said *Triathlete Magazine*'s Aaron Hersh in a telephone and e-mail conversation, is a trend to make the top tubes longer from front to back and thinner side to side than the standard that has held for the last 10 years.

For the past decade, says Hersh, most triathlon bikes have been using one of the standard National Advisory Committee for Aeronautics (NACA) specifications regarding airplane foil shapes, which measure aspects such as maximum camber, chord position from the leading edge, and maximum thickness. The new trend in triathlon bike frames, says Hersh, forgoes the old narrower and deeper foil shape for one that is wider and shallower, chopping off the rear portion of the top tube by 40 percent.

### Aero Wheels

For many years, aero wheel manufacturers thought a narrow and deep rim shape was the best way to go. But with new frame shape theory came new, wider aero wheels and the challenge of creating a wheel shape that would synchronize the whole package. Aero wheel rivals Hed and Zipp joined forces on this evolutionary project. For years, explains Hersh, 19 mm wide wheels with narrow brake tracks and wide, football-shaped oval rims had been the industry standard. The new wheels designed by Hed and Zipp eliminated the 19 mm brake track and made it distinctly wider. Other companies tried to adjust to this trend by making wheels with rims 21 to 22 mm wide. But Hed and Zipp made their new rims 25 to 27 mm wide.

The reason for doing this was all aerodynamics. The old football-shaped rims weren't just a fashion statement—that is the most aerodynamic shape. The problem is that the old wheels could not mesh with the new wide tires on top of the old, narrow brake track. The combination created a figure eight rather than a true, fast toroidal (three-dimensional donut hole) shape, reducing aero performance especially in crosswinds. "The new generation of very wide wheels integrates the brake track and the rim into one unified, fast, true toroidal shape," said Hersh in a telephone conversation.

These new wheels are very fast and expensive. A Hed Stinger set ranges from $2,100 to $2,200, plus $1,600 for a single Stinger disc wheel. A new set of the Zipp Speed Weaponry models costs roughly $1,900 to $2,100.

### Electric Shifters

While Shimano, Campagnolo, and SRAM continue to improve their already excellent shifters, Shimano has made a totally unique component group that seems as if it belongs in a Formula One race car. The Shimano DuraAce Di2 is an electric, motor-driven shifter that costs roughly $4,000 to $5,000. Why so expensive? It is better because the rider is shifting electronically. It takes little effort, the shifting is faster and very precise, and it does not come out of adjustment as easily as a traditional drive train. Not many use it because of the price. But two-time Ironman world champion Craig Alexander is quite happy with his sponsor-provided model. In the couple of years it has been on the market, it has proven to be very reliable—and it weighs only 150 grams (5 ounces) more than the regular DuraAce.

### High-End Power Meters

The full-on $4,000 CycleOps PowerTap and SRM DuraAce models that are integrated with the bike can be worth it for expert-level competitors. Although they grew enormously in popularity when it became known that Lance Armstrong used them, along with top triathletes, the reason was that coaches considered them an important and efficient tool. One key measurement that is crucial to high performance is lactate threshold, which reflects the muscles' ability to match energy supply to energy demand. Lactate threshold, measured in terms of power output, is the single most important physiological determinant of performance and holds true for sprints as well as Ironman stages. More specifically, functional threshold power (FTP) is the highest power an athlete can maintain in a quasi-steady state for an hour without fatiguing. One key advantage of the power meter is it can determine lactate threshold and FTP without invasive blood sampling. And the information provided both indoors on a bike trainer and riding outside and in races is crucial for performance-enhancing goal setting. Although many elite professionals use the acutely precise high-end models, average age-group performers with more discretionary income can easily benefit from more affordable basic power meters.

---

### ▶ High Tech or Low Tech: Putting It Into Perspective

Cory Foulk is 52 years old and has finished 47 Ironman races and 21 Ultraman events. He is an architect and a fine athlete with a wicked sense of humor, and at the same time he has a firm grip on the spirit of the sport. And he is a good person to talk to if you get too caught up in the obsession with the high-tech wonders that are a part of the sport of triathlon—or have an old-school fixation that cannot see the value in the beautiful modern machinery. Foulk has been involved in the sport from its first decade and is still going strong. He did Ironman Hawaii riding barefoot on a $200 neon green, 60-pound (27 kg) Schwinn beach cruiser with foam flames attached to his helmet with Velcro. And he has done the same event on a modern bike he says cost him $12,000. And he found joy and meaning in both experiences.

"Absolutely the greatest thing about doing an event like Ironman on a stone-age piece of equipment is that there is absolutely no pressure," says Foulk, who did that feat in 1996—the year that Luc Van Lierde set the still-standing course record of 8:04:08. "On a bike like that you can sit back and enjoy the race—because that is your only option. You can take your type A personality and throw it out the window. While a PR is not in play, there is always a challenge on a bike like that just to finish within the cutoff time. On a bike like that, there is always a point where I realized that maybe I had bitten off more than I could chew. Maybe I would not make it. And that is a cool feeling. Back in the old days, the finish was not guaranteed. And that was what attracted me to it. That is what I came to triathlon for.

"My 12k bike is a great bike, there is certain almost impossible to describe enjoyment to even have a piece of equipment like that. It's like if you own a BMW, wow the precision and it's so easy to drive. For me honestly I think it is even cooler that I can ride both ends of the spectrum. After I ride the big old fixed gear bike, I really notice the difference." Both his beach cruiser and his very modern, cutting-edge bike sit comfortably together in his Kailua-Kona condo. "My $12,000 bike is a great bike," he says with equal enthusiasm. "It is almost impossible to even describe the pleasure to even have a piece of equipment like that."

Foulk's appreciation for modern technology runs deep. In 2005 he had BHR hip replacement surgery, which rescued him from triathlon retirement and enabled him to do a dozen Ironman and Ultraman races since the procedure.

## PowerCranks

One of the most efficient high-end tools is PowerCranks, devised by Frank Day, a Naval Academy graduate with an engineering background—and one of the original 12 Ironman finishers in 1978. PowerCranks are independent bicycle cranks that replace regular cranks found on typical bicycles or exercise machines. Independent means one leg cannot help the other in making the pedals go around; to pedal the bike, you cannot simply relax on the back stroke but must actively raise the pedal using your hip flexor and hamstring muscles. This change ensures that your leg muscles will become balanced (both right and left, fore and aft) and will train additional muscles for coordination important for health and improved athletic performance. Basically, PowerCranks demand the athlete pedal with virtually perfect form. The company claims PowerCranks can improve both cycling and running, citing not only Tour de France cyclists but also marathon legend and coach Alberto Salazar and many triathletes, including Paula Newby-Fraser, Chris McCormack, Mirinda Carfrae, and Conrad Stoltz, seeking to perfect their form. The cost ranges from $999 for PowerCranks Basic to $1,299 for PowerCranks X-Lite.

## Altitude Tents

By limiting the percentage of oxygen, an altitude tent simulates the effect of living and training at altitudes ranging from 5,200 feet (1,600 m) up to 30,000 feet (9,000 m). The body's adaptation to those conditions stimulates the natural production of red blood cells crucial for endurance sport performance. A decade ago, these tents and hypoxic air generators cost nearly $10,000, but now competitive firms offer tents for as little as $2,500. A clue to their effectiveness? The Union Cycliste Internationale (UCI) seriously considered banning them.

In summary, there are a lot of equipment considerations to be made in the sport of triathlon, which can sometimes be overwhelming for many athletes. What type of bike should you buy? Do you need a power meter? Should you have race wheels and areobars? Many equipment choices will depend on your experience level and budget. I hope the information in this chapter will help you better choose the swimming, cycling, and running gear that is right for you.

# CHAPTER 23

# Choosing a Coach

## Linda Cleveland

A question I get asked a lot by USAT members and athletes is "Why should I hire a triathlon coach? What can a coach do for me that I can't do myself?" Many athletes train themselves with decent success, but many more are missing something in their programs. This can range from a nutrition issue to an inefficient swim stroke that is preventing them from reaching their full potential. Also, unless you've gone to college to learn about anatomy, biomechanics, nutrition, and exercise physiology, it's really hard to understand what might be going on with your body and how to train specific energy systems. It's also challenging to put together a periodized training plan to peak for key races if you're not familiar with what periodization is. Add to that a full-time job and family commitments, and you can see how difficult it is to piece together a solid training plan for yourself. I've spent the past 7 years educating coaches and have learned a lot from the coaches themselves and their athletes. This chapter discusses all the things you need to consider before choosing a triathlon coach as well as how a coach can help you reach your full triathlon potential.

## Qualities to Look for in a Coach

There are many areas of your training and racing that a coach can help you with, and there are also several qualities you need to consider before choosing a coach.

### Education and Background

First, you will want to find out a potential coach's education background. Does the coach have a bachelor's or master's degree in exercise science, exercise physiology, or biomechanics? These particular degrees focus on anatomy, physiology, biomechanics, exercise testing, exercise prescription, and nutrition. They are usually 4-year degrees that require classroom time, lab work, and practical application. If the coach has a master's degree or PhD in a related field, she was most likely required to complete a thesis or dissertation that involved conducting a study related to exercise, analyzing the results, and then reporting those results in a formal paper as well as a defense. Therefore, the person earning the degree should have a good understanding of energy systems, how the body works, and how to apply exercise and training to achieve optimal results.

In addition to the coach's education background, what related certifications does he hold? Is he certified through the national governing body for the sport? For example, USA Triathlon, USA Cycling, USA Swimming, and USA Track and Field all offer coaching certification courses. Does the coach have a personal training certification from the American College of Sports Medicine (ACSM), a certified strength and conditioning specialist or personal trainer certification from the National Strength and Conditioning Association (NSCA), or a certified personal trainer certification from the National Academy of Sports Medicine (NASM)?

If a coach is claiming she can provide specific nutrition advice, make sure she is a registered dietitian (RD). To ensure the coach has experience working with athletes, look for someone who is a certified specialist in sports dietetics (CSSD). This certification is specifically for professionals who have at least 2 years of experience as a registered dietitian and at least 1,500 hours of experience in the specialty practice. If you have a specific metabolic or cardiovascular disease, it is imperative that you work with a registered dietitian. The term *nutritionist* is becoming more common, but there are no regulations or requirements for anyone claiming to be a nutritionist. So make sure you find someone who is an RD or CSSD.

Regardless of what certification a coach claims to hold, ask to see if the certification is current. All the previously listed certifications require coaches to earn some type of continuing education credits to further enhance their skills and knowledge. This requires attendance at conferences, seminars, or webinars to earn these credits. This will help you identify coaches who are willing to spend time and money to maintain their credentials by learning and therefore are better equipped to help their athletes.

## Experience

How do you know if a coach has the necessary skills to work with you? You can start by asking him what his experience is with different types of athletes. Has he worked with beginners training for their first sprint, someone who's been racing a while but trying to improve her time, or any longer-distance athletes training for a half or full Ironman? For those of you racing or thinking about racing the International Triathlon Union (ITU) circuit, does the coach have any experience working with those types of athletes? Does the coach understand how you would qualify to race in a Continental Cup? The ITU points system is also important for your coach to understand if your goal is to race in World Championship Series events and eventually the Olympic Games. If you are an up-and-coming athlete and are working toward your elite license, having a coach who knows the qualification criteria and what races to send you to that would allow you to qualify for your elite card will be extremely helpful. Or you might be looking for a coach who specializes in working with beginners, women, or masters athletes, or maybe you want to work with someone who has coached a variety of athletes. Does the coach have experience working mostly with age-groupers, or does she also coach any elite athletes? Coaching a short-course athlete who races as a profession is very different from coaching a long-course athlete who has a full-time day job. A few of the differences include training time available, training time needed to cover the distance successfully, physical abilities and skills, goals of workouts, and specific workouts given.

You will also want to ask a coach about some of his current and previous athletes' accomplishments in various race distances. This will give you some insight into the coach's record of success. On another note, many professional athletes go into coaching either during their own careers or at the end of their racing careers, but this does not automatically make them good coaches. Yes, elite racing experience is very helpful when a coach is trying to explain something technical to an athlete, but you still want to look for a coach with the education background and related certifications discussed earlier.

## Personality

To be able to work with an athlete closely and help an athlete achieve his goals, a coach's personality must complement the athlete's. At the very least, the coach and athlete need to have a mutual level of respect for each other and be able to get along. We all know it's very difficult to work with type A, driven people if you have a completely opposite personality. However, most triathletes are type A and need a coach who can give them reasons for a particular workout, honest feedback when things don't go as planned, and continued encouragement and motivation to perform at their best. It's important to conduct an interview or have a lengthy conversation with a potential coach to get a feel for whether or not you would work well together.

Other qualities to look for in a coach are integrity and trust. Is the coach honest about how she works with athletes and how she recruits athletes? Is he up front with you about whether or not your goals are realistic? You will most likely be spending a lot of time and money to work with this coach, so can you trust her with the personal information you share and know she will not share any of it with her other athletes, some of whom may be your competitors or friends? There are many different coaching styles, and athletes respond differently to various types of coaching. If you are looking for a coach who will give you the hard truth about why you have not progressed in the past or tell you that your goal of a sub-10-hour Ironman with your current abilities is unrealistic, make sure you ask those types of questions during the interview process.

Some athletes find a coach that they work really well with for several years. Other athletes seem to jump around to several different coaches, looking for someone who is the right fit. You should be completely comfortable with your coach, and if things aren't working out, be sure to discuss it with your coach. There are times when an athlete leaves a coach or a coach needs to leave an athlete because they just aren't getting along or seeing eye to eye on things. This happens more frequently with elite-level athletes who may not be having the best performances and are searching for answers as to why. They will usually place the blame on their coach and possibly seek someone else to work with.

## Philosophy

Before hiring a coach, be sure to ask what his coaching philosophy is. Does the coach believe in giving you recovery days? Is she willing to work around your work and family schedule? Does the coach want you to have fun and enjoy your training? If you are sick, does the coach recommend rest or make you feel guilty for missing a day of training? There should be two-way communication between you and your coach. Your coach should ask you what your goals are for the season and then, based on a current assessment of your fitness, skills, and time available to train, let you know if those goals are realistic or not. A coach should be honest with you and let you know that signing up for your first Ironman without any prior triathlon training and only 5 hours per week to train was not the best idea and, in this case, recommend adjusting your goals to focus on a shorter-distance event. Many coaches will take a stand and refuse to train a young athlete for a long-distance event because it isn't physically safe. This is the kind of coach you want, one who will put your health and safety before your triathlon goals. Other coaches may be willing to provide you with any type of training you ask for, but in the end, it is the coach's responsibility to make sure you are training safely and injury free.

## Programs

When choosing a coach, you'll need to decide whether you want someone who will work with you face to face or someone who works with you mainly online or by phone. The benefits of having regular face-to-face meetings with a coach are tremendous. The coach will be able to analyze your swim stroke, bike technique, and run mechanics, giving you pointers to correct your technique as you are training, which gives you immediate feedback. Many coaches offer weekly group workouts for all the athletes they are training, so it's a chance for you to see your coach and also train with other like-minded athletes. Another benefit of working face to face with a coach is that the coach can look at your face and body language and determine if you're ready for a really hard workout or if it would be more beneficial to take it easier that day or take a day off. Many athletes enjoy the immediate feedback a coach can give by being on the pool deck, riding alongside on a bike, or being at the track with them.

Although there are benefits of working face to face with a coach, there are also challenges. One challenge is coordinating schedules. If your schedule doesn't mesh well with your coach's or you travel a lot, it might be difficult to set up those one-on-one sessions. Another challenge might be cost. Coaches normally charge more for face-to-face sessions with their athletes, so if you're on a budget, you might ask if your coach will meet with you a few times per month in addition to creating your training plan and communicating with you via e-mail, which might save you some money. Another option would be to attend any of the group workout sessions your coach is offering, which is usually a cost-effective way to get face-to-face coaching and a group training atmosphere.

In addition, a few of the main services you are looking for when considering a coach are the training programs and communication methods. Many coaches set up training plans and programs in various levels. The highest level might allow you unlimited phone and e-mail access on a monthly basis in addition to unlimited adjustments to your program, which comes at a higher price. A lower-level program might still include a customized training plan but maybe only a few calls or e-mails per week. So, you'll need to ask yourself what you can afford and what services you want the coach to provide. If you want your coach to attend your first long-distance race, be prepared to pay his travel expenses. Several coaches offer one-on-one training sessions for an additional fee, so you might consider this if you would like a biomechanical analysis of your swimming stroke, cycling mechanics, or running form.

On the other hand, if you need a coach to help you get the most out of your available training time and organize your training into a progression that helps you reach your goals, you should be able to find someone within your budget to do that for you. There are coaches that offer online training plans where you pay for a plan but never actually communicate with the coach. Although this might work for some very motivated athletes, be careful because the plan may not be specifically written for you. You don't want to become overtrained or injured by following a plan that wasn't personalized. Remember that coaching is a profession, and many coaches do this full time for a living, so don't expect a coach to offer you everything you want for $20 a month.

## Support Network and Referrals

An integral part of many coaches' businesses that will benefit their athletes is a great referral and support network. Many smart coaches have a network of professionals in areas they are not experts in. Ask your coach about which doctors, massage therapists, sport psychologists, registered dietitians, or bike-fit specialists they can refer you to. Often these other experts are being coached by your coach and enjoy the referrals. For example, your coach is probably really good at writing training plans and giving you basic fitness tests. However, what if you need specific dietary advice or have a nagging injury you would like professional advice about? Ask your coach, and she should be able to help.

---

### ▶ Questions to Ask a Potential Triathlon Coach

Here is a list of questions that are helpful to ask a coach you are considering hiring.

- Are the training plans customized to meet my needs?
- How often will you be reviewing my training plan?
- Can the plan be modified, and if so, how often?
- How often can I e-mail and call you?
- Do you require a minimum time commitment?
- Do you offer an injury or pregnancy clause?
- Am I required to sign a contract?
- Are there any other services included in the fees?
- How much does it cost to meet with you one on one?
- How much does nutrition advice cost?
- What exactly is included in my training program?
- How will I be billed for the program (e.g., monthly, quarterly)?
- Who are some of your most successful athletes, and how did you help them achieve their goals?
- What is your coaching philosophy?
- How many athletes do you currently work with?
- Do you travel to any of my races? If so, who funds that?
- What is your educational background and what certifications do you currently hold?

---

Also, most coaches have a website and will often post athlete testimonials there. You might read those to see what athletes have to say about the coach. Another great way to learn more about a coach is to hear by word of mouth from a few of his current athletes. It might be as simple as asking someone in your next spin class who her coach is or talking to some of the people in your local running club to see if they are working with anyone. Athletes are likely to give you honest feedback and are usually more than willing to give you the contact information of the coach they are working with.

# How a Coach Can Help You

Training for a sporting event that involves three disciplines is complicated. Most of you work full time and have a family life and a social life, so you have to make the most of the time you do have available to train (see chapter 21 on fitting triathlons into your busy life). And maybe you haven't swum in 15 years or been on a bike since you were a kid, and you don't know where to start. A good coach can help you with everything from your training plan to getting over your fear of swimming in open water.

## *Physical Ability*

A coach will be able to analyze your swimming stroke, biking technique, and running form, which are the first steps in getting you started on the right path. A good coach will develop a structured training plan that will address any areas of weakness, balance your training with the rest of your life, and help you cross the finish line of your race with a smile on your face. She can create workouts that will keep you motivated, challenged, and excited about getting up at 5:00 a.m. to get a training session in before work. Having someone create a customized plan to fit your life is great and takes the stress out of trying to figure out how you should train each day. You want to work with a coach who is flexible and realizes that a training plan is an ever-changing document. Even athletes with the best intentions of getting workouts in will have something come up such as a big project at work, a sick kid, or a family vacation that will prohibit them from completing their training as scheduled.

A coach with an exercise science background will have a better understanding of the physiological changes in your body as a result of training and what stressors are needed to push your body further to improve and adapt. For example, if you're hoping to swim 10 minutes faster during your next half Ironman, your coach might have you swim a test set and then take a look at how much time you have between now and the goal race to determine what pace you need to be swimming each week. He can set up a progressive training plan including swim sets that would be done at your desired pace. As you continue to train and improve in your swimming ability and fitness, you will hopefully reach that goal.

Your coach will also be able to give you basic nutrition advice to help fuel your training and make healthier food choices. As mentioned earlier, anyone with a metabolic or cardiovascular disease needs to seek the advice of a registered dietitian. However, a coach should be able to give a healthy adult general nutrition advice such as what food groups to be eating from, what foods contain a lot of fiber and should therefore be avoided before a long run or race, and how to best hydrate during training. The USA Triathlon certification clinics teach coaches what information they are allowed to give as well as how to calculate an athlete's sweat rate in order to prescribe the amount and types of fluid replacement an athlete will need during training and racing. Again, utilizing an expert in the field will help take the guesswork out of your training plan.

## Mental Skills

When is the last time you swam in a cold, dark body of open water? If you are nervous about swimming, especially in open water, I recommend you find a coach who can meet with you one on one at the pool, lake, or ocean to help you address any fears. You will most likely need to overcome mental barriers that come with preparing for your first race. Maybe the thought of having to swim, bike, and run two or three times per week is a bit overwhelming at first. If you are just getting back into exercise after not doing much, your coach will help keep you motivated to train and prescribe workouts that will challenge you but that you will be able to accomplish. If you've been training and racing for a while but are not satisfied with your results, your coach should be able to assess if some of your limiters include the mental side of training. One of the benefits of having a good coach is that she will explain your overall training plan and the reasons behind each workout as well as give you advice to help you overcome those negative thoughts. Coaches can work with you to develop mantras during tough workouts and low motivation times that help you keep the end goal in sight.

Many coaches prescribe training plans and then ask their athletes to record when the workout was completed, how everything went, and how they felt that day. This helps the coach keep track of fatigue, moods, and signs of possible burnout. There are several questionnaires coaches can use to assess how your training is affecting your mood and overall state of well-being. One is the Recovery-Stress Questionnaire for Athletes (Kellmann and Kallus 2001). This questionnaire asks athletes to rate answers to mood-related questions on a scale system to determine if they are overreaching or overtraining. It is a very useful tool to help a coach determine if he needs to back the training down for an athlete or give her some extra rest and recovery time. USA Triathlon also addresses mental skills training in its coaching certification clinics, so coaches leave with specific tools that can be implemented with their athletes.

## Fitness Assessments and Testing

Most coaches will ask that the first thing you do after filling out a health history questionnaire is perform some baseline tests to determine your current state of fitness. This helps the coach not only assess where you currently are but also, with repeated tests, make sure you are on the right track and adjust your training as needed. A great coach knows that an effective way to show an athlete she has made improvements is by testing in the beginning of the program and then testing after a period of time has gone by to show the athlete her visible fitness gains. Tests that can be done in a lab or gym include lactate threshold, $\dot{V}O_2$max, anthropometric measurements, and strength tests. If you don't have access to a gym or lab, your coach can have you perform field tests while you are out swimming, biking, or running. An example of a field test your coach might use when you first start working with him is a timed 5K run on a track. You simply do a warm-up run and then time yourself or your coach times you while you run the distance on the track. After several months of training, you might be able to run that 5K in less time.

## Time Management

When you work with a coach, you'll also have the benefit of someone managing your training time for you. You will have a purpose for each workout and can spend less time doing more high-quality workouts. In most cases, you will need to discuss with your coach ahead of time what your available hours are to train, what your daily schedule looks like, and when you can commit to a few longer workouts. Athletes tend to overestimate their time availability each week, so it's important to take a look at your current schedule and see what is actually realistic for you. You'll also want to tell your coach which days are best for getting to the pool and which days you have other obligations that you simply can't miss, such as your kid's weekly soccer game.

---

### ▶ Where Do I Find a Coach?

Now that you've decided you want to hire a coach to help you complete your first triathlon, record a personal record at your next Ironman, or simply help you start exercising to get more fit, where do you find a qualified coach? There are several places you can start. USAT offers a find-a-coach function on its website that lists USAT-certified coaches who have chosen to post their contact information. If you want a coach who lives in your area, you can search by state and find someone nearby. You can also do an Internet search for triathlon coaches, and you'll come up with more choices than you'll know what to do with. It might be helpful to narrow the search by area of specialty, physical location, and education background. In addition, you can head down to your local YMCA, fitness center, or gym to see if there are any triathlon programs or clubs. More than likely if a facility is offering a triathlon program, there is a coach who is overseeing the program, writing training plans, and conducting group workouts.

Another great way to find a coach is by word of mouth. You can ask fellow masters swimmers if they have a coach, talk to your friends, or start a conversation at your next race with other competitors to see if they are working with anyone. Interestingly, several coaches who have attended the USAT certification clinics have done so because a group of people in their area was looking for a local coach, so they decided to get certified and become one. Coaching companies also offer either online coaching or sometimes one-on-one coaching depending on where you live. There are athletes who do fine with an online coach and others who need some face-to-face interaction. It's up to you to decide what type of coaching you want.

---

The purpose of this chapter is to show you how a qualified triathlon coach can help with your training and to help you find one. Qualities you want to look for in a coach include education background, related certifications, coaching philosophy, and what type of programs the coach offers. A good coach will help you manage your time, schedule your training plan, test your progress, and give you physical and mental advice. She will provide you with not only a solid training program but also motivation to reach your goals and an environment where training for triathlon is fun. Be sure to ask a lot of questions, and make sure your personality will complement your coach and that you can trust him.

# CHAPTER 24

# Developing Young Triathletes

**Karl Riecken**

The mother of a young member of a triathlon team comes up to one of the coaches and says, "Why are you training her to play soccer? I want her to be an Olympic triathlete!" The coach, who is an expert in adolescent physiology, responds, "You're right. If your child is going to be an Olympian, she will never have to kick a soccer ball during a race or learn the skill of stopping the ball on her chest to avoid touching it with her hands. But, she is learning how to respond quickly at the age when it is easily developed. Imagine your child is in the final qualifying race for the next Olympic Games. She is on the bike, and her rival from another country forcibly nudges her from the side. Because she learned to balance while moving and controlling a soccer ball at age 6, her body will remember that at age 24."

Developing young triathletes is about more than teaching children to swim, bike, and run. Most athletes who are successful professionals as adults were not specialists in their sport from an early age. At 10 years old, Matt Chrabot was not on a developmental triathlon team. Instead, he was playing hockey with his friends and delivering papers once a week in suburban Chicago (Chrabot, 2011). In fact, after he was done with his paper route, he would grab his hockey stick and his rollerblades and pedal over to his friend's house. At the time, he was far more interested in building forts, playing video games, and being outside. Matt's family eventually moved to the east coast and while Matt was swimming on the high school swim team, he was also finding time for surfing. The first hint of specialization came during Matt's senior year. The team had a new coach that year who was tough and demanded the best from his swimmers. After swim practice the swim coach had the young athletes running two to three miles. This means that not until 17 years old was Matt becoming a triathlete. Before that, he was a kid who loved sports with parents who encouraged him to be athletic, which frequently turns out is a winning combination in the world of professional athletics.

In this chapter, we examine how to develop young triathletes in the order of practical importance to their growth as humans. First, children must be children. Then, they can become athletes. Last, they can specialize in a sport. We also call on current triathletes to reflect on their early development, revealing the foundation on which their successes stand.

# Promoting an Athletic Childhood

Today, with the typically overprogrammed lives that youths lead, it is easy to lose sight of what it means to be a child first and an athlete or musician or actor second. What is fascinating about young people is a natural drive to play and compete that is often lost on adults. Being outside and playing with friends in an unstructured environment gives children the opportunities to develop skills on their own and be reinforced for those talents they may naturally possess while uncovering unforeseen ones. Let's take Olympian Sarah Haskins as an example. Before Sarah had chosen triathlon as her sport, she would constantly seek out competition (Haskins, 2011). She recalls when she was 8 years old, she would challenge her high-school-age cousin to a race around the neighborhood. She would be able to keep close to him up to the finish line, where she would start throwing elbows to ensure the win. They do not allow that sort of behavior at the Olympics, but the competitiveness that was fostered when she was young in those races around the neighborhood, when she challenged her siblings to a race to the car at the grocery store, or when she started a game of tag at the bus stop all shaped the athlete she is today.

A simple game of tag that children learn to play at a very young age will develop an aerobic foundation, anaerobic strength, speed, agility, and coordination as well as or possibly better than any organized training activity even the best coaches could produce. Why is this? Because the game of tag introduces real-world unpredictability and competition. The children are left with two choices: (1) get tagged or (2) avoid being tagged by being faster and more agile than the child who is it. The game is simple, with rules that are easy to follow, and the objective is clear. Of course, a coach or other adult supervisor is vital to ensure the safety of the competitors. Nonetheless, with very young athletes, the focus should be on enjoying being active. In fact, before the developmental age of about 7, a prudent coach will expose athletes to a broad range of athletic, skill-based, and tactics-based activities from soccer to swimming and from bowling to chess.

Athletes who train through their adolescent development will go through three very broad stages as they progress toward high performance. Exercise physiologists have special names for each of these stages, but they are fairly easy to understand. Each stage corresponds to different age ranges in each sport, but the principles remain the same.

## Practicing

At this stage, young people are having fun being active and exploring all sports. Children will find the sports that are reinforcing to them through healthy competition in play. Here, they will learn general athletic movements that will lay the foundation for progress by setting up optimal biomechanics and energy pathways.

## Specializing

Once young people begin to get involved in more organized sports such as soccer clubs, swim teams, tennis leagues, and baseball leagues, they will begin to learn skills that are specific to each sport. These skills will go beyond generalized athletic movements to more specialized techniques that prepare them to get stronger, faster, and more agile once they decide on the sport or sports they would like to pursue further. As young people progress through this stage, each sport will get more and more competitive. Additionally, this stage for most sports occurs during puberty, which means that athletes will be maturing at different rates throughout the specialization stage. It is important for young people to specialize in a sport or sports while they are in a good environment for healthy competition and proper development.

### Performing

This is the final stage in the development of an adolescent athlete. This is where we see athletes reach the highest levels of sport. However, athletes will be able to perform at the highest level of the sport only if they have progressed through the former stages by being an active child, then being an athletic adolescent, and then choosing a sport at which to excel. All the techniques and skills the athlete learned as a young person will be utilized.

It is important to keep in mind that not every young person who is in sports will one day become an elite athlete. However, it is also important to understand that athletics are wonderful tools to teach young people about the importance of lifelong fitness, enjoyment of an active lifestyle, and the reality of competition in everyday life. That level of maturity will carry over into all aspects of a young person's life including school, family, relationships, and other extracurricular activities.

# Starting Triathlon

As each child progresses to a stage of early specialization, many parents who understand athletics will begin to put their children in programs such as soccer leagues, karate dojos, and swim teams. These are wonderful places for young athletes to foster great skills. As youth triathlon becomes more popular, there will be an increased demand for programs for these athletes. Soon, these triathlon programs will likely be part of the aforementioned sampling of popular sports for young people. This means there will be increased opportunity for young people to have access to our sport and gain the skills it provides. With knowledgeable and practical coaches, young athletes will be able to join a triathlon team at an early age and progress to any athletic activity they choose. Finding a good coach at this stage is critical. Good coaches will know how to appropriately develop young people to participate and excel in any sport. Great coaches will know how to appropriately develop young people to excel outside of sport as well.

### Swimming

All dreams and aspirations of athletic glory aside, all young triathletes must be able to swim, even in the most basic sense, and be comfortable in the water. Of course, this chapter is about more than making sure little Johnny and Sally can swim to the other side of the pool, but the discussion would be incomplete without mentioning what basic aquatic skills are necessary to prevent drowning. From an early age, children need to be exposed to water and should be able to safely play and enjoy being in and around it. This means children should attend swim lessons as soon as they are able (typically when they are potty trained). Swim lessons not only give the child and parents the confidence to be around water but also give the child another medium in which to play with friends, encouraging fun and competition.

According to Bob Seebohar, one of the foremost experts on childhood development in triathlon, practicing swimming can begin as early as age 7 in both males and females. From this time, athletes can be learning the skills and drills that lay the foundation for competitive swimming. Most professional triathletes today will tell you that knowing how to swim well at a young age is crucial. In fact, most age-group triathletes would probably agree that learning how to swim at an early age is critical for becoming a successful triathlete. Not learning swimming technique when young can be a real pain when trying to learn at 45. For those age-groupers who are reading this, know that it "happens to the best of us," however. It is actually fairly common to see world-class runners come to the Olympic Training Center in Colorado Springs to train with the resident triathletes in hopes of success in triathlon. They assume they can just pick up the swim in a few months or a year and be competitive. In spite of their often phenomenal athletic abilities, these athletes typically find that because they did not establish swimming technique early, the boundaries to learning it after they are fully developed are immense and many times insurmountable.

Of the three sports, swimming is the one that needs to be mastered first, but it offers huge benefits for the budding athlete. While swimming, children lay a foundation for a powerful aerobic engine. A good coach will center short practices on technique so that later in the athlete's development, the aerobic engine will not be too powerful for the body. To draw on a metaphor, if Ferrari were to put all its research and monies into a great engine, but did not bother to spend any resources on a solidly built frame and chassis, then the car would fall apart before the engine even put out any high power. Young athletes need to establish great stroke mechanics from an early age to prepare for when their bodies are ready to be fast.

As athletes get older, training and practicing shift closer and closer to specialization. Although it is ultimately the coach's decision how to structure his team, generally speaking, young swimmers are typically grouped by a careful combination of chronological age (time since birth) and developmental age (physiological maturity). According to the USA Triathlon youth and junior coaching manual, youth athletes (ages 7 to 15) are grouped in four age groups (USA Triathlon, 2011). Each age group has a specific focus:

- *Ages 7 to 8*: One or two practices per week of about 30 minutes each, usually during the summer, focusing on enjoying swimming and working on basic techniques such as breathing and balance in the water.

- *Ages 9 to 10*: Two or three practices per week of about 30 minutes each, usually during the summer, focusing on enjoying swimming, mastering basic techniques, and adding more advanced techniques such as diving.

- *Ages 11 to 12*: Two or three practices per week of about 30 to 45 minutes each, usually year-round, where sets can get a bit longer while still focusing on technique development and mastery.

- *Ages 13 to 15*: Three or four practices per week of about 45 to 60 minutes each, year-round, focusing on technique and energy system development.

With all categories, but especially with the 13- to 15-year-olds, having a good coach to guide the learning of each athlete is very important. During the 13 to 15 age range, athletes are experiencing the height of pubertal changes. This is also where critical development takes place, and having a coaching professional who is knowledgeable about athlete development is vital to the future success of the athletes.

## *Cycling*

It is practically required that all children learn to ride a bicycle, even to simply play in the neighborhood. It is also nearly a given that children will participate in an informal bicycle race "to the end of the street" or "back home from the park" not long after learning to ride a bike. However, it is rare that a child obtains the necessary skill set to be able to stay upright in a pack of 20 other riders when the rider next to him swerves to avoid a pothole. And this is not solely for draft-legal triathlon racing. Many nondrafting racers, who may have had no one around them, have crashed because of improper bike-handling skills that were not obtained as a young athlete. Before specialization can begin in the sport of cycling, proper techniques and confidence in abilities must be learned. Generally these skills include, but are not limited to, the following:

- Grasping and drinking from a water bottle while riding in a straight line
- Shifting gears
- Riding around and through obstacles
- Cornering (making sharp turns)
- One-hand riding
- Riding in different hand positions (hoods versus drops on a road bike; hoods versus aerobars on a time-trial bike)

Cycling is a relatively late-specialization sport. This means athletes will not see much benefit and may even see negative consequences from specializing too early. According to Tudor Bompa, who wrote *Total Training for Young Champions* (Bompa, 1999), among other influential books in modern exercise physiology literature, athletes should not begin practicing cycling until the age of 12. In most cases, children will know how to ride a bike long before they turn 12 and will likely experiment with many of the previously listed skills. Although these are practical abilities that riders of any level would benefit from having, many adult athletes have trouble with them. Therefore, as young people join triathlon clubs, going beyond simply racing with their friends, they will certainly develop fitness but will also have the skills to ride fast and safely as they race more and more. This way, they reach a point where they can begin to specialize by age 16 and reach their performance peaks after age 18 or when puberty is completed.

## *Running*

Imagine yourself at 8 years old. Think about what you were doing. Think about the games you were playing and the activities in which you were participating. What did you love to do? What did you love to do with your friends? If I were to guess, I would imagine the answer was not "I was out with my training partners doing a 3-hour run; we were practicing our nutrition, and we were having a great time going slow and completing the distance we needed to finish our upcoming marathons in under 4 hours."

In fact, I do not even need to guess because I know the answer to those questions in a very general sense. At 8, there is still recess at school, and you were likely out playing on the jungle gym, you may have been playing tag, and your parents may have put you in an after-school soccer league. While playing in the after-school soccer league, you and the rest of your team chased the soccer ball around the field like a swarm of pushy reporters around a movie star. But what happened when you misbehaved while at practice? More likely than not, your coach had you run laps for punishment. And if you were instructed to run those laps, it's not likely the coach required you to do intervals or anything interesting while you ran. Fortunately, this sort of punishment is changing as coaches understand more about adolescent psychology, but there is still a prevailing idea that running is associated with punishment. Ask any adult who is not active (and even some who are) how they feel about distance running or maybe even running in general. At least some of those people will tell you it "sounds like torture."

To get young people to embrace running as an enjoyable activity, it must actually be enjoyable. Again, this does not mean every running training session must be filled with fun and games, but there should be a healthy balance between fun, competition, skill development, and learning so that as many young athletes as possible are reinforced for running performance.

It is vital that parents and coaches see a young athlete not as a current high-performance competitor but as a "26-year-old in the making" according to internationally renowned running expert Bobby McGee (McGee, 2011). McGee cites the constant possibility of burnout from running too hard, too much, and for too long without positive outcomes. For these and for many other physiological reasons that are beyond the scope of this chapter, running has the latest specialization time frame of the three disciplines. In fact, according to Tudor Bompa, athletes should not even start practicing the sport of running until about age 13 (Bompa, 1999). This means they will not start specializing in the sport until about age 16, while high performance is not expected until at least age 22.

## Creating Champions

"I thought it was the coolest thing in the world that I got my name in the paper," said two-time Olympian Hunter Kemper (Kemper, 2011). He won his first IronKids race in 1986 and was thrilled to see his name highlighted in the local paper in Orlando, Florida. Getting that kind of recognition is what let him see he was really good at what he was doing. Does this mean it should be the objective of all parents to see that their child gets her name in the paper for every little thing? Absolutely not. That level of recognition needs to be earned, according to Hunter. He recounted the story of the first racing bicycle his father bought him. He remembers knowing his father would need a guarantee that Hunter would be putting in the time and the effort to make his investment worthwhile. "This was no cheap bike," Hunter recalled, "and I wanted to make my parents proud." The value of hard work was not lost on Hunter, and that is something his parents instilled in him from a young age. Hunter's father wanted Hunter to understand that if he was going to do something, he had better do it 100 percent. That early familiarization with what success means has helped make Hunter Kemper the world-class triathlete he is today.

Success plays a tremendous role in the development of any person, but the point that is often lost in today's society is that success still must be earned. It is not enough to simply reward young athletes for every effort made if the objective is to improve and not be complacent with current performance. That interpretation of positive reinforcement is unfortunately oversimplified. It is correct to say that positive reinforcement for a success, however it is measured, will elicit an increased frequency in the behavior or behaviors that led to the success (Luiselli & Reed, 2011). Let's take a look at what Hunter was saying. First, Hunter was put in a variety of sport programs that let him explore at which activities he could excel. He had met a fair bit of success being a swimmer and even playing soccer. But when his name was published in the paper, he realized something: "Hey, I'm pretty good at this." This, he said "bred his excitement" for doing triathlons. Young athletes will find what is reinforcing to them, whether it's because they are good at the sport, or they enjoy it because that's what all their friends are doing, or because there is something intrinsic about the sport that is reinforcing to them.

Here is where development comes in. It may be up to coaches and parents, along with their young athletes, to answer some tough questions. For instance, let's assume you know a child, let's call him James. James is 12 years old and is swimming on a local swim team, is playing soccer for his middle school, and has great grades in his academic classes. On the swim team, he regularly performs in the top 10 percent of the events in which he is entered and has won a heat in the last two meets in which he swam. Let's also say his coach is good, but she has a very large team, which makes it quite challenging to focus on individual athletes. His middle school soccer team, on the other hand, is ranked about halfway down the list in the district. James's coach is always applauding him for being the best player on the team because he is a great runner and is always trying to get better. However, his teammates lack the same dedication, and because of recent tax shortcomings in the county, the school is cutting back on funding for the soccer team. James often gets frustrated with how the team performs because he knows they could do better. Additionally, he's an A student, but there are quite a few other students who outperform him on some tests in the classroom. His teacher gives more attention to those who get perfect scores than to those, like James, who usually miss just one or two questions.

Now you know some basic facts about the environment in which James is spending some of his formative years. It's hard to predict which direction James will eventually pursue with the most vigor. He performs well at all these disciplines but is not the best at any one of them.

Now let's continue the story a little bit. One day James comes home from school and tells his mother he beat his best friend in a neighborhood bike race even though his best friend is really fast. Seeing how excited he is, his mother suggests that James enter the youth triathlon that's taking place in a few weeks near their home. James, however, is reluctant. He says he doesn't have any friends to do it with. He would rather keep playing for his soccer team because that's what all his good friends are doing. He is reinforced for being with his teammates because even though they are not the best, they have a great time together.

Consider for a moment the effect the environment has on a young athlete. Think back to yourself at age 12. Try to remember the aspects of your life that you enjoyed, the ones that motivated you. Think also about aspects you did not enjoy or that made you uncomfortable. What is important for the development of James and any young person is the environment of which they are a part. Once you have identified what was enjoyable or motivating and what was not enjoyable, think about why those qualities were attributed to those aspects of your life. Now, put yourself in James's shoes.

There are countless possibilities for how he and his family will proceed. He could continue to be the best on a mediocre soccer team and may never get the chance to play in high school or any further because his team is not one that many would notice. He may do very well on a few math tests and in a competition, and his teacher gives him more attention. He could also do the youth triathlon, win, and then be completely sold on becoming a triathlete. Any of these possibilities could be true, as could countless others. The takeaway message is that young people will respond to what is around them. They will shy away from what they do not enjoy and will gravitate toward what they do enjoy. Yes, it is ultimately up to the young person which activities to pursue, but those decisions come from experiences within her environment. It is up to parents, teachers, coaches, friends, siblings, or anyone else in the life of a young person to set up the best environment for the development of a child, then an athletic young person, and then an athlete.

Physiologically, young people are generalists before they are specialists. Building a great athletic foundation is critical for eventual success as an athlete at any level. Allowing each child to love being athletic is the best way to solidify success when he eventually does choose his athletic specialization. No matter what role you play in a child's life, especially as it pertains to athletics, the basic ideas are the same: Provide and foster the best environment possible. Elite-level athletics requires the same dedication, passion, and attention to detail that are valued highly in society for achievement in any field. Those values, if instilled from an early age, will give any child the tools for success in whichever pursuit he or she chooses.

# CHAPTER 25

# Dealing With Common Injuries

## Suzanne Atkinson, MD

Three out of four people reading this chapter have already suffered an injury while training for, or competing in, a triathlon. Although many of you are former runners, cyclists, or swimmers, becoming a triathlete will not lower your risk of injury. In fact your injury risk is higher than it was before you took up triathlon.

## Cumulative Stress of Cross-Training

Triathletes tend to train more hours per week than their single-sport counterparts. Triathletes training at both the lower and higher ends of the spectrum are more likely to be injured, meaning there is a "sweet spot" in which injuries are least likely to occur. In one study of nonelite triathletes, those training a total of 8 to 10 hours per week were less susceptible to injury (Shaw et al. 2004).

That being said, overuse injuries are more common in triathletes than in single-sport athletes because of the cumulative stress of training concurrently for three sports (Tuite 2010). Nearly 75 percent of triathletes have sustained at least one injury since starting the sport (Vleck 2010; Egermann 2003). When looking at goal-race distances, Ironman-distance triathletes have about twice as many recurrent injuries as Olympic-distance triathletes (Vleck 2010). One study of Hawaii Ironman finishers revealed an incredible 90 percent injury rate in the year before the event (O'Toole et al. 1989).

Also, triathletes may be more likely to train through a minor injury—leading to chronic pain or recurrent problems—especially if the pain is viewed as minor or a nuisance such as a grade 1 shoulder separation. Triathletes tend to increase training time in another activity rather than decrease training overall when suffering from overuse injuries. Many overuse injuries from cycling, especially of the knee, are also caused by running and vice versa. Adding additional hours of cycling when someone has runner's knee may not actually lead to any improvement in pain (Tuite 2010; Vleck 2010).

Surprisingly, the presence of coaching or seeking out medical care made no difference in the injury rate of a group of German Ironman finishers. Egermann (2003) found no difference in the injury rates of coached versus noncoached athletes. Although a coach can help an athlete improve technique and design good training plans, the athlete is the one who must pay close attention to her body and take action toward recovery as soon as an injury pattern is identified.

In addition, triathletes may have suboptimal technique or equipment than their single-sport counterparts (Tuite 2010). Taking up a new sport as an adult makes it extremely difficult to develop good muscle memory in the same way as an athlete who has been coached for years. Swimming provides probably the best example of technique differences among adult triathletes and competitive swimmers of any level. Young swimmers benefit from daily poolside coaching, with every stroke monitored. Those who start swimming competitively as adults, however, usually don't have the benefit of technique feedback in the same way.

# Types of Injuries

The spectrum of injuries in triathletes is similar to the spectrum of injuries seen in the single-sport events. In a study of the British Elite Squad comparing event distance with injury patterns (Olympic distance vs Ironman distance), most injuries were attributed to running (65 vs 60 percent), followed by cycling (26 vs 32 percent) and then by swimming (15 vs 16 percent). In some cases athletes attributed more than one sport to an injury (Vleck 2010).

The location of injury seems to vary depending on the race distances being trained for. Elite athletes focusing on Olympic-distance triathlon complained of injuries to the lower back (18 percent), Achilles tendon (14 percent), and knees (14 percent), whereas long-course triathletes complained primarily of pain in the knees (44 percent), followed by the calf (20 percent), hamstrings (20 percent), and lower back (20 percent). In other groups, the knee seems to account for more than half the injuries reported (Tuite 2010).

## Swimming Injuries

Swimming injuries account for 5 to 10 percent of all injuries in triathlon (Tuite 2010). Freestyle swimming requires two motions that can be stressful for the shoulder joint, including overhead reaching and internal rotation of the joint. This can result in three varieties of overuse injuries that cause shoulder pain in swimmers: shoulder impingement syndrome, rotator cuff tendinitis, and swimmer's shoulder. The shoulder is a highly mobile ball and socket joint that is sometimes described as "a golf ball on a tee." The upper part of the arm bone is shaped like a large ball several inches in diameter. This ball sits in the shoulder socket nestled underneath the collarbone, in front of the shoulder blade and adjacent to a tiny cup called the glenoid. The glenoid is "the golf tee."

### Shoulder Impingement Syndrome

Impingement refers to the pinching or trapping of the rotator cuff tendons between the head of the humerus and the part of the shoulder blade that extends forward and over the top of the shoulder joint. Reaching overhead; slouched, rounded shoulders; and internal rotation of the upper arm can all narrow this space and cause repetitive irritation of the small tendon. Impingement pain can be worsened while riding in the aero position on the bike (Tuite 2010).

### Rotator Cuff Tendinitis

Tendinitis is a more general inflammation and swelling of the rotator cuff tendons. Because these rotator cuff muscles are much smaller than the muscles which help move the arm overhead (deltoids), across the chest (pectoralis) and pull it back down to the side (latissimus), these larger movements can cause the ball-and-socket alignment to shift, especially when the rotator cuff is relatively weak. In swimming this happens when the pulling force is too strong relative to the ability rotator cuff muscles to stabilize the joint. Rotator cuff tendinitis frequently causes pain when the arm is lifted to the side or when lowering the arm from the same position. In more severe cases it may be impossible to lift the arm more than a few inches (several centimeters) away from the side of your body.

### Swimmer's Shoulder

Swimmer's shoulder is more common in competitive swimmers and refers to a combination of rotator cuff tendinitis and impingement along with laxity (looseness) of the shoulder joint. Excessive and aggressive stretching of the shoulder joint is common in competitive swimmers and may contribute to joint laxity.

If you begin to develop shoulder pain while swimming, don't ignore it. If you have just started swimming after a layoff period, consider taking a few days off. Resume swimming at a much lower volume and intensity, and build up gradually. Swimmers of all abilities can benefit from having their technique evaluated. One of the most common swimming errors is pushing down on the water with your arm in full extension (i.e., when your arm is extended towards the wall in the direction you are swimming), placing high forces on the shoulder joint. Correcting this common error with improved technique will not only relieve pain and pressure in the shoulder joint but lead to more enjoyable swimming as well.

Here are a few tips for good shoulder health:

- First and foremost have your swim technique evaluated, looking for common errors.

- Ice the area that's painful. A typical regimen is ice for 20 minutes on and 20 minutes off for three cycles. Some recommend icing once per hour for 20 minutes at a time.

- Consider *short-term* use of over-the-counter pain relievers such as ibuprofen or naproxen. Always use the smallest dose that is effective.

- When initial pain resolves, add shoulder-stabilizing exercises to your training on alternate days from swimming. In other words, don't fatigue your rotator cuff muscles in the gym and then go swim hard or you'll be asking for trouble.

- If your pain doesn't resolve within 7 to 10 days (the length a typical sprain or strain lasts), see a medical professional.

## Bicycling Injuries

Bicycling injuries account for 10 to 20 percent of injuries in triathletes. Most are overuse injuries, but each year, about one-third of cyclists fall off their bikes either in training or competition. Common traumatic versus overuse injuries are discussed in this section.

## Traumatic Cycling Injuries

Traumatic cycling injuries result from falls or crashes while riding the bicycle. Whether from a collision with another rider, falls due to road or trail hazards, or automobile collisions, the injuries range from minor scrapes to catastrophic injuries. Traumatic cycling injuries can be minimized by improving bike-handling skills, practicing communication with riding partners, and riding predictably in traffic while being very visible to automobiles. One rider I know waves at drivers at every stop sign intersection to be sure they see her.

Traumatic cycling injuries include injury to the skin, sprains, and fractures. If you have severe pain and swelling over a joint or decreased movement after a fall, seek medical evaluation.

### *Skin*

Your skin is your body's largest organ. It protects you from outside elements, it's waterproof, it keeps out bacteria, it keeps in fluids, it regulates body temperature by sweating, it has built-in glands to keep the skin hydrated and nourished, and it contains the tiny factories that produce hair. Common cycling injuries to the skin include abrasions and cuts. This section also discusses sunburn and increased risk of skin cancer.

### Abrasions

An abrasion results from contact with the ground while moving at high speeds. The friction between the skin and the road surface tears away layers of the skin, sometimes very deeply. "Road rash" typically refers to a large area of skin that is scraped away in a high-speed fall, frequently over the hip, thigh, calf, shoulder, or shoulder blades. Treatment of abrasions and road rash is something every cyclist should be well versed in.

1. Clean the wound and surrounding skin.

    The first step is to clean the area with soap and water. As soon as you can get to running water, irrigate open wounds for a few minutes to further decontaminate the area. Gentle soap will help lift out dirt particles that may be embedded in the skin. Putting full-strength peroxide and iodine directly onto a wound is not recommended because they can damage healthy skin cells that are needed for repair. Both are safe to use on the surrounding intact skin, or they can be used on the wound if they are diluted with water. Surrounding skin should be cleaned and scrubbed.

2. Apply a three-layer dressing.

    The next step is to protect the abraded area from further contamination and allow the body's natural healing process to begin.

    — *Layer one: the nonstick layer*. Because open wounds usually leak clear to yellowish or yellow-red fluid in the first few days, you'll need to use a nonstick dressing as the first layer on the injury. If none is available, you can also spread a very thin layer of antibiotic ointment on a plain gauze pad and place that over the wound to provide both protection from bacteria as well as prevent sticking.

    — *Layer two: the absorbent layer*. Use an even layer of additional plain gauze squares to cover the entire injured area. The purpose of this layer is to absorb the fluids that ooze from the injured skin. If the fluid becomes cloudy, white, or greenish, the wound may be infected, and you should see a health professional right away.

- *Layer three: holding it all together.* Paper tape can be used to hold down the edges of the top layer of gauze. For larger wounds, an ABD pad can be placed on top. ABD pads are large dressings frequently used after abdominal surgery that can be taped down at the edges. Stretchy tubular netting is perfect for arms and legs. It comes in several diameters and can be cut to the length needed and stretched over the entire wound dressing to hold it in place.

**3.** Maintain ongoing care.

Wash the wound daily with soap and water, and redress as needed. The wound will heal the best if the surface of the injury is not allowed to dry out and scab. The new cells require a lubricated surface as they grow and slide into place from the edges of the wound. A bright red appearance at the bottom of the wound is healthy and normal and does not indicate infection. However, if you see bright red or pink skin surrounding the wound, then you may have a wound infection and should see your physician.

## Cuts

Cuts, also called lacerations, can be caused by an impact over a bony area such as the chin, elbow, or knee resulting in the overlying skin splitting open. They can also be caused by cutting forces such as broken glass, metal, or other road debris.

Cuts should be immediately assessed for rapid bleeding; if present, apply firm, direct pressure over the bleeding area for about 10 minutes at a time until bleeding has stopped. If sterile gauze is not available, pressure can be applied with any clean fabric including a jersey or T-shirt. Use the fingers to compress directly over the bleeding wound. In severe cases, you may need to apply pressure over a nearby artery to slow bleeding. Tourniquets are no longer recommended because other methods almost always suffice. If bleeding can't be stopped, continue holding direct, firm pressure and call 911, or go directly to medical care such as the ER or an urgent care center.

Once bleeding is well controlled, the cut should be cleaned with running water if possible in order to remove both visible as well as smaller particles in the wound. Holding the injured part under running tap water for a minute has been shown to be as effective as high-pressure sterile irrigation.

Once the wound has stopped bleeding and has been cleaned, you have a few hours to get to medical care before the window for stitches has passed. A good rule of thumb is, if you think it might need stitches, it probably does. In addition, personnel at a clinic or ER can numb the wound, do further cleaning if needed, and evaluate for related injuries.

## Sunburn and Skin Cancer

Outdoor athletes are at a higher risk for skin cancer. Ultraviolet radiation from the sun is one of the biggest risk factors for several different types of skin cancer. Studies have shown extreme ultraviolet exposure in cycling and triathlon. In addition, sweating while participating in sports has been shown to increase the sensitivity of the skin to injury from ultraviolet rays. Endurance athletes with sun exposure have more abnormal skin findings including melanocytic nevi (developing moles, not present at birth) and solar lentigines (flat areas of darker pigmentation, commonly referred to as age spots caused by the sun). Although both of these findings are nonharmful by themselves, they are both risk factors for melanoma, a type of skin cancer.

Always use skin protection of at least SPF 30, especially in the colder weather when you can still get burned from UV rays even though it's not hot out. Don't forget to use lip balm with SPF protection as well, and reapply frequently during a ride. Seek a medical opinion for any skin changes including new moles or spots or discolored patches of skin, particularly if they are growing in size.

### *Sprains*

Common sites of sprains include the shoulder and the wrist. A separated shoulder is a sprain of the acromioclavicular (AC) joint, where the collarbone and shoulder blade meet on the top outer edge of the shoulder. Wrist sprains can occur in a variety of locations depending on the position of the wrist and site of impact during a fall. A fall on an outstretched hand, humorously referred to as FOOSH by ER physicians, is the most common mechanism resulting in sprains and fractures.

## Separated Shoulder

A separated shoulder is an injury to a small band of tissue (ligament) that holds the end of the collarbone down against the top of the shoulder on the outside edge. When a triathlete falls to the side and lands directly on the outside of the shoulder, this ligament can get stretched to varying degrees. The mildest form of a separated shoulder is simply a sprain of the ligaments with no tearing. This causes pain immediately over the acromioclavicular joint and may cause pain with overhead arm use. Treatment is rest, ice, and anti-inflammatory medicine.

More severe shoulder separations involve tearing of the ligaments holding the collarbone down, resulting in a bump at the far end of the collarbone where the torn ligament is no longer able to hold the collarbone in contact with the shoulder blade. Treatment is usually the same as for a mild separation, but healing time is longer. Rarely do shoulder separations require surgery.

If you think you have suffered a shoulder separation or related shoulder or collarbone injury, place your arm in a sling to gently rest it at the side of your body, and proceed to medical care as soon as possible. Icing the most painful area will help reduce the pain as well as the swelling.

## Wrist Pain After a Fall

Wrist pain after a fall deserves special discussion. The navicular or scaphoid bone is a small triangular bone at the base of your thumb. This bone gives your thumb its full range of motion. Since having opposable thumbs is one of the great things about being human, taking care of an injury to this area is important.

The navicular bone is different from most others in that it has a narrow "waist" and receives its blood supply from the distal (far) end of the bone. If there is a fracture across the narrow waist, it's possible that the bone won't heal properly. If you have persistent pain in the "snuffbox" area of the wrist after a fall, it's vital that you have it examined by a physician. You'll probably be placed in a spica splint and asked to follow up with an orthopedic doctor if the initial X-rays show no fracture.

### Fractures

Common fractures include fractures of the wrist, the elbow, and the collarbone. Many people know immediately if they have broken a bone because they hear a "snap," feel the bone break, or see an obvious deformity of the bone or joint. However, small cracks in certain places may not be so obvious. Almost all broken bones will cause immediate pain, but some may not begin to ache until after a few hours and over the next day.

If you are unable to move a joint in its normal range of motion, if there is obvious deformity of the bone or a joint, or if there is angulation of a long bone in the arm or leg, a broken bone is a strong possibility. Obvious fractures with the bone protruding through or "tenting" the surface of the skin require immediate care by a trained professional such as a paramedic followed by a visit to an emergency or orthopedic physician. Left untreated for too long, angulated or open fractures (bones sticking through the surface of the skin) can cause permanent nerve damage or infection. In addition, severe pain or persistent aching that is undiminishing should be a signal that an X-ray is warranted even if no deformity is seen initially.

Immediate treatment for broken bones includes evaluating for good pulses and movement of the hand or foot beyond the injury, as well as immobilizing the injured area with a temporary splint or sling. These can be improvised from many items you may have with you such as a frame pump and arm warmers to splint an arm or a wrist until medical help can be reached.

## Overuse Injuries in Cyclists

It follows that triathletes have the same knee problems that pure cyclists do. Although pedaling technique is certainly important, there is much less variation in technique on a bicycle as compared with swimming and running. If the bike is not properly fit to the rider, the repetitive motion can accumulate stress on the hips, knees, ankles, and feet, with the knee being the most common area of complaint for a triathlete (Tuite 2010).

**Knee**   The knee is a hinge joint. Although the motion is simple, the structure is somewhat complex. In addition to the contact areas of the upper and lower leg bones (the femur with the tibia), there are two discs of cartilage on either side of the joint called menisci (singular: meniscus), a protective kneecap (the patella) embedded in the tendon of the quadriceps muscle, ligaments that run on either side and through the middle of the joint, and many different groups of muscle attachments from both the upper and lower leg.

Common causes of knee pain in cyclists and triathletes are overuse, a poorly fitting bike, or a combination of both. The top three knee injuries are patellar tendinitis, patellofemoral syndrome, and iliotibial band syndrome.

### Patellar Tendinitis

Patellar tendinitis is an inflammation of the tendon just below the kneecap. When the quadriceps contracts, such as on the downstroke of the pedal, the knee straightens as the force is transmitted through the patellar tendon to the attachment at the tip of the tibia (shinbone). This can cause irritation of the patellar tendon, especially in the spring when enthusiastic cyclists embark on too much mileage or intensity too soon.

### Patellofemoral Syndrome (PF Syndrome)

Patellofemoral syndrome refers to a misalignment of the kneecap in relation to the groove at the end of the femur (thigh bone). When biking causes PF syndrome, it's called biker's knee. When the same syndrome occurs from running, it's called runner's knee. PF syndrome is caused by a relatively stronger lateral (outside) group of the quadriceps muscles. The patella (kneecap) is pulled toward the outside of the knee with every pedal stroke.

Over time, this causes pain from repeated wear and tear. The condition is more common in women because of a larger angle of the thighbone from the pelvis to the knee. Treatment can include adjustment of cleats and shoes as well as strengthening the medial or inside group of the quadriceps muscles with physical therapy exercises.

### Iliotibial Band Syndrome

Iliotibial band syndrome is also known as ITBS or IT band syndrome. The IT band is a thick band of tissue that originates at the hip and connects below the knee. During cycling, the IT band rubs against the outside of the thighbone just above the knee near the bottom of the pedal stroke. A seat that is too high or too far back can make this condition worse (Tuite 2010; Farrell, Reisinger, and Tillman 2003).

**Head and Spine**   The head, neck, and low back are quite literally at the core of your function as a human. The bony skull and vertebrae house your brain and spinal cord, which make up the central nervous system. Protecting the head and spine is important for triathletes in preventing both traumatic and overuse injuries.

### Low Back Pain

In a study of triathlon injuries, 17 to 20 percent of triathletes reported low back pain in the previous training year. More long-distance triathletes reported pain than Olympic-distance triathletes, suggesting a relationship with overall time spent training (Vleck 2010). In another study of Hawaii Ironman finishers, an incredible 72 percent reported low back pain in the previous year (Villavicencio 2007). Finding ways to evaluate, treat, and prevent low back pain is a big concern for all triathletes.

### Neck Pain

Up to 45 percent of triathletes experience neck pain at some point in their careers (Villavicencio et al. 2007). Sources of pain in the neck can be any of the structures mentioned for the low back. Pain can begin as a result of injury (falling off the bike) or strain from looking forward while hunched (hyperlordosis) in the aero position. Triathletes who have had previous sports-related injuries and have been participating in triathlons longer are at higher risk for neck pain.

If you begin to experience low back or neck pain, first take a few days off from training the activity that flared up the pain. Consider the use of over-the-counter anti-inflammatory medications and ice for the first 48 hours. If your pain is severe and does not respond to rest and anti-inflammatories, your physician may recommend a short course of steroids with or without muscle relaxants.

Have your bike fit evaluated by a professional or a knowledgeable friend or coach. If you've been riding a triathlon or aero bike frequently in recent weeks, consider switching to a more upright position, possibly cross-training on a mountain bike or touring bike to maintain fitness.

Getting to the root of pain in the neck and back can be difficult, even for experienced physicians. Although such pain is often minor, there are some warning signs that should prompt you to see a physician right away. In three-quarters of triathletes experiencing low back pain, the pain resolves on its own within a few weeks. About one-quarter of triathletes had low back pain that lasted longer than 3 months, and about 10 percent had neck pain that lasted longer than three months (Villavicencio et al. 2007).

Pain that lasts longer than 3 months is most likely originating from either the discs or the joints that make up the spine. As people age, the disc material can get brittle and develop small tears. If severe, the tear can cause fluid to leak from the disc itself and put pressure on the spinal nerves. This is commonly known as a herniated disc (herniated nucleus pulposus, or HNP, in medical terms).

If at any time you experience sharp, shooting pain; numbness; or weakness from your spine to your extremities, see a doctor immediately for evaluation because this could suggest a herniated disc with pressure on a nerve. Red flags for back pain include difficulty urinating, loss of control of your bowel movements, or numbness around the anus. These symptoms are rare but require you to proceed immediately to the nearest emergency room for evaluation.

**Head Injuries and Concussions**   Your brain is arguably the most important organ in your body. Helmets help prevent brain injuries by dissipating the impact of falls to the helmet instead of to your skull. A concussion causes a complex spectrum of symptoms as a result of a head injury, and it cannot be identified with X-rays, cat scans, or MRIs. Symptoms can include problems with memory, judgment, reflexes, speech, balance, coordination, and sleep patterns (PubMed Health 2011).

Seek immediate medical evaluation if you or a training partner has one or more of the following symptoms. This is not an exhaustive list; if in doubt, go to the hospital.

- Persistent vomiting
- Prolonged loss of consciousness
- Trouble with coordination
- Difficulty speaking
- Difficulty seeing
- Seizures
- Pupils of unequal size
- Clear or bloody fluid draining from the nose, ears, or mouth

Once more significant head injury such as bleeding of the brain and fractured skull are ruled out, treatment of a concussion involves brain rest.

Stay safe when riding, and keep your brain intact! Always wear a helmet when riding, even when riding on trails without traffic. Be predictable, and do not weave in and out of traffic or bike lanes. Learn traffic hand signals. Be visible. Wear bright and reflective clothing. Use flashing LED blinker lights when riding at night.

**The Ankle**   The most common ankle injury from bicycling is Achilles tendinitis. The Achilles tendon is a thick band of fibrous tissue that connects both calf muscles (the gastrocnemius and the soleus) to the heel bone. The Achilles transmits all the force of the downstroke to the pedal.

In triathletes, one possible contributor to Achilles pain is swimming followed by biking. In swimming, the Achilles is shortened because the toes are pointed during the swim. Transitioning immediately to bicycling, where the tendon is stretched, can cause irritation. Severe cases of Achilles tendinitis can progress to a painful lump or swelling that is liable to rupture if the cause is not addressed (Tuite 2010).

If you are suffering from Achilles pain, in addition to treatment with rest, ice, and anti-inflammatories, you should have your bike-fit evaluated to make sure your seat height, fore and aft saddle placement, and cleat adjustment are not contributing to ongoing strain of the Achilles.

## Running Injuries

Because running involves full-body-weight support with every foot strike, it's also the most likely to cause long-term injury or overuse. Running injuries account for up to three-quarters of all missed workouts in triathletes.

### Knee

Just as in cycling, the knee accounts for the majority of reported injuries in running. Running causes one-third of reported overuse injuries in triathletes. The spectrum of injuries is similar to those reported by cycling and includes patellofemoral syndrome, iliotibial band syndrome, and runner's knee (patellar tendinitis), which were discussed under cycling injuries.

Aside from what was already mentioned about these three knee conditions in the section on cycling, factors contributing to running injuries include the following:

- Rapid increase in mileage on hard surfaces (patellar tendinitis)
- Running on a crowned road with a slope (ITBS)
- Hill running (patellofemoral syndrome) (Tuite 2010)

### Foot and Ankle

The ankle is a hinge joint that connects the lower leg with the foot. Ankle injuries can be acute (sprained or twisted ankle) or chronic, such as Achilles tendinitis. Ankle injuries are common in runners and triathletes and account for 15 to 25 percent of running injuries reported by triathletes (Tuite 2010). Foot injuries include metatarsalgia and plantar fasciitis.

#### Metatarsalgia

Metatarsalgia is a general term for pain that occurs in the long bones of the foot, typically on the underside of the foot just behind the toe joints. Either running or cycling can cause this injury. The foot bones (metatarsals) absorb a lot of energy, and repetitive stress can cause a stress reaction of localized injury along the shaft of the bone. Occasionally, a stress fracture can occur. Cycling cleats can also cause increased pressure in this area, contributing to pain. Pedal and cleat combinations with a larger surface area may help diminish pain. One of the treatments for metatarsal pain and stress fractures is a shoe that does not flex along the sole, a characteristic of many high-end cycling shoes. Wearing stiff-soled shoes while cycling with a pedal and cleat combination that provides a large surface area can be good cross-training while the metatarsal injury heals.

### Plantar Fasciitis

Plantar fasciitis accounts for about 50 percent of running injuries in the foot and ankle (PubMed Health 2011). The plantar fascia is a tough sheath of tissue that runs along the sole of the foot, helping it maintain the arched shape, providing some shock absorption for the foot, and allowing for elastic recoil to return energy to the stride. When this tissue becomes inflamed, it can cause pain and burning along the sole of the foot, particularly right in front of the heel. The pain is usually worse in the morning, especially when getting out of bed, and tends to improve as the day goes on.

Treatments for plantar fasciitis include wearing shoes with arch support, especially when first getting out of bed in the morning or when getting up at night. You can stretch the plantar fascia by rolling the foot on a tennis ball or on a can of soda. Keeping several cans of soda in the refrigerator lets you combine cold therapy and stretching at once.

Tight calf muscles can contribute to the pain since the foot will tend to naturally point downward when sleeping because the calf muscle pulls on the heel. Night splints can be used; they work by keeping the plantar fascia stretched in a neutral position overnight.

## Lower Leg

Lower leg injuries account for about 10 percent of injuries seen in triathletes. The lower leg consists of two bones, the tibia and the fibula. The two most significant injuries to the lower leg are shin splints and stress fractures to the tibia.

### Shin Splints

Shin splints cause pain in the front part of the shin. The pain can be caused by irritation and swelling of the covering of the shinbone, known as the periosteum, where muscles attach. With each stride, these muscles pull against the area of the bone where they are attached and can cause the underlying tissue to become tender and swollen. The most common area is usually along the inner edge of the middle portion of the shin. Treatment includes rest and modification of activity (cycling and swimming are probably fine), ice, and anti-inflammatory medication.

### Tibial Stress Fractures

Shin splints can sometimes progress to a stress fracture in the tibia if the underlying cause is not treated and if adequate rest isn't obtained. The pain will be sharp and very focused in a small area. Differentiating between a stress fracture and shin splits requires an MRI. Treatment of stress fractures includes rest for 4 to 6 weeks or even longer.

## Upper Leg, Hip, and Groin

Injuries to the pelvis, hip, and upper leg account for about 10 to 20 percent of injuries in triathletes (Tuite 2010). The hip is a ball and socket joint with far more stability than the shoulder, the other ball and socket joint in the body.

The most important injury to be aware of in this area is a femoral stress fracture. Stress fractures from overuse can occur in the neck of the femur where the bone narrows just before entering the hip socket. An undiagnosed femoral neck stress fracture can result in long-term damage to the hip. In severe cases, athletes may need to have hip replacement surgery to regain full function.

Femoral neck stress fractures are most common in long-distance and ultradistance runners and triathletes. These athletes are used to running through discomfort, and it can be very difficult for them to modify their activity level enough when pain first appears. By the time a stress fracture is diagnosed, the athlete will not be allowed to do any running at all until full healing takes place, which can take 6 weeks or longer.

Injuries in triathletes tend to mirror the injuries seen in single-sport athletes. Even though triathletes are always cross-training, they tend to have higher injury rates than their counterparts in single sports. Triathletes with the fewest injuries tend to train in the range of 8 to 10 hours per week. Those training fewer than 8 or more than 10 hours had higher injury rates. Hopefully these brief descriptions of various injuries in triathletes will help guide you in discovering the cause when you experience symptoms and in seeking medical treatment when needed.

# CHAPTER 26

# Nutrition for Endurance Athletes

## Bob Seebohar

Most triathletes know that nutrition is important for race-day planning, but what you should remember is that nutrition has a profound impact during your daily training sessions, and this can affect how you adapt and prepare for race day. There certainly is a fine balance between what foods and beverages you eat, when and why you consume them, and how you implement a nutrition plan to support your individual health and physical needs. Sport nutrition has evolved quite a bit over the years, and nowadays, it is necessary to look at the big picture to properly implement a nutrition plan for achieving good health and optimal performance, and this means aligning your nutrition plan with your physical training plan. A properly periodized nutrition plan that supports your physical periodization plan will allow you to achieve better health and a higher level of performance.

*Nutrition periodization* is the term that describes matching your nutrition intake to your training sessions. Your nutrition program should vary, with the goal of closely matching your physical training needs so you can enter training sessions well fueled and hydrated and recover adequately in order to continue your performance improvement. It does not matter if you are training for short or long triathlons, adopting nutrition periodization will help you become a better athlete. Nutrition supports training, or as I like to say, "Eat to train, don't train to eat."

## Using the Nutrition Periodization Concept

If you are not nutritionally prepared before a training session, you will not get the same positive physiological training adaptations as other triathletes who pay attention to what, when, how much, and why they eat. Most triathletes follow similar training phases that usually include preparatory (base and build), precompetitive, competitive (race), and transition (off-season) phases. In this chapter, I present the quantitative method of nutrition periodization, which focuses on utilizing numbers within a nutrition plan, but other methods such as qualitative (not relying solely on numbers and counting calories and grams) are also highly recommended. These methods use hunger and satiety responses as well as teach athletes about biological, habitual, and emotional hunger. They are often chosen by athletes who prefer configuring a nutrition plan based on their emotional connection with food rather than with numbers.

The quantitative method gives information about how much carbohydrate, protein, and fat you should eat on a daily basis (in calories per kilogram of body weight). The ranges are provided by scientific research of the amount of each macronutrient that cyclists, runners, swimmers, and triathletes need each day. There is a large range for these nutrients because they cover athletes from very short distances and durations to the very long-duration athletes who qualify as ultraendurance athletes. These ranges give you some background knowledge about how and, more important, why to follow a periodized nutrition plan. I have further separated these ranges in each training phase to give you a better idea of how your macronutrients should change based on your training changes and goals. Keep in mind that understanding the quantitative part of nutrition periodization is important at first, but it is limiting because it does not teach you the qualitative characteristics associated with eating, such as the psychological connection to food and your body's hunger and satiety responses. Eventually, you will migrate to using fewer numbers and relying more on qualitative eating habits.

Here are the goals associated with the nutrition periodization concept to help you better understand it:

- *Manipulate body weight.* Some triathletes have a goal of losing or gaining weight, and this can be a main focus of a nutrition plan.
- *Manipulate body composition.* Some triathletes aim for a certain body fat percentage and will manipulate their nutrition plans accordingly.
- *Improve metabolic efficiency.* Nutrition periodization improves the body's ability to utilize stored fat as energy during exercise while preserving carbohydrate stores.
- *Promote a healthy immune system.* Following a good nutrition plan will help support the immune system, especially during a heavy training load.
- *Support physical periodization.* A nutrition plan should support all the physical fluctuations of volume and intensity in a training year, and thus periodizing the nutrition plan should be the first goal when it comes to looking at a triathlete's nutrition needs.

It is extremely rare for me, as a sport dietitian, to find a triathlete who does not have the goal of losing body fat or improving lean muscle mass. These goals definitely rank high among triathletes, and it just so happens that nutrition periodization supports these goals very well. Remember, this concept implies that you change your food intake based on your training, and by doing this, you can manipulate your body weight and body composition throughout the year. Keep eating the same volume of food when you are training more and you will run out of energy. Eat the same amount of food when you are not training much and you will gain weight. Neither is the goal under the nutrition periodization concept. As your training ebbs and flows, so should your nutrition.

Now for the numbers. The macronutrient ranges that endurance athletes eat on a daily basis, as have been cited in scientific research, include 3 to 19 grams of carbohydrate per kilogram of body weight, 1.2 to 2.0 grams of protein per kilogram of body weight, and .8 to 3.0 grams of fat per kilogram of body weight. If you measure your body weight in pounds, divide that number by 2.2 to get kilograms of body weight. Then, simply multiply the ranges throughout this chapter to individualize your plan. These ranges are large, and they reinforce the underlying message of providing these numbers to you: to let you see that an endurance athlete's daily eating plan (1) does not stay the same throughout the year and (2) has a great amount of variance. How you interpret and use these numbers is the most important thing, and the first step is having an understanding of your physical training plan.

# Eating Based on Your Physical Training

Before using nutrition periodization, you must first have a good understanding of what you are trying to accomplish physically in each of your training phases. Will you be following a traditional physical periodization program that emphasizes improving endurance, flexibility, and strength during base training and later adding intensity, power, and speed during the build phase? Or will you be trying to increase your speed during your base training season? It may sound odd to think about your physical training goals in a nutrition chapter, but remember, nutrition supports your physical training, so you must know where you are headed physically before you can develop your nutrition plan. Specific hydration strategies are presented in the next chapter, and thus they will not be discussed here.

## *Eating During the Preparatory Phase*

More than likely you will be trying to improve your endurance, strength, flexibility, and technique during the preparatory (base) phase. You may also be thinking of shedding a few pounds or some body fat since base-season training often begins after the holidays. All these goals reinforce the fact that you must periodize your nutrition to support your training. It can be a bit tricky at first because your training load (a product of volume and intensity) will not be that high in the early part of this phase if you follow a traditional periodization model. That said, it will be extremely important for you to slowly increase the amount of food you eat as your training increases. Remember, nutrition supports your daily training. If you are not training much in the early part of this phase, then you certainly cannot justify eating a lot. If you misalign your nutrition and your training, you will actually notice weight gain. It is quite common in new triathletes who do not understand the basic idea of periodizing their nutrition programs.

Bringing the numbers back into the story, nutrition periodization for this training phase states you should eat anywhere between 3 and 7 grams of carbohydrate per kilogram of body weight. Until your training volume increases to more than 3 hours for a session, you do not need to eat very much. Try to get most of your carbohydrate from fruits and vegetables, as they are great sources of vitamins, minerals, antioxidants, and fiber. Do not worry about consuming sport nutrition products such as energy bars, gels, and sports drinks. You will not need these extra calories until you start training more.

The protein recommendation is to eat between 1.2 and 1.7 grams per kilogram of body weight. Choosing protein can be difficult because some sources are higher in fat; try to choose the leanest sources such as low-fat dairy products and lean cuts of meat without skin or visible fat. Nonanimal sources of protein such as tofu, edamame, nuts, and beans are also good choices. Fat should not be thought of as the enemy of your diet. Your body requires a certain amount of healthy fat to function properly. Try to eat a lower to moderate amount of fat, .8 to 1.0 gram per kilogram, and make sure the majority is healthy fat such as monounsaturated (avocados, olives, nuts) and polyunsaturated, specifically omega-3 fats (salmon, trout, walnuts, flax). Try hard to minimize your consumption of saturated and trans fats found in processed foods, snack foods, and high-fat meats.

If one of your main goals during the base season is to lose weight or change your body composition, then you are in good company because it is one of the more popular goals among triathletes. For weight loss, I recommend shifting the numbers around a bit so your carbohydrate intake decreases to 3 to 4 grams per kilogram per day, protein increases to 1.8 to 2.0 grams per kilogram per day, and fat remains low at .8 gram per kilogram per day. The key is to decrease your carbohydrate intake to a lower (but still safe) level and increase protein to improve your blood sugar control and keep you fuller longer.

Stabilizing and controlling blood sugar can also help you become more metabolically efficient, which benefits any triathlete, young or old, recreational or professional. Metabolic efficiency is the relationship of carbohydrate oxidation (burning) to fat oxidation throughout different intensities of exercise. As the intensity of exercise increases, your body needs more carbohydrate to fuel the workout. Although this is certainly true, the take-home message is not to overfeed yourself with too much carbohydrate (especially simple sugars) throughout the day or during training. Repeatedly feeding your body a high amount of simple and refined carbohydrate may lead to adverse health issues, such as diabetes, through the development of insulin resistance; can create abnormal blood lipids, such as high triglycerides; and can create a heavier body weight. Balancing your daily nutrition while controlling blood sugar is a key goal in maintaining good health. This can be done by periodizing your nutrition plan throughout the year.

From a performance perspective, improving your body's ability to use fat can lead to a greater use of your stored fat as energy to fuel your training sessions and even your competitions. This reduces your need for calories during training, which will significantly decrease your risk of gastrointestinal (GI) distress. This is extremely important for long-course (half Ironman and longer) athletes since athletes sometimes overeat on the bike in an effort to stay fueled during the bike and run. That is a recipe for disaster, often resulting in GI distress in the form of vomiting or diarrhea. It is also important for short-course (sprint and Olympic distance) athletes because the intensity during competitions is greater, and with that comes a decreased ability to digest and process the calories you eat during exercise. This is due to the body's blood shunting response where, during exercise, blood is carried to the working muscles (to fuel locomotion) and away from the gut. However, if you are exercising at higher intensities and consume too many calories, the body must redirect this blood from the muscles to the gut for proper digestion. When this happens, there is a high risk for GI distress. Thus, no matter if you are training for long- or short-course triathlons, it is to your benefit (from a health and performance perspective) to become more metabolically efficient to teach your body to use more of its internal fat stores and preserve your carbohydrate stores until they are really needed (during higher-intensity exercise). By training your body to do this, you will increase your fat burning at higher intensities, which means you will be able to use more fat to fuel your training at higher intensities.

One of the easiest ways to develop better metabolic efficiency, besides training aerobically, is through proper nutrition—more specifically, implementing a good nutrition periodization plan that supports your training load as it increases and decreases throughout the year. Far too many athletes eat high-carbohydrate diets when their training load does not support it. This simply teaches your body to use more carbohydrate as energy and to store fat, which can lead to weight gain in some cases. Eating a higher-carbohydrate diet will lead to an increase in carbohydrate oxidation. This will decrease the body's ability to oxidize fat because of a higher insulin response seen with high blood sugar, which, in turn, turns off fat oxidation. Therefore, to properly teach your body to use fat more efficiently, carbohydrate intake should be lower in the beginning of this base training phase. This does not mean you should follow a low-carbohydrate diet. Rather, the goal is to balance your carbohydrate, protein, and fat intake through proper blood sugar control so positive metabolic changes can happen.

By focusing on balancing your daily nutrition and eating good sources of lean protein and fiber from fruits and vegetables during this training phase, you can improve your metabolic efficiency in approximately 4 weeks. It does not take long to teach the body how to use fat as an energy source. However, remember that once you develop it, you must maintain it. It is very similar to your fitness level. In the beginning of your training program, you typically have the goal of improving your aerobic fitness, and then throughout the year, you maintain it with different training sessions. Developing and maintaining metabolic efficiency follow the same principles you use in your training program as you prepare your body for the race season. It is not a change that happens overnight, and it is not something you can forget about once you have it. That is why periodizing your nutrition throughout the entire year to support your physical training is so important.

## Eating During Preparatory-Phase Training Sessions

One of the most important things to remember during each training phase is that the calories you put in your body immediately before, during, and after training will be different throughout the year. Your energy needs will vary because of higher and lower training loads based on your goal-competition distance. Most sprint- to Olympic-distance training programs do not exceed 2- or 3-hour training sessions, while half Ironman and Ironman training will easily exceed the 3- or 4-hour mark for individual training sessions. However, even for long-course training, volume will not be that high in the early to middle part of this preparatory training phase, and thus not many calories are needed during training.

The body normally has enough stored carbohydrate to supply 2 to 3 hours' worth of exercise at moderate intensity. Thus, for any training session during this phase that is less than 3 hours, you will not need to consume calories. Be sure you have a metabolically efficient meal or snack (for example, scrambled eggs with fruit, peanut butter mixed with yogurt) before your training session, and then simply drink water and possibly consume extra electrolytes depending on your climate.

If you are training for long course and exceed 3-hour training sessions, you should still eat a metabolically efficient meal or snack beforehand, and there are a few guidelines you can follow after the 3-hour mark during a training session. First, eat between 10 and 50 grams of carbohydrate per hour of training. The range is large because there are many determining factors depending on your training volume and state of metabolic efficiency. Current sport nutrition research recommends eating between 30 and 90 grams per hour, but the research does not periodize nutrition recommendations. As mentioned previously, you do not need that many calories during this training phase since energy expenditure is lower. Additionally, if you have developed good metabolic efficiency, you will not need to eat as many calories during training since your body can use more fat as fuel during these lower-intensity training sessions. Depending on how sensitive your digestive system is, you can choose a wide variety of foods such as crackers, bananas, nuts, and even sandwiches. Many of the higher-calorie sport nutrition products are not needed during this training phase. Save those for the next training cycle when your intensity and energy expenditure are higher.

Second, very few triathletes even think about eating protein during a training session, but especially since this is the base training phase, it is really not necessary to consume protein because calorie expenditure is lower and thus a high number of calories is usually not needed. And, finally, fat is not needed and should not be consumed unless you are training for ultraendurance competitions and training sessions are longer than 6 hours.

After most training sessions during this phase, a well-balanced snack or meal. This could be a combination of lean protein, fruits and vegetables, a small amount of carbohydrates and a little fat, and will give you all the nutrients you need, particularly if you are training for short-course triathlons. It is simply not necessary to follow a postworkout nutrition regimen after training sessions of less than 3 hours with no high-intensity intervals. Choose a well-balanced snack, or time it so you will have your meal in the hour after you finish training, and you will be set.

## Eating During the Competitive Phase

For triathletes, the competitive phase means more intensity. Whether it is sprint sets in the pool, hill repeats, threshold or $\dot{V}O_2$max intervals, or track sessions, the body's thermostat is turned up, and more calories will be expended during these types of training sessions. Short-course triathletes will not increase volume of training too much, while long-course triathletes will begin to extend past the 4- or 5-hour training session mark. The typical physical goals associated with this training phase are to improve speed, power, and economy. This adds more stress to the body and increases energy expenditure, making nutrient timing more important.

The biggest mistakes triathletes make during this training phase are overconsuming calories (not using a periodized nutrition approach) and choosing foods that do not support metabolic efficiency. The worst thing you can do during your competition season is to significantly alter your nutrition plan. Small deviations that account for fitness level, environment, or duration of competitions are fine, but changing your daily plan too much will backfire on you.

Because of the higher intensity and frequency of glycogen-depleting workouts, carbohydrate intake can increase to 5 to 10 grams per kilogram. However, this is dependent on the specific training session. For example, a higher carbohydrate intake on a recovery or easy day is not necessary and will not be in your best interest in controlling blood sugar (and body weight). Aim to closely match your macronutrient intake based on the daily training you perform. Training of higher intensity and volume may require more carbohydrate and vice versa. This is how a periodized nutrition plan fits in the competitive training phase. The range for protein remains at a moderate level, 1.4 to 1.6 grams per kilogram. Focus on lean sources and those that are rich in branched-chain amino acids, found in animal products such as meat and dairy as well as in protein powders such as whey and soy.

The range for fat is similar to that of the preparatory phase, with the exception of athletes training for ultraendurance races. However, very few triathletes fall into this category, which is defined as distances greater than Ironman. Daily fat intake can increase up to 1.5 grams per kilogram for these athletes since they will likely need additional fat in their eating program because of the higher energy loss from longer-duration training sessions (more than 8 hours). Fat is more energy dense and will help these athletes remain in energy balance more effectively. Of course, healthier fats such as polyunsaturated (specifically omega-3) and monounsaturated fats with minimal amounts of saturated and trans fat should be the focus.

## Eating During Competitive-Phase Training Sessions

During competitive-phase sessions, there is not only an increased energy expenditure from more intense workouts but also an increased risk for GI distress as discussed previously. The main goals of eating during training sessions and races during this phase are to prevent or reduce GI distress and recover nutritionally from high-intensity training sessions. From the previous training phase, you should have determined what food combinations work for you before your training sessions, and these should be carried over into this phase. Some of the meal and snack combinations that worked well in the previous phase may not work as well for higher-intensity training sessions. In some athletes, the gut becomes more sensitive during speed and power training. In this case, metabolically efficient meals and snacks should be consumed in liquid form, such as smoothies, 1 to 2 hours before a workout. This will normally decrease the risk of GI distress during a training session, although if you have a more sensitive stomach, try consuming a liquid source of calories about 3 hours before a workout.

Refueling the body after intense training sessions is important, but even more important is knowing when refueling is needed and when it is not. Recovery nutrition is not necessary after each of your training sessions. Replenishing glycogen stores is the main reason for following the scientific postworkout nutrition recommendations, with rehydrating a close second. However, keep in mind that glycogen stores can be replenished within 24 hours with just normal eating, so you may not need the extra calories from sport nutrition products after some of your training sessions. Here are some guidelines to follow for implementing a postworkout nutrition plan for training sessions longer than 4 hours or at high intensity for more than 90 minutes or for when you have a second workout that day or early the next morning.

Within 60 minutes after one of these workouts, consume 1.0 to 1.2 grams of carbo-hydrate per kilogram of body weight. This usually works out to 50 to 100 grams or 200 to 400 calories. Also, consume 6 to 20 grams of lean protein (essential amino acids). Be sure to minimize fat intake immediately after these training sessions because fat competes with carbohydrate absorption. After this initial feeding, it is then recom-mended to get back on track with your normal blood-sugar-controlling nutrition plan 2 to 4 hours afterward. On nonquality (not specific to race intensity or not specific to race duration) training days or even quality training days when you do not need to recover glycogen stores in under 24 hours, you can simply go back to following your normal daily nutrition plan.

## Eating During the Transition Phase

For most triathletes, the off-season is a welcome time of year since it brings rest, recovery, and lack of structure. Unfortunately, it is also a time of year when triathletes make nutrition mistakes and see their body weight and body fat rise. Your primary nutrition goal in the off-season should be controlling the amount of food you eat by shifting the number of macronutrients you consume. You cannot eat the same way as you did in the previous training phase because you are no longer adhering to a training program and thus are not burning as many calories. The goal of controlling blood sugar is extremely important now, and focusing on eating lean protein, fruits, and vegetables as the mainstay of your daily nutrition is the main objective. Since you are not training, you do not need all the sport nutrition products you were using during your race season. Eliminate such supplements, and focus on controlling your blood sugar with real food.

Your daily carbohydrate intake should decrease to 3 to 4 grams per kilogram, with most of the emphasis on fruits and vegetables and less on whole grains and starches. Because of reduced energy expenditure, you do not need to eat as much carbohydrate as you did during your racing season. Protein intake should range from 1.6 to 2.0 grams per kilogram, while fat remains low at .8 to 1.0 gram per kilogram, with an emphasis on healthy omega-3 fats.

## Eating During Transition-Phase Exercise Sessions

Eating during this phase is simple: You do not need to methodically plan as you did earlier during race season. Remember, you are exercising for fun now, possibly working on improving technique and recovering from your race season. Focus on being well nourished before exercise with a light, well-balanced meal or snack. During exercise, if you consume anything, it should be water, and don't worry about following a specific postworkout nutrition plan. Eat a snack or plan a meal within 2 hours after a workout.

Table 26.1 summarizes the quantity and fluctuation of carbohydrate, protein, and fat throughout your annual training year.

**TABLE 26.1**

### Suggested Macronutrient Amounts Based on Training Phases

| Training phase | Carbohydrate | Protein | Fat |
|---|---|---|---|
| Preparatory | 3-7 g/kg (or 3-4 g/kg for weight loss) | 1.2-1.7 g/kg (or 1.8-2.0 g/kg for weight loss) | .8-1.0 g/kg (or .8 g/kg for weight loss) |
| Competitive | 5-10 g/kg | 1.4-1.6 g/kg | .8-1.5 g/kg |
| Transition | 3-4 g/kg | 1.6-2.0 g/kg | .8-1.0 g/kg |

Implement a year-round nutrition program in the same way as you plan a training program and reap the benefits of enhanced health, improved performance, and better body composition and weight control. Your eating program should ebb and flow just as your training does, and your physical performance will be much better supported when nutrition matches your physical training needs. Enjoy the journey of nutrition periodization and metabolic efficiency throughout your physical training phases.

# CHAPTER 27

# Hydrating During Training and Competition

## Alicia Kendig

Hydration is one of the most important factors in the ability to train and compete at the highest level. And for some reason, it continues to be one of the most challenging aspects to control and stay in tune with. Athletes of all disciplines, ages, and levels struggle with finding the proper balance to meet their needs. To better understand the needs of any given athlete, it's important to realize the purpose of fluid in the body.

## Physiological Role of Water and Hydration

It is common knowledge that water plays a vital role in health and wellness and that water itself makes up a large portion of overall body mass. From 65 to 75 percent of muscle mass is water, and 10 percent of fat mass is water, leaving anywhere between 40 and 70 percent of overall body weight to be in the form of water weight, depending on body composition.

Water is found in various places within the body, and 60 percent is intracellular (fluid inside the cell) and 40 percent is extracellular (water found outside each cell). Extracellular fluids include plasma, fluid in the eyes, secretions in the digestive system, fluid around the spinal column, and fluid created by the kidneys and skin. Plasma makes up most (approximately 20 percent) of the extracellular fluid. When cooling the body, most fluid lost in the form of sweat draws from this extracellular plasma fluid. The amount of fluid in these various places will be in constant flux.

Other properties of water in the body include the following:

- All exchanges of gases in the body occur over membranes moistened by water.
- The delivery of oxygen and nutrients to working muscles and the excretion of waste in the form of urine and feces require water.

- Water and various other components lubricate the joints and cushion the vital organs.
- Water has an unalterable density, creating a structured environment for muscle and various other body tissues. Muscles and tissues therefore require water to maintain their size and integrity.
- Water's resistance to temperature change makes it ideal for withstanding both environmental and internal changes in temperature. If water changed temperatures easily, then exercise in hot temperatures would be impossible because of the body's tendency to overheat. The same would be true for exercising in cold temperatures; the body would freeze too quickly. Having water as a main ingredient in the body is crucial for coping with many environmental factors it is faced with.

Euhydration, the normal state of fluid balance, ensures that all these functions continue to run smoothly and efficiently. If provided with adequate amounts of fluid in food and beverages, as well as electrolytes, a healthy working system will monitor and control the proper amount of fluid retained and excreted. Electrolytes, in the form of charged ions, establish an electrical balance between the interior and the exterior of every cell. In other words, they help the cells in the body retain the proper amount of fluid to balance losses. These charges then facilitate nerve impulses to activate and contract muscle fibers. It makes sense that this cascade of events is very important for exercise and performance, but it is also important that these electrolytes, specifically sodium, be in balance for survival. The intake of fluid without the inclusion of key electrolytes to replace losses can actually be fatal. Sodium, potassium, and chloride are the three primary charged electrolytes found in the cell and are all dissolved in bodily fluids. Sodium and chloride are the two key electrolytes in plasma and extracellular fluid that aid in fluid balance of the cells of the body.

# Fluid Needs for Athletes

Hydration needs will vary from athlete to athlete depending on individual factors. Aside from genetic variances, a few known trends are seen in various populations engaging in sport. For starters, female athletes typically have lower sweat rates than their male counterparts. This is largely due to less surface area or smaller body size. Another reason is a smaller amount of muscle mass generates less heat, requiring less fluid in the form of sweat to maintain adequate core temperature. On the contrary, some research indicates that women have a higher water turnover than men, resulting in more urine fluid loss and an increased fluid need to replace losses. Last, there have been more reported cases of hyponatremia in women than in men, which could be attributed to many factors, both physiological and psychological. Hyponatremia is excessive fluid intake without necessary electrolytes, causing a fluid imbalance (more about hyponatremia later in this chapter).

Age also plays a factor. With increasing age (greater than 65 years), a decreased thirst perception can lead to an increased overall risk of dehydration. Along with that, older athletes recover from dehydration and exercise more slowly than their younger counterparts, creating the need for adequate recovery time. Impaired health and function of the kidneys in older athletes could lead to water retention and high blood pressure.

## ▶ Factors of Dehydration

In the ideal world, euhydration will always be achieved during training, during competition, and throughout the day. However, to be realistic, some degree of dehydration will occur as a result of the imbalance between sweat losses and the amount of ingested fluid consumed in the effort to replenish those losses. Often endurance athletes are dehydrated at the onset of activity because of improper recovery from previous training sessions or events, lack of awareness of actual needs, or an effort to cut down on weight.

In response to the stress of decreased availability of body fluid, the body reacts by altering normal biological markers. This leads to increased core body temperature, increased heart rate, decreased stroke volume (amount of blood pumped with each beat of the heart), and increased perceived exertion (mentally, activity feels much more difficult). The greater the overall dehydration, the greater the degree of these stress alterations.

There is a general agreement, supported in many research studies of trained athletes, that reductions in body water need only be minimal to cause detrimental effects on performance. Walsh et al. (1994) reported that a reduction in body mass of as little as 2 percent resulted in a reduction in performance of up to 44 percent. A level of dehydration as great as 3 percent (caused by diuretics) produced a 3 to 5 percent reduction in 1,500- to 10,000-meter running times (Armstrong, Costill, and Fink 1985). A few more recent studies indicate that well-trained athletes tolerate hypohydration to a certain degree. Laursen et al. (2006) found that a body loss of up to 3 percent was tolerated in well-trained triathletes during an Ironman competition without risk of thermoregulatory failure. This percent reference range is merely an average of observed tolerance levels. The magnitude of the effect on performance is determined by many factors, such as environmental temperature, the current exercise task, and an athlete's unique biological characteristics. All these factors working together, and not merely in isolation, have a negative effect on athletic performance.

To add to the altered body functions caused by dehydration, cognitive processing and levels of motivation may become affected. In the sport of triathlon, concentration is vital and can be degraded by dehydration and hyperthermia, the latter being shown to have a greater effect. The cognitive effects of dehydration include a hindrance of short-term memory, working memory, and visuomotor abilities. Long-term memory is greatly decreased in athletes with exercise-induced heat-stress dehydration (Cian et al. 2000).

For age-group athletes, observed sweat rates are lower before adolescence than at a mature age. This should be considered, especially if exercise and competition will be conducted in hot and humid environments.

When determining how much fluid you need, let's start with sedentary people in order to establish a baseline. A sedentary person, in a nonstressful environment, requires approximately 2.5 liters of water daily. As stated already, this depends on size and body composition. Sedentary men need closer to 3 liters of water a day, typically because of greater body size and higher muscle mass, which has a higher water content. Sedentary women need closer to 2 liters. Fluid losses for these people average about 2 to 3 liters, with 50 percent of that fluid in the form of urine. In an active person, this percentage of water losses can easily be offset by sweat losses or, in a person living at altitude, respiration losses.

Active people in a warm, humid environment can easily need 5 to 10 liters a day depending on increased sweat and other cooling-method fluid losses. During intense exercise, the 2 to 3 liters lost in 1 day in sedentary adults can be lost in 1 hour in athletes. This amount of sweat will greatly vary from athlete to athlete, even when fitness level, exercise intensity, and environmental factors are similar. Typical sweat values for athletes vary greatly, due both to individual and temperate conditions. An Australian study observing the sweat rates of water polo players found an average rate of .29 liter per hour, whereas a study of tennis players showed a sweat rate of 2.60 liters per hour. Here's a look at how different sports compare in terms of sweat losses (USDA 2010):

- Male water polo athletes lost .29 liter per hour in training and .79 liter per hour in competition.
- Male half-marathon athletes lost 1.49 liters per hour in winter competition.
- Male and female Ironman athletes lost .81 liter per hour in a temperate bike leg and 1.03 liters per hour in a temperate run leg.

To keep your body working at its best, for triathletes especially, hydration is a link to all other pieces of the puzzle. Without it, they won't fit together, and peak performance is out of the question. For that reason, you should follow hydration recommendations not only in competition but also in everyday training. Following are the recommendations for before, during, and after training and competition, with the goal of always supporting euhydration, or hydration balance.

## Before Training and Competition

As stated numerous times already, proper hydration is important from the beginning of activity. The goal of euhydration is to start the physical activity with normal plasma electrolyte levels, which can be achieved with sufficient beverage intake and normal food consumption. However, if recovery time after prior training sessions is suboptimal (less than 8 hours), then it is very common for endurance athletes to start the next session dehydrated. In this case, a vigorous preworkout hydration program is necessary before the onset of activity. For triathletes specifically, drinking enough fluid during activity is difficult because of accessibility or excessive losses outweighing ingestion. Proper hydration can improve thermoregulation by minimizing increases in core temperature, thereby decreasing sweat losses and improving exercise performance in the heat.

The American College of Sports Medicine (Sawka et al. 2007) recommends 5 to 7 milliliters of fluid per kilogram of body weight 4 hours before exercise. In general, 400 to 600 milliliters (13 to 20 ounces) is advised in this 4-hour preparation time. So a 165-pound (75 kg) person would multiply 5 milliliters by 75 kilograms (for a total of 375 milliliters) to determine the lower range and multiply 7 milliliters by 75 kilograms (for a total of 525 milliliters) to determine the higher range. This recommendation stands for an athlete close to the euhydration state. In the case that urine production is nonexistent or production is dark or highly concentrated, then additional fluid is recommended. Two hours after the onset of exercise, an additional 3 to 5 milliliters per kilogram of body weight is recommended. The same 165-pound (75 kg) person would need an extra 225 milliliters (3 ml × 75 kg) to 375 milliliters (5 ml × 75 kg) of fluid. By determining fluid needs before exercise, an athlete can be assured that urine production can occur and be eliminated.

Including electrolytes in preexercise fluid intake is important for longer training sessions, especially for athletes who sweat excessively. The addition of 500 to 1,000 milligrams of sodium (about a quarter teaspoon of table salt) per liter of fluid, or simply eating a small snack of salty foods, will be plenty to help the body prepare for exercise. Forgetting to include these electrolytes, especially when high sweat losses may occur, can increase the risk of hyponatremia. Attempting to hyperhydrate (by using glycerol or drinking too much water) with fluids that expand the extracellular and intracellular spaces will greatly increase the risk of having to void, as intestinal absorption will be limited. Little evidence on the physiological or performance advantage of hyperhydration has been shown in research. This hyperhydration substantially dilutes plasma sodium before the onset of exercise.

## During Training and Competition

Again, the goal for hydration during exercise is to balance losses to maintain euhydration. The American College of Sports Medicine recommends a loss of no more than 2 percent of overall body weight in the form of fluid (Sawka et al. 2007). In addition, fluid losses are accompanied by electrolyte losses, which should be compensated for by the addition of sodium in a replacement beverage. Exactly how much fluid and electrolytes an athlete needs depends on individual sweat losses and exercise duration. For this reason, it is important for athletes to monitor sweat losses, especially for exercise sessions lasting longer than 3 hours. The longer the workout, the greater the chance that fluid and electrolyte replacement may be insufficient and lead to deteriorations in performance.

Recommendations for hydration during exercise stem from the amount of fluids lost during a set amount of time, which will vary depending on climate, level of fitness, acclimatization, prior hydration status, and workout apparel. With all this variability, simple recommendations are difficult to make. Observed sweat losses in athletes vary from .4 to 1.8 liters per hour of exercise. With this broad range, it is imperative that athletes monitor their personal responses to varying training situations and develop their own customized fluid replacement programs that prevent losses of more than 2 percent of overall body mass at the start of exercise.

A simple way to do this is as follows:

1. Before exercise, weigh yourself without clothing and equipment.
2. Monitor fluid consumption during exercise.
3. Weigh yourself after activity without clothing and equipment.
4. Determine body mass loss during exercise.
5. Add to losses the amount of fluid consumed during activity, as the amount of loss is an indication of fluid needs during a set time of activity.

For exercise lasting more than 60 minutes, the inclusion of carbohydrate in addition to sodium will not only replace fluid losses but also provide fuel for ongoing activity. The rate of fluid absorption is closely related to the carbohydrate content of the drink. Too much carbohydrate can slow absorption. The absorption of water through the intestine wall is greater in the presence of sugars and sodium. Carbohydrate and sodium sports drinks are absorbed more rapidly than water or sodium and water alone. The optimal carbohydrate concentration (grams of carbohydrate per milliliter of fluid), according to research, is 5 to 8 percent. Along with this, sodium concentration should be 10 to 30 millimoles per liter for optimal absorption and prevention of hyponatremia. For this reason, sports drinks are certainly beneficial for activities lasting longer than 60 minutes.

Although most triathletes are well informed of the necessity of hydration, logistical factors involved in the sport of triathlon can make fueling and hydrating more challenging. Fluid intake during the swim is most often impossible, and depending on how long it takes to get on the bike, athletes may start the second leg of the race in a dehydrated state. Proper hydration on the bike is then crucial, as the running leg of the race creates problems for carrying enough water to support needs.

When trying to balance fluid losses, it is important to realize that fluid is not lost only in the urine and sweat but also via respiration. Although relatively low in shorter triathlons, these losses are quite significant in an Ironman. In an observation study of Ironman athletes, fluid losses were estimated as 940 milliliters (32 ounces) per hour lost in sweat, 41 milliliters (1.5 ounces) per hour lost in urine, and 81 milliliters (3 ounces) per hour lost through respiration. Thus, it is crucial that these athletes work toward ingesting approximately 1 liter per hour of fluid for the duration of their race.

---

### ▶ Replacing Sodium Losses

Sodium losses in sweat depend on the overall sweat rate and the concentration of the fluid lost. Sweat sodium concentrations typically range from 250 to 1,500 milligrams per liter. Given the variable sweat rates of different athletes, there is a large reference range for sodium needs. One thing is for certain: For a triathlete training and competing for numerous hours a day, sodium needs may be greater than realized. Athletes engaging in endurance and ultraendurance events may need to monitor their sodium intake and be conscious of replacing losses appropriately. In addition to sodium, other essential electrolytes may be lost. Next in line, in order of concentration in sweat, are potassium, calcium, magnesium, and chloride. Although these nutrients are essential in the diet, the amount lost in sweat does not warrant doses as high as the sodium content of sports drinks. In races lasting long enough to significantly deplete these electrolytes, solid foods should be used for replenishment.

Most of the dietary recommendations available for public reading address the sedentary population. In the 2005 dietary guidelines released by the U.S. Department of Agriculture, the recommendation for sodium intake was no more than 2,300 milligrams a day. Every 5 years the USDA updates these recommendations, and sodium was reevaluated and changed to 1,500 milligrams a day in 2010 to address the rapidly growing population living with various chronic diseases such as diabetes, heart disease, and obesity. The USDA estimated that the average American diet contained 3,400 to 4,000 milligrams of sodium.

A distinction must be made between the difference in needs of those with chronic diseases and those living the lifestyle of an endurance athlete. An endurance athlete's diet is stereotypically "healthier" and includes less sodium than the diet of the average sedentary American. In reality, this is far from the truth. A diet containing only 1,500 milligrams of sodium a day would sustain an Ironman athlete for less than 1 hour of high-intensity activity.

The cycling portion of a triathlon is the best opportunity for optimizing fluid balance. Fluid is the most readily tolerated and available during this time. However, high-intensity activity slows absorption compared to at rest. In a study performed by Robinson et al. (1995), gastric emptying was limited to .5 liter per hour when exercising at intense levels. The excess fluid ingested remained in the stomach, leading to feelings of fullness.

## After Training and Competition

Recovery after exercise is important for the health of the body as well as for preparation for the next training session. Training and racing in a hot and humid environment can put a lot of stress on the body. Effective rehydration after exercise is achieved only by replacing both fluids and sodium. In fact, water alone for hydration is less efficient.

The American College of Sports Medicine (Sawka et al. 2007) recommends replacing 150 percent of sweat losses in the form of fluid for complete rehydration. The extra amount above what is lost allows for the flushing out of fluid through urine production. The inclusion of sodium (more than 1,000 milligrams) allows for increased fluid retention and the restoration of fluid balance in the extracellular and intracellular spaces.

Sodium in sports drinks has its benefits, but palatability is a consideration. Too much sodium is often not palatable for many athletes. For this reason, it is often recommended that you try many different sports drinks to find one that both provides the nutrients you need for proper hydration and that you are inclined to drink so you will achieve the intended goals of recovery time.

# Adverse Health Effects Related to Hydration

Many athletes are familiar with the constant instructions to hydrate but often don't consider why this is important or what the serious consequences could be if hydration is overlooked. Numerous published research findings show the importance of a certain hydration level for maintaining peak performance or preventing deteriorations in performance caused by sweat losses and dehydration. Adverse health effects can occur if the body's natural method of releasing heat is impaired. Peripheral vasodilation, or increased blood flow at the surface of the skin, allows for heat dissipation, but it decreases blood flow to the central nervous system. Sweat production increases this heat dissipation but also increases the risk of dehydration. The presence of sodium in the sweat increases the risk of electrolyte imbalance. Given these various conditions, the role of fluid in the body of an athlete is vitally important.

Following is an overview of the possible conditions occurring as a result of chronic dehydration as well as the signs and symptoms to look for to identify the problem before it spirals out of control. These are listed in order of mild to severe.

## Heat-Related Illness

Proper hydration should always be the goal, not just during training and competition but throughout the day as well. As already stated, when hypohydration, or underhydration, occurs, adverse effects on training and performance are quickly apparent. Without the ability to cool the body in a properly hydrated state, varying levels of heat illness can easily occur in prolonged intense activity or shorter high-intensity sports. This condition stereotypically occurs only in hot and humid climates, but realistically it can also happen in cooler, dryer climates.

A graded continuum of heat illness has been established, ranging from mild, to performance-inhibiting, to life-threatening conditions, such as heatstroke. It is difficult to say which athletes are more susceptible to heat exhaustion, and it is not confirmed that all mild forms will inevitably progress to heatstroke. Although research is still ongoing in this area, all endurance athletes should be aware of the signs and symptoms of heat-related illnesses.

## Heat Edema

Heat edema is classified by noticeable swelling around the feet, ankles, and hands. It can occur as a result of the body's effort to dissipate heat away from the working muscles to the skin. This peripheral vasodilation leads to the accumulation of interstitial fluid in the distal extremities, such as the wrists, ankles, hands, and feet. Core temperature is not affected by this condition, but athletes should be aware of it, especially if they are predisposed to its development. Older persons and unconditioned athletes not acclimatized are at highest risk.

## Heat Rash

Heat rash is another condition that arises from the effort to remove heat via excessive sweating. Also referred to as "prickly heat," heat rash develops when clothing obstructs the secretion of the sweat ducts on the skin, causing irritation of the epidermis. Common areas for this to occur are the trunk, groin, neck, and areas covered by a sports bra in female athletes. Generally heat rash has a rapid onset and presents itself frequently in athletes who sweat excessively and those with a history of its appearance.

## Heat Syncope

Heat syncope is classified by feelings of weakness and dizziness that disappear quickly after resting, sitting, or lying down. Core temperature is normal. This condition typically occurs immediately after the completion of exercise. Hypotension, caused by rapid peripheral vasodilation, decreases blood flow to the central nervous system, causing fainting or mental confusion. This can also occur with prolonged standing after strenuous activity and changes in body position from sitting to standing after strenuous activity. Sudden stopping and standing allows for venous pooling. Lying down after experiencing these symptoms can quickly increase blood flow to the brain and relieve symptoms.

## Heat Cramps

Heat cramps are classified by the onset of painful muscle contractions, often in the calf or quadriceps, that are alleviated by rest, complete recovery, and stretching. Core temperature is normal or slightly elevated. Muscle spasms or cramps are one of the earliest signs of heat illness noticed by athletes. These cramps typically appear after exposure to excessive heat without appropriate hydration and electrolyte repletion. In this condition, the muscle begins to spasm, resulting in rapid, painful contractions. Sodium loss has been shown to exacerbate these spasms, but the role that other electrolytes such as magnesium, potassium, and calcium play is not yet clear. Other possible causes of heat cramps are chronic dehydration and overstimulation of muscle contraction beyond what the trained muscle is accustomed to.

## Heat Exhaustion

Heat exhaustion is classified by core temperature elevated up to 104 degrees Fahrenheit (40 degrees Celsius). Malaise, fatigue, and dizziness are classic symptoms, along with nausea, vomiting, headache, fainting, weakness, and cold and clammy skin.

## Heatstroke

Heatstroke is the most dangerous form of heat illness and is classified by core temperature elevated higher than 104 degrees Fahrenheit (40 degrees Celsius). The skin is hot to the touch, without much sweating. The athlete experiences an altered mental state and may even be unconscious. Irritability, ataxia (loss of coordination), confusion, and coma are all possible results. Given the severity of these symptoms, prompt recognition and treatment are vital for the best chance of recovery.

There are two kinds of heatstroke, classic and exertional, based on the underlying cause of the excessive heat exposure. Classic heatstroke occurs mostly as a result of environmental factors such as high ambient temperatures and increased humidity preventing evaporative cooling. Exertional heatstroke is more due to internal heat production by the contracting muscles in the body, usually in the case of strenuous activity. Despite the variations in their causes, the treatment of these two conditions is the same.

## *Hyponatremia*

Excessive fluid intake without necessary electrolytes causes a fluid imbalance called hyponatremia. Hyponatremia is, in essence, a water toxicity. The low sodium concentration in the plasma creates an osmotic imbalance across the blood brain barrier, causing too much water to flow into the brain. This leads to brain swelling, causing symptoms such as headache, confusion, nausea, and cramping.

With the increase in popularity of ultraendurance sports (greater than 3 hours), the occurrence of hyponatremia in athletes is also on the rise. Typically, athletes are more concerned about dehydration and replenishing fluid losses in these events. Relying on water and sports nutrition products without an appropriate electrolyte load will eventually result in a dilution of electrolytes in the body, or hyponatremia.

The following groups are at higher risk of developing hyponatremia:

- Athletes with high sweat rates, especially in hot and humid climates
- Poorly conditioned athletes with highly concentrated sodium losses
- Athletes consuming low-sodium diets
- Athletes on diuretic medications for hypertension
- Athletes ingesting high amounts of sodium-free fluid during prolonged exercise (greater than 3 hours)

## *Rhabdomyolysis*

Given the known functions of fluid in the body, such as maintaining the integrity of cell membranes and facilitating normal reactions in the working muscles, it makes sense that dehydration can be harmful to the health of the muscle at the cellular level. Rhabdomyolysis is a syndrome causing the breakdown and destruction of muscle fibers. It is most often seen in new exercisers, strenuous exercisers, and athletes who overexert themselves. Clinical evidence suggests that dehydration can increase the consequences of this condition.

Clinically, creatine kinase levels (up to five times higher than the normal reference range) and reported muscle pain are indicators of this condition. Dehydration combined with heat stress and novel training can induce serious health problems. Soldiers and service men (e.g., police officers) engaging in a sudden increase of activity—typically in the form of physical training—without proper hydration are frequently treated for symptoms of rhabdomyolysis. The condition can lead to renal failure, and treatment often includes hemodialysis. Fatal cases with complications of heatstroke, rhabdomyolysis, and acute renal insufficiency have been reported.

Proper hydration is necessary for all types of athletes to train and compete at their best. Replacing fluid and electrolyte losses before, during, and after training and competition will ensure that physical and psychological performance is not compromised in any type of environment. Just how much fluid and other nutrients, specifically sodium, are needed will vary from athlete to athlete. Realizing the importance of proper hydration will help triathletes assess and monitor their losses to help them create a personalized hydration plan that works best for them.

# CHAPTER 28

# Beyond Swim, Bike, Run

## Katie Baker

There comes a time in many triathletes' competitive lives when the daily routine of a swim–bike–run routine becomes too monotonous. When this happens a little change is needed. This is a perfect time to throw additional multisport options into the mix, enabling athletes to take a mental and physical break from the sometimes monotonous training of swim, bike, and run.

## What Is Multisport?

Multisport is the term used to describe sporting events made up of just that: multiple sports. In this format, athletes race in a continuous series of stages, often referred to as legs, and rapidly switch, or transition, from one athletic discipline to another, with the objective of completing the entire series in the least amount of time. Usually multisport events are endurance races, which can include swimming, biking, running, skiing, and kayaking. Triathlon, the most common multisport, consists of swimming, biking, and running at various distances, ranging from the sprint up to the Ironman. Yet, multisport captures much more than just these three sports. It has grown to encompass many combinations of multiple disciplines. We now see many types of multisport events inside the United States as well as around the world. Some of the more common types include duathlon (run, bike, run), off-road (swim, mountain bike, trail run), and winter triathlon (run, mountain bike, skate ski, all occurring on snow). Additionally, multisport is not limited to the more common "tri" options. Athletes can find events consisting of more than three disciplines that fall into more of the adventure racing category. These events tend to be composed of anything and everything and are not limited to kayaking, rappelling, orienteering, mountain biking, and trekking.

Events from the Olympic Games, such as the pentathlon, decathlon, and modern pentathlon, are not usually considered multisport because their individual components are not held back to back. Multisport events are a great way to learn a new sport, improve base fitness, and expand skills that can be applied to other multisport activities. It is not unusual to see crossover between the various formats. For instance, many athletes competing at the highest level in winter triathlon are the same athletes consistently finishing at the top of the podium in off-road triathlon events.

In 2010, USA Triathlon, the national governing body of triathlon and multisport, sanctioned 2,265 events of which 26 percent were disciplines other than swim, bike, run. Nontraditional events are included in this 26 percent. Nontraditional events have a multisport component but do not fit into any of the categories mentioned previously (e.g., a 5K beach run, 4-mile board paddle, or 4-mile surf ski). Obviously an event such as this deviates from the norm, and therefore it falls into the nontraditional category. USAT sanctioned 156 off-road events in 2010. These off-road events included both triathlons and duathlons. Additionally, 28 events of a similar nature were held for youth.

Multisport continues to morph and grow each year, supplying all endurance athletes the opportunity to showcase their talents, whether during single-track technical mountain biking, cross-country skiing, rappelling down a rock face, or kayaking across a body of water. Whatever it may be, multisport continues to welcome new formats into its family. This chapter discusses the history of multisport events such as duathlon, off-road triathlon, winter triathlon, and adventure racing as well as the equipment needed to complete these events and some training suggestions.

# Types of Multisport

Many single-sport endurance athletes turn to multisport for that mental break or even just to try something new and challenge themselves in novel and exciting ways. Following are a few of the most common types of multisport.

## Duathlon

Duathlon combines the sports of running and biking, usually in the format of a run, a bike, and then another, sometimes shorter, run. This format is often considered a more demanding event than the triathlon. Many triathletes will tell you that duathlons are more grueling. Athletes begin with a hard run, jump on their bikes more fatigued than after a swim, and then finish the race with another run of the same distance as the first run (or slightly shorter). Athletes tend to agree that a duathlon requires considerably more recovery time than a triathlon completed in the same amount of time. Organizers sometimes produce events with just a run and bike, eliminating the second run leg in an attempt to not scare participants off.

USAT sanctioned 383 duathlons in 2010. One of the first U.S. duathlon series was the Coors Light Series, which had regular stops in big cities such as Phoenix, Chicago, and Denver. It wasn't uncommon to see big-name triathletes competing at these events, not to mention ESPN televising them. The Coors series offered athletes experience, money, and exposure. Some of the more popular duathlons in the United States are Powerman Alabama and the Desert Sun Duathlon in Arizona. The Dannon Duathlon Series once provided duathletes an opportunity to race frequently against the most competitive duathletes in the country.

Many athletes consider Powerman Zofingen, in Switzerland, the world's most demanding duathlon event. The race consists of a hilly 10K run, mostly on trails; a hilly

150-kilometer road bike of three 50-kilometer loops; and finally a very hilly 30-kilometer two-loop trail run. Mark Allen, six-time Ironman Hawaii champion, has been quoted as saying Powerman Zofingen is the hardest race he ever participated in.

Many athletes turn to duathlon because they are proficient runners and cyclists but are not comfortable in the water. Greg Watson was a duathlon world champion in 2004. He came to duathlon in 1988 with a running background as a member of a biathlon team—Greg ran and his teammate biked. After a few wins, Greg decided to branch out and try to tackle both the run and bike himself. He immediately found success and enjoyment and set his sights on the 1991 Duathlon World Championships in Palm Springs, where he did earn the title of overall age-group champion. The following year, Watson decided to race as a professional.

## Duathlon Equipment

Fortunately, the equipment needs of duathlon are not as complicated as other multisport events. Athletes simply need a bike and running shoes. You can choose any type of bike to compete on. I recall my first, and last, duathlon experience when I chose to ride my 40-pound (18 kg) 10-speed Huffy I had received for my 12th birthday. I finished what was probably one of the most grueling events I have competed in to date, but my bike split was nothing worth raving about. It is helpful to know the course when considering what type of bike to race on; if it's a hilly course, athletes may choose a road frame, while a time-trial bike frame is great for a flatter, less technical course. Off-road duathlons are another option, in which case a mountain bike is your desired type of bicycle.

## Duathlon Training

Of all the multisport categories, duathlon training may be more structured than other formats for the simple reason that the event consists of only running and cycling. Depending on the goals and ability level of the athlete as well as the length of the event, training plans may vary.

For a beginner, training should remain fun and unintimidating. By training for both running and cycling, the athlete is not risking the same overuse injuries as a single-sport athlete. As an athlete's competitiveness level increases, training sessions may become more frequent, with increased intensity within each session. Duathletes at the top of their game average 60 running miles (97 km) per week as well as 300 cycling miles (483 km). Many variables dictate training including available time, the athlete's goals, and what his body is able to withstand in terms of training load. Figure 28.1 provides a suggested training week for the average duathlete trying to maintain fitness as well as keep weight off. Keep in mind this athlete works 40 hours a week and has a family but is competing at the USA Triathlon Duathlon National Championships (5K run, 35K bike, 5K run).

## *Off-Road Triathlon*

Off-road triathlon is often referred to as Xterra, the name of the race series that has helped launch and grow this style of racing. Xterra has been the title sponsor of the race series produced and developed by Team Unlimited, an events and marketing group based out of Honolulu, Hawaii. Xterra has more than 100 events in 16 countries and

**FIGURE 28.1**

## Midseason multisport training week.

| | Monday | Tuesday | Wednesday | Thursday | Friday | Saturday | Sunday |
|---|---|---|---|---|---|---|---|
| **Bike** | 90 min easy spin | Day off | 60 min moderate effort over rolling hills | Interval session: 20 min warm-up; 6 × 3 min hill repeats with 2 min recovery on downhill; 20 min easy cool-down | Day off | Combo workout: 60 min bike with last 30 min at 85-90% intensity and followed immediately by 20 min run at 90% effort;10 min easy cool-down jog | Day off |
| **Run** | Day off | Interval session: 20 min warm-up; 5 × 1K at 5K race-pace effort with 2 min recovery jog between each effort; 15 min cool-down | Easy 45 min with last 10 min to include 10 × 30 pickups; run to occur before bike (ideally, athlete is running in a.m. and biking in p.m.) | Day off | Tempo run: 15 min warm-up; 25 min at 10K pace; 10 min cool-down | | Long run: 90 min run with middle 45 min at half-marathon pace |

continues to add new events to the calendar each year. These events culminate at the Xterra World Championship in Maui, Hawaii, each October.

Before Xterra there were mountain bike triathlons with no set distances or specified rules. Athletes rode their mountain bikes on grueling technical courses, and when finished they rode down to the ocean and jumped in the water to wash the mud off. Eventually a run element was added, and voila, off-road triathlon was born. The off-road events tend to appeal to cyclists, unlike the road triathlon where runners generally have the advantage. During a road triathlon 50 to 55 percent of the total time is spent biking, while during an off-road event this tends to be at least 60 percent. As for the run during a road triathlon, 35 percent of the event tends to be running, whereas during an off-road event this is lower, closer to 25 percent.

## Off-Road Equipment

The equipment needs in an off-road triathlon are fairly similar to a road triathlon in that the same three disciplines are being contested: swim, bike, and run. The swim equipment remains the same. Like any swimming event, you will need goggles and something to swim in. It is very common for off-road events to be held at higher altitudes, which means the water temperatures will be cooler. USAT rules state that wetsuits are permitted when water temperatures are 78 degrees Fahrenheit (26 degrees Celsius) and below. Therefore, you may want to invest in a USAT-approved wetsuit. It is not an enjoyable experience to swim in cold water without a wetsuit. Just as the classification indicates, the biking leg is contested off-road, and therefore a mountain bike is needed to negotiate the trails. Depending on the course, some trails may be more technical than others, and you will want to consider whether a full-suspension or a hard-tail mountain bike is the better option. A full-suspension bike adds more weight that may be less forgiving on major climbing sections, but it may be optimal on a hairy, technical downhill with a lot of rocks and roots.

   Both types of mountain bikes are ridden at these events, so the option is yours. As far as shoes, this depends on your level of mountain biking expertise. More advanced mountain bikers may choose to ride clipless pedals with special mountain bike shoes, while some athletes are more comfortable with pedals that have cages. If the latter is desired, then athletes can ride with a running shoe, which eliminates the need to change shoes between the bike and the run. Athletes must wear helmets during the bike leg according to competition rules. Some athletes choose to wear cycling gloves, especially for a technical mountain bike course that may find people off their bikes as much as on. As for the run, athletes may choose to lace up their trail running shoes for a more technical running course, but normal running shoes will always suffice.

## Off-Road Training

Athletes tend to move into off-road triathlon to escape the sometimes overly intense attitudes of road triathletes. Off-road triathletes are usually more laid back and easy-going, and therefore their training schedules may lack the structure that most people assume is needed to be competitive. At the end of the day, it's about having fun and enjoying the company you keep on those longer training days. As mentioned already, cyclists tend to be drawn to off-road triathlon because the distances are more suited to their strengths. Most athletes will spend most of their time biking and running, sometimes both on and off the road, with little time spent training for the swim, not to say this is the best way to train for an off-road event. It depends on the athletes and what their objectives may be. Figure 28.2 provides a sample week of off-road training.

**FIGURE 28.2**

### Off-road triathlon training week.

|  | Monday | Tuesday | Wednesday | Thursday | Friday | Saturday | Sunday |
|---|---|---|---|---|---|---|---|
| *Swim** | Easy 60 min swim | Day off | Day off | 90 min swim with intervals | Day off | Day off | Day off |
| *Bike* | Day off | 45 min spin on road bike | 90 min mountain bike ride with group pushing pace | Day off | Intervals on road bike: 20 min warm-up; 5 × 5 min hard effort with 3 min recovery spin; 20 min moderate pace; 10 min cool-down | Day off | 180 min long mountain bike ride |
| *Run* | Day off | 10 min easy warm-up; 3 × 10 min at race pace on trail with 5 min recovery jog; 10 min cool-down | Easy 30 min run | Intervals: 20 min warm-up; 8 × 400 m with 200 m recovery jog; 10 min cool-down | Day off | 90 min long trail run | 15 min run at 85% immediately after bike |

*Alternate between 2 swims per week and 3 swims per week. Athletes can determine whether that third workout will be an easy 60 min swim or a more challenging 90 min swim with intervals based on their swimming fitness level and how they are feeling across the board. If an athlete is feeling extremely fatigued in general, then an easy 60 min workout to concentrate on technique is advised. If an athlete is fit but feeling speed is lacking, more intervals as well as speed work may be required.

## Winter Triathlon

For those athletes who prefer chillier temperatures and some good competitive interaction during the typical off-season, there's winter triathlon. The sport of winter triathlon consists of a 5 to 8K run on a hard-packed snowy surface, a 10 to 15K mountain bike on snow, and an 8 to 12K cross-country ski. Winter triathlon was likely introduced by the Europeans back in the late 1980s, as there are reports of winter triathlons being organized in France and Spain. It wasn't until 1997 that the ITU hosted the first Winter Triathlon World Championships. The first few world championships were contested on asphalt with the exception of the ski, but the races eventually moved to snow after some trial and error. Unfortunately, Mother Nature can be fickle, and some events are contested on nonsnow surfaces, although this is not ideal.

In 2010, the first winter world championship title was won by an American athlete, Rebecca Dussault, a 2006 Winter Olympian in Nordic skiing. She was recruited by fellow athlete and friend Brian Smith to give winter triathlon a try and petition for a slot on the worlds team despite not having ridden a bike or run in many months. Her athletic resume earned her a spot on the 2008 team that competed in Freudenberg, Germany. Rebecca, not 14 months after giving birth, took up the challenge despite having never competed in a winter triathlon. According to a conversation with Rebecca, it was a year of no snow, which made for a brutal and awesome introduction at the same time. "I never before had done multisport racing other than adventure racing and was excited to put my 'jack of all trades' endurance skills to the test. I say it was brutal because the run was very painful on the hard, dry surfaces since I hadn't been running at all that winter, and the bike favored the power riders since it was also contested on a huge dry loop. I am a climber, so this also posed a great challenge to me. I would have to wait until the following year to find out about my winter running and biking skills! I ended up sixth despite this being my first winter triathlon, which left me hungry for more. I knew with the right training and course conditions that I could one day be world champion."

### Winter Triathlon Equipment

Depending on the conditions, you may want to consider the following equipment for the optimal winter triathlon experience. For the run you can wear any type of running shoe. More competitive athletes may want to consider some sort of trail shoe that provides better traction. Some athletes may even wear a cross country spike or a racing flat equipped with one-eighth-inch (3 mm) sheet metal screws. You need to consider if the snow is hard packed or loose and deep to determine what shoe will provide that competitive advantage. For the biking leg, athletes tend to ride a mountain bike, although some may choose a cyclo-cross bicycle. Always check with the event organizer to confirm any rules in regard to tire size and width restrictions, as this may vary event to event. Because of the softer surface that snow usually provides, consider running 10 to 20 psi in your mountain bike tires. Running the lower tire pressure allows athletes more forgiveness when attempting to maneuver the unpredictable surface snow often provides. You may wear cycling shoes or regular running shoes; the choice is yours. Helmets are a must because you can never foresee when a tire will choose to be uncooperative, leading to a trip over the handlebars.

For the last leg, the ski, you can use either skate or classic skis. Skate skiing tends to be a quicker, more efficient means of Nordic skiing. It is not as easy as it looks, however, so some athletes prefer to strap on the classic skis and take a little longer. Depending on an athlete's competitive level, it usually comes down to comfort and what he hopes to accomplish. In most situations, athletes take on such athletic challenges with the simple goal of finishing—even if they finish last—and therefore comfort wins out. Most winter triathlons are contested at Nordic centers, so you do not need to own your own ski equipment but can rent before investing in equipment you are unsure you will enjoy and use.

Dussault reminds athletes to not be intimidated by the gear. "It really all makes sense and falls into place when you're out there racing. Enjoy the fact that there are so many elements to master, and if you are good or better at most, then you'll be great at this sport. There's waxing, tire selection and pressure, running shoes, technical skills, strength, stamina, feeding and fueling, transitioning, balancing, problem solving, uphills, downhills, flats, and so on. With all these elements and more, there is a fit for everyone."

## Winter Triathlon Training

Training for winter triathlon, like other multisports, is appealing because it can be so diverse, which leads to a more well-rounded and balanced athlete. Athletes do not find themselves with the same overuse injuries that are often experienced in other sports.

Start training now because you never know if and when winter triathlon will be added to the Winter Olympic program. The ITU has been pushing the IOC hard to add winter triathlon. If added, it will be the first sport to appear in both the summer and winter Olympics. The main concern from an IOC perspective is the lack of participation internationally. The IOC wants sports that are universal, with participation on at least four continents and in at least 25 countries. Unfortunately this sport is not there yet, but as participation grows and the sport becomes more mainstream, winter triathlon will find its way into the Olympic Games. Figure 28.3 provides a sample training week for an athlete participating in winter triathlon.

**FIGURE 28.3**

### Winter triathlon training week.

|  | Monday | Tuesday | Wednesday | Thursday | Friday | Saturday | Sunday |
|---|---|---|---|---|---|---|---|
| *Run* | Day off | Easy 30 min run before ski | 45 min run on trail or snow | Day off | Combo workout: 15 min warm-up run; 3 × 5 min run/10 min bike/5 min ski at 85% effort, with 5 min recovery between each; easy 20 min cool-down ski | 90 min long run, with last 25 min at 10K run effort | Day off |
| *Bike* | 60 min easy spin | Day off | 90 min at moderate effort | Intervals: 20 min warm-up; 4 × 10 min at 90% effort, with 5 min recovery spin; 10 min cool-down | | 60 min mountain bike ride | 45 min at moderate effort |
| *Ski* | Day off | Intervals: 20 min warm-up; 5 × 5 min at 95% effort, with 3 min recovery ski; 10 min cool-down | Day off | 30 min easy ski after bike | | Day off | 120 min long ski after bike |

## Adventure Racing

Adventure racing can also fall under the umbrella of multisport, although it does not fall under the purview of USA Triathlon but rather the United States Adventure Racing Association (USARA). When hearing the words *adventure racing*, most think of such events as Primal Quest and Eco-Challenge. They differ from the multisport events describes already because they tend to include team competition. Depending on the race, you may have teams of up to five, and therefore you are never stronger than your weakest racer.

Mike Kloser personifies the multisport athlete. Mike's accolades include four-time adventure racing world champion, three-time Eco-Challenge champion, and five-time Primal Quest champion as well as multiple national adventure racing series titles. In an October 13, 2003, *Sports Illustrated* article, Mike was nicknamed "the Intimidator." Barry Siff is another legend of multisport. When asked if he believes adventure racing falls within multisport, his response was, "It honestly personifies multisport. Its very definition is basically that of any nonmotorized sport or activity; thus, we climbed mountains, trekked through jungles, ran, mountain biked, rappelled up to 1,200 feet, in-line skated, Nordic skied, swam, scuba dived, rode horses, and probably more." What is so attractive about this sport to athletes? Siff said in a telephone conversation he was drawn to the sport largely because of its multisport nature. "I would awake each morning, call my teammate Liz, and we'd discuss what sports or activities we'd do that day—no structure, no regimen, no schedule . . . we just got out there and had fun while typically doing two sports a day, for a total of 2 to 5 hours per day."

### Adventure Racing Equipment

Most adventure races will give racers a list of required and suggested gear depending on what sports are being contested within the event. Following is a sample gear list.

#### Mandatory Equipment

Hydration system
Emergency blanket
Bike helmet
Bike
Climbing harness
Rappel device
Life vest

Kayak
Kayak paddles
Compass
Cell phone
Maps and grids
Guidebook and passport

#### Highly Recommended Equipment

Wetsuit or paddle jacket and pants
Tire pump
Knife or multitool
Lighter
Spare tubes, patch kit, bike tools
Gloves for bike and rappel
Long-sleeved polypropylene or fleece top

Headlamp
Dry bag for maps and gear
Rain gear and layering clothes
Survival mirror
Whistle
First aid kit

As you can see from these lists, adventure racers need a fair amount of equipment in order to safely complete an event.

## Adventure Racing Training

The beauty of adventure racing is the diversity of the training. Depending on what race you are preparing for, training can range from mountain bike riding to kayaking to rock climbing. The same principles of training apply here. Try to squeeze in two activities each day. Intensity, frequency, and duration should vary each day for each activity. You may want to add a weight training regimen when preparing for adventure races because overall strength will cross over to most activities, especially when you do not have the time to train for each activity multiple times each week. Weight training allows athletes to be more efficient and useful with limited training time.

Multisport is not limited to duathlon, winter triathlon, off-road triathlon, and adventure racing. Other formats are emerging all the time. They say variety is the spice of life, so spice up your training regimen, and jump into a new multisport event today.

# CHAPTER 29

# Long-Term Triathlete Development

## *Gordon Byrn*

Triathlon is a sport that people can do for a lifetime, so proper long-term development, regardless of when an athlete begins training and racing triathlons, is key to longevity in the sport. Long-term development is important for athletes to reach their potential and prevent performance plateaus, so triathletes must develop the proper skills and fitness in swimming, cycling, and running at the beginning of their triathlon training in order to be successful over the years. Within the discussion of long-term development, it's essential to keep in mind the nature of the athlete. The vast majority of athletes do not require sophisticated planning and workout structuring; rather, they will benefit from a straightforward focus on the topics explored in this chapter.

## Developing and Improving Fitness

There are building blocks of athletic performance that factor into athlete development. In order, these are as follows:

1. Movement skills and the ability to perform these skills quickly
2. Aerobic threshold stamina, known more commonly as endurance
3. Sport-specific strength, or the ability to apply force effectively
4. Lactate threshold stamina, or the maximum pace, power, or duration that an athlete can produce aerobically
5. Functional threshold performance, or the athlete's performance for a 60-minute best-effort maximal performance
6. $\dot{V}O_2$max performance, or the athlete's maximal pace and power for a 5-minute best-effort performance

These building blocks form a pyramid, where one block builds on the other. The first three building blocks provide the platform on which race-specific training is built.

## ▶ Performance Limiters

When you train for a specific goal race, there will inevitably be factors that limit performance. For illustration, I have matched certain limiting concepts to each sport in triathlon, but bear in mind that all limiters can apply to any sport. (Later in this chapter, I outline specific workouts that can be used to assess, and address, an athlete's current stage of development.)

*Swimming* is the most skill-dependent sport, and therefore, long-term development requires consistent training and a commitment to technical improvement. Although it makes sense to limit total time invested in swimming, for most of the year, it is essential to get the most from the time invested, because time is limited. Skills improve most quickly through workout frequency (practice) and informed video review (directed technical improvement). When skills are well established, triathletes have a mixture of strength and fitness which can help their swimming performance.

Understanding a swimmer's pace versus duration curve, across distances of 50, 400, and 1,500 meters, will help the coach assess limiters, as will an understanding of an appropriate stroke for the swimmer's body type and fitness. Smaller, and fitter, athletes should train to support a higher stroke rating (functional threshold fitness and movement skills will dominate how well they swim). Conversely, larger, and less fit, athletes should focus on distance per stroke (specific strength and movement skills will dominate how well they swim).

In terms of return on work, *cycling* is probably the fairest sport in triathlon. The skill component, and injury risk, is far less than in swimming, and running, respectively. Although body type has an influence on approach, far more important is understanding the specific performance and duration requirements of an athlete's goal triathlon, both in terms of terrain and distance. The bike can, and should, be used to train for the entire duration of the triathlon (total time, swim–bike–run) as well as the specific duration on the bike leg (total distance, bike). For both these goals, an intimate understanding of the energy expenditure across the day (total) and per hour (rate) is required. Total work limiters are most classically seen in long-distance racing with larger athletes (e.g., moving 200 pounds across a 14-hour event requires considerable work, at *any* pace). Work-rate limiters are usually seen with experienced athletes, especially smaller and over shorter distances.

Typically, when we talk about fitness, we gravitate toward a work-rate discussion: the power or pace an athlete can produce. However, depending on athlete size, movement economy, metabolic efficiency, and event duration, the total output required for the event can be a fundamental performance limiter, most especially in amateur athlete populations. Put simply, many athletes, especially large and novice, build sufficient fitness to exhaust their fuel supply on race day. A fuel supply limiter can be identified, then addressed, on the bike—where work and work-rate information can be easily captured through the use of a power meter.

Long-term *running* development requires an athlete to run frequently for a long time. Athletes, particularly highly motivated triathletes, are often in a rush to get to "real" run training, or what they consider high-intensity running. Before embarking on a block of high-intensity training, consider if top-end sustained speed is truly limiting performance.

Although athletes have an intrinsic attraction to painful training, in triathlon running, capacity to administer pain rarely limits performance. Instead, I recommend addressing the following:

- Build *connective tissue strength* and address personal *biomechanical limiters* through frequent running, strengthening exercises (calf raises, hip bridges), and appropriate muscle tension (taut, rather than tight, muscles).

- Improve *skills*, and *speed*, in terms of movement economy, and quickness, respectively. Skills need to be learned in a low-stress, low-intensity environment and gradually progressed in terms of pace and stress.

- Train the ability to operate efficiently in all the energy systems outlined in chapter 9, with a focus on *progressive aerobic stamina*. Most important, benchmark performance at, and slightly over, specific race pace. Assess race pace on actual, not goal, performances, and make sure the training program is rooted in reality.

- Consider the role of *body composition* on overall performance. When body composition is limiting long-term development, total stress loads (training and life) should be reduced in order to create space for the athlete to build new habits. Be aware that endurance sports can feed the psychology of disordered eating, and seek professional medical help when needed.

Consider these blocks the foundation for building a fit athlete. When an athlete's skills break down, or the athlete fails to deliver training performance on race day, the cause is typically underdeveloped movement skills, stamina, and sport-specific strength. The final three building blocks are focused on creating a race-fit athlete who is prepared for competition at a specific event. Another way of looking at these two classes of fitness—athletic and race-specific—is this: The capacity to do work must be well established before an athlete will be able to absorb work-rate training. An effective mantra to remember is "Work before work rate."

By consistently applying a plan that is balanced between the three sports (swim, bike, run) as well as focused, primarily, on athlete-specific fitness, you will go a long way toward achieving your full athletic potential. As well, being committed to giving 110 percent in your training and competition can greatly increase the probability of success in the larger picture of your overall life.

To appropriately progress through these stages of development, you need to integrate techniques to improve your fitness. Consider the following five techniques as you strive to improve long-term fitness.

### Variable Stimuli

It is recommended that you follow a consistent, moderate training program for as long as you continue to improve. When plateaus are reached, it can be tempting to add to training load in an effort to improve. Although this is effective, in experienced athletic populations, improvement can come from varying the stress rather than increasing the stress. This technique is very important with fragile and injury-prone athletes.

### Mental Freshness

Improvement takes time, and persisting across time requires motivation. Variation in approach within a season, and between seasons, is effective for maintaining motivation.

### Specific Overload

Triathletes in general, and working triathletes in particular, often lack the single-sport volume to make dramatic progress in any one area of their athletic portfolios. As well, it is far easier to sustain a higher performance level than reach a new performance level. Therefore, smart application of specific overload periods can take you to higher single-sport performance levels, which are maintained across your competitive season.

### Athletic Longevity

Athletes and coaches need to consider—and address—the attributes required for long-term success. Agility, flexibility, muscle balance, and maximal strength may not affect short-term performance, but their absence will impair long-term performance, particularly in veteran athletes. In the United States, the median age of triathletes is relatively high. Within adult populations, consider what will be required for athletic performance in 10, 20, and 30 years. Be very careful with training strategies that might mortgage future athletic performance. As a species, we share a weakness toward favoring the present over maximizing long-term returns.

### Aerobic Development

For most triathletes, the greatest limiter to performance is stamina at appropriate race effort. Triathlon appeals to highly motivated athletes, and they often don't want to do the training or put in the hard effort of the training required to develop superior strength and stamina. A coach can achieve a material increase in short-term performance by appealing to the athlete on a long-term development basis.

Although the previous techniques focus on developing your athletic abilities, keep in mind that your performance in a specific goal race—in all three triathlon events—also relies on a simple progression of improvement:

1. Completing the race distance across multiple days
2. Completing the race distance in a single day
3. Completing the race distance in a single day, without stopping
4. Completing the race distance in a single day, without stopping, and with pace changes designed to optimize finishing time (or position)

The steps in this progression should be addressed while you work on improving your economy, as well as the mental skills to optimize your race experience.

## Assessing Athletic Range and Depth of Fitness

The best technique I know for constant athletic development is consistent repetition of a plan that is balanced between the swim, bike, and run and focused, primarily, on athlete-specific fitness.

In amateur athletic populations, plateaus frequently arise from a lack of consistent training load. Adding variability or intensity to an inconsistent athlete's program is a distraction from what matters, which is establishing consistent training. The optimal strategy is to stay focused on a simple, balanced plan that removes habits and choices that impair your ability to do work. That said, what should this balanced plan focus on, and how can you assess your progress? To determine this, first consider these questions:

- What is my stage of development right now?
- What are my goals?
- How much time do I have available for training?
- Does an increased focus on triathlon make sense for my overall life?

Make sure the answers to these questions are consistent and in harmony with your life. Before spending a lot of energy improving athletic performance, you need to ensure that triathlon fits within your overall life goals.

The following assessments allow you and your coach to examine your fitness, and they provide benchmarks for tracking improvement. Always consider benchmark performance relative to goal-race duration as well as goal-race performances. Moderate aerobic performances can be benchmarked daily. High-intensity and sustained best-effort performances need only be tested every 3 to 6 weeks.

To help you out as you work through these assessments, consider that you have five gears within your aerobic engine:

1. Easy
2. Steady
3. Moderately hard (mod-hard)
4. Threshold
5. $\dot{V}O_2$max

These five gears correspond with the energy systems outlined in chapter 9 and are used to help you understand how intensely to perform each segment of these assessments.

| RPE number | Breathing rate/ability to talk | Exertion | Gears |
|---|---|---|---|
| 1 | Resting | Very slight | Easy |
| 2 | Talking is easy | Slight | Easy |
| 3 | Talking is easy | Moderate | Steady |
| 4 | You can talk but with more effort | Somewhat hard | Steady |
| 5 | You can talk but with more effort | Hard | Mod-hard |
| 6 | Breathing is challenged or don't want to talk | Hard | Mod-hard |
| 7 | Breathing is challenged or don't want to talk | Very hard | Threshold |
| 8 | Panting hard or conversation is difficult | Very hard | Threshold |
| 9 | Panting hard or conversation is difficult | Very, very hard | $\dot{V}O_2$max |
| 10 | Cannot sustain this intensity for too long | Maximal | $\dot{V}O_2$max |

## Swim Assessment 1: Descending 400s and 200s

This workout assesses athlete awareness of pace control and benchmark pace at different efforts. Swim this workout so it progresses from easy to max as the intervals progress. Although rest times of 10 and 15 seconds are noted, well-trained swimmers will achieve a more accurate assessment with rests of 5 and 10 seconds, respectively.

- 12 × 25 *easy* on 10 seconds' rest
- 6 × 50 *steady* on 10 seconds' rest
- 4 × 75 (25 *easy*, 25 *mod-hard*, 25 *steady*) on 10 seconds' rest
- 3 × 100 *steady* on 10 seconds' rest
- 5 × 400 *threshold* on no more than 15 seconds' rest
- 5 minutes *easy*
- 5 × 200 *max* on 10 seconds' rest
- Cool-down

## Swim Assessment 2: Pace Change 200s

This workout assesses athlete awareness of pace control and benchmark pace at different efforts. Use the paces derived from assessment 1 to set the send-off (the time you leave for each interval) for each step of the main set (these are the sets of 200 in the workout). The longer main-set duration, and its sustained nature, will give an insight into your depth of swim fitness, or your capacity to hold pace over time. Well-trained swimmers will achieve a clearer benchmark by setting their send-offs based on expected pace for the final 200 and adding 10 seconds per set. For example, a fit athlete expecting to swim 2:40 for the final swim would set the send-offs at 3:20, 3:10, 3:00, 2:50, and 2:40, respectively, for the five 200s of the main set. Another way to complete this set is to take 10 seconds' rest after each 200.

- 16 × 50, all on 10 seconds' rest, with this pattern: 3 *easy*, 1 *threshold*, 1 *steady*, 1 *mod-hard,* 1 *easy*, 1 *threshold* (2×)
- 200 relaxed swimming, athlete's choice
- 5 × 200 *easy* on 10 seconds' rest
- 4 × 200 *steady* on 10 seconds' rest
- 3 × 200 *mod-hard* on 10 seconds' rest
- 2 × 200 *threshold* on 10 seconds' rest
- 200 $\dot{V}O_2$max
- Cool-down

## Swim Assessment 3: Long Descending Intervals

This workout assesses an athlete's ability to hold aerobic paces over long durations. Use pace data from the previous benchmarking swim workouts to set goal paces. Until you have sufficient endurance for a total swim distance of 5,000 meters, adjust the swim interval distance by using 400s, 600s, or 800s. Most athletes should aim to move from easy to moderately hard paces. Well-trained swimmers will be able to move from easy to threshold paces.

- 5 × 1,000, descending 1 to 5 on 15 seconds' rest:

- 1st 1,000: moderate pace, with 15 seconds' rest
- 2nd 1,000: faster than the first 1,000, with 15 seconds' rest
- 3rd 1,000: faster than the second 1,000, with 15 seconds' rest
- 4th 1,000: faster than the third 1,000, with 15 seconds' rest
- 5th 1,000: faster than the fourth 1,000, with 15 seconds' rest

An alternative structure, where pace is increased on each set, can be used for this assessment as follows:

- 10 × 100 on 5 seconds' rest
- 8 × 125 on 10 seconds' rest
- 4 × 250 on 15 seconds' rest
- 2 × 500 on 20 seconds' rest

## Swim Assessment 4: Prescribed-Pace 100s

The previous three swim workouts assess pace and the capacity to hold pace over time. This workout lets you see how long you can sustain threshold paces and higher. To assess this, the total main-set duration should be 40 to 60 minutes long. Use a fixed send-off that is slightly longer than threshold pace. For example, if threshold pace is 1:27 per 100, then a send-off of 1:30 would be appropriate, and the main-set structure could be 30 × 100, holding on 1:27 and leaving on 1:30. Note that most athletes overestimate their speed at threshold and use a pace that is closer to velocity at $\dot{V}O_2$max. If you are seeking to train $\dot{V}O_2$max pace, then use a main set of 12 to 30 minutes' duration, with rest intervals of between 35 and 100 percent of work intervals. For example, if $\dot{V}O_2$max pace is 1:20 per 100, then an appropriate main-set structure would be 12 × 100, leaving on 1:40 and coming in on 1:20.

- 500 *easy* on 20 seconds' rest
- 4 × 100 descend on 15 seconds' rest
- 4 × 75 (as 25 build, 25 *steady*, 25 *easy*) on 10 seconds' rest
- 4 × 50 *threshold* on 15 seconds' rest
- 100 *easy*
- 12-40 × 100 with prescribed pace and rest
- Cool-down

## Bike Assessment 1: Progressive Bike Test

The goal of this workout is to assess aerobic range as well as top-end performance. The test can be done maximally or submaximally. If you do not have access to a power meter or other power measuring device, then the best way to do this test is to start 10 beats per minute below the bottom of your steady heart rate zone and track distance per step. Use 5 beats per minute as your step height, and continue until one step past functional threshold heart rate (FTHR).

First, you'll need a rough estimate of your functional threshold power (FTP), and then you warm up for 20 to 30 minutes, with your power remaining under 50 percent of FTP. The actual test should start at 50 percent of FTP. This is a very easy intensity on purpose. To get a clear reading of your aerobic zones and break points, you need to start quite low. The most common mistake in benchmarking is a fast start because it skews the data.

If your FTP is less than 125 watts, then use 10-watt steps; from 125 to 174 watts, use 15-watt steps; from 175 to 249 watts, use 20-watt steps; from 250 to 349 watts, use 25-watt steps; and for 350 watts, use 30-watt steps. Be aware that step height is another area where you can skew your data. If the step heights are too large, then you could pass right through an important break point or training zone. So it is better to use smaller steps if you are unsure.

When performing the test, each step should last for 5 minutes. Record your heart rate at 1-minute intervals. The main things you want to track are heart rate, power, and effort (how it feels)—these are most important within your likely race power range. How far you progress will depend on you. There are benefits of taking the test all the way to failure (checking for fatigue and seeing top-end heart rates); however, these aspects do not need to be tested often. If you plan on doing the test often, then you need only go to failure once per quarter. The rest of the time, build to slightly past FTP.

## Bike Assessment 2: Progressive Field Assessment

The goal of this test is to assess your progression over longer durations. If you have a power meter, then this workout will let you check on your power zones. If you don't have a power meter, then you can still test by benchmarking distance traveled for each segment of the test set. Rather than fixed times, you can use a fixed-distance course and note your split. It's not perfect, but on a calm day, your average speed will be a meaningful number.

The warm-up should be about 45 minutes; include about 15 minutes of steady effort as well as some 4 × 2-minute builds where you lift effort gradually from steady to just under functional threshold (effort, not HR). Spin easy between the warm-up intervals. The main set is a 45-minute continuous effort split into thirds. Aim for 15 minutes' worth of effort at each of aerobic threshold (AeT, bottom of steady), lactate threshold (LT, top of mod-hard), and functional threshold (FT, top of threshold). A 45-minute main set is a short test for an endurance athlete—races and long workouts will let you see how much you decouple (during a race, or long workout, how far away from your benchmark tests are you performing?). When endurance is well established, you should be able to stay within 7 percent of these benchmarks when racing as well as in your long workouts.

Another way to approach the test is to benchmark off a target heart rate. Use the HR that corresponds with aerobic threshold, lactate threshold, and functional threshold, respectively. Give yourself 5 minutes to gradually build to each target HR. If you don't have access to a power meter, then use the target HR method and track distance covered. Although distance is influenced by wind speed and direction, you will still be able to gather useful data. These field data are useful for comparison against progressive bike sets that are often done in the lab or indoors.

## Bike Assessment 3: Long Progressive Intervals

The goal of this workout is to assess the depth of aerobic stamina over race durations as well as the impact of periods of higher intensity. To perform the test, start with 10 minutes at easy pace, then move into a 2-hour continuous main set where you alternate 40 minutes of steady effort with 20 minutes of mod-hard effort. Finish with 5 minutes of easy cycling, and then go into your run.

Another option is to start with 10 minutes at easy pace and then move into a 2-hour continuous main set, where the first hour is 40 minutes of steady effort and 20 minutes of mod-hard effort. For the second hour, start with 20 minutes of steady effort, and then do 10 minutes of mod-hard effort; for the final 30 minutes, progress in 10-minute blocks from steady to mod-hard to threshold effort. Immediately after the threshold block, insert 20 minutes at steady effort—bring your heart rate down gradually while spinning slightly faster than normal time-trial cadence.

## Run Assessment 1: Progressive Run Test

The goal of this workout is to assess aerobic range as well as top-end performance. The test can be done maximally or submaximally. Perform this test at a track; one lap = 400 meters or one-quarter of a mile, and the total test distance is 10 to 12 kilometers (continuous).

To perform the test, warm up with 15 to 20 minutes of recovery-effort running or cycling. Run increasing 2,000-meter repeats. Start the first 2K at 20 beats per minute (bpm) below the bottom of your steady zone, and increase effort by 10 bpm for each successive 2K interval. Track your average pace and maximum and average HR for each 1,000-meter leg, and continue until 2K beyond functional threshold heart rate.

Note that if you have access to lactate testing, then you can take lactates at the end of each 2K stage. If you are taking lactates, the baseline lactate (before starting the test) needs to be under 1.5 millimoles. If lactate is elevated, then continue an easy warm-up for a further 10 minutes and test again. If still over 1.5 millimoles, you'll have to try another time to achieve accurate lactate values. If most of your steps would take longer than 10 minutes, drop the interval duration to 1,600 meters. If most of your steps would take longer than 12 minutes, drop the interval duration to 1,200 meters.

## Run Assessment 2: Long Progressive Intervals

The goal of this workout is to assess progression over longer durations. This workout is best done in the field rather than on a treadmill or track. Choose a course you can easily access. The precise durations are not all that important; when doing this session myself, I use a trail around a small local lake.

To perform this test, think about this set as 5 × 12 minutes, as follows:

- 12 minutes *easy*
- 12 minutes *steady*
- 12 minutes *mod-hard*
- 12 minutes *threshold*
- 12 minutes *steady*
- End with strides

Note that you can extend the duration of the final steady block to assess decoupling (explained in bike assessment 2). For a long benchmarking workout, repeat the main set twice. Use effort the first time through the main set, and use heart rate the second time. Compare the average pace achieved with the two methods to assess the accuracy of your pace perception.

This chapter has been written assuming a goal of developing athletic performance. In fact, it was my mission to share what I've learned on this subject with you. However, in my years of coaching, training strategy rarely limits performance.

Most athletes are driven by something other than race-day performance, and the value in athletics flows from an area other than the finish line. When building a long-term plan, coaches and athletes should consider all areas of personal and athletic development: performance relative to others, performance relative to self, long-term personal health and longevity, and life skills learned through athletics.

Even with elite sport, the value of competition comes from its ability to increase an athlete's drive to be the very best he can be. In learning to maximize your ultimate athletic potential, you will learn valuable skills you can apply to your life long after you are finished competing in sport.

# USA Triathlon University

USA Triathlon University is focused on bringing together the educational functions of the organization under one umbrella. USA Triathlon University expands educational functions in new directions; establish across-the-board quality standards for various educational functions; publish materials, both in print and on the web, in support of various educational programs; and engage in public education about the various educational components of USA Triathlon, as well as put an exclamation point on our role to fuel the multisport lifestyle. USA Triathlon University includes programming in coaching education, race director certification, sport development, research, and multisport development.

The coaching education program includes coaching certifications levels I to III, youth and junior certification, community certification, webinars, elite coaching mentorship opportunities, art and science symposiums, and USAT-certified performance and training centers. The race director certification program includes race director certifications level I and II. The sport development program includes clubs and growing grassroots disciplines such as duathlon, aquathlon, and off-road triathlons. The research program focuses on research for all constituents of USA Triathlon. The multisport development program includes medical provider certification and youth programming.

The purpose of USA Triathlon University is to be the one-stop shop for all things educational at USA Triathlon, including all the programs just identified. USA Triathlon University will continue to grow and offer programs that affect everyone involved in the multisport lifestyle. Please visit www.usatriathlon.org for more information.

# BIBLIOGRAPHY

## Chapter 1

Bompa, T., and G. Haff. 2009. *Periodization: Theory and methodology of training*. Champaign, IL: Human Kinetics.

USA Triathlon. 2000. Level I coaching clinic manual. Colorado Springs, CO: USAT.

## Chapter 2

American College of Sports Medicine. 2009. Nutrition and athletic performance. *Med Sci Sports Exerc* 41(3):709-31.

Bangsbo, J., T.P. Gunnarsson, L.N. Wendell, and M. Thomassen. 2009. Reduced volume and increased training intensity elevate muscle Na + /K + pump {alpha}2-subunit expression as well as short- and long-term work capacity in humans. *J Appl Physiol* 107(6):1771-80.

Benardot, D. 2006. Gender and age: The young athlete. In *Advanced sports nutrition*, 199-204. Champaign, IL: Human Kinetics.

Bernhardt, G. 2008. *Bicycling for women*. Boulder, CO: VeloPress.

Clapp, J.F., III. 2002. *Exercising through your pregnancy*. Omaha: Addicus Books.

Edwards, S. 1992. *Triathlon for kids*. New York: Winning International.

Fournier, M., J. Ricci, A.W. Taylor, R.J. 1982. Skeletal muscle adaptation in adolescent boys: Sprint and endurance training and detraining. *Med Sci Sports Exerc* 14(6):453-6.

Friel, J. 2009. *The triathlete's training bible*. Boulder, CO: VeloPress.

Gandolfo, C. 2004. *The woman triathlete*. Champaign, IL: Human Kinetics.

Habash, D.L. 2006. Child and adolescent athletes. In *Sports nutrition: A practical manual for professionals*, ed. M. Dunford, 229-68. Chicago, IL: American Dietetic Association.

Kowalchik, C. 1999. *The complete book of running for women*. New York: Pocket Books.

LeBlanc, J. 1997. *Straight talk about children and sport: Advice for parents, coaches, and teachers*. New York: Mosaic Press.

Lepers, T., F. Sultana, C. Hausswirth, and J. Brisswalter. 2010. Age-related changes in triathlon performances. *Int J Sports Med* 31(4):251-6.

Marti, B., and H. Howald. 1990. Long-term effects of physical training on aerobic capacity: Controlled study of former elite athletes. *J Appl Physiol* 69(4):1451-9.

Nelson, S. 2007. *Nutrition for young athletes*. 5th ed. Falls Church, VA: Nutrition Dimension.

O'Toole, M., and P.S. Douglas. 1995. Applied physiology of triathlon. *Sports Med* 19(4):251-67.

Petersen, S.R., C.A. Gaul, N.M. Stanton, and C.C. Hanstock. 1999. Skeletal muscle metabolism in short-term, high intensity exercise in prepubertal and pubertal girls. *J Appl Physiol* 87(6):2151-6.

Ratey, J.J., and E. Hagerman. 2008. *Spark: The revolutionary new science of exercise and the brain*. Boston: Little, Brown.

Sharkey, B.J., and S.E. Gaskill. 2006. *Sport physiology for coaches*. Champaign, IL: Human Kinetics.

Shephard, R.J. 1982. *Physical activity and growth*. Chicago: Yearbook Medical.

Taaffe, D. 2006. Sarcopenia: Exercise as a treatment strategy. *Aust Fam Physician* 35(3):130-4.

Trappe, S., D.L. Costill, M.D. Vukovich, J. Jones, and T. Melham. 1996. Aging among elite distance runners: A 22-year longitudinal study. *J Appl Physiol* 80(1):285-90.

Tudor, B.O. 2000. *Total training for young champions*. Champaign, IL: Human Kinetics.

Weinberg, R., and D. Gould. 2007. *Foundations of sport and exercise psychology*. Champaign, IL: Human Kinetics.

Williams, M. 2008. Nutrition for the school aged child athlete. In *The young athlete: The encyclopaedia of sports medicine*, ed. H. Hebestreit and O. Bar-Or, 203-17. Vol. XIII. Malden: Blackwell.

# Chapter 4

Aagaard, P., and J.L. Andersen. 2010. Effects of strength training on endurance capacity in top-level endurance athletes. *Scand J Med Sci Sports* (Suppl 2):S39-47.

Aspenes, S., P.-L. Kjendlie, J. Hoff, and J. Helgerud. 2009. Combined strength and endurance training in competitive swimmers. *J Sports Sci Med* 8:357-65.

Bell, G.J., S.R. Petersen, J. Wessel, K. Bagnall, and H.A. Quinney. 1991. Physiological adaptations to concurrent endurance training and low velocity resistance training. *Int J Sports Med* 12(4):384-90.

Bentley, D.J., G.J. Wilson, A.J. Davie, and S. Zhou. 1998. Correlations between peak power output, muscular strength and cycle time trial performance in triathletes. *J Sports Med Phys Fitness* 38(3):201-7.

Chtara, M., K. Chamari, M. Chaouachi, A. Chaouachi, D. Koubaa, Y. Feki, G.P. Millet, and M. Amri. 2005. Effects of intra-session concurrent endurance and strength training sequence on aerobic performance and capacity. *Brit J Sports Med* 39(8):555-60.

Cronin, J., and G. Sleivert. 2005. Challenges in understanding the influence of maximal power training on improving athletic performance. *Sports Med* (Auckland, NZ) 35(3):213-34.

Durell, D.L., T.J. Pujol, and J.T. Barnes. 2003. A survey of the scientific data and training methods utilized by collegiate strength and conditioning coaches. *J Strength Cond Res* 17(2):368-73.

Ebben, W.P., A.G. Kindler, K.A. Chirdon, N.C. Jenkins, A.J. Polichnowski, and A.V. Ng. 2004. The effect of high-load vs. high-repetition training on endurance performance. *J Strength Cond Res* 18(3):513-7.

Folland, J.P., C.S. Irish, J.C. Roberts, J.E. Tarr, and D.E. Jones. 2002. Fatigue is not a necessary stimulus for strength gains during resistance training. *Brit J Sports Med* 36:370-3.

Girold, S., D. Maurin, B. Dugue, J.C. Chatard, and G. Millet. 2007. Effects of dry-land vs. resisted- and assisted-sprint exercises on swimming sprint performances. *J Strength Cond Res* 21(2):599-605.

Hoff, J., J. Helgerud, and U. Wisloff. 1999. Maximal strength training improves work economy in trained female cross-country skiers. *Med Sci Sports Exerc* 31(6):870-7.

Izquierdo, M., J. Ibanez, J.J. Gonzalez-Badillo, K. Hakkinen, N.A. Ratamess, W.J. Kraemer, D.N. French, J. Eslava, A. Altadill, X. Asiain, and E.M. Gorostiaga. 2006. Differential effects of strength training leading to failure versus not to failure on hormonal responses, strength, and muscle power gains. *J Appl Physiol* 100(5):1647-56.

Jung, A.P. 2003. The impact of resistance training on distance running performance. *Sports Med* (Auckland, NZ) 33(7):539-52.

Kraemer, W.J., and K. Häkkinen. 2010. Strength training in endurance runners. *Int J Sports Med* 31(7):468-76.

Kraemer, W.J., N. Ratamess, A.C. Fry, T. Triplett-McBride, L.P. Koziris, J.A. Bauer, J.M. Lynch, and S.J. Fleck. 2000. Influence of resistance training volume and periodization on physiological and performance adaptations in collegiate women tennis players. *Am J Sports Med* 28(5):626-33.

Kraemer, W.J., and R.U. Newton. 1994. Training for improved vertical jump. *Sports Sci Exchange* 7(6):1-12.

Li, L. 2004. Neuromuscular control and coordination during cycling. *Res Q Exerc Sport* 75(1):16-22.

Marx, J.O., N.A. Ratamess, B.C. Nindl, L.A. Gotshalk, J.S. Volek, K. Dohi, J.A. Bush, A.L. Gomez, S.A. Mazzetti, S.J. Fleck, K. Hakkinen, R.U. Newton, and W.J. Kraemer. 2001. Low-volume circuit versus high-volume periodized resistance training in women. *Med Sci Sports Exerc* 33(4):635-43.

Mikkola, J., H. Rusko, A. Nummela, T. Pollari, and K. Hakkinen. 2007. Concurrent endurance and explosive type strength training improves neuromuscular and anaerobic characteristics in young distance runners. *Int J Sports Med* 28(7):602-11.

Mikkola, J.S., H.K. Rusko, A.T. Nummela, L.M. Paavolainen, and K. Hakkinen. 2007. Concurrent endurance and explosive type strength training increases activation and fast force production of leg extensor muscles in endurance athletes. *J Strength Cond Res* 21(2):613-20.

Millet, G.P., B. Jaouen, F. Borrani, and R. Candau. 2002. Effects of concurrent endurance and strength training on running economy and $\dot{V}O_2$ kinetics. *Med Sci Sports Exerc* 34(8):1351-9.

Nader, G.A. 2006. Concurrent strength and endurance training: From molecules to man. *Med Sci Sports Exerc* 38(11):1965-70.

Paavolainen, L., K. Hakkinen, I. Hamalainen, A. Nummela, and H. Rusko. 1999. Explosive-strength training improves 5-km running time by improving running economy and muscle power. *J Appl Physiol* 86(5):1527-33.

Paavolainen, L.M., A.T. Nummela, and H.K. Rusko. 1999. Neuromuscular characteristics and muscle power as determinants of 5-km running performance. *Med Sci Sports Exerc* 31(1):124-30.

Paton, C.D., and W.G. Hopkins. 2005. Combining explosive and high-resistance training improves performance in competitive cyclists. *J Strength Cond Res* 19(4):826-30.

Rhea, M.R., S.D. Ball, W.T. Phillips, and L.N. Burkett. 2002. A comparison of linear and daily undulating periodized programs with equated volume and intensity for strength. *J Strength Cond Res* 16(2):250-5.

Spennewyn, K.C. 2008. Strength outcomes in fixed versus free-form resistance equipment. *J Strength Cond Res* 22(1):75-81.

Spurrs, R.W., A.J. Murphy, and M.L. Watsford. 2003. The effect of plyometric training on distance running performance. *Eur J Appl Physiol* 89(1):1-7.

Stone, Michael H., M.E. Stone, W.A. Sands, K.C. Pierce, R.U. Newton, G.G. Haff, and J. Carlock. 2006. Maximum strength and strength training: A relationship to endurance? *Strength Cond J* 28(3)44-53.

Sunde, A., Ø. Støren, M. Bjerkaas, M.H. Larsen, J. Hoff, and J. Helgerud. 2010. Maximal strength training improves cycling economy in competitive cyclists. *J Strength Cond Res* 24(8):2157-65.

Taipale, R.S., J. Mikkola, A. Nummela, V. Vesterinen, B. Capostagno, S. Walker, D. Gitonga, B.R. Rønnestad, E.A. Hansen, and T. Raastad. 2010. Effect of heavy strength training on thigh muscle cross-sectional area, performance determinants, and performance in well-trained cyclists. *Eur J Appl Physiol* 108(5):965-75.

Tanaka, H., and T. Swensen. 1998. Impact of resistance training on endurance performance: A new form of cross-training? *Sports Med* (Auckland, NZ) 25(3):191-200.

Taylor-Mason, A.M. 2005. High-resistance interval training improves 40-km time-trial performance in competitive cyclists. *Sportscience* 9:27-31.

Turner, A.M., M. Owings, and J.A. Schwane. 2003. Improvement in running economy after 6 weeks of plyometric training. *J Strength Cond Res* 17(1):60-67.

Willardson, J.M., L. Norton, and G. Wilson. 2010. Training to failure and beyond in mainstream resistance exercise programs. *Strength Cond J* 32(3):21-29.

Yamamoto, L.M., R.M. Lopez, J.F. Klau, D.J. Casa, W.J. Kraemer, and C.M. Maresh. 2008. The effects of resistance training on endurance distance running performance among highly trained runners: A systematic review. *J Strength Cond Res* 22(6):2036-44.

# Chapter 6

Allen, H., and A. Coggan. 2010. *Training and racing with a power meter.* 2nd ed. Boulder, CO: VeloPress.

Friel, J. 2006. *Your first triathlon.* Boulder, CO: VeloPress.

Friel, J. 2009. *The triathlete's training bible.* Boulder, CO: VeloPress.

Friel, J., and G. Byrn. 2009. *Going long.* Boulder, CO: VeloPress.

# Chapter 8

Allen, H., and A. Coggan. 2010. *Training and racing with a power meter.* 2nd ed. Boulder, CO: VeloPress.

Allen, M. 2010. Working your heart. Available: www.markallenonline.com/maoArticles.aspx?AID = 2.

Björling, C. 2008. Welcome. Available: www.clasbjorling.com/en/index.html.

Borg, G. 1998. *Borg's perceived exertion and pain rating scales.* Champaign, IL: Human Kinetics.

Goss, J. 1994. Hardiness and mood disturbances in swimmers while overtraining. *J Sport Exerc Psychol* 16:135-49.

Kellmann, M. 2002. Underrecovery and overtraining: Different concepts, similar impact? In *Enhancing recovery: Preventing underperformance in athletes,* ed. M. Kellmann, 3-24. Champaign, IL: Human Kinetics.

Kellmann, M. 2010. Preventing overtraining in athletes in high-intensity sports and stress/recovery monitoring. *Scand J Med Sci Sports* 20(Suppl 2):S95-102.

Kellmann, M., and K.W. Kallus. 2001. *The Recovery-Stress Questionnaire for Athletes: User manual.* Champaign, IL: Human Kinetics.

Kellmann, M., T. Patrick, C. Botterill, and C. Wilson. 2002. The Recovery-Cue and its use in applied settings: Practical suggestions regarding assessment and monitoring of recovery. In *Enhancing recovery: Preventing underperformance in athletes,* ed. M. Kellmann, 301-11. Champaign, IL: Human Kinetics.

Kenttä, G., and P. Hassmén. 1998. Overtraining and recovery. *Sports Med* 26:1-16.

Kenttä, G., and P. Hassmén. 2002. Underrecovery and overtraining: A conceptual model. In *Enhancing recovery: Preventing underperformance in athletes*, ed. M. Kellmann, 57-79. Champaign, IL: Human Kinetics.

Löhr, G., and S. Preiser. 1974. Regression und Recreation: Ein Beitrag zum Problem Streß und Erholung [Regression and recreation: A paper dealing with stress and recovery]. *Zeitschrift für experimentelle und angewandte Psychologie* 21:575-91.

McNair, D., M. Lorr, and L.F. Droppleman. 1971/1992. *Profile of Mood States manual*. San Diego: Educational and Industrial Testing Service.

Peterson, K. 2003. Athlete overtraining and underrecovery: Recognizing the symptoms and strategies for coaches. *Olympic Coach* 18(3):16-17.

Selye, H. 1974. *Stress without distress*. Philadelphia: Lippincott.

# Chapter 9

Armstrong, L. 2000. *Performing in extreme environments*. Champaign, IL: Human Kinetics.

Austin, K.G., and B. Seebohar. 2010. *Performance nutrition: Applying the science of nutrient timing*. Champaign, IL: Human Kinetics.

Bompa, T., and G. Haff. 2009. *Periodization: Theory and methodology of training*. Champaign, IL: Human Kinetics.

Foster, C. 1998. Monitoring training in athletes with reference to overtraining syndrome. *Med Sci Sports Exerc* 30(7):1164-8.

Gibala, M.J., and S.L. McGee. 2008. Metabolic adaptations to short-term high-intensity interval training: A little pain for a lot of gain? *Exerc Sport Sci Rev* 36(2):58-63.

Kellmann, M., ed. 2002. *Enhancing recovery: Preventing underperformance in athletes*. Champaign, IL: Human Kinetics.

Laursen, P.B. 2010. Training for intense exercise performance: High-intensity or high-volume training? *Scand J Med Sci Sports* 20(Suppl 2):S1-10.

Sleivert, G.G., and D.S. Rowlands. 1996. Physical and physiological factors associated with success in the triathlon. *Sports Med* 22(1):8-18.

Snyder, A.C., A.E. Jeukendrup, M.K. Hesselink, H. Kuipers, and C. Foster. 1993. A physiological/psychological indicator of over-reaching during intensive training. *Int J Sports Med* 14(1):29-32.

# Chapter 10

Al Haddad, H., P.B. Laursen, S. Ahmaidi, and M. Buchheit. 2010. Influence of cold water face immersion on post-exercise parasympathetic reactivation. *Eur J Appl Physiol* 108:599-606.

Ali, A., M.P. Caine, and B.G. Snow. 2007. Graduated compression stockings: Physiological and perceptual responses during and after exercise. *J Sports Sci* 25:413-9.

Almeras, N., S. Lemieux, C. Bouchard, and A. Tremblay. 1997. Fat gain in female swimmers. *Physiol Behav* 61:811-7.

Armstrong, L.E. 2006. Nutritional strategies for football: Counteracting heat, cold, high altitude, and jet lag. *J Sports Sci* 24:723-40.

Armstrong, L.E., and C.M. Maresh. 1991. The induction and decay of heat acclimatisation in trained athletes. *Sports Med* 12:302-12.

Armstrong, L.E., C.M. Maresh, J.W. Castellani, M.F. Bergeron, R.W. Kenefick, K.E. LaGasse, and D. Riebe. 1994. Urinary indices of hydration status. *Int J Sport Nutr* 4:265-79.

Banister, E.W., J.B. Carter, and P.C. Zarkadas. 1999. Training theory and taper: Validation in triathlon athletes. *Eur J Appl Physiol Occup Physiol* 79:182-91.

Bosquet, L., J. Montpetit, D. Arvisais, and I. Mujika. 2007. Effects of tapering on performance: A meta-analysis. *Med Sci Sports Exerc* 39:1358-65.

Bringard, A., R. Denis, N. Belluye, and S. Perrey. 2006. Effects of compression tights on calf muscle oxygenation and venous pooling during quiet resting in supine and standing positions. *J Sports Med Phys Fitness* 46:548-54.

Bringard, A., S. Perrey, N. and Belluye. 2006. Aerobic energy cost and sensation responses during submaximal running exercise: Positive effects of wearing compression tights. *Int J Sports Med* 27:373-8.

Buchheit, M., J.J. Peiffer, C.R. Abbiss, and P.B. Laursen. 2009. Effect of cold water immersion on postexercise parasympathetic reactivation. *Am J Physiol Heart Circ Physiol* 296:H421-7.

Burke, L.M., G. Millet, and M.A. Tarnopolsky. 2007. Nutrition for distance events. *J Sports Sci* 25 (Suppl 1):S29-38.

Busso, T., H. Benoit, R. Bonnefoy, L. Feasson, and J.R. Lacour. 2002. Effects of training frequency on the dynamics of performance response to a single training bout. *J Appl Physiol* 92:572-80.

Busso, T., R. Candau, and J.R. Lacour. 1994. Fatigue and fitness modelled from the effects of training on performance. *Eur J Appl Physiol Occup Physiol* 69:50-54.

Butterfield, G.E., J. Gates, S. Fleming, G.A. Brooks, J.R. Sutton, and J.T. Reeves. 1992. Increased energy intake minimizes weight loss in men at high altitude. *J Appl Physiol* 72:1741-8.

Casa, D.J., R.L. Stearns, R.M. Lopez, M.S. Ganio, B.P. McDermott, S. Walker Yeargin, L.M. Yamamoto, S.M. Mazerolle, R.W. Roti, L.E. Armstrong, and C.M. Maresh. 2010. Influence of hydration on physiological function and performance during trail running in the heat. *J Athl Train* 45:147-56.

Cheung, K., P. Hume, and L. Maxwell. 2003. Delayed onset muscle soreness: Treatment strategies and performance factors. *Sports Med* 33:145-64.

Cheuvront, S.N., R.W. Kenefick, S.J. Montain, and M.N. Sawka. 2010. Mechanisms of aerobic performance impairment with heat stress and dehydration. *J Appl Physiol* 109:1989-95.

Coutts, A.J., K.M. Slattery, and L.K. Wallace. 2007. Practical tests for monitoring performance, fatigue and recovery in triathletes. *J Sci Med Sport* 10:372-81.

Farr, T., C. Nottle, K. Nosaka, and P. Sacco. 2002. The effects of therapeutic massage on delayed onset muscle soreness and muscle function following downhill walking. *J Sci Med Sport* 5:297-306.

Fein, L.W., E.M. Haymes, and E.R. Buskirk. 1975. Effects of daily and intermittent exposure on heat acclimation of women. *Int J Biomet* 19:41-52.

Fitz-Clarke, J.R., R.H. Morton, and E.W. Banister. 1991. Optimizing athletic performance by influence curves. *J Appl Physiol* 71:1151-8.

French, D.N., K.G. Thompson, S.W. Garland, C.A. Barnes, M.D. Portas, P.E. Hood, and G. Wilkes. 2008. The effects of contrast bathing and compression therapy on muscular performance. *Med Sci Sports Exerc* 40:1297-1306.

Garet, M., N. Tournaire, F. Roche, R. Laurent, J.R. Lacour, J.C. Barthelemy, and V. Pichot. 2004. Individual interdependence between nocturnal ANS activity and performance in swimmers. *Med Sci Sports Exerc* 36:2112-8.

Halson, S. 2008. Nutrition, sleep and recovery. *Eur J Sport Sci* 8:199-126.

Hickson, R.C., C. Kanakis, Jr., J.R. Davis, A.M. Moore, and S. Rich. 1982. Reduced training duration effects on aerobic power, endurance, and cardiac growth. *J Appl Physiol* 53:225-9.

Hilbert, J.E., G.A. Sforzo, and T. Swensen. 2003. The effects of massage on delayed onset muscle soreness. *Br J Sports Med* 37:72-75.

Hirai, M., H. Iwata, and N. Hayakawa. 2002. Effect of elastic compression stockings in patients with varicose veins and healthy controls measured by strain gauge plethysmography. *Skin Res Technol* 8:236-9.

Ibegbuna, V., K.T. Delis, A.N. Nicolaides, and O. Aina. 2003. Effect of elastic compression stockings on venous hemodynamics during walking. *J Vasc Surg* 37:420-5.

Ingjer, F., and K. Myhre. 1992. Physiological effects of altitude training on elite male cross-country skiers. *J Sports Sci* 10:37-47.

Jakeman, J.R., C. Byrne, and R.G. Eston. 2010. Efficacy of lower limb compression and combined treatment of manual massage and lower limb compression on symptoms of exercise-induced muscle damage in women. *J Strength Cond Res* 24:3157-65.

Kimber, N.E., J.J. Ross, S.L. Mason, and D.B. Speedy. 2002. Energy balance during an Ironman triathlon in male and female triathletes. *Int J Sport Nutr Exerc Metab* 12:47-62.

Kraemer, W.J., J.A. Bush, R.B. Wickham, C.R. Denegar, A.L. Gomez, L.A. Gotshalk, N.D. Duncan, J.S. Volek, M. Putukian, and W.J. Sebastianelli. 2001. Influence of compression therapy on symptoms following soft tissue injury from maximal eccentric exercise. *J Orthop Sports Phys Ther* 31:282-90.

Lind, A.R., and D.E. Bass. 1963. Optimal exposure time for development of heat acclimation. *Fed Proc* 22:704-8.

Mancinelli, C.A., D.S. Davis, L. Aboulhosn, M. Brady, J. Eisenhofer, and S. Foutty. 2006. The effects of massage on delayed onset muscle soreness and physical performance in female collegiate athletes. *Phys Therap* 7:5-13.

Millet, G.P., A. Groslambert, B. Barbier, J.D. Rouillon, and R.B. Candau. 2005. Modelling the relationships between training, anxiety, and fatigue in elite athletes. *Int J Sports Med* 26:492-8.

Millet, G.P., B. Roels, L. Schmitt, X. Woorons, and J.P. Richalet. 2010. Combining hypoxic methods for peak performance. *Sports Med* 40:1-25.

Minors, D.S., and J.M. Waterhouse. 1981. Anchor sleep as a synchronizer of rhythms on abnormal routines. *Int J Chronobiol* 7:165-88.

Moraska, A. 2007. Therapist education impacts the massage effect on postrace muscle recovery. *Med Sci Sports Exerc* 39:34-37.

Mujika, I., A. Chaouachi, and K. Chamari. 2010. Precompetition taper and nutritional strategies: Special reference to training during Ramadan intermittent fast. *Br J Sports Med* 44:495-501.

Mujika, I., A. Goya, S. Padilla, A. Grijalba, E. Gorostiaga, J. Ibanez. 2000. Physiological responses to a 6-d taper in middle-distance runners: Influence of training intensity and volume. *Med Sci Sports Exerc* 32:511-7.

Mujika, I., J.C. Chatard, T. Busso, A. Geyssant, F. Barale, and L. Lacoste. 1996. Use of swim-training profiles and performances data to enhance training effectiveness. *J Swim Res* 11:23-29.

Mujika, I., and S. Padilla. 2000. Detraining: Loss of training-induced physiological and performance adaptations. Part I: Short term insufficient training stimulus. *Sports Med* 30:79-87.

Mujika, I., and S. Padilla. 2003. Scientific bases for precompetition tapering strategies. *Med Sci Sports Exerc* 35:1182-7.

Mujika, I., S. Padilla, and D. Pyne. 2002. Swimming performance changes during the final 3 weeks of training leading to the Sydney 2000 Olympic Games. *Int J Sports Med* 23:582-7.

Mujika, I., T. Busso, L. Lacoste, F. Barale, A. Geyssant, and J.C. Chatard. 1996. Modeled responses to training and taper in competitive swimmers. *Med Sci Sports Exerc* 28:251-8.

Pandolf, K.B. 1998. Time course of heat acclimation and its decay. *Int J Sports Med* 19(Suppl 2): S157-60.

Pedlar, C., G. Whyte, S. Emegbo, N. Stanley, I. Hindmarch, and R. Godfrey. 2005. Acute sleep responses in a normobaric hypoxic tent. *Med Sci Sports Exerc* 37:1075-9.

Pichot, V., F. Roche, J.M. Gaspoz, F. Enjolras, A. Antoniadis, P. Minini, F. Costes, T. Busso, J.R. Lacour, and J.C. Barthelemy. 2000. Relation between heart rate variability and training load in middle-distance runners. *Med Sci Sports Exerc* 32:1729-36.

Pitsiladis, Y.P., C. Duignan, and R.J. Maughan. 1996. Effects of alterations in dietary carbohydrate intake on running performance during a 10 km treadmill time trial. *Br J Sports Med* 30:226-31.

Pyne, D.B., I. Mujika, and T. Reilly. 2009. Peaking for optimal performance: Research limitations and future directions. *J Sports Sci* 27:195-202.

Reilly, T., G. Atkinson, W. Gregson, B. Drust, J. Forsyth, B. Edwards, and J. Waterhouse. 2006. Some chronobiological considerations related to physical exercise. *Clin Ter* 157:249-64.

Reilly, T., and J. Waterhouse. 2007. Altered sleep-wake cycles and food intake: The Ramadan model. *Physiol Behav* 90:219-28.

Reilly, T., J. Waterhouse, and B. Edwards. 2005. Jet lag and air travel: Implications for performance. *Clin Sports Med* 24:367-80, xii.

Reilly, T., J. Waterhouse, L.M. Burke, and J.M. Alonso. 2007. Nutrition for travel. *J Sports Sci* 25(Suppl 1): S125-34.

Reilly, T., and P. Maskell. 1989. Effects of altering the sleep-wake cycle in human circadian rhythms and motor performance. Proceedings of the First IOC World Congress on Sport Science, Colorado Springs, CO.

Rusko, H.K., H.O. Tikkanen, and J.E. Peltonen. 2004. Altitude and endurance training. *J Sports Sci* 22:928-44; discussion 945.

Shepley, B., J.D. MacDougall, N. Cipriano, J.R. Sutton, M.A. Tarnopolsky, and G. Coates. 1992. Physiological effects of tapering in highly trained athletes. *J Appl Physiol* 72:706-11.

Sherman, W.M., D.L. Costill, W.J. Fink, and J.M. Miller. 1981. Effect of exercise-diet manipulation on muscle glycogen and its subsequent utilization during performance. *Int J Sports Med* 2:114-8.

Thomas, L., I. Mujika, and T. Busso. 2008. A model study of optimal training reduction during pre-event taper in elite swimmers. *J Sports Sci* 26:643-52.

Thomas, L., I. Mujika, and T. Busso. 2009. Computer simulations assessing the potential performance benefit of a final increase in training during pre-event taper. *J Strength Cond Res* 23:1729-36.

Thomas, L., and T. Busso. 2005. A theoretical study of taper characteristics to optimize performance. *Med Sci Sports Exerc* 37:1615-21.

Trenell, M.I., K.B. Rooney, C.M. Sue, and C.H. Thompson. 2006. Compression garments and recovery from eccentric exercise: A 31P-MRS study. *J Sport Sci Med* 5:106-14.

Walker, J.L., G.J. Heigenhauser, E. Hultman, and L.L. Spriet. 2000. Dietary carbohydrate, muscle glycogen content, and endurance performance in well-trained women. *J Appl Physiol* 88:2151-8.

Waterhouse, J., A. Nevill, B. Edwards, R. Godfrey, and T. Reilly. 2003. The relationship between assessments of jet lag and some of its symptoms. *Chronobiol Int* 20:1061-73.

Waterhouse, J., G. Atkinson, B. Edwards, and T. Reilly. 2007. The role of a short post-lunch nap in improving cognitive, motor, and sprint performance in participants with partial sleep deprivation. *J Sports Sci* 25:1557-66.

Waterhouse, J., T. Reilly, G. Atkinson, and B. Edwards. 2007. Jet lag: Trends and coping strategies. *Lancet* 369:1117-29.

Weber, M.D., F.J. Servedio, and W.R. Woodall. 1994. The effects of three modalities on delayed onset muscle soreness. *J Orthop Sports Phys Ther* 20:236-42.

Weerapong, P., P.A. Hume, and G.S. Kolt. 2005. The mechanisms of massage and effects on performance, muscle recovery and injury prevention. *Sports Med* 35:235-56.

Wendt, D., L.J. van Loon, and W.D. Lichtenbelt. 2007. Thermoregulation during exercise in the heat: Strategies for maintaining health and performance. *Sports Med* 37:669-82.

Wenger, H.A., and G.J. Bell. 1986. The interactions of intensity, frequency and duration of exercise training in altering cardiorespiratory fitness. *Sports Med* 3:346-56.

Wilson, J.M., and G.J. Wilson. 2008. A practical approach to the taper. *Strength Cond J* 30:10-17.

# Chapter 14

Bentley, D.J., G.R. Cox, D. Green, and P.B. Laursen. 2008. Maximising performance in triathlon: Applied physiological and nutritional aspects of elite and non-elite competitions. *J Sci Med Sport* 11(4):407-16.

Bentley, D.J., S. Libicz, A. Jougla, O. Coste, J. Manetta, K. Chamari, and G.P. Millet. 2007. The effects of exercise intensity or drafting during swimming on subsequent cycling performance in triathletes. *J Sci Med Sport* 10(4):234-43.

Chatard, J.C., and B. Wilson. 2003. Drafting distance in swimming. *Med Sci Sports Exerc* 35(7):1176-81.

Chatard, J.C., D. Chollet, and G. Millet. 1998. Performance and drag during drafting swimming in highly trained triathletes. *Med Sci Sports Exerc* 30(8):1276-80.

Delextrat, A., J. Brisswalter, C. Hausswirth, T. Bernard, and J.M. Vallier. 2005. Does prior 1500-m swimming affect cycling energy expenditure in well-trained triathletes? *Can J Appl Physiol* 30(4):392-403.

Delextrat, A., T. Bernard, C. Hausswirth, F. Vercruyssen, and J. Brisswalter. 2003. Effects of swimming with a wet suit on energy expenditure during subsequent cycling. *Can J Appl Physiol* 28(3):356-69.

Delextrat, A., V. Tricot, C. Hausswirth, T. Bernard, F. Vercruyssen, and J. Brisswalter. 2003. Influence of drafting during swimming on ratings of perceived exertion during a swim-to-cycle transition in well-trained triathletes. *Perception and Motor Skills* 96:664-6.

Delextrat, A., V. Tricot, T. Bernard, F. Vercruyssen, C. Hausswirth, and J. Brisswalter. 2003. Drafting during swimming improves efficiency during subsequent cycling. *Med Sci Sports Exerc* 35(9):1612-9.

Delextrat, A., V. Tricot, T. Bernard, F. Vercruyssen, C. Hausswirth, and J. Brisswalter. 2005. Modification of cycling biomechanics during a swim-to-cycle trial. *J Appl Biomech* 21(3):297-308.

Guezennec, C.Y., J.M. Vallier, A.X. Bigard, and A. Durey. 1996. Increase in energy costs of running at the end of a triathlon. *Eur J Appl Physiol* 73:440-5.

Hausswirth, C., A.X. Bigard, and C.Y. Guezennec. 1997. Relationships between running mechanics and energy cost of running at the end of a triathlon and a marathon. *Int J Sports Med* 18(5):330-9.

Hausswirth, C., A.X. Bigard, M. Berthelot, M. Thomaidis, and C.Y. Guezennec. 1996. Variability in energy cost of running at the end of a triathlon and a marathon. *Int J Sports Med* 17(8):572-9.

Hausswirth, C., Y. Le Meur, F. Bieuzen, J. Brisswalter, and T. Bernard. 2010. Pacing strategy during the initial phase of the run in triathlon: Influence on overall performance. *Eur J Appl Physiol* 108(6):1115-23.

Heiden, T., and A. Burnett. 2003. The effect of cycling on muscle activation in the running let of an Olympic distance triathlon. *Sports Biomech* 2:35-49.

Hue, O., A. Valluet, S. Blonc, and C. Hertogh. 2002. Effects of multicycle-run training on triathlete performance. *Res Q Exerc Sport* 73(3):289-95.

Hue, O., D. Le Gallais, A. Boussana, D. Chollet, and C. Prefaut. 1999. Ventilatory responses during experimental cycle-run transition in triathletes. *Med Sci Sports Exerc* 31:1422-8.

Levine, B.D., L.D. Lane, J.C. Buckey, D.B. Friedman, and C.G. Blomqvist. 1991. Left ventricular pressure-volume and Frank-Starling relations in endurance athletes: Implications for orthostatic tolerance and exercise performance. *Circulation* 84(3):1016-23.

Millet, G., D. Chollet, and J.C. Chatard. 2000. Effects of drafting behind a two- or a six-beat kick swimmer in elite female triathletes. *Eur J Appl Physiol* 82(5/6):465-71.

Millet, G.P., and D.J. Bentley. 2004. The physiological responses to running after cycling in elite junior and senior triathletes. *Int J Sports Med* 25(3):191-7.

Millet, G.P., G.Y. Millet, M.D. Hofmann, and R.B. Candau. 2000. Alterations in running economy and mechanics after maximal cycling in triathletes: Influence of performance level. *Int J Sports Med* 21(2):127-32.

Peeling, P.D., D.J. Bishop, and G.J. Landers. 2005. Effect of swimming intensity on subsequent cycling and overall triathlon performance. *Br J Sports Med* 39(12):960-64; discussion 964.

Privett, S.E., K.P. George, N. Middleton, G.P. Whyte, and N.T. Cable. 2010. The effect of prolonged endurance exercise upon blood pressure regulation during a postexercise orthostatic challenge. *Br J Sports Med* 44(10):720-4.

Whyte, G., N. Stephens, R. Budgett, S. Sharma, R.E. Shave, and W.J. McKenna. 2004. Exercise induced neurally mediated syncope in an elite rower: A treatment dilemma. *Br J Sports Med* 38(1):84-85.

Winter, E.D., A.M. Jones, R.C. Davison, P.D. Bromley, and T.H. Mercer. 2009. *Sport and Exercise Physiology Testing Guidelines*. New York, NY: Routledge

# Chapter 16

Silva, A.J., A. Rouboa, A. Moreira, V.M. Reis, F. Alves, J.P. Vilas-Boas, and D.A. Marinho. 2008. Analysis of drafting effects in swimming using computational fluid dynamics. *J Sports Sci and Med.* 7(60-66). www.jssm.org/vol7/n1/9/v7n1-9pdf.pdf.

# Chapter 18

Cosgrove, A. 2005. Metabolic power training for MMA. www.elitefts.com/documents/mma2.htm.

# Chapter 22

Sumner, J. September 2007. Industrial revolution: Three innovators who changed triathlon. *Inside Triathlon.* 22(9): 48-51.

USAT John Martin provided survey material.

# Chapter 23

Kellmann, M., and K.W. Kallus. 2001. *The Recovery-Stress Questionnaire for Athletes: User manual.* Champaign, IL: Human Kinetics.

# Chapter 24

Bompa, T. O. 1999. *Total Training for Young Champions.* Champaign, IL: Human Kinetics.

Chrabot, M. 2011, February. (K. Riecken, Interviewer) Colorado Springs, Colorado.

Haskins, S. 2011, February. (K. Riecken, Interviewer) Colorado Springs, Colorado.

Kemper, H. 2011, February 10. (K. Riecken, Interviewer) Colorado Springs, Colorado.

Luiselli, J. K., & Reed, D. D. (Eds.). 2011. *Behavioral Sport Psychology: Evidence-Based Approaches to Performance Enhancement* (1st Edition ed.). New York, New York: Springer.

McGee, B. 2011. Developing the Run. *USA Triathlon Youth & Junior Coach Certification Course*. Colorado Springs, CO.

USA Triathlon. 2011. *Youth & Junior Coaching Manual*. Colorado Springs, CO: USA Triathlon.

# Chapter 25

Egermann, M., D. Brocai, C. A. Lill, and H. Schmitt. 2003. Analysis of injuries in long-distance triathletes. *Int J Sports Med*. 24(4): p. 271-6.

Farrell, K.C., K.D. Reisinger, and M.D. Tillman. 2003. Force and repetition in cycling: possible implications for iliotibial band friction syndrome. *The Knee*. 10(1): p. 103-109.

Moehrle, M. 2008. Outdoor sports and skin cancer. *Clin Dermatol*. 26(1): p. 12-5.

O'Toole, M. L., W. D. Hiller, R. A. Smith, and T. D. Sisk. 1989. Overuse injuries in ultraendurance triathletes. *Am J Sports Med*. 17(4): p. 514-8.

PubMed Health. 2011. *Concussion*. 2011 Jan 11, 2011 [cited 2011 September 26th]; Available from: http://www.ncbi.nlm.nih.gov/pubmedhealth/PMH0001802/.

Shaw, T., P. Howat, M. Trainor, and B. Maycock. 2004. Training patterns and sports injuries in triathletes. *J Sci Med Sport*. 7(4): p. 446-50.

Tuite, M.J. 2010. Imaging of triathlon injuries. *Radiol Clin North Am*. 48(6): p. 1125-35.

Villavicencio, A. T., T. D. Hernandez, S. Burneikiene, and J. Thramann. 2007. Neck pain in multisport athletes. *J Neurosurg Spine*. 7(4): p. 408-13.

Vleck, V.E., D. J. Bentley, G. P. Millet, and T. Cochrane. 2010. Triathlon event distance specialization: training and injury effects. *J Strength Cond Res*. 24(1): p. 30-6.

# Chapter 26

Seebohar, B. 2011. *Nutrition periodization for athletes*. 2nd ed. Boulder, CO: Bull.

# Chapter 27

Armstrong, L.E., D.L. Costill, and W.J. Fink. 1985. Influence of diuretic induced dehydration on competitive running performance. *Med Sci Sports Exerc* 17:456-61.

Bergeron, M.F., C.M. Maresh, L.E. Armstrong, J.F. Signorile, J.W. Castellani, R.W. Kenefick, K.E. LaGasse, and D.A. Reibe. 1995. Fluid and electrolyte balance associated with tennis match play in a hot environment. *Int J Sport Nutr* 5:180-93.

Burke, L. 2007. *Practical sports nutrition*. Champaign, IL: Human Kinetics.

Cian, C., N. Koulmann, P.A. Barraud, C. Raphel, C. Jimenez, and B. Melin. 2000. Influence of variation in body hydration on cognitive function: Effect of hyperhydration, heat stress and exercise-induced dehydration. *J Psychophysiol* 14:29-36.

Cox, G.R., E.M. Broad, M.D. Riley, and L.M. Burke. 2002. Body mass changes and voluntary fluid intake of elite level water polo players and swimmers. *J Sci Med Sport* 5:183-93.

Howe, A.S., and B.P. Boden. 2007. Heat related illness in athletes. *Am J Sports Med* 35:1384-95.

Laursen, P.B., R. Suriano, M.J. Quod, H. Lee, C.R. Abbiss, K. Nosaka, D.T. Martin, and D. Bishop. 2006. Core temperature and hydration status during an Ironman triathlon. *Br J Sports Med* 40:320-5.

Maughan, R.J., and R. Murray. 2001. *Sports drinks: Basic science and practical aspects*. Boca Raton, FL: CRC Press.

McArdle, W.D., F.I. Katch, and V.L. Katch. 2009. *Exercise physiology: Energy, nutrition, and human performance*. Philadelphia, PA: Lippincott Williams & Wilkins.

Robinson, T., J. Hawley, G. Palmer, G. Wilson, D. Gray, T. Noakes, and S. Dennis. Water ingestion does not improve 1-h cycling performance in moderate ambient temperatures. *Eur J of App Phys* 71:153-160.

Sawka, M.N., L.M. Burke, E.R. Eichner, R.J. Maughan, S.J. Montain, N.S. Stachenfeld. 2007. Exercise and fluid replacement. *Med Sci Sports Exerc* 39:377-390.

United States Department of Agriculture. 2005/2010. Dietary reference intakes: Recommended intakes for individuals.

Walsh, R.M., T.D. Noakes, J.A. Hawley, and S.C. Dennis. 1994. Impaired high intensity cycling performance time at low levels of dehydration. *Int J Sports Med* 15:392-8.

Founded in 1982, **USA Triathlon** is proud to serve as the national governing body for triathlon in the United States. The organization is the sanctioning authority for more than 4,000 diverse events, ranging from grassroots to high-profile races nationwide. USA Triathlon works to create interest and participation in a variety of programs, including camps, clinics, races, and educational opportunities. USA Triathlon's 150,000 members are made up of athletes of all ages, coaches, race directors, officials, parents, and fans striving to strengthen multisport.

On the elite level, USA Triathlon is responsible for the selection and training of teams to represent the United States in international competition, including the world championships, Pan Am Games, and Olympic Games. It conducts national camps and clinics and provides coaching education programs. On the developmental level, USA Triathlon fosters grassroots expansion of the sport, which is facilitated by the sanctioning of age-group events and triathlon clubs and certification of coaches and race directors. National and regional championships are held for triathletes from junior to senior age divisions.

The USA Triathlon mission is to encourage, support, and enhance the multisport experience in the United States while promoting fitness and health through exercise, the spirit of competitiveness, and the pursuit of excellence.

**Linda Cleveland MS, CSCS**, is a USA Triathlon LII certified coach and the coach development manager at USA Triathlon. She has a BS degree in exercise fitness management with a minor in health promotion from the University of Wisconsin–Oshkosh and an MS in exercise and wellness from Arizona State University. She has been an adjunct faculty member at Arizona State University; worked in corporate wellness at Motorola in Phoenix; and coached triathletes, cyclists, and runners since 2004.

Linda has been with USA Triathlon since 2005. As the coach development manager, she is responsible for overseeing a variety of programs in the education department, including coaching certification clinics and curriculum, mentorship opportunities in elite coaching, performance coaching newsletters, USAT University, webinars, and youth clinics. Since joining USAT, she has made the coaching education program one of the most highly regarded in any national governing body. Linda offers high-performance coaches the opportunity to learn what it takes to work with world-class athletes. She has also served as a head coach at several ITU races, including continental cups, world cups, and world championship series races.

Linda keeps her skills fresh by coaching age-group triathletes and training for triathlons herself. Linda resides in the mountains of Colorado with her husband, son, and two big dogs. She enjoys hiking, camping, mountain biking, skiing, snowshoeing, fishing, and spending time in the great outdoors.

# ABOUT THE CONTRIBUTORS

**Alicia Kendig, MS, RD, CSSD,** has worked with various national governing bodies, the USOC, and the United States Anti-Doping Agency to educate athletes on both sport nutrition and dietary supplements. She holds a bachelor's degree in nutrition and a master's degree in public health nutrition from Case Western Reserve University in Cleveland, Ohio. As a collegiate varsity swimmer and during her time as an assistant coach, she lent her expertise in sport and nutrition to numerous athletes and teams. She has helped athletes of all ages, levels, and backgrounds achieve their performance goals by focusing on fuel for optimal performance. She is currently a sport dietitian with the Winter Sports Group and is the athlete performance lab coordinator with the U.S. Olympic Committee. Alicia enjoys swimming, road and mountain biking, running, hiking, and snowboarding.

**Barb Lindquist** is one of the best U.S. triathletes of all time. She raced for 10 years as an elite, was ranked No. 1 in the world from 2003 to 2004, represented the United States at the Olympics in 2004 (9th), and is a member of the USAT Hall of Fame. Of her 134 elite races at all distances, she won 33 and was on the podium 86 times. Since retirement from racing in 2005, Barb coaches and works part time for USAT recruiting collegiate athletes. She lives in Wyoming with her husband and coach, Loren, together tackling their most important venture to date: raising twin boys.

**Bob Seebohar** is a board-certified specialist in sport dietetics, an exercise physiologist, a strength and conditioning coach, and a USA Triathlon certified elite, youth, and junior coach and a competitive endurance athlete. Seebohar was the director of sport nutrition at the University of Florida and the sport dietitian for the U.S. team at the 2008 Summer Olympics. He is the author of the books *Nutrition Periodization for Endurance Athletes: Taking Traditional Sports Nutrition to the Next Level* and *Metabolic Efficiency Training: Teaching the Body to Burn More Fat*.

**Christine Palmquist, MS, MBA,** is an elite-level III USAT coach, an expert USAC coach, and an elite coach for TrainingBible Coaching. Chris was a four-year rower for Cornell University. After working for IBM in Chicago, Chris obtained her MS in education from Northwestern University and began her coaching career as a science and math teacher and track and cross country coach at the middle and high school levels. After her children were born, Chris expanded her coaching and writing responsibilities, eventually coaching for Joe Friel at TrainingBible Coaching, where she has been a regional manager, a coaching mentor to new coaches, and an elite-level master coach since the start of the company. Chris is a coach with the Multisport Madness triathlon team, coaching youth ages 7 to 19 in the Chicago suburbs. Chris has written regularly for *Chicago Amateur Athlete* and *Chicago Athlete* magazines since 1994. She is currently a contributing editor for *Chicago Athlete*. Chris has also written for numerous magazines and contributed to USAT's coaching education manuals and Youth Championship guides.

**George Dallam** is a professor in the department of exercise science, health promotion, and recreation at Colorado State University in Pueblo. A triathlete since 1981, Dr. Dallam initiated the USA Triathlon national teams program in 1996 and has served as coach, physiologist, and consultant to numerous elite U.S. triathletes since that time. Athletes coached by Dr. Dallam have included national elite and age-group champions, Olympians, Pan American Games medalists, world age-group champions, and the top-ranked male triathlete in the world in 2005-2006, Hunter Kemper. Dr. Dallam has been involved in numerous research studies and the publication of their results examining various aspects of triathlon as well as diabetes risk factor modification. He has authored numerous articles applying training principles to triathlon and is the coauthor, with Steven Jonas, of *Championship Triathlon Training*. He is regularly sought as a speaker and expert writer on exercise-related topics, having provided insights to publications such as *Runner's World* and the *New York Times*.

**Gordon Byrn** is a husband, father, and triathlete based in Boulder, Colorado. He is a champion of Ultraman Hawaii and founder of Endurance Corner.

**Graham Wilson, MS,** is a USAT level III coach, chair of the USAT National Coaches Commission, and a USAT certified race official. He has been racing and coaching for over 25 years and has completed over 200 triathlons, including 8 Ironman events. He was a member of the British triathlon team before moving to the United States. Graham assists each of his clients in reaching their athletic potential. His oldest client took up triathlon at age 72 and has twice won world championship medals at the Olympic distance.

**Ian Murray** has been a full-time triathlon coach for over a dozen years. His is certified by USAT as an elite coach as well as USAC and ASCA. Ian is the host and writer of *Triathlon Training Series DVD* and head coach for the LA Tri Club. He has served as head coach for the USAT elite athletes at 2010 ITU WCS Madrid, 2010 ITU PATCO Championships, and 2009 Duathlon World Championships. He was named USAT's Development Coach of the Year in 2006.

**Iñigo Mujika** earned PhDs in biology of muscular exercise (University of Saint-Etienne, France) and physical activity and sport sciences (University of the Basque Country). He is a level III swimming and triathlon coach. His research interests include training methods and recovery, tapering, detraining, and overtraining. He has performed extensive research on the physiological aspects associated with endurance sport performance, published over 80 articles in peer-reviewed journals and 2 books and 13 book chapters, and given over 160 lectures in international conferences. Iñigo was senior physiologist at the Australian Institute of Sport, physiologist and trainer for Euskaltel Euskadi cycling team, and head of research and development at Athletic Club Bilbao football club. He is director of physiology and training at USP Araba Sport Clinic, physiologist of the Spanish Swimming Federation, associate editor for the *International Journal of Sports Physiology and Performance*, and associate professor at the University of the Basque Country.

**Jackie Dowdeswell** was born in the UK, where she earned a BSc honors degree in physiology and biochemistry. Being fit and motivating people have always been Jackie's passions. She is a triathlete who enjoys competing locally. Jackie is a USA Triathlon level

II coach, ASCA level 2 coach, USA Cycling level 3 coach, ACE personal trainer, ACE lifestyle and weight management consultant, and certified stroke technician. Jackie also has many athletic achievements: overall female winner of Pittsford Triathlon 2009 and 2010, 4th in age group at Sprint National Championships 2008, qualifier for intermediate-distance national championships 2008, and Lake Placid Ironman Triathlon 2007 and 2010.

**Jess Manning** is an athlete, coach, founder, co-owner, and CEO of Bricks MultiSport and Fitness and head coach for Team Bricks, the leading multisport team in the Mid-Atlantic region. As a business leader, Jess has inspired others to reach their potential as athletes. As USAT race director, Jess offers many race and fitness opportunities in which athletes of all abilities can participate. He is a USAT level II coach, USA Cycling and AFFA personal trainer, and Spin instructor. He has concentrations in elite and youth multisport coaching. His personal athletic highlights include three-time consecutive winner of Trisports Events Super Ultimate Challenge running series, Boston Marathon finisher, fastest first-time triathlete, New Jersey Genesis Sprint Triathlon finisher, fastest first-time ultradistance triathlete, Ford Eagleman Ironman finisher, 2009 and 2010 Piranha Sports age-group champion, and Florida Ironman finisher.

**Joe Friel, MS,** has trained endurance athletes since 1980. His clients have come from all corners of the globe and included national champions, world championship competitors, and an Olympian. He is the author of 11 books on training for endurance athletes, including the popular and best-selling Training Bible series. He holds a master's degree in exercise science and is a founder and past chairman of the USA Triathlon National Coaching Commission.

**Joe Umphenour** has been a professional triathlete since 1997. He is a USA Triathlon level I certified coach. His top racing results include 2008 Hong Kong ITU Triathlon (1st), 2008 Asian Aquathlon Championships (1st), 2008 Elite National Championships (2nd), 2001 ITU World Championships (11th), 3-time Ironman Hawaii finisher (best finish 53rd in 1994), 2004 ITU Cornerbrook and Newfoundland World Cups (2nd), and 12 top 12 World Cup finishes.

**Karl Riecken** earned a master's degree in health and wellness and applied exercise physiology from the University of Central Florida. During his undergraduate years he was a cross-country runner but fell in love with triathlon before he graduated. Karl has worked for the sport performance departments of both USA Swimming and USA Triathlon, conducting research and helping to coach world-class athletes at the Colorado Springs Olympic Training Center. He has been an assistant coach for youth triathlon teams and for USA Triathlon Elite Development Camps. Karl coaches and provides coaching education for Vanguard Triathlon, working with all levels and all ages of athletes and coaches. Karl holds certifications from the National Strength and Conditioning Association, USA Triathlon, USA Track and Field, USA Cycling, USA Weightlifting, and the Road Runners Club of America.

**Katie Baker, MS,** started working for the United States Olympic Committee in 2011 as the sport performance manager, serving as a liaison between the USOC and various national governing bodies, including USA Triathlon. Before working at the USOC, Katie was employed by USA Triathlon for over 11 years in various capacities, including membership coordinator, national teams program coordinator, and national teams program manager. During her time as national teams manager, Katie served as the team leader for duathlon, long-course triathlon, Winter Olympics, and Olympic triathlon. She also served as the 2008 Beijing Olympic triathlon team manager. Katie earned a BS in journalism with a minor in fine arts from Indiana University and an MS in sport administration from the University of Northern Colorado. Katie coaches high school swimming and works with a local kids' triathlon club. She is a USAT level II certified coach.

**Krista Austin, PhD, CSCS,** is a distinguished physiologist and nutritionist who has worked for the United States Olympic Committee and consults for the Nike Oregon Project, top-tier track and field athletes, USA Triathlon, and USA taekwondo. Her expertise includes exercise training, performance nutrition, dietary supplements, obesity, diabetes, and elite athletes. She has worked for and achieved tremendous success as a performance nutritionist for the English Institute of Sport and England's cricket team.

Austin authored the book *Performance Nutrition: Applying the Science of Nutrient Timing*. As a member of the American College of Sports Medicine and National Strength and Conditioning Association, Austin writes for accredited industry publications and serves as a referee for multiple scientific journals. As an associate editor, Austin contributed to the *International Journal of Sports Nutrition and Exercise Metabolism*.

**Kristen Dieffenbach, PhD,** is an assistant professor of athletic coaching education at West Virginia University and is a consultant certified by the Association of Applied Sport Psychology. Currently she is the coaching education representative on the NASPE sport steering committee and is on the board for the National Council for Accreditation of Coaching Education. She also serves as an advisory board member with the USA Cycling coaching education committee. Kristen is a professional coach with a category 1 (elite) USA Cycling license and a level II endurance specialization from USA Track and Field. She has coached for over 15 years at the high school, collegiate, recreational, and elite levels.

**Kurt Perham** is a lifelong endurance athlete and coach. Starting as an elite cyclist, Kurt transitioned to multisport in the 1990s. He has competed at both national and world championship events in multiple cycling disciplines. Kurt has coached for nearly 15 years, and his athletes' accolades include IM world champions, AG worlds medalists, and national champions in cyclocross. He holds the highest coaching credentials from USA Triathlon and USA Cycling. He guides athletes worldwide.

**Mathew Wilson** is a cardiovascular exercise physiologist at Aspetar, Qatar's orthopaedic and sports medicine hospital. He was the laboratory director at the Research Centre for Sport and Exercise Science at the University of Wolverhampton, UK. He was also the screening manager for the CRY Centre for Sports Cardiology at the Olympic Medical Institute for 5 years. In conjunction with Professors Sharma and Whyte, he has screened over 10,000 athletes for cardiac conditions.

**Michael Kellmann** is head of the sport psychology unit in the faculty of sport science at Ruhr-University Bochum in Germany. Michael served six years on the executive board of the German Association of Sport Psychology and is on the editorial board of *The Sport Psychologist*, the *Zeitschrift für Sportpsychologie*, and the *Deutsche Zeitschrift* *für Sportmedizin*. Michael's current research activities include prevention of overtraining and recovery enhancement, sport psychology diagnostics and intervention, coach behavior during competition and practice, and personality and performance competence of coaches in sports. Michael's work has appeared in several publications. He is coauthor of *Recovery-Stress Questionnaire for Athletes: User Manual* and edited the book *Enhancing Recovery: Preventing Underperformance in Athletes*.

**Mike Ricci** is a level III USA Triathlon certified coach and has been coaching endurance athletes since 1989. Mike has coached multisport athletes, swimmers, and runners of all abilities from all over the world. Mike is the head coach for Team D3 Multisport, the University of Colorado triathlon team (2010 national champs) and has been the track coach for the Boulder Triathlon Club since its inception. Mike has coached hundreds of athletes to their first triathlons and more than 70 one on one who have earned the right to call themselves an Ironman. Mike also wrote the training programs for the USA World Championships from 2003 to 2009.

**Sage Rountree** is a USA Triathlon level II certified coach and author of *The Athlete's Guide to Yoga*, *The Athlete's Pocket Guide to Yoga*, and *The Athlete's Guide to Recovery*. A frequent contributor to *Runner's World*, she co-owns the Carrboro Yoga Company and coaches triathletes from her hometown of Chapel Hill, North Carolina. She competes in triathlons of all distances and raced with team USA at the 2008 Short-Course World Championships.

**Sara McLarty** is the fastest swimmer in triathlon. She was a 15-time NCAA All-American swimmer at the University of Florida and collegiate triathlon national champion. After narrowly missing the 2004 Olympics in the 400-meter freestyle, she won a silver medal in that event and bronze in the 5K open water at the world championships. Sara is currently training to qualify for the Olympics, writing the swim training column for *Triathlete* magazine, and coaching triathletes in Clermont, Florida, at the National Training Center.

**Scott Schnitzspahn** has been a coach for more than a decade at USA Triathlon, where he has held various volunteer and salaried positions, including sport performance director for the 2006 through 2010 seasons. He was responsible for the development of elite triathletes and coaches and served as team leader for the 2007 Pan American Games and 2008 Olympic Games. Scott moved from USAT to the U.S. Olympic Committee as the high-performance director overseeing triathlon and cycling among other endurance sports.

**Sergio Borges** is a top age-group triathlete. Since 1994 he has been dedicated to studying the art and science of triathlon training. He has competed in hundreds of races of all distances, including 20 Ironman races around the world and over 50 half Ironmans, qualifying for the Hawaii Ironman World Championships seven times. Sergio has also been nominated as All-American by USA Triathlon 6 times. After over 10 years of investment banking, he decided to apply his expertise to triathlon coaching. Sergio is a certified level III USA Triathlon coach and level II USA cycling coach. He coached the U.S. elite, junior elite, and U23 team at the World Duathlon in Switzerland in 2003 and the U23 Tri national team in 2004. He also has worked with USAT at the collegiate national camps and recruitment camps. He lectures at the levels I and II coaching clinics and writes for three sport magazines. Sergio was involved in the first-ever paratriathlon camp organized by CAF and is the founder of the JCC Triathlon Master Program and the Kids XTeam Triathlon Club.

**Sharone Aharon** holds an MS in exercise sciences. He is a USA Triathlon level III coach and the founder and head coach of Well-Fit Triathlon & Training, a coaching company in Chicago. Sharone started coaching in 1988, focusing on endurance athletes and in the past few years elite athletes.

**Steve Tarpinian** is the president of Total Training, Inc., a fitness consulting company specializing in swim, bike, run, and triathlon workshops. He was a member of the USAT National Coaching Committee and a certified USAT level II coach.

**Suzanne M. Atkinson, MD, FACEP,** is an emergency medicine physician who founded Steel City Endurance in 2005. She has been coaching triathletes, cyclists, and swimmers for events of all distances from supersprint to Ironman triathlons and endurance mountain bike races, including 24-hour racing and the Leadville 100. She founded two women's bicycle racing teams in Pittsburgh and specializes in swim technique and stroke mechanics as well as bicycling skills development for road racers and triathletes. Her continuing education includes certification by USA Triathlon level II, USA Cycling level II, and total immersion teaching professional. Suzanne worked as an instructor for Outward Bound School from 1991 to 1998 before attending medical school at the University of Pittsburgh.

**Timothy Carlson** has finished 40 triathlons, including 6 half Ironmans. He wrote a series of columns of interviews with experts who offered advice for beginning triathletes on equipment and training strategies. He also ran dozens of road races, finished 10 marathons, and wrote about his successful quest to qualify for the Boston Marathon, which involved heart rate training under internationally renowned coach Dick Brown. He wrote an extensive feature for *Inside Triathlon* on the physiological effects of triathlon training.

**Yann Le Meur, PhD,** is a sport scientist at the research department of the National Institute of Sport, Expertise and Performance in Paris. He earned a PhD in physiology of exercise (University of Nice-Sophia Antipolis) by working on the factors of performance in Olympic-distance triathlon. His research interests focus on performance analysis, fatigue, overtraining, and recovery. Dr. Le Meur has published in prominent peer-reviewed journals in sport and exercise science. He is involved in the scientific following of several French Olympic teams, including triathlon, cross-country mountain bike, synchronized swimming, modern pentathlon, and track cycling (team pursuit).